STP 1129

Slurry Walls: Design, Construction, and Quality Control

David B. Paul, Richard R. Davidson, and Nicholas J. Cavalli, editors

ASTM Publication Code Number (PCN)
04-011290-38

ASTM
1916 Race Street
Philadelphia, PA 19103

Library of Congress Cataloging-in-Publication Data

Slurry walls : design, construction, and quality control / David B.
Paul, Richard R. Davidson, and Nicholas J. Cavalli, editors.
  (STP ; 1129)
  "ASTM publication code number (PCN) 04-011290-38."
  Includes bibliographical references and index.
  ISBN 0-8031-1427-3
  1. Hazardous substances—Environmental aspects. 2. Slurry trench
construction. I. Paul, David B., 1956- . II. Davidson, Richard
R., 1953- . III. Cavalli, Nicholas J., 1949- . IV. Series:
ASTM special technical publication ; 1129.
TD195.H39S58   1992
628.4 ' 2—dc20   92-32908
                                                      CIP

Photocopy Rights

Peer Review Policy

Each paper published in this volume was evaluated by three peer reviewers. The authors addressed
all of the reviewers' comments to the satisfaction of both the technical editor(s) and the ASTM
Committee on Publications.

The quality of the papers in this publication reflects not only the obvious efforts of the authors and the
technical editor(s), but also the work of these peer reviewers. The ASTM Committee on Publications
acknowledges with appreciation their dedication and contribution to time and effort on behalf of ASTM.

Printed in Fredricksburg, VA
September 1992

Foreword

This publication, *Slurry Walls: Design, Construction, and Quality Control,* contains papers presented at the symposium of the same name, held in Atlantic City, NJ on 27–28 June 1991. The symposium was sponsored by ASTM Committee D-18 on Soil and Rock. David B. Paul of the U.S. Bureau of Reclamation in Denver, CO, Richard R. Davidson of Woodward-Clyde Consultants in Denver, CO, and Nicholas J. Cavalli of Wehran Envirotech in Middletown, NJ presided as symposium chairman and co-chairmen, respectively, and are all editors of the resulting publication.

Contents

Overview

The first International Symposium on Slurry Walls: Design/Construction/Quality Control was held on 27–28 June, 1991 in Atlantic City, NJ. The purpose of this symposium was to bring together an interdisciplinary and international group of engineers and scientists to: (1) provide a forum to exchange experiences and findings related to the design, construction, and quality control methods for slurry walls; (2) learn from both successful and unsuccessful case histories; (3) promote technology transfer between the various disciplines and countries represented; and (4) provide an education resource for those attending. In fact, due to the large attendance from a truly international group of engineers, scientists, and practitioners, a broader perspective was provided by the authors.

Eighteen papers presented at the symposium and 12 other papers that were not presented due to time constraints, are included in this volume. The thirteen papers, in addition to several others, were presented at a poster session. They are grouped into four main categories: (1) State-of-the-Art; (2) Hazardous Waste; (3) Seepage Control; and (4) Structural.

The state-of-the-art presentations included a history of slurry wall development by Ressi which describes the techniques and equipment typically used for slurry wall construction. Vanel presented several innovations including a new joint system between panels. Tamaro and Poletto described the importance of construction quality control and pointed out that there are no national standards for the design and construction of slurry walls. Millet and Perez provided an update to a paper they presented 10 years ago on the then state-of-the-practice of slurry wall construction specifications in the United States.

The importance of dealing with hazardous waste has grown tremendously in the last decade and slurry cutoff walls have been the primary method for preventing underground migration of pollutants. Grube provided the perspective of the Environmental Protection Agency (EPA) on the use of slurry cutoff walls for environmental pollution control. Cavalli presented a composite vertical barrier system that utilizes a geomembrane installed through slurry. The recent introduction into practice of biodegradable slurries was discussed by Ryan and Tallard. Instead of bentonite slurry, guar-gum based slurries are used to maintain the open trench. They have been used in recent projects to allow for the installation of deep drains that eliminates sheeting, shoring, and dewatering. The effects of soil pollution interaction on the stability of geosynthetic composite walls was presented by Fang, Chaney, and Pamukcu.

Davidson et al. discussed the use of plastic concrete to construct a seepage barrier at a large copper mine in Vancouver, B. C. Construction of a 400-foot-deep wall through the Corps of Engineers Mud Mountain Dam outside of Seattle was described by Davidson et al. Compaction grouting was utilized by the contractor to restress the dam to allow for excavation of the deep panels without large slurry losses.

Papers were also presented which describe the use of cutoff walls for unique structural applications. Johnson et al. presented two case studies where barrettes or load-bearing elements (LBEs) were installed for projects constructed by the "up/down" method. Schoenwolf presented very interesting results from a monitored reinforced concrete wall utilized for the deepest building excavation ever undertaken in Boston. Bruce and Tamaro presented a valuable case history of the use of a cutoff wall to construct a 165-foot-deep shaft, 52 feet in diameter, within two city blocks of the ocean.

The editors are grateful to the authors for their efforts in preparing the excellent papers included in this volume. They provide a valuable contribution to the state-of-practice not only in the United States, but all over the world.

David B. Paul

U.S. Bureau of Reclamation, Denver, CO; chairman.

Richard R. Davidson

Woodward-Clyde Consultants, Denver, CO; co-chairman.

Nicholas J. Cavalli

Wehran Envirotech, Middletown, NY; co-chairman.

State-of-the-Art Papers

Arturo L. Ressi di Cervia

HISTORY OF SLURRY WALL CONSTRUCTION

REFERENCE: Ressi di Cervia, A.L. "History of Slurry Wall Construction", Slury Walls: Design, Construction, and Quality Control, ASTMSTP1129, David B. Paul, Richard R. Davidson, and Nicholas J. Cavalli, Eds., American Society for Testing and Materials, Philadelphia, 1992.

ABSTRACT:The slurry wall industry started in Italy in the 40's and spread throughout the world in three decades. It has divided into three distinct markets: Structural Walls, Deep Cut-Offs and Slurry Trenches. Each market has followed a different development pattern. Progress has been made in design, equipment and technology to fulfull the needs of each of those segments of the industry.

KEYWORDS:bentonite, clamshell, hydromill, percussion, rotary

INTRODUCTION

The task of outlining the history of slurry wall construction requires first and foremost the definition of the subject matter.

The best definition I can think is the following:

A slurry wall is an excavation in unstable soil supported by a fluid which is constantly kept at the ground level, later backfilled with an engineered substance.

This definition covers all the subject matter that I want to discuss with the exception of cement bentonite walls where the mud used during the excavation for support purposes hardens in the trench and becomes the backfill.

Outside of the scope of this paper are alternative techniques, some of which will be discussed in subsequent papers.

Arturo Ressi is the President of ICOS Corporation of America, 151 Grand Avenue, P O Box 749, Englewood, New Jersey 07631

3

Techniques like vibrating beam walls, secant pile walls, deep soil mixing and jet grout barriers, although from time to time can be utilized in lieu of slurry walls, are really not germane to this type of construction, since they employ a different construction method and different principles.

Having defined the subject let us discuss where it all began.

It was in Italy in the late forties that ICOS first acquired patents on slurry wall construction. The discovery of the technique stems from the use of bentonite mud during the drilling of piles which was done at the time in a rather primitive fashion.

The observation that bentonite mud, first utilized as a means to keep solids in suspension, was also stabilizing the excavation and obviating the need of casing the hole, prompted ICOS' engineers to experiment with rectangular excavations filled with bentonite to see whether they could be stable.   Initial successes led to the acquisition of patents and the performance of the first underground concrete walls in the late forties.

The clamshells designed for this purpose, aptly named crocodiles, were a far cry from what is in use today but were effective enough for the budding industry to encourage ICOS to continue to experiment and develop the technique.

At this time also extensive laboratory research was done on the factors effecting trench stability, on mud configuration, on concrete placement and on bond of reinforcing bars with concrete placed under bentonite.

Having satisfied first themselves, and then the engineering community on the validity of the system, ICOS began in earnest to seek application for its new technique in the civil engineering field.

With the spread of the technique and with the expiration of the original patents, a score of foundation companies, mainly in Europe and Japan begun to develop equipment and techniques in this field of construction. Today there are a scope of international contractors, mostly European, who will work anywhere in the world, and in every developed country there is usually a number of local contractors capable of performing all but the most difficult work.

If we look at the development of this industry we can prepare an evolutionary chart which shows that the slurry wall process has branched out in three different and distinct areas:

Structural Walls
Deep Cutoff Walls
Slurry Trench

Although obviously there are overlaps in the three categories, nevertheless they are sufficiently distinct to be treated separately since they have evolved in three different markets.

Before entering into a discussion of the three main areas of slurry wall construction, I want to explain briefly how the companies active in this field operate, since their structure and contractual posture is significant in both the development and the diffusion of the technique.

By and large the slurry wall field has been dominated by specialized contractors who perform the work either as their main activity or as a part of their more diversified panoply of foundation techniques.

With some limited exceptions, no general contractor has in the long run successfully developed and maintained an in house capacity to perform this type of work.

The reason for this is probably found in the fact that this technique requires a high degree of specialization in the field personnel, a sizable capital investment in specialized equipment and an attitude toward the performance of this high risk work which is more in line with the mentality of a specialist contractor.

Let us now examine the three separate areas of slurry wall construction and generally define their characteristics.

Structural Walls: They are the ones with the longest history. Typically, since the walls are part of much larger structures, the specialist contractor is a subcontractor on the project and he performs his work in contractual arrangements which cover the whole spectrum between providing only technical assistance to being a full subcontractor who is totally in charge of his aspect of the foundation work. Typically the specialist contractor will be responsible for the design of the slurry wall portion of the work almost everywhere in the world, except in England and the U.S. where he will be involved in the design only if the walls are used as temporary structures.

The major developments for this type of work have been in the design and in the integration of this structure in the overall project, since there is very little difference in the walls built 30 years ago to the ones built today with the notable exceptions of a couple of developments which will be more fully explored in detail.

One of the main characteristics of this type of construction is that it is mostly done by clamshells, and today mostly by mechanical ones.

Deep Cutoff Walls: They are typically procured as a separate contract especially if they are utilized for remedial work or to protect an excavation.   Typically the specialty contractor is in charge of the whole project and he will take under his umbrella any accessory work connected with the project, thus acting as a General Contractor for the slurry wall installation.

In this area equipment has made the greatest advances and techniques of constructing those deep cutoffs have evolved steadily from the first job to the present time.

Another area where there has been evolution in the deep cutoff is the area of the backfill material.

Slurry Trenches: It is an area of relatively low technology and of lesser difficulty.   This type of work is characterized by a continuing search for the most cost effective method of excavation.   The advances in this area have been made in the backfill composition as well as in the utilization of composite barriers to contain hazardous and non hazardous leachates.

Let us now discuss the three areas in detail, tracing the genealogy of each of these as if we were exploring the evolution of a sub-species.

Structural Walls: The first applications of slurry wall construction were structural ones,   where the technique was utilized to create reinforced underground concrete walls.

The branching out of different techniques within this specialty is depicted in Figure 1.

The initial work was done with rudimentary clamshells which evolved from the first "crocodiles"   which weighed less than two tons and were operated by a wooden tripod. To the present, highly sophisticated RW clamshells which weighed approximately 11 tons are operated by a 100 ton crawler crane.

In the last 30 years several companies have attempted to introduce hydraulic clamshells, either cable suspended or kelly mounted.   Such clamshells have excavation rates superior to those achieved by mechanical clamshells, but are costly, have more frequent breakdowns, are more cumbersome to utilize and require skilled mechanics to be kept in good working order.

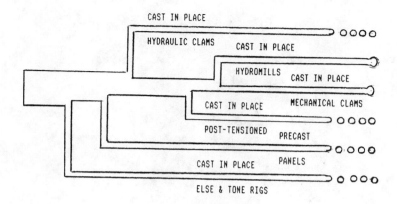

FIGURE 1:   The Breakdown of Structural Walls

Although this type of equipment has been widely utilized in the past, and still is in some parts of the world,
presently the major specialized companies are reverting to
mechanical clamshells, especially in structural work, an
example of which is shown in Fig. 2.

The fact that structural walls are mostly used in urban areas with tight constrictions, difficult geometries
and strict verticality requirements has basically induced
the majority of the companies to revert to mechanical
clamshells which, in the meantime, have been developed to
obtain a very high rate of production while remaining essentially a very simple piece of equipment.

Throughout the development of the technique several
companies have designed other types of equipment for
slurry wall construction and they have from time to time
been utilized in structural walls, sometimes successfully.
On the whole though, there is now a general consensus
that the majority of the urban structural work should be
done by cable hung mechanical clamshells.

A lot of work has been done in the area of the joint
between panels. Ideally the vertical joint between panels
should be watertight, act as a guide for the tool excavating the adjacent panel and allow for continuity of
reinforcement through the joint.

While the first two requirements have been met in
several practical ways, the continuity of reinforcement
still remains difficult and costly to achieve.

Over the years great advances have been made in the
design field, with the result of extending the use of this
technique to a broader range of structures.

FIGURE NO. 2:   Cable Hung Mechanical Clamshell

Without getting into a detailed discussion of a subject which would be covered by other speakers, let me men-
tion that the use of post tensioned walls capable of
retaining unsupported spans,   the design of circular and
elliptical structures for deep excavation, where the wall
acts like a ring in compression and the use of top down
techniques where the structure is built from the ground
floor up, while the foundation is being excavated down at
the same time, thus resulting in the elimination of any
temporary supporting system for the wall, have greatly extended the economic application of this technique.

The one other area of development in this field which
enjoyed greater popularity in Europe a few years back but
has never much caught on in the United States is the use
of precast panels set in a self hardening cement bentonite
mud.

Another development that is not very new but only
recently has begun to be applied widely in the United
States is the use of load bearing elements in lieu of
caisson or piles, especially when they are planned in conjunction with a perimeter slurry wall.   The simultaneous
construction of the perimeter wall and the foundation ele

ments with the same type of equipment in congested urban areas results in substantial savings of time, less confusion on site and thus in an overall economy.

   Deep Cutoff Walls: This is the area where the development of equipment and techniques has been the most dramatic.

   Fig. 3 shows how the field of deep cutoffs has evolved.

   The first deep cutoffs were done by either secant piles or interlocking piles as illustrated in the attached figure. This first technique was followed by more sophisticated methods involving the use of "primary" and "secondary" elements. The "primary" elements were circular, drilled by direct circulation percussion tools and the "secondary" elements were bioconcave excavations drilled with winged percussion tools both fixed and expandable, with direct circulation of mud. This technique allowed cut-off walls to be built in the early sixties to the depth of over 400'. The same concept of primary piles connected by secondary elements excavated by a movable wing tool was the base of the construction of the Wolf Creek Dam Phase I and Phase II.

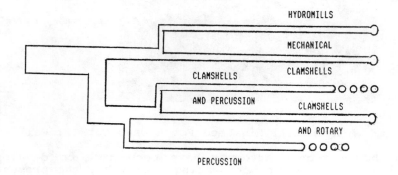

FIGURE 3:   The Breakdown of Deep Cut-Offs

   The most recent developments in the field of deep cut-offs consist in the utilization of a new generation of excavation tools, called hydromills, consisting in a frame with counterotating cutter wheels at the bottom, equipped with a system of reverse circulation of the mud. One such piece of equipment is shown in Figure 4.

   In the last decade a series of projects has been built by hydromills.

Presently the deepest cutoffs have been built with
this technique and this type of equipment is likely to
remain the standard of the art for deep cutoffs in certain
types of soils.

FIGURE 4:   A Hydromill Rig Used For A Deep Cut-Off Wall

Although recent attempts have been made to develop
hydro mills capable of perforating hard rock, the present
limitation of those machines consists in the fact that
they cannot operate in all soil conditions, albeit at a
slow progress rate, like other type of equipment.   Large
hard boulders and/or layers of hard rock necessitate the
withdrawal of the machine and the use of other means to
continue the work.

It is therefore concurrent with the use of this new
machine the utilization of more standard techniques which
are a combination of percussion and rotary drilling and
the use of mechanical clamshells.   The choice of one system versus another is dictated by many factors, of which
soil parameters, maximum depth and size of the work are
the most important ones.

Later papers will give examples of the utilization of all the techniques above indicated in different deep cutoffs.

Since the relationship between need and technology is a symbiotic one (a need opens the development of a new technology, and its availability creates new areas of application) it's very probable that in the near future deep cutoffs will be utilized more and more in a variety of projects.

The absolute reliability and verifiable performance of a positive, continuous cutoff cannot be matched by any other type of underground barrier.

Since positive cutoffs are being specified more and more, it must be understood that the purpose of a water cutoff is very different than that of a structural wall. Consequently, some of the requirements which are important for a structural wall are not meaningful for a deep cutoff while others may be harmful.

Although deep cutoffs initially were almost exclusively done with structural concrete the tendency in the last decade has been to develop a variety of plastic mixes to be used as a backfill which are capable of accommodating movement of the cutoff without cracking. This is particularly important when the cutoff is built in seismic areas and when large movements are anticipated due to changing load conditions, as is the case of dams subjected to big oscillations of the reservoir level.

It is also important to note that while verticality is a critical element in a structural wall because it has design implications, verticality "per se" is meaningless in deep cutoffs where continuity of the wall and maintenance of a minimum section are what is required. Consequently techniques which address those two requirements are inherently more desirable. The use of stop end pipes or guides which assure continuity and uniformity of section are therefore inherently better than procedures relying solely on verticality control to achieve the stated end.

Typically on a given job both techniques may be used, but a more critical decision is whether to use stop end pipes or not. If stop end pipes or guides are not used, a portion of the previously poured panels have to be reexcavated and the guarantee of continuity and maintenance of the minimum section is based on the verticality measurements of the machine (less and less reliable at greater and greater depths) and on the tendency of the machine to follow the path of least resistance, that is the previously poured plastic concrete, (which may not always be true).

Figure 5 illustrates the sequence in which panels can be constructed, either in a "primary/secondary" sequence, or in a "following" sequence.

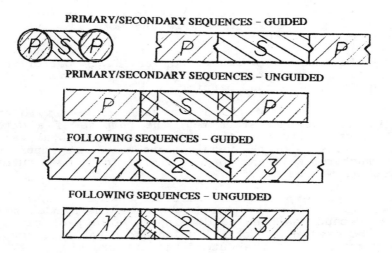

FIGURE 5:   Possible Panel Sequences

Slurry Trenches:

The origin of slurry trenches is actually a bit murkier than I led you to believe in my introduction.

Although modern slurry trenches are an extension of slurry wall technology which started in the United States in the early seventies under the auspices of the Corps of Engineers, there is evidence that some early shallow slurry trenches were built in California in the mid forties by the Navy.

Since, on the other end, such early work did not continue and the method was "lost" for 25 years,   we could consider it a dead branch in the evolutionary tree of slurry wall technology.

Slurry trench construction is essentially a dirt moving job; it requires, in its simpler cases, very little specialized equipment and it is therefore accessible to the greatest variety of contractors.

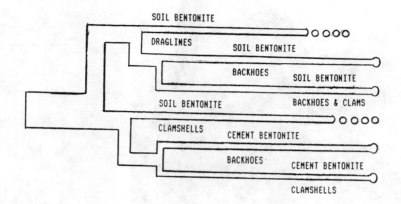

FIGURE 6:   The Breakdown of Slurry Trenches

It is generally the entry door for contractors who want to become involved in slurry wall construction.

In this segment of the industry techniques have ranged from the initial use of clamshells, (since such type of construction was considered an offshoot of structural and deep cutoff walls) to the use of draglines to finally the use of backhoes as shown on Figure 7 which are the most efficient and economical excavating machines up to depths of approximately sixty feet.   Figure 6 shows the evolution of this technology.

When slurry trench cutoff requires deeper penetration a first pass by backhoe is supplemented with additional excavation of clamshells or, alternatively, a specially designed long boom is fitted on backhoes to increase their reach.

Other than the progressive utilization of more efficient excavating tools to optimize costs the only substantial development in the slurry trench technology has been the utilization in the last decade of liners in the trench to supplement the backfill material for long term resistance to chemically aggressive water contaminants.   The resulting composite barriers gives further assurance of the lasting performance of the underground barrier.

One characteristic of slurry trenches that must be remembered, is that since the excavation proceeds from beginning to end in a continuous fashion, the primary requirement for a water cutoff (continuity) and the secondary requirement (minimum size) are automatically guaranteed by the construction technique.

FIGURE 7: Backhoe Excavating A Slurry Trench

The later consideration is the reason why alternative methods like deep soil mixing, jet grouting barriers, vibrating beam barriers, although from time to time competitively priced, do not in reality provide a product with a same degree of certainty provided by a slurry trench.

Under the slurry trench category we must discuss cement bentonite cutoffs. In this technique the backfill and the supporting mud are one and the same, since the mixture of cement and bentonite used during excavation hardens over time in the trench. Although it has its applications, in my opinion it has become limited by its higher costs and higher permeability which do not justify its use unless special circumstances forbid the utilization of soil bentonite walls.

In summary having reviewed the history and state of the art of the industry I venture the following forecasts:

1.   Top down techniques will become the standard of the industry in the construction of foundations in tight urban areas.

2.   We will see a new generation of more agile and less costly hydro mills, probably operating on somewhat different principles, and the market for deep cutoffs will expand.

3.   The utilization of composite barriers with liners in slurry trenches will increase; this will result in an increased level of sophistication and technology in this segment of the industry.

Paul Vanel

MAKING DIAPHRAGM WALL JOINTS WATERTIGHT WITH THE CWS SYSTEM

REFERENCE: Vanel, P., "Making Diaphragm Wall Joints Watertight
with the CWS System," Slurry Walls: Design, Construction, and
Quality Control, ASTM STP 1129, David B. Paul, Richard R.
Davidson, and Nicholas J. Cavalli, Eds., American Society for
Testing and Materials, Philadelphia, 1992.

ABSTRACT: Diaphragm walls are discontinuous structures composed
of individual panels. Making the joints between the panels
watertight has been a problem for decades. The CWS system is a
technique that allows the construction of geometrically well
defined joints equipped with watertight devices such as waterstop
blades.

CONSTRUCTION OF DIAPHRAGM WALL- CLASSICAL METHODS

Underground diaphragm walls are composed of panels cast in place
in an alternate or successive order.

1. Alternate order method

In this case, (see Fig.1), the construction begins by excavating
and concreting primary panels (i.e. 1, 3, 5, ...) regularly spaced
along the axis of the structure wall.

The construction is then completed by excavating and concreting
secondary panels (i.e. 2, 4, 6, ...) in the space left between primary
panels.

2. Successive order method

In this case, (see Fig. 2), the panels are excavated and concreted
one after another, i.e. panel n + 1 against panel n.

Paul Vanel is expert engineer at Entreprise Bachy, 4, rue Sainte-
Claire Deville, 92563 Rueil-Malmaison, France.

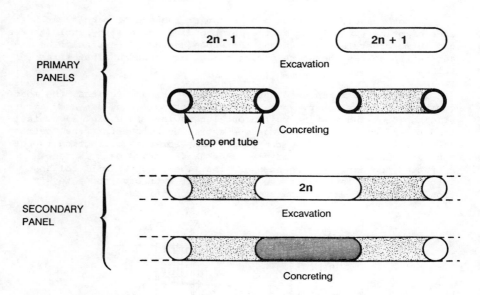

Fig. 1 - Construction scheme with alternating panels.

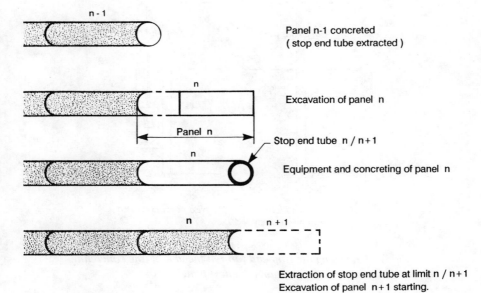

Fig. 2 - Construction scheme with successive panels.

In both cases, end forms are set up at the end of panels, at both ends of primary panels or at the earth end of successive panels. These end forms create a hollow along the whole depth of the panel. The adjacent panel is therefore excavated and concreted against this hollow.

The stop end forms used until now have various sections, the most common being a cylinder. Whatever their sections, they are used as sliding forms and must be pulled out lengthwise. (see Fig. 3). This condition implies that they must be extracted before the final setting of the concrete. Selecting the proper time for this extraction is not easy and takes some skill mainly when the diaphragm wall is deep. Extracted too early and chances are that the concrete will collapse into the hollow left under the end form. If extracted too late, friction may prevent extraction under normal conditions.

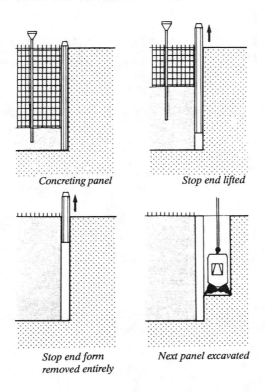

Concreting panel   *Stop end lifted*

Stop end form   *Next panel excavated*
removed entirely

Fig. 3 - Extracting the stop end form at the end of the concreting and before excavating the next panel.

Whichever method is selected, a diaphragm wall ends up in being an assembly of elementary independent panels placed side by side. Concerning watertightness and mechanical strength, there is a lack in continuity at each joint, despite the tongue and groove effect provided by the shape of the end forms.

In addition, practical construction of the joints calls for special care to ensure :

- a correct geometrical continuity of the wall,

- a correct quality of the joint itself concerning geometry and surface finish.

DIAPHRAGM WALL WITH CWS JOINT

General principle

The CWS end form is not extracted as a sliding form before excavating the adjacent panel. It is extracted laterally after the adjacent panel has been excavated. It took about three years to complete the development and give the method its present state of simplicity. It is the lateral extraction after excavating the adjacent panel which allows the presence, while the excavation is carried out, of an actual rail temporarily sealed in the concrete of the previous panel. This rail is a guide for the excavating tool which can be a grab or a rock mill. It secures a perfect geometrical continuity of the wall and good quality of the joint between panels.

The lateral extraction after excavating the adjacent panel allows installation in the joint of additional equipment restoring mechanical continuity and watertightness of the diaphragm wall.

Implementation of the system

The CWS end form is composed of a caisson beam made of high strength steel. After a panel is excavated, the CWS form is installed against the ground at one end of the excavation. Concreting is carried out and the form is not extracted as a sliding form. It is left in place until completion of the excavation in the adjacent panel (see Fig. 4).

The end form is then pulled aside by the excavating tool, especially equipped with blades adapted to slide down the wings of the form. The progression of the blades thus pushed between metal and concrete from top to bottom of the panel secures the detachment of the form, allowing its lifting out. As the CWS form is left in place while the next panel is excavated, it can be used as a guide, guaranteeing the geometrical continuity of the wall. To this effect, the excavating tool is locked onto the form at regular intervals throughout the excavation operations. Any tendency to deviation is thus corrected as soon as it appears. At the end of the excavating operation, the form is practically free and can be extracted.

An additional advantage is the fact that the metal form protects the surface of the concrete in the joint against the impacts of the excavating tool.

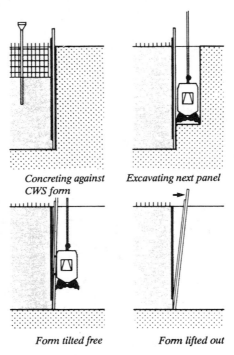

Concreting against
CWS form

Excavating next panel

Form tilted free

Form lifted out

Fig. 4 - Pulling aside the stop end form after concreting and after excavating the next panel.

Securing watertightness of joints

The positive protection that the CWS form provides at the end of the previous panel secures an excellent geometry of the joint between panels and the lateral extraction allows the installation of watertightning devices such as plastic or rubber waterstop blades. This is achieved with varied design depending on the degree of guarantee specified (see Fig. 5 and 6). Twin blades is the usual arrangement.

To install the waterstop blades, the CWS form is fitted with an additional grooved caisson in which the blades are inserted. They are jammed in the grooves owing to the elasticity of the central duct (see Fig. 7).

The free half of the blades is sealed in concrete when the panel is concreted. The lateral extraction uncovers the other half which is then sealed in the concrete of the adjacent panel (see Fig. 8).

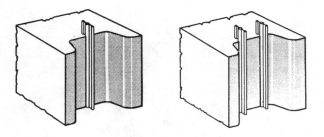

Fig. 5 - One blade and two blade systems of waterstops.

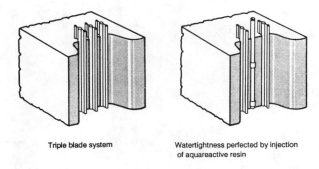

Triple blade system   Watertightness perfected by injection
                                       of aquareactive resin

Fig. 6 - Systems for high security projects.

Fig. 7 - Insertion of t he waterstop blades in the grooved CWS stop end form.

Fig. 8 - Waterstop blades sealed in concrete of primary panels.

Versatility of the system

With time and practice, the system has shown its versatility and more than one million square meters of diaphragm walls have been successfully constructed with the CWS joint system. The following examples in Figs. 9 through 14 show that the technique has been applied to practically all the fields of civil engineering construction.

CONCLUSION

The CWS joint technique results from a radical change in the concept of construction of diaphragm wall. It improves the quality of the diaphragm walls and is the initiator of a trend among contractors who try to develop equivalent systems.

Fig. 9 - Car park constructed under a canal.

SETE - FRANCE

Fig. 10 - Subway system.

PARIS - VILLEJUIF - FRANCE

Fig. 11 - Urban deep excavation.
PARIS − FRANCE

Fig. 12 - Circular diaphragm wall for liquefied natural gas underground storage.
MONTOIR DE BRETAGNE − FRANCE

Fig. 13 - Harbour quay wall.

LE HAVRE – FRANCE

Fig. 14 - Very high inertia diaphragm wall.

PARIS – FRANCE

George J. Tamaro, Raymond J. Poletto

SLURRY WALLS-CONSTRUCTION QUALITY CONTROL

REFERENCE: Tamaro, G. J. and Poletto, R. J., "Slurry Walls--Construction Quality Control," Slurry Walls: Design, Construction, and Quality Control, ASTM STP 1129, David B. Paul, Richard R. Davidson, and Nicholas J. Cavalli, Eds., American Society for Testing and Materials, Philadelphia, 1992.

ABSTRACT: Structural slurry walls[1] have become a standard method for the construction of deep underground structures in the United States. Structural slurry walls have been excavated to great depth and have been installed to plan dimensions from approximately 10 meters in diameter for circular shafts to hundreds of meters for walls for tunnels or large commercial basements. Slurry walls have been installed through a variety of difficult geological formations with varying success, and have been used as temporary walls, permanent walls, water cutoff walls, load bearing elements or in lieu of underpinning.

Currently there are no United States standards for the design and/or construction of slurry walls. Government agencies, private consultants, contractors and trade groups have prepared and, from time to time, published and distributed specifications for the construction of slurry walls [1]. These specifications vary in degree of complexity and quality standards. Some specifications place excessive emphasis on the preparation and control of bentonite slurry used for excavation, with insufficient emphasis placed on quality control of the tremie concrete placement or requirements for the finished product. This paper will discuss the slurry wall construction process, identifying those areas which require special scrutiny by the contractor and owner.

KEYWORDS: Slurry Walls, Bentonite Slurry, Excavation, Quality Control

---

INTRODUCTION

The quality of structural slurry walls is very much dependent upon the skill, experience and personnel of the specialty subcontractor. No amount of quality control can assure a good quality end product if the contractor is unskilled, unknowing, or willfully intending to construct other than the highest quality wall. A good, field quality control program can not guarantee a well constructed end product; however, good quality control can identify poor construction practices at an early stage of construction and hopefully encourage the contractor to conduct the work in a skillful and high quality fashion. Good quality control and record keeping will also assist the owner in identifying problem areas which may occur as a result of either subsurface or construction problems during the installation of the slurry wall. Certain construction or site restraints or particular geologic conditions can prevent the contractor from achieving specified wall tolerances, finishes and steel reinforcing cover. Good quality control in the field should minimize the detrimental effect of these problems.

George J. Tamaro is a Partner and Raymond J. Poletto is an Associate at Mueser Rutledge Consulting Engineers, 708 Third Avenue, New York, NY 10017

[1]The name "Slurry Wall" (USA) and "Diaphragm Wall" (Europe & Asia) is interchangeable.

Quality control in the field is the primary obligation of the contractor. Quality control (quality assurance) by the owner's designated representative should be established to assure that the contractor is executing the work in a workmanlike manner and that the contractor will achieve the desired end results.

This paper will describe the essential elements and steps in slurry wall construction and will suggest controls which should be implemented by the contractor and/or the owner.

GUIDE WALLS

Guide walls are essential for the accurate control of line and grade of the slurry wall. They initially serve as a guide for the excavation and later as a support for the reinforcing cage during concrete placement. The excavation of guide walls should be carried down to the elevation of the lowest utility or to the level of the foundations of adjacent structures without undermining them. Guide walls should be cast on a stable, compact subgrade. All abandoned utilities should be removed and plugged and all openings through adjacent basement walls should be sealed. In the case where guide walls are not provided against existing structures, those structures should be protected by a cement plaster coating and then lined with plywood or a steel plate. The trench for the guide walls should be excavated to remove all loose materials and backfilled to the underside of the guide walls with lean concrete or a clean, well compacted backfill. Guide walls are usually 150mm to 300mm thick and 1m to 2m deep and are normally reinforced with only 4 to 7 13mm diameter bars running longitudinally. As a practical manner only the inside face of the guide walls should be formed while the back face of the guide walls should be cast against the soil to the sides of the excavated trench. The inside face of the guide wall should be set at the theoretical line of the inside face of the slurry wall. The outside face of the guide wall may be set at a dimension larger than the width of the wall in order to provide clearances for excavating tools (Figure 1).

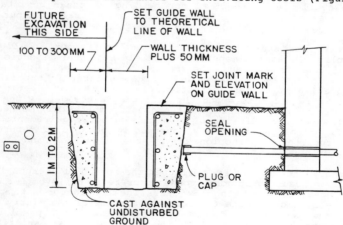

Figure I – TYPICAL GUIDE WALL DETAILS

In many locations, guide walls will be removed after final construction is completed. In other cases the guide wall on the unexcavated side of wall could remain in place while the guide wall on the inside or excavated side of the wall is removed during general excavation.

Prior to the start of the site work the contractor should provide a detailed drawing showing all the survey baselines and geometry of the guide walls, the guide wall construction procedures and methods for control of field measurements.

Guide walls are necessary for both the support of the ground during excavation, support of cages and other equipment and for the full vertical and horizontal control of the construction. All measurements of the panel will be made from the guide walls. An accurate survey is required to establish the location of panel ends, as well as the elevation of the top of guide wall so that the contractor and the inspector can measure from the guide walls to assure the geometry of the excavation is as intended. Guide walls should be blocked at adjacent panels during excavation so that the movement of the clamshell or collapses under the guide walls do not permit unnoticed shifting of the guide walls. The surveyor should perform periodic rechecks of line and grade in order to assure that undetected movements have not occurred during panel excavation.

PANEL DIMENSIONS AND ARRANGEMENTS

Panel dimensions and arrangements are usually controlled by the technical requirements of the design and the type and size of the equipment that is available to the contractor performing the work. It is obvious that the panel thickness and length can be no thinner or shorter than the width and length of the bucket. Short panel lengths, usually in the range of 2m, should be used at areas of unstable soils or where very high surcharge loads result from adjacent structures. Longer panels, ranging up to 10m in length, can be used in stable soils. Panel lengths can vary anywhere from 2m to 10m; however, many panel sizes are dictated by the location of internal framing, temporary bracing, the interior column layout, the location of adjacent footings or the length of the contractor's buckets.

Walls are usually 600mm, 750mm or 900mm thick. However, thicker walls are available if required for bending or shear resistance or if required to support vertical loads. Other structural configurations are possible for geometric or load capacity requirements (Figure 2).

Prior to the start of excavation the contractor should provide a detailed plan of panel dimensions, wall elevations and sections showing details of the panels and the reinforcement. Wall dimensions are established initially by design and sometimes later in the field if the precise location of target soil strata is uncertain. In some cases the contractor is required to embed the wall to greater depths than required for basic design requirements. These greater depths may be necessitated by lateral support conditions or by water cutoff requirements. The top of the wall elevation is usually governed by details of future subgrade or superstructure construction or by the elevation and location of adjacent footings.

The contractor is usually permitted the option of overpouring the top of the wall to assure that good, sound concrete is achieved for connection to future construction. In many cases the contractor sets the top of guide wall elevations to the finished top surface of the slurry wall, thus permitting the continuous placement of concrete in the panel until such time as sound concrete reaches the surface. As an alternative, contractors have placed the guide walls at a higher elevation, overpoured beyond the theoretical top of the panel (but not to the top of the guide walls) and then cut down the excess concrete to the correct elevations. The latter procedure is less certain to yield quality concrete at the top of the wall.

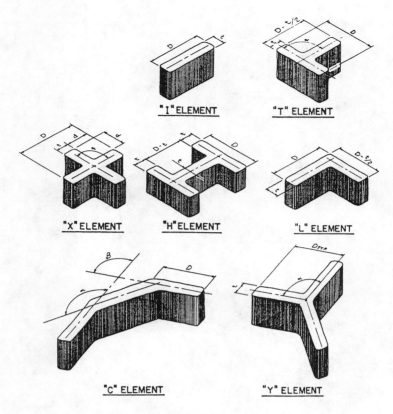

"I" ELEMENT   "T" ELEMENT

"X" ELEMENT   "H" ELEMENT   "L" ELEMENT

"C" ELEMENT   "Y" ELEMENT

Dmin. = LENGTH OF CLAM SHELL BUCKET

tmin. = WIDTH OF CLAM SHELL BUCKET

α VARIES FROM 60° TO 120° BUT TYPICALLY 90°

$\alpha \geqq$ 90° FOR "C" ELEMENT

β VARIES FROM 0° TO 180°

d VARIES FROM 0 TO (D-t)

Figure 2 – TYPICAL CONFIGURATIONS

Construction joints between panels are achieved in a variety of ways. The most basic and simplest method uses a round pipe to form a half round joint at the ends of the primary panels. Some contractors have attempted to improve upon this detail by using combinations of angles or plate stock attached to smaller round or rectangular tubes. Other contractors have used special end stops which permit the incorporation of waterstops into the joint. On many occasions steel wideflange beams are used to form panel joints and/or to provide structural capacity to the wall (Figure 3). Complicated joint details are expensive, difficult to install and can affect the installation of the reinforcing steel cages.

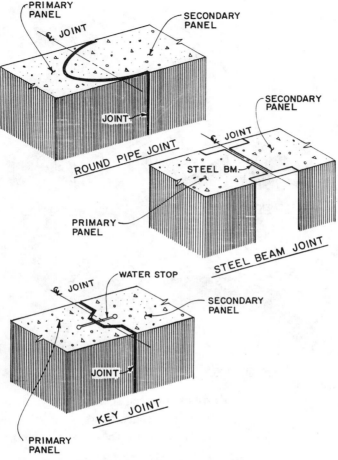

Figure 3 - PANEL JOINTS

REINFORCING STEEL CAGES

In general, reinforcing steel cages should be detailed as simply as possible. The same details should be repeated as often as possible. The design should require one layer of horizontal and vertical reinforcing steel on each face of the wall. Vertical splices should be minimized and, if possible, totally eliminated by special coupling devices available in the industry. Plates for bracing or tieback sleeves for rock or soil anchors are usually attached to reinforcing cage. Special care must be taken to tie and align the sleeves at the correct orientation and clear of the main reinforcing (Figure 4). A complete set of shop drawings should be prepared by the contractor for the inspector and steel fabricator's use.

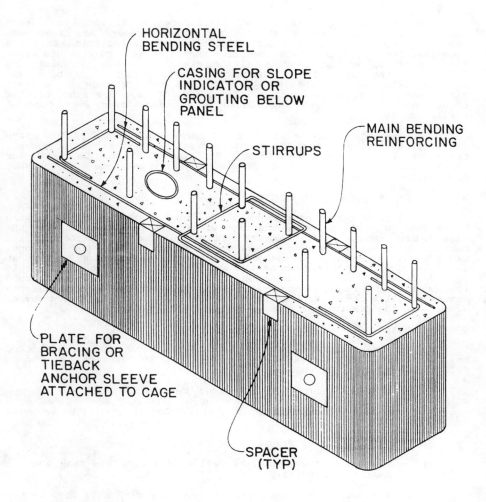

HORIZONTAL
BENDING STEEL

CASING FOR SLOPE
INDICATOR OR
GROUTING BELOW
PANEL

MAIN BENDING
REINFORCING

STIRRUPS

PLATE FOR
BRACING OR
TIEBACK
ANCHOR SLEEVE
ATTACHED TO CAGE

SPACER
(TYP)

Figure 4 – TYPICAL REINFORCING

Provision should be made for field alteration of the cages. Unforeseen site conditions usually require a greater or less depth or thickness of wall. The cage may also have to be altered in order to accommodate the revised panel length resulting from layout changes or panel digging errors. Accessories may be added or moved to accommodate changes in design or construction. The inspector should not permit the field alteration of the cages without the approval of the designer.

Welding of cages is to be discouraged. Welding can cause metallurgical changes to the steel and erection stresses can cause even the best made welds to fail during lifting and installation into the excavated trench. Cages and accessories should be secured with tie wire. The contractor should provide all supplemental steel necessary to strengthen the cage during handling and placement. U bars and supplemental steel should be securely tied to the cage to prevent misalignment or distortion during lifting and setting. A minimum of 75mm cover should be required and should be provided over each face of reinforcement.

The owner's representative must check each step of the cage fabrication, verifying that the required steel has been installed and all components are correctly positioned. The cage should not be lifted for installation into the excavation if not fully in compliance with the shop drawings.

SPACERS, SKIDS AND SPACING DEVICES

An adequate number of spacers, skids or other spacing devices should be used to properly position the cage within the panel and to hold the cage in that correct position during concrete placement. The position and details of the spacing devices should be shown on the shop drawings. Cages should be securely suspended from the guide walls and be kept at least 1m clear of the bottom of the excavation. The contractor should provide details showing the location of all inserts. The inspector should spot check all cage construction assuring that the contractor has installed all accessories and inserts and has placed the required number of bars in the correct positions.

CONCRETE MIXES

The concrete mix should be designed by the contractor and submitted to the owner's representative for approval. The concrete mix should follow several specific rules:

1. Design mixtures should range between 20 mpa and 35 mpa ultimate strength and should be designed and tested with enough water to guarantee that a 200mm slump will be achieved in the field.

2. Natural gravel is preferred to crushed stone.

3. The aggregates should be well graded and less than 20mm in maximum dimension.

4. A sandier mix, similar to a pumpcrete mix, will flow better through the tremie pipe as well as throughout the panel.

5. Plasticizers, water reducing agents, air entrainment agents and fly ash are recommended, however, super plastersizers, which only remain workable for a short period of time, should be used with caution.

Workability is the most important feature of tremie concrete. Every effort should be made to achieve as workable a mix as possible at the plant and to retain such workability throughout placement; 200mm slump concrete is essential for proper casting of slurry wall panels. Efforts by the contractor to provide greater slump or by the inspector to provide lesser slump should be resisted. Stiff unworkable concrete will assure that the panels will be honeycombed, joints will be irregular and leaks will occur. It is extremely difficult to place low slump concrete through a tremie pipe and into a long narrow excavation.

BENTONITE SLURRY

Fresh bentonite slurry should consist of a mixture of sodium bentonite and potable water and should exhibit as a minimum; specific gravity of about 1.03, viscosity of about 32 seconds using the Marsh Cone Funnel, maximum filtrate loss of 20 cc using a standard filter press and a pH between 7 and 11. After mixing, bentonite should be stored on site for at least one day, either in tanks or in a reservoir, in order to permit proper hydration. The contractor should establish a small bentonite quality control laboratory on site to assure that the bentonite slurry is suitable for its intended use. The contractor should then perform periodic testing of the bentonite at the trench to assure that bentonite is continuing to serve its intended purpose and will be sufficiently clean and workable to permit placement of tremie concrete. The contractor should always have at least one panel volume of mixed slurry available in storage in order to permit a rapid replacement of slurry should major losses occur.

Prior to the placement of tremie concrete, bentonite slurry in the excavated trench should exhibit a specific gravity of no more than 1.10, viscosity of no more than 50 seconds, sand content of no more than 5% measured 1.5m above the bottom of the trench. The contractor should provide suitable desanding equipment including air lifts, screens and cyclones in order to meet these requirements.

EXCAVATION

The contractor shall provide excavation equipment that is capable of removing all materials encountered within the alignment of the wall. Excavation can be done by either clamming, drilling, scraping or grinding, or a combination of these methods. The tools used may be subject to environmental constraints such as excessive noise and vibration. The excavation should be done in a continuous manner to the lines and grades established on the guide walls. The bentonite slurry should be pumped from the storage facilities in a continuous manner in order to assure that the excavated trenches can always be filled to within 1.5m of the top of the guide walls. Verticality of wall should be checked during excavation; if not within tolerance backfill with lean concrete and re-excavation maybe required. Depths should be checked at the start of each day to determine if cave-ins occurred overnight.

PLACEMENT OF REINFORCING STEEL CAGE INTO PANEL

Prior to the placement of the cage into the trench the bentonite slurry should be tested, cleaned and modified as necessary to meet specified requirements and to assure that the bentonite slurry is suitable for tremie concrete and the bottom should be sounded by a weighted line or rod to verify that the required depths have been achieved and that there is no sand residue or rock fragments on the bottom. Reinforcing steel cages and the end stops should be placed within the panel as soon after cleaning the trench as practical. The stop end devices should be securely fastened in position and the cage should be supported properly to assure that no movement will occur during concrete placement. Construction joints should be cleaned where fresh concrete is to be placed against previously placed concrete.

PLACEMENT OF CONCRETE

Concrete should be placed as soon after the installation of the reinforcing steel cages as practical and when started, concrete placement should proceed continuously until uncontaminated concrete has reached the required top of wall elevation. The contractor should maintain detailed records of the quality, quantity, and rise of concrete in the panel for each truck delivery (Figure 5) and should provide adequate equipment to assure that an uninterrupted supply and placement of concrete will occur even if a breakdown occurs somewhere within the system.

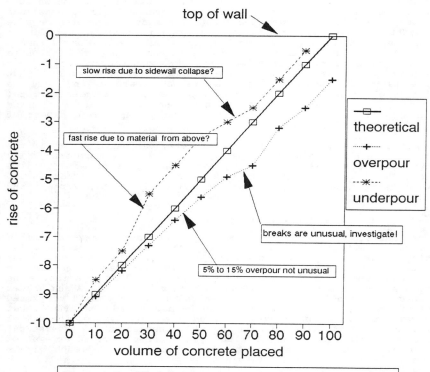

Figure 5 - Field record of concrete placement

Concrete should be placed by tremie methods in such a manner that the concrete displaces the slurry progressively from the bottom and rises uniformly to the surface and that the concrete and the slurry do not intermix.   The writers prefer the use of a single tremie pipe and short panels and do not recommend the use of "go devils" or plugs in an attempt to prevent concrete segregation or mixing of concrete with bentonite at the start of the placement.   The problem resulting from entrapment of the "go devil" or the plug within the panel is greater than the perceived benefit of initially separating the concrete from the slurry.   The tremie pipe must always be embedded within fresh concrete a minimum of 2m and a maximum of 5m.

The tremie pipe may have to be surged during placement.   If such is the case, great care must be taken to assure that the pipe is always embedded in fresh concrete and that the tremie seal is not lost.

In many cases contractors insist upon the use of two tremie pipes. Contractors should not be prevented from the use of two pipes; however, the contractors must then accept full responsibility for any   defects within the panel which may occur under those conditions.   The writers hesitate to prohibit the use of two tremie pipes if the contractor insists on their use. The writers prefer to impose restrictions on the use of two tremie pipes to minimize occurrences of defects resulting from entrapment of laitence or contaminated bentonite within the center of the panel.   As a minimum a sufficient number of trucks must be available to charge each tremie hopper uniformly and the concrete level at each tremie must be raised essentially level.

Normal practice permits the extraction of end pipes during the later stages of the concrete placement.   In many cases concrete is still being placed at the upper level of the panel while end stops are being slowly lifted from the bottom.   End stop withdrawals should be done in a smooth and continuous manner just after the initial set of the concrete occurs. Set times can be estimated by testing small batches of concrete retained from each truck.

A single 200mm or 250mm tremie pipe centrally located within a panel is recommended. Tremie hopper should be sufficiently large to receive the occasional surge of concrete and to prevent spillage of concrete from the hopper into the trench.   It is wise to provide a 75mm x 75mm or 100mm x 100mm mesh screen at the hopper inlet in order to prevent the entry of large balls of concrete which are occasionally found in poorly mixed and/or high cement content concrete mixes.   Once the concrete has been properly mixed and placed it is almost impossible for the concrete to not achieve its specified strength.

It has been the writers experience that cylinders taken during placement usually show concrete strengths 10 to 15 percent greater than the strengths specified. Cores taken later from the wall are apt to have strengths equal to or greater than 150 percent of the strengths specified. Defects in placed concrete are usually the result of problems which occur during placement of concrete by tremie methods.   Delays in delivery, overly stiff concrete mixes, loss of tremie charge, intermixing of concrete resulting from the use of two tremie pipes can cause such defects. The placement of concrete by tremie is the most critical element of the whole operation and must be closely controlled by both the contractor and inspection personnel at the site.   Once a concrete placement starts it should proceed to its conclusion unless means are taken to insure that a second stage of concrete placement can be undertaken without detrimental effect.

ACCURACY, TOLERANCES AND FINISHES

Construction accuracy and wall finishes usually depend upon the geology of the site and the contractor's skills and tools. Verticality tolerance is usually specified as 1% but may vary from 0.5% to 1.25% depending on design requirements and ground conditions (Figure 6). Tolerances should be increased by 50 to 100 percent in case the walls are to be excavated through loose soils or fills, containing piles, timbers or other loose debris.   The finish of the wall will be a direct reproduction of the soil surface against which the wall is cast. A loose boulder removed at the face of the excavation leaves an indentation at the side of the excavation. Concrete will fill the indentation, appearing as a protrusion on the finished wall.

Upon exposure of the wall the contractor should clean and removing all soil and weak concrete. The surveyor should check the wall against specified tolerances and mark out of tolerances areas for removal and defects for repair. All loose bentonite and soil should be removed from the top of the wall and from the face of the wall. The top of the wall should be trimmed to the finished elevations, and a key cut out for extension of the wall if needed. Keys and inserts should be exposed and prepared for subsequent use. Occasional bumps should be trimmed from the face of the wall and void areas should be filled. Occasionally a wall is parged or shotcreted to provide a "smooth" finish. In many cases the as cast walls serve as the final finished wall.

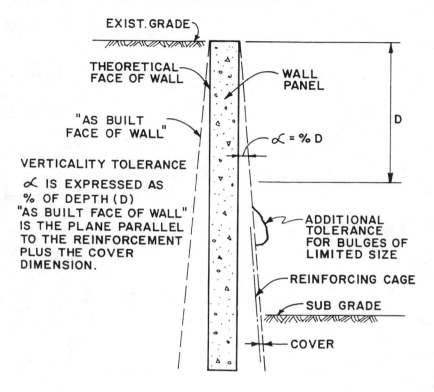

Figure 6 — WALL TOLERANCES

Properly executed slurry walls are watertight throughout the panel. Occasionally seepage will occur at the vertical joint between panels, at cold joints or at tieback locations. Sealing of seepage at inserts or through a vertical joint is the responsibility of the slurry wall contractor and must be performed by the contractor after the wall is exposed. The inspector should check all joints or defects to determine if they are watertight and will not blow at a later stage of construction. Defective joints or cracks are chipped out, cleaned and packed with rapid setting cement grout mixes. Occasionally it is also necessary to grout the soil directly behind the wall at the location of the leak.

RECORDKEEPING

The contractor and the inspector should maintain accurate records of all field operations. The contractor should prepare and maintain a true scale drawing showing the elevation of the wall, panel by panel, with dimensions, numbering scheme, sequence of panel installation, location of adjacent structures and utilities and the detail of inserts and other items that are embedded in the wall. The drawing should be updated daily by the contractor's supervisory personnel, recording excavation progress, material passed through and difficulties encountered during that day's operations. The drawing should be coded in such a manner that the strata lines of the various materials passed through can be readily determined. The contractor should also provide, on a daily basis, his bentonite slurry testing reports and concrete placement records including rate of placement and rise of concrete diagrams. If the quality of the soil or rock at the bottom of the wall is verified by either spoon sampling or core boring, that information should be provided as obtained and recorded on the wall elevation drawing. The inspector should maintain a set of drawings and documents for his own use. Report forms (Figures 7 and 8) used by the writers in their quality control program are attached to this report as a guide to the minimum data which the inspector should observe and collect.

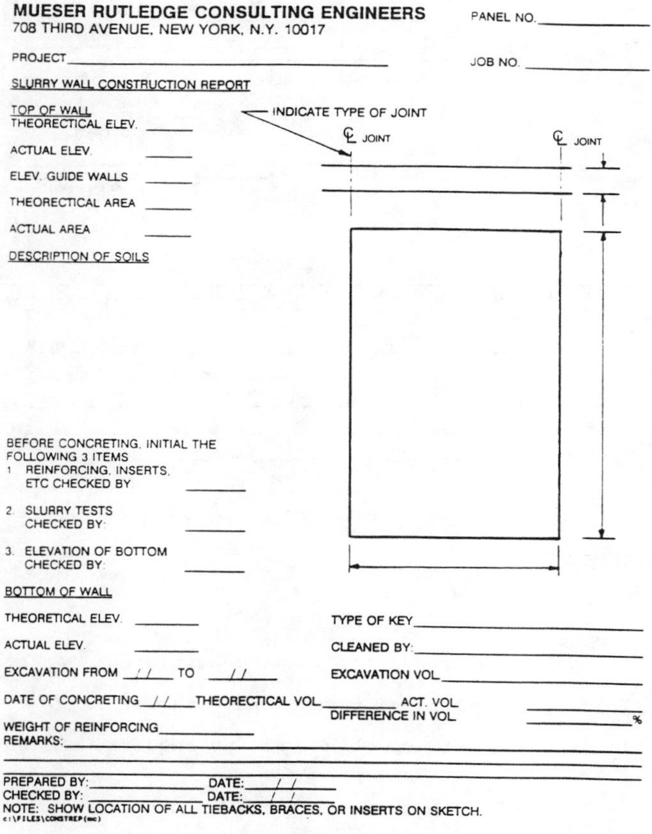

MUESER RUTLEDGE CONSULTING ENGINEERS
708 THIRD AVENUE, NEW YORK, N.Y. 10017

PANEL NO. _____

PROJECT _____

JOB NO. _____

SLURRY WALL CONSTRUCTION REPORT

TOP OF WALL
THEORECTICAL ELEV. _____
ACTUAL ELEV. _____
ELEV. GUIDE WALLS _____
THEORECTICAL AREA _____
ACTUAL AREA _____

DESCRIPTION OF SOILS

INDICATE TYPE OF JOINT

℄ JOINT   ℄ JOINT

BEFORE CONCRETING, INITIAL THE FOLLOWING 3 ITEMS
1. REINFORCING, INSERTS, ETC CHECKED BY _____
2. SLURRY TESTS CHECKED BY: _____
3. ELEVATION OF BOTTOM CHECKED BY: _____

BOTTOM OF WALL
THEORETICAL ELEV. _____
ACTUAL ELEV. _____
EXCAVATION FROM __/__ TO __/__
DATE OF CONCRETING __/__ THEORECTICAL VOL. _____ ACT. VOL _____
DIFFERENCE IN VOL _____ %
WEIGHT OF REINFORCING _____
REMARKS: _____

TYPE OF KEY _____
CLEANED BY: _____
EXCAVATION VOL _____

PREPARED BY: _____ DATE: __/__
CHECKED BY: _____ DATE: __/__
NOTE: SHOW LOCATION OF ALL TIEBACKS, BRACES, OR INSERTS ON SKETCH.
c:\FILES\CONSTREP(mc)

Figure 7 - INSPECTORS SLURRY WALL CONSTRUCTION REPORT

MUESER RUTLEDGE CONSULTING ENGINEERS

708 THIRD AVENUE, NEW YORK, NEW YORK 10017

FIELD INSPECTION REPORT - BENTONITE SLURRY TESTS (API - RP13B)

PROJECT _____   JOB NO._____

LOCATION _____

PANEL NO. _____

1)	DENSITY	SPECIFIED	MIN.		MAX	
	TEST NO. _____	MEASURED	ELEV. _____		DENSITY _____	
	_____		_____		_____	
	_____		_____		_____	

2)	VISCOSITY	SPECIFIED	MIN.	SEC	MAX	SEC
	TEST NO. _____	MEASURED	ELEV. _____		TIME	____ SEC
	_____	MARSH FUNNEL	_____			____ SEC
	_____		_____			____ SEC

3)	FILTRATION	SPECIFIED			MAX	CC
	TEST NO. _____	MEASURED	ELEV. _____		VOLUME ____ CC	

THICKNESS OF FILTER CAKE _____

4)	SAND CONTENT	SPECIFIED	MAX	%		
	TEST NO. _____	MEASURED	ELEV. _____	SAND CONTENT ____ %		
	_____		_____	____ %		
	_____		_____	____ %		

5)	pH	SPECIFIED	MAX		MIN	
	TEST NO. _____				pH _____	

REMARKS_____

_____

_____

PREPARED BY:_____ DATE:_____

CHECKED BY:_____ DATE:_____
C:\FILES\SLURTEST(mc)

Figure 8 - INSPECTORS BENTONITE SLURRY TEST REPORT

INSPECTOR'S CHECKLIST

GUIDE WALLS

1)   Are guide walls carried down to sufficient depth?

2)   Is subgrade material compact and stable?

3)   Is distance between guide wall as required and sufficient to accommodate bucket?

4)   Is line and grade accurately and "permanently" marked on guide walls?

5)   Are all abandoned utilities and penetrations of adjacent walls located and adequately sealed?

EQUIPMENT

1) Check length, width and weight of excavating tools.

2) Check mixing plant capacity and condition.

2) Check size of screens on desander. Check cyclones if used.

3) Check capacity of slurry storage tanks or reservoir. If tanks under pressure check certification.

4) Record size and type of tremie pipe, check for leaks, check lengths.

SHOP DRAWINGS & SUBMITTALS

1) Has contractor provided adequate shop drawings and details for the layout of the wall and for the fabrication of the reinforcing steel cages?

2) Has contractor provided required material submissions (concrete mix design, steel mill reports, bentonite test reports)?

3) Has contractor provided required building condition surveys, settlement level surveys and instrumentation?

REINFORCING STEEL CAGE

1) Has the contractor provided the required type, size and grade of steel?

2) Is the cage fabricated correctly (correct number and position of bars)? Are all inserts, keys and blockouts in place and correctly located? Are adequate lifting bars or cable connections provided to lift and support the cage?

3) If necessary to alter cage during installation, record changes.

4) Check that spacers and support system is adequate to hold cage in position when concrete is placed.

5) Check cages for buoyancy, extensive blockouts may resist the rise of concrete and cause the cage to float.

CONCRETE MIX AND PLACEMENT

1) Check delivery ticket for mix proportions; visually check for conformity as concrete is placed into hopper. Record arrival of truck, start and completion of placement. Work with contractor to assure continuous placement with no delays.

2) Check slump and prepare cylinders for testing.

3) Measure rise of concrete at completion of truck discharge, plot rise vs. volume, compare with theoretical.

4) Record length of segments of tremie pipe, record embedment of pipe, record time and length of pipe segments removed.

5) Check that end stops are correctly located and secured against movement during concrete placement.

BENTONITE SLURRY

1) Check slurry quality at plant, at trench, at intervals specified or when a change in slurry quality is noted.

2) Check that slurry has been properly desanded prior to concrete placement.

3) Perform final tests prior to placement of reinforcing cages.

4) Check that waste bentonite has been properly disposed.

PANEL EXCAVATION

1) Visually classify excavated material removed from panel, check if in agreement with geologic profile.

2) Check verticality and alignment at specified intervals.

3) Check depth of excavation at end of shift each day and at beginning of new work day. Check surface area adjacent to excavation.

4) Check that contractor is maintaining adequate excavation records.

5) Record unusual occurrences.

6) Is contractor prepared to maintain bentonite level at all times (overnight and weekends) and able to backfill in an emergency?

7) Check area at spoils stockpile to make sure waste slurry is contained.

8) Check condition of bottom of panel prior to placement of concrete; is wall embedded adequate distance into specified soils or rock? Is bottom of panel level sloped or stepped; has bottom surface been adequately cleaned? Is the end stop "hole" from the primary panel deeper than the level of the secondary panel?

9) Check slurry in panels for excess water at top of panel after heavy rains.

DURING GENERAL EXCAVATION

1) Review excavation and concreting records for possible wall defects at each stage of excavation.

2) Is contractor inspecting wall for defects as general excavation proceeds downward?

3) Is contractor performing adequate repairs?

4) Is surveyor highlighting alignment and tolerance problems?

5) Are keys, inserts, etc. correctly located, cleaned and prepared for subsequent use?

6) Is contractor performing required surveys and instrumentation measurements?

7)   Be prepared for surprises; have excavation and grouting equipment and wood wedges readily available, a little flow of water can move a lot of fine grained sandy soils.

GENERAL

1)   Is there adequate fencing around trenches and covers over open panels?

CONCLUSIONS

While quality control and quality of the slurry wall end product are the sole responsibility of the contractor it is essential that the owner and his inspection forces be at all times aware of the quality of the work installed by the contractor. The contractor and the inspectors should work together to achieve a high quality end product which will ensure the continued successful use of slurry walls in the United States.

REFERENCE

[1]   Millet, R.A. and Perez, J-Y, "Current USA Practice: Slurry Wall Specifications," Journal of the Geotechnical Engineering Division, ASCE Vol. 107, No. GT, August 1981.

Richard A. Millet,[1] Jean-Yves Perez,[2] and Richard R. Davidson[3]

USA PRACTICE SLURRY WALL SPECIFICATIONS 10 YEARS LATER

REFERENCE: Millet, R.A., Perez, J.Y. and Davidson, R.R., "USA Practice Slurry Wall Specifications 10 Years Later," Slurry Walls: Design, Construction and Quality Control, ASTM STP 1129, David B. Paul, Richard R. Davidson and Nicholas J. Cavalli, Eds., American Society for Testing and Materials, Philadelphia, 1992.

ABSTRACT: Ten years earlier the authors prepared a paper on the then beginning state of practice regarding slurry wall specification in the USA. Changes (or lack thereof) and developments in the basic building blocks of specification criteria for the two types of walls constructed by the slurry wall technique; i.e., structural diaphragm walls and cutoff walls are reviewed. Specific recommendations and overview guidance for specification content are made for each wall type. Conclusions are presented concerning the present needs and likely future developments in this rapidly expanding specialty construction field.

KEYWORDS: Slurry wall, diaphragm, cutoff, permeability, permanence, deformability, structural integrity, slurry properties, plastic concrete, soil-bentonite, and cement-bentonite.

INTRODUCTION

In 1981 the authors prepared a paper on the "Current USA Practice: Slurry Wall Specifications" (Millet and Perez 1981). The state of practice of slurry wall has gone through a significant growth period since that time. This paper will look at the USA practices in slurry wall specifications in 1991 and reflect on things that have changed and things that have not.

Two basic underground walls are constructed by the slurry wall technique: (1) the structural diaphragm wall, and (2) cutoff barrier wall. The structural diaphragm walls act as retaining walls and/or a foundation-bearing wall. The cutoff barrier walls are used to provide a hydraulic barrier to water seepage beneath dams, and within dams and dikes and beneath canals, etc., a barrier for water inflow into construction excavations, and a barrier to contain hazardous waste and its leachate. This latter use has been one of the areas of significant use and technology change in the last ten years.

---

[1]Executive Vice President and Chief Practice Officer, Woodward-Clyde Consultants, Stanford Place 3, Suite 1000, 4582 South Ulster Street, Denver, CO 80237.

[2]President and CEO, Woodward-Clyde Group, Inc., Stanford Place 3, Suite 1000, 4582 South Ulster Street, Denver, CO 80237.

[3]Senior Associate, Woodward-Clyde Consultants, Stanford Place 3, Suite 1000, 4582 South Ulster Street, Denver, CO 80237.

To establish diaphragm and cutoff slurry wall design criteria and, thus, specifications, the designer must clearly establish the objectives or end results that are to be obtained. This paper considers the critical design criteria and the resulting specifications for both slurry diaphragm walls and cutoff walls.

Diaphragm and cutoff walls are initiated with a common process. This process is the excavation of a narrow trench without the use of significant lateral support other than that provided by a bentonite-water slurry which is pumped into the trench so that the slurry level is maintained at or near the top of the trench throughout the excavation process.

In the diaphragm wall process, after completion of a segment of excavated trench, either cast-in-place concrete (tremie process) or precast panels are used to displace the stabilizing mud and construct a load-bearing wall (vertical and lateral).

There are four basic types of slurry cutoff walls: (1) soil-bentonite, (2) cement-bentonite, (3) plastic concrete, and (4) concrete. In the soil-bentonite cutoff process, the bentonite slurry is displaced by a soil-bentonite mixture similar in consistency to high slump concrete. The soil backfill forms a low permeability, highly plastic cutoff wall. In the cement-bentonite cutoff process, cement is added to a fully hydrated bentonite-water slurry. The cement-bentonite-water slurry is then used to both stabilize the slurry wall during excavation, and upon setting of the cement, for the permanent cutoff wall itself. The plastic concrete backfill is similar to cement-bentonite mix, but aggregate is added to the backfill to form a stronger but still "plastic" wall. The plastic concrete backfill is placed by a tremied process which displaces the bentonite slurry. Concrete cutoff walls are backfilled with structural concrete using a tremie process.

Prebid identification of potential contractor experience and qualifications for slurry wall construction are important, but even more critical is the experience and qualification of the key contractor site personnel; i.e., site superintendent and foreman or crew chief. It is these personnel who can "make or break" a project, and specifications should require both minimum years and project type experience for these individuals as well as giving the owner the right of approval for these key personnel.

End-result (performance-guaranteed) specifications are acceptable if (and this is an important if) the owner, engineer, and contractor truly understand and can agree on what end results are to be obtained. Until owners and engineers become more familiar with slurry trench techniques, applications, and limitations, some method specification will continue to be used. However, these specifications should be tailored to the true needs of the owner. With this philosophy, we shall examine in more detail the basic criteria for slurry wall construction.

The critical design criteria for the two types of slurry walls are:

Diaphragm walls:
- structural strength and integrity,
- permanence, and
- permeability.

Cutoff walls:
- permeability,
- deformability, and
- permanence.

These critical criteria can be subdivided and the corresponding building blocks of a specification developed. It is important to realize that specifications should be no more restrictive than is necessary to achieve the desired end product. To make specifications more complex and restrictive than necessary only results in raising the bid prices, delaying the progress of the work, and increasing the potential of contract litigation. Restrictive specifications may also tend to inhibit the specialty contractor from trying new ideas in difficult situations in this still developing field.

DIAPHRAGM WALL

The following text examines the three critical building block criteria for a specification for a diaphragm wall:
- (1) structural strength and integrity,
- (2) permanence, and
- (3) permeability.

Structural Strength and Integrity

Eight sub-criteria are recommended for consideration: (1) continuity and stability of excavation; (2) steel reinforcement or precast panel placement; (3) concrete placement (tremie process); (4) concrete fluidity (slump test); (5) concrete strength (water-cement ratio); (6) panel connections; (7) support systems (struts, rakers, tiebacks, etc); and (8) internal excavation procedures (control of maximum soil and groundwater pressures).

Continuity and Stability of Excavation--For the diaphragm wall to function as planned, it must be continuous. In turn, the excavated trench must remain open and be stable until the bentonite slurry is replaced with the applicable backfill. Many factors can affect the continuity and stability of the excavated trench. The following text provides a summary of the significant factors.

Soil, bedrock, and groundwater conditions--It is important to thoroughly investigate and understand the subsurface soil and/or bedrock conditions in the area of the proposed trench excavation. Problem excavation areas, such as boulders, dense sands and gravels, cemented layers, man-made obstacles (piers, bulkheads, old foundation elements, etc.) must be thoroughly understood and presented to the contractor if the diaphragm wall is to be properly bid, excavated, and constructed (i.e., proper excavation tools and technical procedures are planned and used).

It is extremely important that groundwater conditions in the area of the trench be thoroughly understood. This will include a sound understanding of the seasonal variations, as well as the potential for dramatic changes in groundwater levels due to anomalous weather conditions. Conditions such as artesian pressures and other geologic anomalies, such as springs and man-made sources of water (such as broken sewers), also should be thoroughly understood in order to avoid difficulties with the stability of the trench excavation. Once groundwater conditions are defined, specifications should require that the slurry in the excavation be kept a minimum of 3 ft (1 m) to 5 ft (1.5 m) above the maximum groundwater level anticipated during the excavation of the trench. The ability to set the minimum distance that the slurry should be above the groundwater level is directly related to the ability of establishing that groundwater level; i.e., the less certain, the greater the distance specified above the estimated groundwater table.

Excavation machines/techniques--Diaphragm walls are generally excavated in panels comprised of 1 to 3 bites of the excavation equipment. The length of these panels is controlled by the excavation equipment used, and the ability to maintain trench stability and place a manageable volume of concrete backfill. Panel lengths typically range from 9 to 30 ft (3 m to 9 m).

The most common excavation method for diaphragm walls is the cable-hung clamshell. This device matches the width of the trench and can weigh between 9 to 13 tons (8.1×10^3 kg to 11.79×10^3 kg). It is flexible and can be easily switched with a cable-hung chisel to excavate harder soils and rocks. Variations on the cable clamshell include clamshells opened and closed hydraulically, and clamshells suspended on the ends of the steel Kelly bars. These modified clamshells can be more effective in excavating harder soils by virtue of the greater force applied in digging.

For harder soils and rocks, the hydrofraise or hydromill devices are commonly used. These machines utilize hydraulic motors to drive rotary drum cutters which excavate the soil or rock, and the cuttings are removed through reverse circulation pumps. The cuttings are removed from the slurry in a desanding plant and fresh or clean slurry is added at the top of the trench. The hydrofraise machines have inclinometers to precisely monitor their verticality, and they can be steered by controlling the cutter torque and rotation speed, and if necessary, by adjusting the orientation of the machine by jacking. These machines can weigh up to 80 tons (72.56×10^3 kg) and be 60 feet (18 m) high. Cutters can have hardened pics or button/disc cutter bits. Hydrofrase machines have difficulty in excavating materials with significant cobble to boulder sizes. Clamshell systems work better in such environments.

Critical excavation tolerances--Specifications normally will indicate the minimum width and depth of the wall. In addition, it is normal to specify a maximum deviation from plumbness for the wall. With respect to depth and width, these criteria are usually established by the structural requirements of the diaphragm wall, the excavating equipment thought most appropriate for the site conditions, and with regard to depth, the geologic formations into which the diaphragm wall is to be founded. In general, the excavation tolerances, and particularly, the alignment of the diaphragm wall, can be better controlled when adequate reinforced concrete guide walls are specified to be constructed ahead of the trenching operations.

With regard to plumbness, structural or potential architectural considerations are important. The state of the art is such that walls have been built to depths of over 400 ft (122 m) with less than 6 in. (15 cm) deviation from the vertical; i.e., 1:800. However, one should specify such severe limitations on verticality only in cases where they are deemed to be a necessary requirement for the intended purpose of the wall. On most projects, 1:100 to 1:400 vertical tolerances have been used and found to be satisfactory. It is necessary (if the vertical tolerances are important to the end results of the diaphragm wall) that number, depth and frequency of verticality measurements be specified. If this is left to the end of the trench excavation process, a great deal of remedial excavation usually is required.

The depth of embedment of the diaphragm wall in bearing or cutoff stratum must be specified, and, more importantly, verified during construction. Typical requirements depending on bearing capacity, seepage, and passive toe resistance design criteria are 6 in. (1.5 cm) in very competent bedrock to as much as 2 to 4 ft (0.6 to 1.2 m) in softer bedrock or competent soil. The bottom of the excavation trench should be thoroughly cleaned with an airlift to remove loose soils, rock debris, and contaminated slurry. The bottom conditions should be checked by probing to confirm cleanliness of the foundation contact, just before concreting.

Acceptable techniques for making verticality measurements include clamshell or chisel plumb lines, reverse pendulum, and Koden sonic measurements. The most common technique is to attach a wire line to the center of the clamshell, lower it in 20 - 40 ft (6-12 m) depth increments and measure the offset from true vertical by a rule placed across the trench. Measurements are made on both ends, and, depending on the length of the panel, possibly at the center of the panel. Reverse pendulum measurements are made in a similar fashion with a circular device the same size as the trench lowered from a frame with winch and scale. The Koden probe is also lowered from the centerline of the trench and provides a strip chart image of the distance travelled by a wave reflected from the trench walls. This technique provides a continuous verticality profile.

Potentially more important than verticality is continuity between adjacent panels. Verticality measurements from adjacent panels can be overlain to ensure that the minimum overlap of concrete backfill has been achieved across the joint. Minimum continuity between panels is typically specified to be 24 in. (60 cm).

Slurry properties--The properties of the trench stabilizing slurry are important in that they control to a great extent the stability of the trench, the removal of excavated material, and the adequacy of concrete placement. A stable thixotropic suspension of Wyoming grade bentonite and water is typically specified. Primary slurry properties that are typically specified are viscosity, density, unit weight or specific gravity, filtrate loss, and pH. These properties can be specified both for newly prepared slurry and for samples of slurry taken from the production trench.

In slurry trench practice, viscosity is generally measured with a Marsh funnel [API Spec 13A, Spec RP 13B (current release date)]. Viscosity is a measure of the ability of a fluid to resist shearing; an average viscosity of approximately forty (40) Marsh seconds is appropriate for slurry wall construction. This value of viscosity has been found to give consistently reasonable results in ensuring the satisfactory excavation, stability, and concreting of the trench. Fresh slurry should have a minimum viscosity of 32 Marsh seconds, while in the trench the slurry viscosity should not exceed 65 Marsh seconds.

Minimum density of freshly prepared slurry has typically been set slightly over that of groundwater. Some specifications have set minimum densities so high that, if prepared with bentonite alone, the mixture would not even flow. Such high densities can only be obtained if fine sands or other excavated material are mixed in with the slurry. Because it is important in a diaphragm wall to minimize the sand content of the slurry so that the eventual tremie concreting operations are not impeded, it is important that a minimum density for a diaphragm wall should not be made a severe limitation (actually, it is probably more appropriate to rely on control of the viscosity and filtrate loss). Specified maximum unit weight typically is on the order of 65 lb/ft^3 (29 kg/m^3) to 75 lb/ft^3 (34 kg/m^3), and is limited to ensure the tremie processes are not impeded.

Another factor considered in slurry trench specifications is the maximum allowable sand content prior to concrete placement. This parameter can be measured directly by sand content tests or, more commonly, indirectly by the density of the slurry. Prior to tremie concreting of the diaphragm wall, it is typically specified that the sand content should not exceed 5%. To reduce the sand content of the slurry, it is normally recirculated through a desanding unit to remove the sand with shakers and cyclones.

Filtrate loss for a bentonite slurry is determined by a standard filter press test [American Petroleum Institute (API) Test PP131B]. The filter press test is used to simulate the formation of filter cake that is built up on the excavated surfaces by the electrokinetic forces and seepage forces pushing the slurry into the sides of the trench. Filtrate loss and corresponding cake thickness are indicative of how much slurry loss will occur during excavation of the trench, and how fast the cake will form or reform on the sides of the trench when damaged; e.g., by the excavating tools.

Filtrate loss is indeed a measurement of the stability of the slurry and its ability to maintain a stable trench. A polluted slurry, be it by cement or by other chemicals such as salts or acids, will have a high filtrate loss and a thick filter cake built up of flocculated slurry.

To ensure a slurry of adequate quality, a reasonable upper limit should be specified for the standard filtrate loss. Normal range of filtrate loss for bentonite slurries both freshly prepared and from samples obtained in the production trench are 15 cm³ to 30 cm³.[1]

Usual range of filtrate loss for cement-bentonite slurries is much higher; in general, from 100 cm³ to 180 cm³. Actually, in this application, it is preferred to measure the filtrate loss of the fully hydrated bentonite slurry before the addition of cement.

The last important control item on slurry properties is pH, especially in an area where the chemistry of the soil excavated or of the groundwater could dramatically change the pH of the bentonite slurry mixture. The most desirable range for the slurry pH is on the order of 6.5 to 10. If the pH becomes greater than 10.5, the slurry should be watched very closely, as it will tend to flocculate and settle out. At this point, it may be necessary to require the addition of a deflocculating agent to ensure continued effectiveness of the slurry.

Of all the slurry properties discussed above, it is our opinion that filtrate loss has demonstrated itself to be the single most useful construction control factor in preventing the failure and collapse of slurry trench excavations. If the filtrate loss is above 30 cm³, then the trench is in danger of collapse. Compounding this problem is stand open time. A sure failure scenario is high filtrate loss and inactive or stand open times in excess of several days. The higher the filtrate loss and the longer the trench is inactive, the higher the risk of failure.

Alternative slurry materials--Other materials are occasionally used in certain applications instead of bentonite to create a stabilizing slurry in the trench. Attapulgite clay can be used in saline water environments because it is less susceptible to flocculation in the presence of high sodium concentrations than bentonite. However, this clay does not form a stable filter cake and is typically not used in unstable granular soils. High yield bentonite (125 barrels per ton) fully hydrated in fresh water may work well in these conditions.

Newly introduced polymer muds are receiving more attention. The polymers are manufactured from organic compounds including bean curds. Their propensity to degrade into water makes them attractive in urban environments where bentonite disposal is costly. However, polymers do not form a stable filter cake and are not recommended for trenches in unstable granular soils.

Steel Reinforcement Placement--The steel reinforcement requirements for a concrete diaphragm wall follow standard American Iron and Steel Institute and American Concrete Institute specifications. In addition to these basic reinforcing specifications, it is important to recognize that the steel should be such that tremie concrete can be easily and thoroughly placed around the steel without honeycombs and slurry-filled voids. Consequently, it is important that steel reinforcement not be so dense and

---

[1] Note: Because of the origin of this test, only metric units have interpretative value.

tightly placed as to present problems in tremie concreting. Spacers on the external reinforcing bars on the reinforcing cage must be installed to ensure proper centering of the reinforcing cage in the slurry wall and ensure proper concrete coverage of the steel on the external faces of the wall. To facilitate future construction, sleeves and trumpets for future tiebacks, bearing plates for future struts and structural members, knockout panels, and shear keys can be included in the reinforcing cage. It is important to remember that, because the reinforcing cage is placed in sections panel by panel, it must be checked to ensure the integrity of the cage while and prior to its placement into the trench. Techniques to connect reinforcing cages across panel joints are available, but not often used.

The adherence of slurry to the reinforcing bars may affect the concrete-to-steel bond, but not sufficiently to control design. Bond reduction factors of 0.8 to 0.6 have been used.

Placement of precast panels into a cement-bentonite slurry or bentonite slurry with tremie placement of a toe embedment concrete is used when specific structural or aesthetic design criteria can only be met by a precast system. As with any diaphragm wall, the most difficult part of the precast panel operation is to ensure panel connections are intact and properly aligned. Proper spacers must again be used and vertical and horizontal alignment of the panels must be monitored, during and after installation. Existing proprietary precast panel techniques usually include a special surface treatment of the excavation side of the panels to facilitate removal of the hardened cement-bentonite slurry.

Concrete Placement Tremie Process--The standard tremie concreting processes are applicable in the placement of concrete in bentonite slurry diaphragm wall construction. The tremie pipe(s) should remain embedded in the fresh concrete a minimum of 10 ft (3.0 m) at all times. When concreting wide panels, e.g., panels wider than 30 ft (9.2 m), it is recommended that more than one tremie pipe be specified. A rule of thumb is to use one tremie per 15 ft (4.6 m) of panel. The design of the concrete mix must ensure that the maximum size of aggregate is appropriate to the tremie process as regards the spacing of steel reinforcement. The tremie process also is affected by the slurry viscosity, density and sand content. It is important that in the tremie process, sufficient concrete be on hand to adequately backfill a panel section without interruption so as not to cause a formation of horizontal cold joints and, thus, slurry seams during the concreting process. Special effort should be made to clean large deviations in panel verticality that may act as overhangs or discontinuities in the trench walls that would entrap contaminated slurry during concreting. If geotechnical data indicate that sandy soils (or bedrock) will be encountered in the trench excavation, then strong emphasis must be placed in the specifications regarding desanding requirements, prior to concrete placement, e.g., maximum sand content of slurry and/or maximum density of the slurry. In some cases it may be necessary to replace contaminated slurry with fresh slurry prior to concreting.

Concrete Fluidity (Slump Test)--It is normally considered good practice to specify concrete fluidity (as measured by the standard concrete slump test) in the range of 7 in. to 9 in. (180 mm to 230 mm). This will ensure adequate flow of the concrete in the tremie system and the displacement of the slurry in the wall panels. Stiffer mixes usually lead to voids and open honeycombs in the panels, particularly where the reinforcing cage is dense. Plasticizers can be specified to increase the workability of the mix without reducing its strength.

Concrete Strength (Water-Cement Ratio)--The strength of the concrete in the backfilled diaphragm wall is directly related to the water-cement ratio of the concrete mix and the structural requirements of the wall.

Consequently, normal American Concrete Institute (ACI) specifications and practice can be followed in specifying the required structural strength of the concrete.

Panel Connections--There are various positive panel construction connection techniques that can be specified to ensure that there is a structural tie between adjacent panel sections and that these sections have adequate strength and integrity to support the design loads imposed upon them. Some of these connections are proprietary, others have become standard practice. In many cases, this is a good place to require an end-result specification, i.e., require that the strength, integrity, and continuity of the joints is maintained and allow the contractor to use his ingenuity to develop an appropriate scheme.

Several types of typical structural panel joints are illustrated in Figure 1. The circular stop end joint is the most commonly used panel connection. By removing the stop end tubes from the primary panels, a semi-circular guide is provided for the adjacent secondary panels. Cleaning of the joint with a scratcher or other device is important to remove any contaminated material from the panel connection. Triangular tongue and groove joints can be constructed in a similar manner. When hydrofraise excavation equipment is used, it can excavate a roughened joint directly into the concrete of the adjacent panel ensuring a clean, tight connection.

Support Systems (Struts, Rakers, Tiebacks, etc.)--The support system needed to provide the temporary or permanent support for concrete diaphragm walls after excavation inside the wall enclosure is very similar to that for any retaining wall. Consequently, struts, rakers, and earth and rock tiebacks are appropriate and have been used successfully with diaphragm walls.

In addition, cantilever design by internal stiffening with vertical structural steel members, enlarged T-panel counterfort shape with or without stem anchors, and by post-tensioning have been used.

Internal Excavation Procedures (Control of Maximum Soil and Groundwater Pressures)--Many times, structural support of diaphragm walls has been determined by the design engineer only in a final excavated condition, whereas internal support systems described previously and groundwater and soil conditions inside the excavation area, are left totally up to the contractor. This can cause difficulties in that there may be certain combinations of construction conditions; i.e., groundwater, excavated soil and rock conditions, and installation procedure of retention system, which can lead to higher stresses during excavation than considered for the permanent conditions.

If the engineer feels this may be the case, it may be necessary to either work out a compatible system with the contractor or place limits in the specification on the procedures that must be followed in installing the support system for the diaphragm wall, and on the sequence of excavation.

A simple example of a possible problem would be permitting total dewatering of the interior of the excavation and removal of a large lift thickness of excavated material without the placement of the first interior support; e.g., tieback, raker, etc. These conditions must be examined in close detail on a job-by-job basis and then the engineer must decide what are the maximum limits he can permit the contractor to develop, and where he must specify control to ensure the structural strength and integrity of the wall.

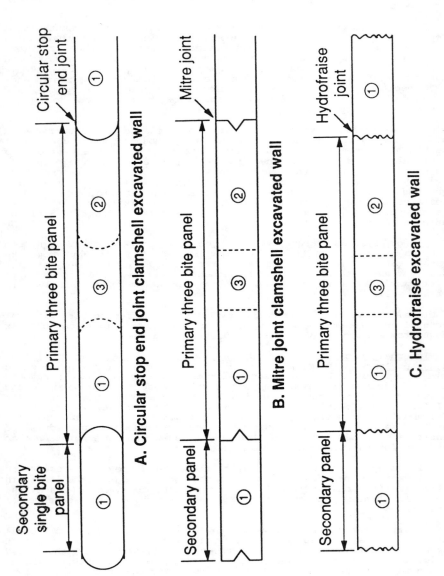

FIG. 1 -- Foundation slurry wall panels: typical layouts.

Permanence

Permanence of a concrete diaphragm wall is of primary importance. In most cases, the concrete diaphragm wall has become a permanent part of the structure and, thus, must endure for the life of the structure. There are four areas of general concern and interest: (1) active role in the foundation, (2) reinforced concrete permanence, (3) tieback permanence, and (4) architectural considerations.

Active Role in the Foundation--As previously identified, many typical concrete diaphragm walls become an integral part of the foundation of the proposed structure, either as a permanent retaining wall or vertical load-bearing member, or both. In this regard, all considerations that are involved in any permanent foundation element must be reviewed and evaluated in controlling and specifying the desired end result.
Reinforced Concrete Permanence--As for any other subsurface structures, time-dependent corrosion must be taken into account for diaphragm slurry walls. The quality of the concrete may be altered with time by aggressive groundwater. In some cases, sulfate-resistant cement may have to be specified. In other cases, the concrete may have to be designed to withstand the long-term corrosive action of saline or acidic waters. Because the concrete in a diaphragm slurry wall is actually cured under rather ideal humidity and temperature conditions, shrinkage cracks are not usually of concern.

Tieback Permanence--A practice that was developed in Europe and now is applied in U.S. practice is the use of permanent earth/rock tiebacks to support permanent concrete diaphragm walls. This practice consists of providing access to the jacking head of anchors; this permits the rejacking and testing of the anchors over the life of the structure.

Corrosion is a concern for permanent stressed tiebacks. The designer should be aware of the corrosion potential of the soil and rock mass surrounding the tiebacks. The specifications should include measures, such as protective coatings and grouting, cathodic protection, etc.

Architectural Considerations--In many applications, the interior portions of concrete diaphragm walls can be left exposed; i.e., subway excavations, basements of parking garages in buildings, etc. Where this is the case, certain limitations on concrete projections into the excavation may be appropriate. There have been many case histories where the interior of the diaphragm walls, when exposed upon excavation, have been found to be quite satisfactory for use without any additional cosmetic applications.

However, when a different aesthetic finish is desired, several facing techniques are available. The surface can be sandblasted or shotcreted to obtain a roughened "sandstone like" texture. Facial panels of different design can also be mounted to the slurry wall interior face. Control of seepage through joints may also be an architectural consideration, and surface sealing techniques work well.

Permeability

With regard to the permeability of the concrete diaphragm wall, it is typical to specify that there be no free-water leakage through the wall, but depending upon the architectural and social use of the interior part of the exposed slurry wall, dampness of the wall may be permitted. It is, of course, possible that in certain applications even dampness needs to be limited. If this is the case, the engineer will have to recognize that the more restrictive the specifications, the greater the likely bid costs.

For permeability, five primary criteria are recommended for consideration: (1) integrity of wall excavation, (2) concrete placement, (3) concrete fluidity (slump), (4) panel connections, and (5) sleeves and other wall inserts.

Integrity of Wall Excavation--Considerations are similar to those listed under continuity and stability of excavation of diaphragm walls; i.e., soil, bedrock and groundwater conditions, critical excavation tolerances, and slurry properties. If the trench is not continuous and stable, then excess seepage, leakage, or dampness is certain. Of particular concern are three items: (1) the foundation contact conditions at the bottom of the wall (ensuring a watertight cutoff), (2) the presence of discontinuities within the wall, and (3) the continuity between panels and the integrity of the joints.

Concrete Placement--Again, the same consideration consistent with structural strength and integrity applies; the tremie process must follow the same good practices as required for any tremie process. Clean joints and clean uncontaminated slurry are of paramount importance.

Concrete Fluidity (Slump)--To ensure low permeability of the wall, a high slump concrete mix (see previous discussion concerning plasticizers) is needed to prevent bad concrete joints and honeycombs.

Panel Connections--The same type of panel joints shown in Figure 1 are used to provide a semi-watertight connection between panels. Although no slurry wall is perfectly watertight, if joints are properly constructed, seepage flows should be very small at first (dampness) and may diminish completely with time as the bentonite thixotropically seals the small opening. Each of the joints in Figure 1 provides an elongated seepage path, and if properly cleaned, should have less than 1 mm thickness of bentonite on the joint surface. Tremie concreting through contaminated slurry may produce a much thicker coating of contaminated clay which could be erodible, leading to potential piping through the joint. These problems generally appear during initial excavation and can be repaired by surface treating or grouting of the joint. Severe joint piping problems can be corrected by freezing or flashed grouting until a permanent seal is installed. Several manufacturers now offer joints with water-stop plastic inserts across the joints. So long as the integrity of the concrete contact between panels is maintained, this technique may provide additional watertight security. Placing too many inclusions and obstructions at a joint makes complete concrete continuity more difficult to achieve.

Sleeves and Other Wall Inserts--For future construction ease, various sleeves and inserts (e.g., for tiebacks, utility penetration, etc.) can be installed in the reinforcing cage prior to concreting. Often these inserts constitute a preferential seepage path for outside groundwater. To avoid unacceptable water inflow, grouting behind the sleeves and inserts may have to be specified. For permanent installations, sealing of these inclusions may be required with expansive grouts or plates.

CUTOFF WALL

Introduction

Since our first paper in 1981, the use of plastic slurry cutoffs (soil-bentonite, cement-bentonite, plastic concrete) has had an exponential growth, especially in hazardous waste applications.

Uses of Cutoff Walls--Figure 2 shows typical applications of the cutoff wall as constructed with the slurry method. As can be seen from Figure 2, applications can range from forming an impervious cutoff for a dam or dike impoundment to the containment of subsurface oil and chemical pollutants.

At the present state of the practice, two general types of plastic cutoff walls are used: (1) walls excavated with a bentonite-water slurry and backfilled with a soil-bentonite or plastic concrete mixture, and (2) walls excavated with a cement-bentonite-water slurry which does not need to be backfilled as cement causes the slurry to harden to strengths comparable to that of a stiff clay.

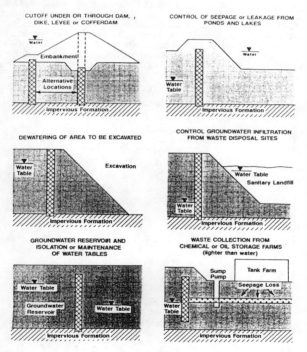

FIG. 2 -- Typical application of slurry trench cutoff wall.

Mix Design Alternatives--A designer has a wide variety of slurry wall backfill mixes available to match the specific cutoff requirements of each project. Backfills can range from soil-bentonite to cement-bentonite to plastic concrete to conventional concrete. As the percentage of cement increases, the strength and performance (erosion resistance) increases, but at the expense of ductility. Figure 3 shows how compressive strength increases with cement-water ratio. The addition of bentonite improves ductility and reduces permeability but may decrease strength. However, the designer must work within a limited range of aggregate size and cement and bentonite content to provide a workable mix with adequate fluidity. Balancing strength, ductility, erodability, permeability and workability is the challenge of slurry wall backfill mix design.

For example, soil-bentonite may be the most ductile backfill available for a seepage cutoff through a dam under construction. It will deform with the embankment without cracking. However, the low tensile strength may not provide adequate resistance to hydraulic fracturing, once the reservoir is filled, leading to seepage. Therefore, cement-bentonite with a higher tensile strength may be preferred or the width of the soil-bentonite cutoff could be increased.

Another example is a seepage cutoff in a large open cut that will be deforming as the slope is excavated. Although cement-bentonite provides a ductile backfill, if cracks develop, it may not have sufficient erosion resistance to prevent their enlargement. A low strength plastic concrete with a higher cement content and a high percentage of bentonite may be a more appropriate balance between ductility and erosion resistance. Various additives may be used to improve concrete behavior including fluidifiers and accelerators. Fly ash has also been used as cementiceous material as a replacement for a certain percentage of cement in the mix. However, the delay in strength gain with fly ash should be considered in its use.

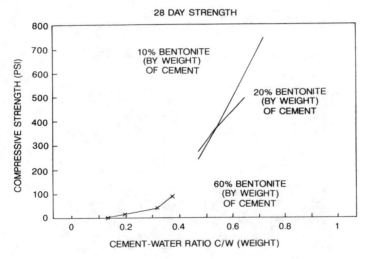

FIG. 3 -- Compressive strength vs. C/W ratio.

With the aforementioned applications and types of cutoff walls in mind, there are three principal design criteria which we believe to be important considerations in the preparation of specifications for construction of plastic cutoff walls. These criteria are permeability, deformability, and permanence.

Permeability

Permeability is, of course, the most important characteristic of the cutoff wall in that the major reason this type of slurry trench/wall is constructed is to minimize the passage of fluid. Cutoffs can prevent infiltration into an excavation, retain water in a reservoir, or prevent a leakage of polluted chemicals, oils, gasoline, etc., out of a containment area. The following five factors are important to the eventual permeability of a slurry trench cutoff wall: (1) continuity and integrity, (2) thickness of wall (hydrostatic head), (3) cutoff backfill properties, (4) backfill placement for soil-bentonite and plastic concrete cutoff, and (5) connection detail with surface structures.

Continuity and Stability Excavation--It is important that the slurry trench excavation and finished wall be continuous so as not to permit seepage zones or zones of pervious material to breach the cutoff. In this regard, the following factors must be considered.

The same factors considered in the diaphragm wall section are applicable here. The depth will be controlled in many cases by the subsurface conditions; i.e., the depth to an aquiclude and the type of containment or permeability barrier that is to be constructed. The width will be dependent upon the required permeability of the cutoff walls, the backfill materials that make up the wall, the hydrostatic pressure across the wall, and the minimum size of available excavation equipment. These latter items will be considered subsequently. The inclination and deviation from verticality will only be important as they affect the continuity and integrity of the wall and should be specified accordingly.

The slurry properties important to ensuring stability of the trench during excavation and backfilling are identical to those specified for diaphragm walls; i.e., viscosity, density, filtrate loss, pH, and sand content.

Groundwater conditions must be thoroughly understood along the entire length of the cutoff wall in order to prevent difficulties with regard to caving of the trench due to high hydrostatic pressures or adverse chemical influences on the slurry encountered during the excavation. As was considered for diaphragm walls, it is important that a minimum of 3 ft to 5 ft (1 m to 1.5 m) of slurry head be maintained in the excavation above the level of the maximum anticipated groundwater conditions. As discussed for diaphragm walls, seasonal and man-made fluctuation of groundwater levels must be established in this regard. Maintaining a filtrate loss of less than 30 cm^3 provides a very useful index on the effectiveness of the filter cake in preventing trench collapse.

Potential anomalous subsurface conditions that will impede either the continuity of the cutoff wall as it is being excavated or the tie-in with the subsurface aquiclude must be understood. The minimum penetration into an aquiclude at the base of the wall must be thoroughly examined before it is specified. If the aquiclude is a competent impervious bedrock, a very minor penetration may be satisfactory. A considerable cost penalty would be imposed on the project by requiring a 2-ft (0.6-m) penetration into a competent bedrock if it is not truly required. If, however, the excavation is to be carried into a clay aquiclude, then it might be reasonable to specify a 2-ft or 3-ft (0.5-m or 1-m) penetration into the aquiclude. Such penetration may avoid problems with regard to cleaning the bottom of the excavation, as essentially a sump has now been provided in which soil which has settled out of the slurry may collect without creating a seepage path at the base of the wall.

Thickness Wall (Hydrostatic Head)--In setting minimum thickness of the cutoff wall, hydrostatic head and permeability of the backfill materials must be evaluated. A typical relationship that has been used for soil-bentonite backfill slurry walls is that the wall should have a thickness of 5 ft (30 m) to 7.5 ft (1.5 m-2.3 m) for walls up to 100 ft (30.5 m) in depth. Detailed studies of arching and hydrofracturing are appropriate for significant deviations from this guideline or for deeper cutoff walls.

For both plastic concrete and cement-bentonite slurry trench cutoff walls, the increased shear strength of the backfilled wall has typically permitted the wall thickness to be set at a minimum physical excavation thickness; i.e., somewhere between 24 in. and 36 in. (610 mm and 910 mm). This width is satisfactory up to a depth of at least 100 ft (30.5 m) of hydrostatic head. Beyond that point, more detailed engineering evaluations should be carried out to evaluate the ability of cement-bentonite or plastic concrete cutoff walls to resist hydrofracturing, cracking and erosion.

A new factor in establishing cutoff wall thickness, which also affects the wall's permeability, is the insertion of a geomembrane into the wall backfill process. Several proprietary installation techniques have been developed by contractors. It is recommended, if a geomembrane is needed, that only a contractor and key personnel with prior experience be used on the project. Specific criteria such as geomembrane physical and chemical properties and general environmental compatibility should follow appropriate ASTM standards.

Cutoff Backfill Properties: Soil-bentonite backfill--In many cases, specifications have established a gradation of soil-bentonite backfill that compares to that of a glacial clay till; i.e., a wide range of particle sizes from coarse to fine with the resultant bentonite content somewhere in the range of 2% to 4% by weight and on the order of 10% to 20% fines (soil particles finer than the openings of a No. 200 standard U.S. sieve). Permeabilities of such mixtures have been measured to be on the order of 10^{-7} cm/s. It must be pointed out that other gradations have been used satisfactorily for soil-bentonite backfill, including fine sands and clays. The density of the backfill should be at least 5 lb/ft^3 (80 kg/m^3) greater than the density of the bentonite slurry.

The second factor with respect to specification of the backfill concerns its consistency. Typically, the consistency of soil-bentonite backfill is controlled by a concrete slump test. To control the slope of the backfill and to ensure that liquid slurry is not trapped in the backfill, it has been found that a slump in the range of 4 in. to 6 in. (100 mm to 150 mm) is appropriate. If the slump is greater than this, then a very flat backfill slope is obtained which can pose problems with regard to efficiency of excavation. If the slump is less, honeycombs, voids, and entrapment of pervious materials may result which can cause breaches in the cutoff wall.

The desired consistency of the backfill is typically obtained by either tracking and blading the soil with bentonite slurry adjacent to the slurry-filled trench, or using an on-site pug-mill to mix the backfill.

Cement-bentonite (self-hardening slurry)--The principal factors affecting the permeability of the cement-bentonite slurry (which is also the slurry used during the excavation process) are cement-water ratio, bentonite-water ratio, and, of course, mechanical procedure in making eventual panel connections between the fresh cement-bentonite slurry and the set cement-bentonite. It is important to recognize that the cutoff wall is formed by the cement-bentonite mixture which is the same material that is used to stabilize the trench during excavation. Typical permeability of cement-bentonite slurry cutoff wall is on the order of 10^{-6} cm/s (10^{-1} ft/yr).

It is important to specify in the cement-bentonite process that the bentonite be fully hydrated with water prior to the addition of any cement. When this procedure is followed, the cement-water ratio typically will be the controlling factor in the eventual strength, deformability, and permeability of the backfill.

It is important, when panel cold joint or work shift connections are made between two excavation units, that a thorough excavated overlap is obtained to ensure that no windows or cold joints are created. Experience has indicated that connections may be made as long as one week later into set cement-bentonite and adequate continuity has been obtained. In some cases, retarder can be added to the cement-bentonite slurry to prevent flash set and cracking and, therefore, permit positive contact between adjacent panel units. Typically, the cement-bentonite slurry trench process is used in a continuous fashion, with connections made along the wall on a daily basis.

The self-hardening characteristics may limit the depth of cement-bentonite walls to that which can be excavated before hardening occurs. However, cement-bentonite walls with depths of over 100 feet (30 m) have been successfully completed.

Plastic concrete backfill--Factors controlling the permeability of plastic concrete backfill is the cement-water ratio, bentonite content, weight, angularity and size of fine and coarse aggregate, and mixing sequence. Workable mixes with a slump of 7 to 9 inches (17.5 to 12.5 cm), can have a bentonite content ranging from 4% to 12% by weight and coarse aggregate up to 3/4 inch (1.8 cm) if rounded and 1/2 inch (1.2 cm) if angular. It is always recommended to fully hydrate the bentonite in the full volume of water before mixing in cement and aggregate. This avoids lumps of dry bentonite and aggregate and promotes a more uniform, low permeability backfill. Permeabilities ranging from 10^{-7} to 10^{-8} cm/s (10^{-2} to 10^{-3} ft/yr) can be achieved depending on cement content.

Conventional concrete backfill--Properties of conventional concrete are similar to those discussed for diaphragm walls. Very low permeabilities as low as 10^{-10} cm/s (10^{-5} ft/yr) have been achieved for conventional concrete.

Backfill Placement for Cutoff--The initial backfilling procedure for a soil-bentonite cutoff wall requires that the soil-bentonite mixture be placed by a tremie process in the slurry-stabilized cutoff trench, or a starter slope trench is used (see Figure 4a). The initial process continues until sufficient material has been placed in the excavation to permit the backfill material to become exposed at the top of the trench.

If tremie is used, standard practices with regard to tremie should be maintained. Soil-bentonite backfill also has been successfully tremied with a clamshell bucket; however, this process is dependent on contractor implementation skills.

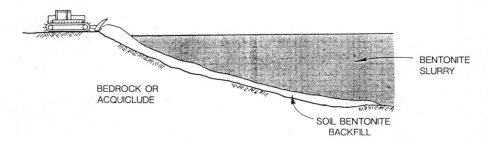

FIG. 4a -- Soil-Bentonite cutoff wall backfill.

After exposure of the backfill material at the top of the trench, the remainder of the backfill is pushed with a dozer onto the exposed backfill at the top of the slurry wall. Free fall through slurry is not permitted. Pushing the backfill forces the material to slide down into the trench under its own weight. This process is continued until the entire excavation has been backfilled. Typical slopes of the backfill surface during the backfilling process range from 5:1 to 10:1 (horizontal to vertical); the slope depends upon the slump of the soil-bentonite backfill material and the gradation of the material involved. The higher the slump and the more uniform the gradation, the flatter the resulting slope of the backfill surface. A low slump and a coarse grade of material will have the steepest slopes. Of course, the steeper the slope and the lower the slump, the greater the possibility of trapping sediment, partially excavated material, or fluid slurry in the cutoff wall.

As discussed above, there is no backfill process for the cement-bentonite cutoff walls; the stabilizing slurry sets up in the trench to form the wall (see Figure 4b). For plastic concrete and conventional concrete cutoff walls, standard tremie process is used as discussed under diaphragm walls (see Figure 4c).

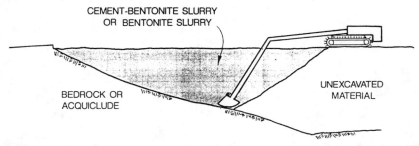

FIG. 4b -- Soil-Bentonite or cement-bentonite cutoff wall excavation.

<u>Connection Detail Surface Structures</u>--Figure 5 demonstrates the application of a soil-bentonite cutoff wall beneath a dam or dike embankment. It is important to recognize in the engineering application of cutoff walls that there will be some settlement and consolidation of a soil-bentonite cutoff wall. Figure 5(a) presents a typical application of a slurry wall in such a circumstance.

Note in Figure 5a that if proper connection details are not carried out, there is potential for a seepage path to develop, due to consolidation of the backfill material, at the top of the soil-bentonite cutoff wall. However, a simple construction detail of forming an impervious dike, which probably would be needed to provide a working platform for the construction of the slurry wall anyway [see Figure 5(b)], reduces the potential risk for such a seepage path to develop. Considerations such as this connection detail are a fundamental part of proper application of slurry wall cutoffs. Similar but less extensive details are required for cement-bentonite and plastic concrete cutoff walls due to their lower compressibility.

<u>Deformability</u>

It is important to recognize that, under major dam embankments, up to 10% foundation strain may occur and that slurry cutoff walls must be capable of sustaining such high levels of deformation without cracking or shear. This is significantly different than conditions typically faced by diaphragm walls. A major factor which controls the deformability of the cutoff wall is the cutoff material properties. The following consideration is thus separated into the four types of basic material; i.e., soil-bentonite, cement-bentonite, plastic concrete and concrete.

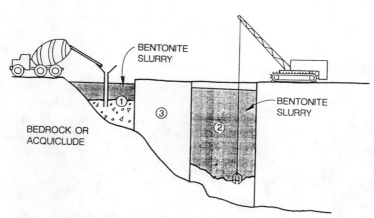

PANEL ① CONCRETE OR PLASTIC CONCRETE TREMIE BACKFILL

PANEL ② EXCAVATION PROCESS UNDER BENTONITE SLURRY

PANEL ③ UNEXCAVATED

FIG. 4c -- Concrete and plastic concrete slurry wall.

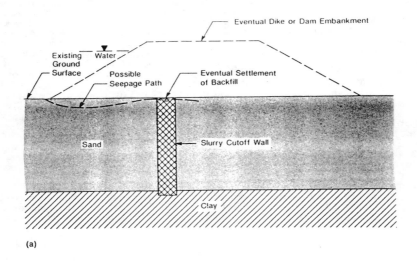

(a)

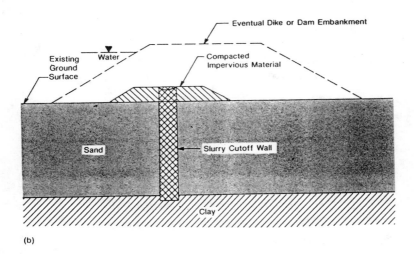

(b)

FIG. 5-- Connection detail for soil-bentonite
slurry trench cutoff under embankment.

Soil-Bentonite--As considered briefly with regard to backfill slope and permeability, backfill strength is affected by gradation and slump of the backfill material. The coarser the gradation of the backfill, the more rigid and firm the eventual performance of the wall. Conversely, the greater the slump, the more flexible the wall will be with regard to potential deformations. With regard to soil-bentonite walls, however, it is suggested that when specifying a reasonable gradation of coarse to fine material and a slump of 4 in. to 6 in. (100 mm to 150 mm), there is little problem with deformation or cracking. Consequently, in general, it can be said that soil-bentonite walls are quite deformable and typically do not have problems with regard to cracking.

Cement-Bentonite--The factors which affect the deformability of cement-bentonite slurry trench cutoff walls are the cement-water ratio and the bentonite-water ratio. Significant laboratory testing has been carried out to relate the cement-water ratio and, to a lesser degree, bentonite-water ratio to the deformability (without cracking) of various cement-bentonite mixtures. It has been determined that the higher the strength (i.e., the higher the cement-water ratio) the stiffer, more rigid, and thus, less deformable, the eventual cement-bentonite wall. Correspondingly, investigation of the bentonite-water ratio indicates that the higher the bentonite-water ratio, the higher the plasticity of the wall. Figure 6a presents a summary of typical test results for a particular application of a cement-bentonite wall. It can be seen from this plot that the cement-water ratio has a dramatic effect on deformability of the cement-bentonite backfill.

In this particular case, a 10% deformation was required. Because of the more complex relationships that must be evaluated in the application of a cement-bentonite slurry trench cutoff wall, more sophisticated testing may be required on a specific project basis to ensure the desired end result will be obtained.

Plastic Concrete--The addition of aggregate to a mixture of cement and hydrated bentonite slurry provides a stiffer, higher strength backfill than cement-bentonite. Strength and stiffness increase with increasing cement-water ratio, while increasing bentonite content reduces strength and increases ductility. An important design guideline is to evaluate and adjust, as practical, the strength and deformability of the backfill to be compatible with that of the surrounding soil or rock mass. Therefore, the slurry wall will deform with the surrounding mass and not form a rigid inclusion that would tend to concentrate bending and tensile stresses leading to cracking. Although in unconfined compression, plastic concrete behaves in a relatively brittle manner (see Figure 6b), in triaxial compression with sufficient bentonite, plastic concrete deforms like a hard clay or glacial till.

Permanence

The use of slurry trench cutoff walls may or may not have a permanent application. If a slurry cutoff wall is used around an excavation to provide a temporary dewatering expedient, then the life of the wall may be only on the order of 1 year to 2 years. If, on the other hand, the slurry wall cutoff has been applied as a cutoff or seepage barrier beneath a dam or around a hazardous waste landfill, then, of course, the slurry wall must last for the life of the facility.

Under normal environmental and geotechnical conditions, properly constructed soil-bentonite, cement-bentonite and plastic concrete backfilled slurry walls can be considered permanent structures.

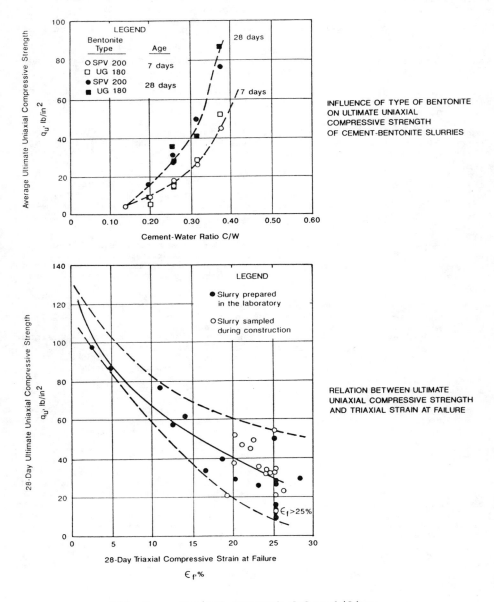

INFLUENCE OF TYPE OF BENTONITE
ON ULTIMATE UNIAXIAL
COMPRESSIVE STRENGTH
OF CEMENT-BENTONITE SLURRIES

RELATION BETWEEN ULTIMATE
UNIAXIAL COMPRESSIVE STRENGTH
AND TRIAXIAL STRAIN AT FAILURE

FIG. 6a -- Typical strength deformability
tests for cement-bentonite slurries.

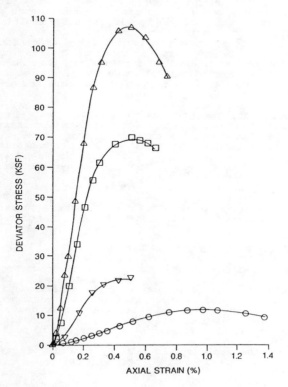

MIX	B/W	C/W	C/A	S/A	B/A	w	γd	AGGREGATE
○ CEMENT BENTONITE	6	0.38	-	-	-	180	28.2	-
□ MIX A PLASTIC CONC.	4.7	0.6	16.7	23.1	1.3	17.5	112.7	45% CWR 55% NS
△ MIX B PLASTIC CONC.	3.5	0.68	16.3	9.8	0.8	15.6	116.5	45% CWR 55% NS
▽ MIX E PLASTIC CONC.	6	0.6	16.7	30.1	1.7	25.3	97.6	OTHER PROJ. PIT RUN

B   BENTONITE WEIGHT   w   WATER CONTENT
W   WATER WEIGHT   γd   DRY UNIT WEIGHT (LB/FT^3)
C   CEMENT WEIGHT   CWR COARSE WASTE ROCK WEIGHT
A   AGGREGATE WEIGHT   NS   NATURAL SAND WEIGHT
S   BENTONITE-WATER WEIGHT

FIG. 6b -- Representative unconfined compression
test results on slurry wall backfill mixes (ICM barrier wall).

Continued research is being carried on by the bentonite producers to develop bentonites that may be used in corrosive environments and, thus, provide permanence even under severe environmental conditions. For specific applications of bentonites for anomalous or corrosive groundwater, soil conditions, or contaminants, it is important that the correct type of bentonite be specified. Compatibility testing with the specific site groundwater or contaminants permeating through samples of the design backfill should provide useful guidance. It may also be useful to seek advice and consultation from bentonite producers and other slurry manufacturers.

Recent research into the permanence of slurry wall backfills in contaminated environments provides the following design guidance. Soil-bentonite samples permeated with aqueous solutions of organic fluids showed no significant increases in permeability. Soil-bentonite samples permeated with concentrated solutions of organic fluids showed significant permeability increases (2 to 4 times). The maximum permeability of soil-bentonite approaches the permeability of the base soil. Therefore, a well graded, low permeability base soil will maintain low permeability even in the most hostile environment. Long-term tests showed a slight decrease in permeability with time for plastic concrete. Plastic concrete samples permeated with concentrated organic base showed no degradation in permeability with time.

CONSTRUCTION QUALITY CONTROL/QUALITY ASSURANCE

It is often required, in specifications, that the contractor be made responsible for running basic quality control tests on the various specified control elements; i.e., viscosity of the slurry, density of the slurry, filtrate loss, slump of the backfill material, verticality of the trench, etc. This testing is usually reported on a periodic basis; typically daily. Depending upon the size, volume, and scope of the project, the number of and time frequency of tests should be defined.

In addition to the contractor's quality control, it is strongly recommended that the owner and engineer provide, through a geotechnical organization, construction quality assurance. This is especially true if the engineer/owner are not familiar with slurry walls and their applications. Such geotechnical quality assurance services would include spot testing of the appropriate specified construction criteria; i.e., again, slurry viscosity, slurry density, slump of backfill, concrete slump, depth of trench, proper tie-in with aquiclude or bearing stratum, verticality, cleaning of trench bottom, etc. The frequency of the spot checks and spot testing would be dependent upon, again, the volume and production of work and the discrepancy, if any, between spot checks and the contractor's quality control testing. Such an independent quality assurance organization provides the owner with the necessary controls over the desired products and criteria that had been established in the specifications. It should be emphasized that there should not be items in the specifications that require quality control if these items are not, in fact, important to the end results or desired objective of the construction. In other words, quality control and quality assurance should be specified only for those items that truly have an affect on the desired end product.

CONCLUSIONS

Looking back at the evolution of the practice of slurry wall construction since the authors' original paper ten years ago, the following observations are offered. The basic specification building blocks are unchanged. Excavation methods have improved. The influence and effects of groundwater chemistry are now an important design consideration of the permanence of a slurry wall cutoff. New muds have been developed with improved performance in adverse environments. Plastic concrete has filled a performance gap between cement-bentonite and conventional concrete.

Important future developments to be considered in slurry wall specifications include new types of composite walls with internal geomembranes. New polymers will be introduced to improve trench stability and chemical resistance. Joint details are likely to improve, affecting permeability performance. Excavation capabilities are likely to continue to improve with rock excavation and greater depth. New chemically active backfills that absorb contaminants will also be introduced.

There are many and varied applications for the use of slurry diaphragm and slurry cutoff walls. Their full application and exposure has not yet been developed in the United States. Because of this fact, the specialty contractors who have engaged in slurry wall construction efforts overseas and, to a limited extent in the United States, have developed a degree of expertise above that of owners and architect/ engineer firms. Consequently, owners and architect/engineers are faced with a process in which they must establish specifications for work in which the specialty contractor is the expert. This can lead to rather awkward contract specifications and relationships, and can often result in specifications that require unnecessary controls and limitations which only generate additional cost and add nothing to the technical performance of the wall or cutoff. It is important, therefore, that in preparing specifications for a slurry wall, a thorough understanding of the desired end result is maintained and only those specific criteria that affect the end result be addressed and controlled by the specifications.

REFERENCES

Millet, R.A., and Perez, J.Y., "Current USA Practice: Slurry Wall Specifications" Journal of Geotechnical Engineering Division ASCTE Vol. 107 No. GT8, August 1981, pp 1041-1056.

BIBLIOGRAPHY

A Review of Diaphragm Walls, Proceedings, Institution of Civil Engineers, London, England, 1977.

D'Appolonia, D.J., "Soil-Bentonite Slurry Trench Cutoffs," Journal of the Geotechnical Engineering Division, ASCE, Vol. 106, No. GT4, Proc. Paper 15372, Apr., 1980, pp. 399-417.

Diaphragm Walls & Anchorages, Proceedings, Conference organized by the Institution of Civil Engineers London, Institution of Civil Engineers, Sept. 18-20, 1974. London, England, 1975.

Evans, J.C., Fang, H., and Kugelman, I.J., "Containment of Hazardous Materials with Soil Bentonite Slurry Walls," Proc. of the 6th National Conference on management of Uncontrolled Hazardous Waste Sites, Washington, D.C., November 1985, pp. 369-373.

Evans, J.C., Fang, H., and Kugelman, I.J. "Organic Fluid Effects on the Permeability of Soil-Bentonite Slurry Walls," Proc. of the National Conference on Hazardous Wastes and Environmental Emergencies, Cincinnati, OH, 1985, pp. 267-271.

Evans, J.C., Stahl, E.D., and Drooft, E. "Plastic Concrete Cutoff Walls,"
    Geotechnical Practice for Waste Disposal '87, Geotechnical Special
    Publication No. 13, ASCE, June 1987, pp. 462-472.

Grouts and Drilling Muds in Engineering Practice, Symposium organized by
    the British National Society of Soil Mechanics and Foundation
    Engineering at the Institute of Civil Engineers, Institution of
    Civil Engineers, May 1963, Butterworths, London, England, 1963.

Kohl, T.W., Kauschinger, J.L., and Perry, E.B., Plastic Concrete Cutoff
    Walls for Earth Dams, Technical Report REMR-GT-15, U.S. Army Corps
    of Engineers, Washington, D.C., March 1991.

Millet, R.A., and Perez, J.Y., "Current USA Practice: Slurry Wall
    Specifications" Journal of Geotechnical Engineering Division ASCTE
    Vol. 107 No GT8, August 1981, pp 1041-1056.

"Principles of Drilling Fluid Control," Petroleum Extension Service, The
    University of Texas, Austin, Tex.

Rogers, W.F., Composition and Properties of Oil Well Drilling Fluids, 3rd
    ed., Gulf, Houston, Tex., 1963.

Ryan, C.R., "Slurry Cutoff Walls--Design and Construction," Resource
    Management Products Slurry Wall Technical Course, Chicago, Ill.,
    1976.

Sherard, et al., Earth and Earth-Rock Dams: Engineering Problems of
    Design and Construction, John Wiley and Sons, Inc., New York, N.Y.,
    pp. 304-308.

Hazardous Waste

Walter E. Grube, Jr.

SLURRY TRENCH CUT-OFF WALLS FOR ENVIRONMENTAL
POLLUTION CONTROL

REFERENCE: Grube, W.E.,Jr., "Slurry Trench Cut-Off Walls for
Environmental Pollution Control," Slurry Walls: Design, Construction,
and Quality Control, ASTM STP 1129, David B. Paul, Richard R.
Davidson, and Nicholas J. Cavalli, Eds., American Society for testing
and Materials, Philadelphia, 1992.

ABSTRACT: Cut-off walls built by the bentonite-clay slurry trench
technique are designed and installed to control flow during site
remediation at hazardous waste sites. Non-aqueous phase liquids
(NAPL's) in the site groundwater are being sought in remedial
investigations as critical contaminants which are likely to significantly
affect cut-off wall design and performance. Testing of backfill
permeability with these liquids is necessary to ensure that the backfill
will resist degradation at elevations where they occur in the
groundwater. Recent research has focused on the impact of ion
diffusion through the completed barrier. Plastic concrete, attapulgite
clay slurries, and biopolymer slurries have been reported in use to
meet job-specific requirements. Field test cells, several tens of feet in
dimension, and extending to the expected depth of the total cut-off
wall structure, are increasingly being required by clients as pre-
construction hydraulic performance demonstrations. Pump-down
measurements applied to these cells provide data from which the
permeability of the walls, built with full-scale field equipment, can be
calculated. Hydraulic fracturing, verification of bottom-key
effectiveness, long-term permeability performance, and significance of
diffusion of solutes through the completed groundwater barrier remain
areas of sparse published data. This paper reviews environmental
slurry wall experience since the early 1980's, with emphasis on
performance evaluation.

KEY WORDS: slurry trench, groundwater, cut-off, wall, barrier,
environmental, bentonite, control, permeability, hydraulic
conductivity, pollutants.

Introduction

Vertical barriers to groundwater and pollutant migration have become
common structures for isolation of groundwater contaminants.

Within the U.S. EPA's Superfund program, containment of liquids within a
site has been accepted as a practical means to meet two goals:

o--   reduce the migration of groundwater pollutants from a site during the
time that a treatment, destruction, or removal technology is being applied,

Dr. Grube was Research Project Manager, USEPA, Cincinnati, Ohio 45268
when this paper was written; he is currently Director, Research &
Development, Clem Environmental Corp., Fairmount, GA 30139.

o--   reduce the volume of groundwater coming into and through a site, so that less total volume needs to be treated for pollutant destruction or removal.

The "slurry trench cut-off wall" has been adapted from standard civil engineering practice as the most common groundwater barrier. This structure consists of a trench maintained open by addition of a clay slurry during excavation; after reaching the desired depth and linear extent, the trench is backfilled with a material of lower groundwater permeability than the original soil or geologic formation which was excavated. The use of suspended clay slurries to maintain open excavation in coarse-grained and saturated soils has been extensively discussed in construction engineering literature (Gill, 1978; Millet, et al, 1981; Ryan, 1976). The trench backfill usually consists of a mixture of soil excavated from the trench with bentonite clay and other fine-grained materials designed to provide a relatively even distribution of many different sized soil particles in the final backfill mix. In specific circumstances other backfill components are selected. Portland cement provides structural rigidity. Use of plastic concrete has been reported. Addition of fly ash has been proposed for its contaminant sorptive properties. Geomembrane sheets or steel sheet-pilings may provide reduced permeability beyond what can be obtained with soil material mixtures. Other vertical barrier excavation or construction techniques, and barrier material formulations have been applied by various commercial companies for particular site conditions.

For about the past 12 years, nearly 100 reports of slurry trench cut-off wall installations to control groundwater and/or pollutant flow at various types of waste sites have been published. Many of these descriptions appeared in Proceedings of a variety of waste Conferences held around the U . S. and other parts of the world. Regularly published technical journals also contain occasional reports of these structures.

The Slurry Trench

This method of excavation is particularly suitable where the soil or shallow geologic formation is so friable that the walls of an open trench will collapse during excavation unless they are shored up by some means. Another advantage accrues where the groundwater table is shallow---within a few feet of the land surface. Slurry trench construction dispenses with sheets of plywood or steel panels, which can become expensive. Ordinary trench excavation equipment can easily operate and dig through a slurry-filled trench.

Traditionally, and in many cases most economically, bentonite clay has been the material mixed with water into a slurry or suspension and placed into the trench to prevent wall collapse until a backfill material has been placed. Numerous reports of experience with this material have been published. Recently, other trench slurry materials have been tested or used. These include attapulgite clay plus surfactants, and protein-rich gum material from organic and biochemistry processes.

The Cut-Off Wall

Slurry trench backfill creates the groundwater barrier desired at a site under remedial action. Soil-bentonite, cement-bentonite, geomembranes, and steel sheet-piling comprise the water migration barriers currently constructed. Few examples of the latter two structures have been described in published papers.

Bentonite clay is the dominant suspension agent used both in slurry trench construction and to reduce the permeability of the backfill mixture.

This clay is the commercial name for naturally occurring clay deposits which contain the clay-sized mineral montmorillonite as the dominant constituent. Physical, chemical, and engineering properties of this clay-mineral were characterized by geologists and clay mineralogists many decades ago. Technical specifications for low-permeability mixtures of soil materials for backfills have been published in numerous papers (Ryan, 1976; Gill, 1978; D'Appolonia, 1980; Millet, et al, 1981).

Soil-cement, cement-bentonite, plastic concrete, and other backfill mixtures designed to harden in place have been reported. These are used either where structural strength is required in the completed barrier, or where there may be inadequate amounts of economically available soil materials.

Placement of interlocked sheets of geomembrane materials into the slurry trench to form a pollutant migration barrier of lower permeability than obtainable with soil materials has been proposed by geomembrane vendors. Such materials have been more commonly used in Europe than in the U.S. One installation in Germany consisting of a geomembrane and steel sheet barrier was described to the author (W. G. Coldewey, DMT, Bochum, Federal Republic of Germany; personal communication). Since the site was underlain by mined-out areas, this barrier was designed to be flexible to accommodate possible subsidence. Installation of "Schmalwand", by the vibrating beam method continues to be seen in Europe. Clients in Germany have accepted this technology in regions of suitable geology.

Pollution Migration Control

Early in the consideration of engineering technologies and structures that could be applied to clean up uncontrolled hazardous waste sites, the slurry trench cut off wall" was included in remedial designs (USEPA, 1984). Various configurations of this structure to control pollutant migration have been proposed. These have been depicted as either keyed-in or hanging, with:
> circumferential placement,
> upgradient placement with drain, or
> downgradient placement.
The circumferential wall, keyed into an underlying aquiclude, is the most common design, and implementation, where groundwater control is desired at a waste site. The incomplete variants of a cut-off wall are uncommon at waste sites.

Acceptance of the "slurry wall" demanded data which describe the degree to which groundwater flow could be reduced, which led to laboratory measurements of the permeability of backfill materials. Traditional methods of measurement of soil permeability were applied, and many data were published. Laboratory permeability testing is a routine part of characterization of a proposed backfill material. Several published reports present the current state-of-the-art in laboratory permeability testing (Carpenter, 1986; Daniel, 1984; Evans, 1986). The actual hydraulic performance of an installed cut-off wall has been documented in only a few cases, discussed later.

Compatibility Testing

A major consideration in barrier selection is whether the site groundwater contaminants are chemically aggressive and will react adversely with backfill components, leading to increased permeability after backfill installation. Reaction with bentonite clay is a major concern. The laboratory permeability test of cut-off wall backfill materials has become the primary measure of compatibility of the barrier with groundwater in which it will be in contact. Although several studies have reported the influence of permeant liquid composition on the hydraulic conductivity of backfill materials, a great deal of the concern for the potential for adverse chemical interactions derives from studies of solvent effects on compacted clay soil landfill liners. Grube, et at, (1987) summarized these numerous studies.

If the groundwater contains solutes that will degrade the barrier, this factor should be determined early in the design stage of the cut-off wall. Acceptance of a cut-off wall within remedial design requires submission of data showing that the permeability of the selected backfill does not increase after the permeant fluid has been passed through. The permeant test liquid is either actual contaminated groundwater from a site or a synthetic mixture created to simulate chemically aggressive groundwater. There is no well-recognized universal formula for mixing laboratory reagents to simulate an aggressive groundwater; each formulation is site-specific. Evans and Fang (1986) describe a laboratory method that is widely applied to determine groundwater/barrier compatibility.

Compatibility testing of both trench slurry and backfill material is essential in two major environmental situations:

o   where the marine environment exerts a strong influence on groundwater composition, and

o   where there is known or potential presence of immiscible liquids sunken or floating in the site groundwater.

Since sodium-bentonite will lose this cation (Na) and corresponding swelling capacity in the presence of cations such as calcium, magnesium, iron, and aluminum from sea water, the extent of this exchange must be determined early in the design of a cut-off wall in this environment. Commercial bentonite clay suppliers claim they have modified bentonite clay formulations to resist ion exchange in marine environments; they also provide laboratory testing services to demonstrate the performance of their products. The cut-off wall designer should be sure that compatibility tests are conducted in an unbiased manner, with procedures well recognized for relevance.

Immiscible groundwater contaminants are widely recognized today as NAPL's, LNAPL's, and DNAPL's(non aqueous phase liquids, light and dense non aqueous phase liquids). Where a groundwater cut-off barrier intersects immiscible pools, the potential for barrier degradation is high, and will not be reflected by tests of trench slurry or backfill materials where normal site groundwater has been used. Detailed characterization of the groundwater regime at hazardous waste sites is essential in order to provide credible data which confirm or refute the presence of immiscible pools.

Where groundwater contaminants are in low concentrations, such as below the solubility limit of the particular organic compounds, concern for backfill permeability degradation is lessened. There are no clear guidelines to define the "low concentration" which would be no cause for concern. For the case of inorganic solutes, there is an indication from laboratory studies of single salt solutions that divalent cation concentrations in the range of 0.1 to 0.5 $\underline{N}$ increase the permeability of soils enriched with sodium bentonite.

In-Situ Performance Monitoring

Data which show the degree to which an installed groundwater control barrier is effective are sparse in well-known and widely distributed technical journals. Barrier effectiveness has been evaluated in terms of decreased solute concentrations in monitoring wells outside the barrier vs inside. Persistence in the decrease in groundwater elevation on the pumped side of a barrier compared with ambient has been another measure.

The U.S. EPA's Office of Research and Development conducted a well-documented study of hydrologic impact of a cut-off wall installation at the Sylvester Site in Nashua, New Hampshire (USEPA, 1987). This report remains the most widely cited example.

Individual Districts of the U. S. Army Corps of Engineers have required pilot-scale construction of groundwater control barriers in order to qualify construction contractors. Data from performance of these test structures reside in the individual District and site files. Private waste management corporations have also required test cell construction prior to enclosing an entire waste site with a cut-off wall. Data from these tests are largely unavailable because of client-confidentiality, however local or state permit files may contain some of this information. A planned 4.5km x 22m depth slurry wall in Germany will be preceded by construction of a test field by the chosen contractor.

Performance of several well-publicized cut-off wall installations at Superfund Remedial Action sites has been documented. These include Rocky Mountain Arsenal, Sylvester Site in Nashua, New Hampshire, Lipari Landfill in New Jersey, Chevron Site in Richmond, California, and others. Published data from these installations are not uniform in approach, field methods, parameters tested, or data analysis. This is because of the lack of standardized performance assessment methods. At the present time, there is little Agency interest in supporting development of standard methods to evaluate groundwater cut-off structure performance. This is because of the expected relatively short performance lifetime of a cut-off wall in environmental applications, the stigma of a slurry trench as a simple containment structure (with its corresponding least preference as a waste management option), and dedication of scarce resources to waste minimization and related efforts.

QA/QC

Barrier integrity, assuming adequate design, depends on two factors: 1) trench continuity, including key into underlying geologic formation and 2) quality and uniformity of the backfill mixture.

In environmental applications, quality control measures associated with the trench slurry should not be considered as important as those which verify the backfill material. Slurry formulations necessary to maintain an open trench are readily devised by experienced geotechnical engineers. Selection and mixing of appropriate clay or other suspensions are generally not problems. The adequacy and performance of bentonite filter cake is not a significant part of the final barrier structure. This is because of two factors: 1) the possibility of damage during backfill placement, and 2) the absence of data which show the extent and hydraulic performance of filter cake regions present in field-scale barrier structures.

Construction specifications state that the slurry trench shall be keyed into a clay layer, rock formation, or other geological material at the base of the barrier (USACOE, 1985). The elevations of the trench base are routinely specified in construction drawings. Because the connection between trench backfill and the foundation material may present a groundwater leakage pathway, this region requires intensive quality assurance. Trench bottom elevations are usually obtained by direct measurement of the depth to which excavation buckets reach; independent data can be obtained by sounding with a long rod or weighted line. Distances between trench bottom elevation data should be governed by the type of geologic material encountered, with minimum of a few meters. Trench bottom samples should be taken directly from the excavating bucket, rather than depending on small soil sampling devices.

Backfill quality is routinely tested by periodic measurements such as unit weight, moisture content, gradation of soil materials, cone slump, and permeability. Soil materials' gradation, unit weight, and similar index properties are important parameters used to indicate when several different soil strata are encountered during excavation. When these vary considerably, it may be impossible to adequately control the quality of a backfill composed primarily of excavated trench soils. Design and construction decisions, in such cases, must be based on an intensive site investigation, and appropriate backfill mixing techniques. Stress applied during permeability testing should not exceed the overburden stress expected near the top of the barrier wall. Studies have shown that decreasing hydraulic conductivities are obtained as hydraulic gradient is increased. Tests for bentonite content, such as the API methylene blue method, have been found not as reliable as permeability tests for backfill acceptance. Testing frequency for backfill quality control is widely accepted at one test per 1,000 cubic yards of backfill.

Daily (or overnight) tests of backfill permeability using a modified API Filter Press are performed by some contractors. This close monitoring is encouraged, but a relationship between field permeability using the API Filter Press and laboratory permeability and compatibility must be established during the design phase of the project.

For compatibility testing, a minimum of two pore volumes of permeant liquid must flow through the sample. This volume is necessary to assure that adequate opportunity for interaction between liquid and the soil under test is obtained.

Verification of the integrity of the slurry trench cut-off barrier after installation remains a task not well standardized. Cone-penetrometer probes of the completed backfill have been used experimentally to determine uniformity. These have encountered some difficulty in maintaining a vertical path through the trench.

Observation wells are common groundwater monitoring structures. Data which should be collected should be specified in detail for applications in slurry trench performance monitoring. Such wells should have groundwater elevations monitored periodically, with pump tests applied to provide supplemental data. Groundwater quality should be periodically monitored downgradient of the cut-off wall, with data compared to baseline (preconstruction) values.

Construction and subsequent excavation and examination of a test cell presents a method to ensure construction quality. Daily construction inspection must then be relied upon to ensure that the major barrier structure is built with the same quality as the test cell. Analyses of the performance of several cut-off walls has shown the need for intensive examination of the initial sections of wall construction. Where new, or inexperienced contractors, or unusual geologic settings are present, it has been found that a "learning curve" exists. It should be anticipated that the first several hundred feet of barrier installed may require re-construction if test data show that this section has not been properly built.

Such aspects as backfill uniformity, concrete cracking, distribution of additives such as flyash, and other backfill properties can be documented both visually and with samples taken for laboratory testing. Logani and Kleiner (1980) excavated 3 to 7 meter deep test pits and 10 to 15 meter deep drill holes to examine a cement-bentonite cut-off wall in Honduras. Filter cake, colored zones, and lack of seepage were observed. The question of tie-in of the cut-off wall with the underlying formation can only be verified by examination of materials during trench excavation.

Problems

The civil engineering construction state-of-the-art for slurry trench cut-off walls is basically the same as was applied several decades ago to restrain water from entering construction sites such as bridges, piers and lock/dam foundation, and associated structures.

Backfills of soil material are placed at saturation and thus provide a ready pathway for diffusion transport of solutes across the barrier region. Gray and Weber(1984) have examined this mode of pollutant transport and published several reports. Based on simulations of a hypothetical soil-bentonite barrier at two limiting cases they suggest that solute migration through soil-bentonite barriers by molecular diffusion can be significant. The role of this transport mechanism has already been shown significant in studies of transport in natural clays (Johnson et al, 1989). Gray and colleagues (1991) have also examined the contribution of flyash containing unburnt carbon in attenuating solute migration. They concluded that the capacity of carbon associated with flyash for sorption of representative low-molecular-weight solutes was at least equivalent to that of naturally occurring carbon. There have been few other studies of solute sorbents incorporated into backfill mixtures. Use of pollutant-capturing additives can be expected to receive careful scrutiny by remediation technology reviewers in regulatory agencies. Many contaminant-sorptive materials have not been evaluated for stability. Uniformity of incorporation into a barrier structure, effective sorption capacity, susceptibility to desorption or other loss of pollutants, and mechanism of pollutant recovery represent some areas of concern which have not been resolved by credible research or experience.

Backfills enriched with Portland cement which hardens are susceptible to cracking, leaving unknown and almost undocumentable preferential pathways for contaminated water flow. Recent designs of plastic concrete may help to relieve this problem.

Some design engineers place a great deal of confidence, in the low permeability of a slurry wall, in the relatively thin filter-cake which develops on the trench sidewalls. The filter cake is susceptible to mechanical dislodging during excavation and backfill operations. This may introduce unknown and nearly undocumentable "windows" in this barrier component.

Data quality remains an area of concern to those both within and outside the Agency who are responsible for slurry wall performance. Nearly every study reviewed is deficient in the primary area of project quality assurance---documenting the quality of the environmental measurements. Absence of a sound experimental design upon which either laboratory or field measurements are based is a nearly universal shortcoming. The majority of published data result from single observations from an array of varied parameters . Thus, no conclusions regarding data variability or confidence intervals can be made. In other cases, physical concepts are modelled using theoretically sound values for variables, and resulting numerical conclusions are proposed as the basis for potential environmental effects. In the latter cases, the design engineer or regulatory approval authority have no practical guidance regarding the importance of modelled results in affecting design and construction. Applications of many model results have not yet bridged the gap to the practicalities of construction economics and materials use.

Conclusions

Although survey of EPA Records of Decision for remediation of Superfund sites shows nearly two dozen slurry trench cut-off wall references, many of these structures may not be built. This is because waste removal and/or destruction remain preferred remedial technology options.

Groundwater control at sites contaminated with hazardous chemicals, however, can be effectively achieved by slurry trench techniques routinely in use by civil engineers for many years. Design, construction, and monitoring of the hydraulic effectiveness of such barriers at uncontrolled hazardous waste sites must be of substantially higher quality than that applied where groundwater cut-off is only necessary for routine construction site dewatering.

Testing the barrier filling mixture to verify that it will not significantly change permeability in the presence of the site-contaminated groundwater relies primarily on laboratory permeability test procedures. Reports of studies of these procedures in geotechnical journals form the basis for conducting such compatibility tests. Methods are being standardized by ASTM Committees.

Data which illustrate the effectiveness of a cut-off wall after installation have not been well summarized. They lie within individual site files at cognizant regulatory offices, or are client-confidential. Uniform methods to reliably measure and document in-situ hydrologic performance of groundwater barriers at hazardous waste sites have not been developed or published.

REFERENCES

[1]   Gill, S. A. 1978. Applications of Slurry Walls in Civil Engineering Projects. Preprint 3355, ASCE Convention, Chicago. 20pp.

[2]   Millet, R. A., et al. 1981. Current USA Practice: Slurry Wall Specifications. J. Geotech. Eng. Div., Proc. ASCE, Vol. 107, No. GT8, 1041-1056.

[3]   Ryan, C. R. 1976. Slurry Cut-off Walls Design and Construction. Technical Course on Slurry Wall Construction, Design, Techniques, and Procedures. Chicago, IL. 20pp. (avail. from author, c/o Geo-Con, Inc., Pittsburgh, PA.)

[4]   D'Appolonia, D. J. 1980. Soil-Bentonite Slurry Trench Cutoffs. J. Geotech. Eng. Div. ASCE, Vol. 106, No. GT4, April, 399-417.

[5]   USEPA. 1984. Slurry Trench Construction for Pollution Migration Control, EPA-540/2-84-001. ORD, Cincinnati, OH 45268. Avail. from NTIS as # PB 84 177831.

[6]   Carpenter, G. W. and R. W. Stephenson. 1986. Permeability Testing in the Triaxial Cell. Geotech. Testing J., GTJODJ, ASTM, Vol. 9, No. 1, 3-9.

[7]   Daniel, D. E., S. J. Trautwein, S. S. Boynton and D. E. Foreman. 1984. Permeability Testing with Flexible-Wall Permeameters. Geotech Testing J., GTJODJ, ASTM, Vol. 7, No. 3, 113-122.

[8]   Evans, J. C. and H. Y. Fang. 1986. Triaxial Equipment for Permeability Testing with Hazardous and Toxic Permeants. Geotech. Testing J., GTJODJ, ASTM, Vol.   8, No. 3, 126-132.

[9]   Grube, W. E., Jr., M. H. Roulier and J. G. Herrmann. 1987. Implications of Current Soil liner Permeability Research Results. in Proc. 13th Annual Rsch. Symp. Land Disposal, Remedial Action, Incineration and Treatment of Hazardous Waste, EPA/600/9-87-015. RREL, USEPA, Cincinnati, OH 45268.   pp9-25.

[10]   USEPA. 1987. Construction Quality Control and Post-Construction Performance for the Gilson Road Hazardous Waste Site Cutoff Wall, EPA/600/2-87 /065.   Avail. from NTIS as # PB88 113295.

[11]   U. S. Army Corps of Engineers. 1985. Civil Works Guide Specification for Soil-Bentonite Slurry Trench Cutoffs. CW-02214.

[12]   Logani, K. L. and D. E. Kleiner. 1980. Cement -Bentonite Slurry Trench Cutoff Walls. in Proc. 7th Pan American Conference on Soil Mechanics and Foundation Engineering. 14 pp.

[13]   Gray, D. H. and W. J. Weber, Jr. 1984. Diffusional Transport of Hazardous Waste Leachate Across Clay Barriers. in Proc. 7th Annual Madison Waste Conference. University of Wisconsin-Extension, Madison, WI.

[14]   Johnson, R. L., J. A. Cherry and J. F. Pankow. 1989. Diffusive Contaminant Transport in Natural Clay: A Field Example and Implications for Clay-Lined Waste Disposal Sites. Environ, Sci. Technol. 23.

[15]   Gray, D. H., W. R. Bergstrom, H. V. Mott and W. J. Weber. 1991. F ly Ash Utilization in Cut-Off Wall Backfill Mixes. in Proc. 9th Intl. Coal Ash Utilization Symp., Orlando, FL.

Nicholas J. Cavalli

COMPOSITE BARRIER SLURRY WALL

REFERENCE: Cavalli, N.J., "Composite Barrier Slurry Wall," Slurry Walls: Design, Construction, and Quality Control, ASTM STP 1129, David B. Paul, Richard R. Davidson, and Nicholas J. Cavalli, Eds., American Society for Testing and Materials, Philadelphia, 1992.

ABSTRACT: For decades systems utilizing various types of vertical flow barriers have had to be constructed to contain polluted groundwater or leachate from contaminated sites or waste disposal areas. Many of the vertical barriers used in these systems were implemented and were assumed, or designed to maintain their impermeable and barrier qualities over the long term. In the years that have passed little data has been available for comparison of predicted long-term effectiveness of vertical barriers with actual results, thus long-term performance of vertical barriers in chemically and physically agressive environments remain uncertain and unproven. Composite barriers are an attempt to overcome these inadequacies and provide a database to go forward.

KEYWORDS: slurry wall, vertical barriers, geomembrane, permeability, bentonite, composite barrier, contaminants

INTRODUCTION

Since the early 1960's slurry walls have been used as hydraulic barriers on numerous civil engineering projects. As environmental concerns grew in the seventies, the use of this technology was transferred to environmental projects. Although environmental barriers will have the same hydraulic conditions as barriers on civil projects, environmental barriers require material to withstand an almost unending attack of chemicals.

In the latter part of the 1970's the EPA recognized this potential for chemical attach in their design of liner systems and hence under the Resource Conservation and Recovery Act (RCRA), changed the standards to deal with this problem. RCRA has since mandated that new liner systems be constructed of composite materials. The typical RCRA liner is made up of two layers of clay and two layers of synthetic membrane separated by drainage material. Although regulatory agencies have addressed chemical degradation problems in horizontal barriers they have not addressed these problems in the vertical barriers.

Vice President, Wehran Construction, Inc, 666 East Main St, Middletown, NY 10940

COMPOSITE BARRIERS

Vertical Barriers

Vertical barriers used to contain contaminated waste or groundwater include:

- Slurry walls
- Vibrating beam thin walls
- Steel sheeting
- Grout curtains
- Jet grouting
- Compacted clay
- Deep soil mixing

All of those mentioned consist of a single impervious element, limiting their ability to be monitored for performance and gradual degradation due to chemical incompatability.

At present, vertical barriers are monitored by placing observation wells on both sides of the barrier. The perimeter of the vertical barrier is not usually determined by the contaminant plume but by geographic conditions such as rivers, hillsides, cliffs, etc., or by property boundaries. When monitoring, wells on both sides of the barrier may indicate contaminated water immediately after construction. We must then ask how long it will take to notice improvement in the water quality outside the barrier.

Existing analytical techniques of approximate travel times are incapable of providing predictions with both a high level of confidence and a narrow range of anticipated values. In addition, these techniques require a known set of conditions as a starting point for analysis. This requires the performance qualities of the installed barrier to be known to a greater degree of certainty than is possible for any of the barriers mentioned.

Considering vertical groundwater flow approximates one foot per year, depending on gradients, soil permeabilities, and other factors, results from existing monitoring systems may be inadequate to determine how these barriers can or will perform.

Composite Geomembrane/Slurry Wall Barrier

In order to eliminate some of the uncertainty in construction quality and to utilize a material that has a known chemical resistance, a composite barrier can be utilized. The composite barrier, shown in Figure 1, is comprised of several layers.

The first layer is a thin filter cake approximately 1/8" thick and comprised of bentonite, with a permeability of 1×10^{-8} cm/sec. The second is an engineered backfill of either soil bentonite, cement bentonite, or plastic concrete, ranging in thickness from one foot to two- and one-half feet. The engineered backfill can be designed to have a permeability of 1×10^{-7} cm/sec. The third barrier is an HDPE geomembrane sheet, 100 mil thick, which has a permeability of 1×10^{-12} cm/sec. The HDPE geomembrane is backed by a geofabric drain which is placed in the center of the system. The first three components of the barrier repeat on the opposite side of the drainage layer.

The slurry wall construction method allows installation of the system in difficult site conditions and to depths greater than 100 feet.

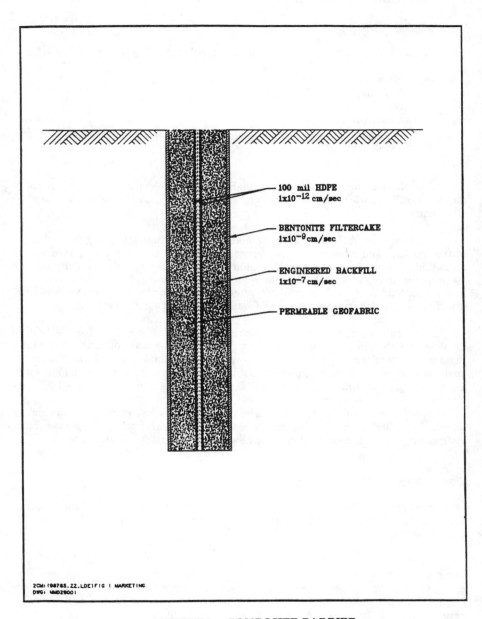

FIGURE 1 – COMPOSITE BARRIER

The bentonite slurry used in the construction maintains the stability of the trench for the installation of the system's HDPE envelope. The slurry also develops a filter cake on the walls of the trench, which provides an additional low permeability bentonite film. The composite system in effect provides three different types of barriers, and a total of six sections to contain the flow of contaminants (Figure 1).

The composite barrier has several features which provide considerable performance advantage over other barriers when used as a "vertical barrier" to form a cut-off wall. The composite barrier adds to a vertical barrier the capabilities for monitoring performance and withdrawal of contaminants from within the cut-off wall. The HDPE envelope provides a stable, low permeability (10^{-12} cm/sec) membrane, and when installed in the trench, provides improved resistance to contaminant migration and low overall permeability of the system.

Development

During the fall of 1982, a full-scale construction test was performed at an existing sanitary landfill in New Jersey to demonstrate the concept and methodology of a composite cut-off wall.

The composite barrier tested had different features than the system previously described. The barrier tested included an envelope of HDPE backfilled with sand and lowered into a bentonite-filled trench (Figure 2).

The test section was designed as a 22-foot deep triangle (Figure 3). Twenty-two feet was chosen because it was deep enough to extrapolate methodology and costs for deeper sections, yet shallow enough to minimize the cost of the test installation. The shape was designed in order to determine the feasibility of the HDPE envelope and to establish a technique to close the barrier.

After several weeks of testing it was determined that the system was constructable. However, it was also discovered that the system was extremely expensive to install since it required several cranes to handle, place and lower the envelope into the slurry trench and its use would be restricted to depths less than 50 feet.

Composite Barrier Construction Methodology

As a result of the experience learned during the test section, a state-of-the-art economic composite barrier was developed.

The construction method was altered to eliminate the need for holding large sections of trench open and handling large cumbersome sheets of HDPE. This installation of the composite barrier was thus broken into a six step process.

The first step was to fabricate a thin HDPE envelope by welding an HDPE sheet to two HDPE pipes connected by a perforated pipe along the bottom of a panel (Figure 4). Geofabric was then placed between the sheets and secured.

The second step required the drilling of a vertical hole to the depth of the proposed subgrade and equal in diameter to the barrier width at each end of the HDPE panel. The

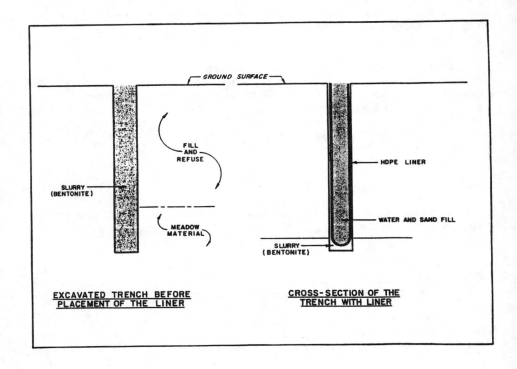

FIGURE 2 – TRENCH CROSS-SECTIONS BEFORE & WITH LINER IN-PLACE

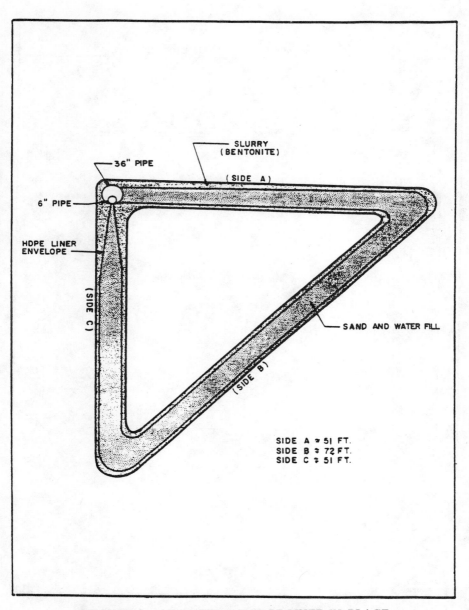

FIGURE 3 – PLAN VIEW OF HDPE LINER IN-PLACE

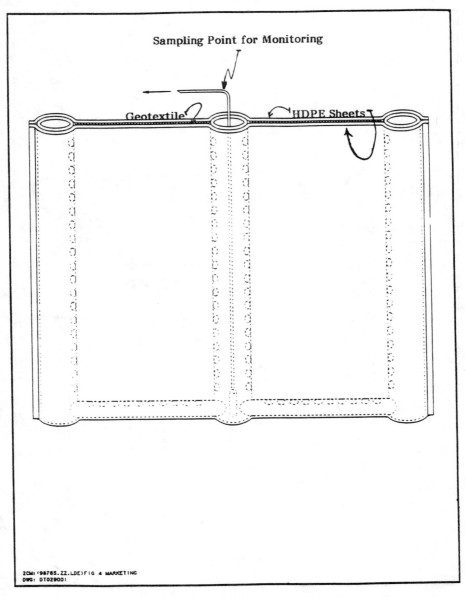

FIGURE 4 – COMPOSITE BARRIER

drilling method chosen would depend upon site soils. The holes would be drilled using either bentonite slurry or cement bentonite.

After the holes are drilled under slurry, a pre-manufactured HDPE connection would be lowered into the open hole. A steel member, the same shape as the connection, would then be placed in the connection to provide vertical stability, weight to counteract the buoyancy, protection for the connection, and a plug to maintain the openings in the connection. Once the connections were in place, the hole would be backfilled with plastic concrete, or if excavated with cement bentonite, the cement bentonite would be allowed to set.

Once the connections were in place and backfilled, the space between the connections would be excavated with bentonite slurry using a slurry wall clamshell. Upon completion of the excavation, the bentonite slurry remaining in the excavation would be circulated and passed through a desander to insure both the removal of all sediments from the bottom of the excavation, and to clean the slurry to a point where the sand content is less than five percent.

With the excavation complete, the steel members are pulled out of the connection opening. The HDPE envelope is then lifted vertically, aligned with the openings of the connection, and lowered into place.

The final step is to backfill with the engineered backfill using a tremie on both sides of the envelope. In this way, the backfill can be placed equally on both sides of the HDPE membrane so that its remains centered. The backfill is continued until the excavation is complete.

CONCLUSION

The composite barrier offers several advantages over a single type of barrier.

A composite barrier will provide resistance to a wider range of contaminants. Since there are two different types of material, their abilities would overlap to withstand degradation.

If desired, this system can also provide a collection and monitoring system in its center. The system can be monitored through the pipes at the end of each panel, and if found leaking, the pollutant can be withdrawn.

Since the system is built in panels, defects, if found, can be isolated and repaired.

The composite barrier is symmetrical, therefore, if degradation should occur it would be detected within the center of the HDPE envelope.

Gilbert R. Tallard

NEW TRENCHING METHOD USING SYNTHETIC BIO-POLYMERS

REFERENCE: Tallard, G. R., "New Trenching Method Using Synthetic Bio-Polymers," Slurry Walls: Design, Construction, and Quality Control, ASTM STP 1129, David B. Paul, Richard R. Davidson, and Nicholas J. Cavalli, Eds., American Society for Testing and Materials, Philadelphia, 1992.

ABSTRACT: For the first time, a radical departure from solidly established concepts and practices based on the use of bentonite for trenching under slurry, is proving itself as a viable alternative . It is even more so in this age of acute environmental sensitivity. The role played by polymers, and in particular a synthetic biodegradable polymer, are taking an increasing role in geotechnical construction: cohesionless sands can be cored with 100% recovery and small and large diameter soft ground tunnels are being bored with greater ease. Of interest to the field of slurry trenched excavations is the new ability to excavate under slurry, be it for continuous deep french drain or for a panelized reinforced concrete diaphragm wall, using a same and totally new kind of slurry. This slurry is a solution of polymers combined with either natural fines or added colloids. Since the slurry is naturally biodegradable, it can be used in all situations. The biodegradation can be deferred by inhibitors and with pH control while regulating it according to needs.

Leachate collection or recharge french drains installed under slurry are presented from the conceptual and QC perspectives. Since most structural slurry wall projects are in urban areas, where working with clay muds is problematic for many reasons, the writer examines the advantages of going from bentonite to polymer slurries. The limitations of the new technology are also discussed.

KEYWORDS: slurry, polymer, bentonite ,colloids , slurry trench, drains, trenching, viscosity, filtrate, cake, pH, biodegradable, diaphragm wall, disposal, spoil, leachate.

[1]President, Envirotrench Co., Pelham, N.Y. 10803

INTRODUCTION:

The practice of bentonite slurries derives from the oil well drilling mud technology, a sophysticated and complex science. The level of technology transfer that has in fact taken place from an oil well application to a slurry trenched excavation application is minimal. The basic principles that are utilized by design engineers or practitioners remain generally rudimentary. This is why slurry specifications are often inadequate. Understandably, a 15,000 ft (4,572 m.) deep well is a different affair than a 50 ft (15.25 m.) slot in the ground!

In this country, the natural sodium montmorillonite clay and API 13B remain the pillars of specifications for most slurry trenched projects, be it structural diaphragm walls or cement bentonite cutoff walls. Other less fortunate countries must manufacture their technical clays through a number of blends and permutations. This leads to a greater variety of clay products which have a greater specificity in their applications. None of this flexibility exists here.

With a limited exposure to chemistry in high school and a lack of formal training at the professional level, the often specified "slurry specialist" is far from being a "mud engineer" in the oil field sense of the term.   An ASTM subcommittee is still laboring with issuing standards that will be indigenous to the slurry trenching industry.

Environmental regulations, in most western nations, are making it ever more onerous to dispose of any form of liquid waste. Slurried trench spoils are not welcome at dump sites and contaminated bentonite slurries hauled away by vac trucks at the tail end of a concrete pour need special processing.

Large civil engineering projects in densely populated cities tend to take the best advantage of the underground space, even at a premium cost. The multitude of publicly funded infrastructure projects using slurries, be it for large caisson work, slurry walls or slurry shield tunneling, requires an approach to mitigate the disposal problems. Further, technical challenges such as sticky clays and mud contamination by either cement, natural chalk or marls have called for alternative excavation fluids.

Bio-polymers for drilling muds have been developed over the past 30 years with the oil well drilling industry in mind. The reduction of mud viscosity in the turbulent flow at the bit level that polymers permit do improve drilling rates[1]. Anti swelling effect in clays is an other attractive property of some polymers.

The US slurry wall industry has been exposed, since the seventies, to bentonite boosters and viscosifiers such as carboxylmethylcellulose (CMC) which are extensively used in Japan, as a bentonite extender and filtrate reducer. Without fanfare, the US bentonite processing industry has prepared some of its products with wetting agents and polymers to either boost less performing clays or to provide a more consistent quality.

Engineers writing specifications who refuse modified bentonite as a blanket mode may want to adjust their judgement. However these less than 100% natural bentonite do not reduce the disposal problems, the slurries remaining essentially clay muds.

BACKGROUND OF CONVENTIONAL BENTONITE SLURRIES:

CAKE FORMATION:
The fundamental requirement for the stability of an excavated face in the wet is the preservation of the equilibrium maintaining the intrinsic soil strengths by providing a constant external force of a fluid column substantially in excess of the soil's pore pressure. This equilibrium is enhanced by the formation of an impervious membrane at the interface between soil and fluid column which is known as the "cake". This cake is the product of filtration of particulates in suspension in the fluid through the soil interface, the thickness and density of which depends on materials and depths. Once a cake has formed into a sufficiently impervious matter, the fluid column's positive head can be maintained at low cost since little fluid addition is required.
At this juncture, the notion of thixotropy and gel strength are not yet relevant.

SLURRY DENSITY:
The notion that the column's increased weight by means of a denser fluid may improve trench stability is an attractive one. It is practiced commonly in oil well drilling. Specifications occasionally call for trenching slurries with densities up to 1.12 to 1.28 g/cm^3 (70 to 80 lbs/CF) compared to a more common 1.04 g/cm^3 (65 lbs/CF). Such well ment intentions are often foiled by adverse side effects on the rest of the work; excess viscosity and unstable solid load are the main drawbacks possibly affecting the quality of the endproduct. Further, it would be wise to shy away from specifying certain slurry trenched excavations altogether if the difference between 1.12 and 1.04 is going to be the difference between stable and unstable trenches.

SLURRY CLEANING:
Once an excavation under bentonite slurry is completed, the preparation for the intended use requires, most often, to assure that the trench be cleaned of settling suspended solids prior to backfilling, be it filter gravel or tremie concrete. Here the gel strength of the bentonite slurry comes into play: since the slurry is rigid, a percentage of excavated soil remains either in suspension or in a state of slow descent. Depending on the slurry viscosity and the types of soils encountered, the proportion can vary between 1 and 20% by volume which amounts to 40 to 900 lbs(23 to 520 Kg) of granular material per cubic meter of slurry. A typical 100 CY (73 m^3) panel could contain as much as 45 tons (41 tonnes) of

sand in suspension in the slurry or about two tuck loads. Hence there is a need to desand the slurry before backfilling to avoid defects in the endproduct. The difficulty in selecting a safe maximum sand content results from the impracticality of separating, at given viscosities and gel strengths, the particle size under which no settlement will occur from the coarser fration that will settle and which is the only cause of concern. Typically, specified sand content values remain in the 1 to 5% bracket.

VISCOSITY:

To reduce the sand content problem, experienced practitioners favor working with slurries in the 32 to 38 Marsh seconds. API 13 B baseline bentonite testing values are ment to compare bentonite qualities not to prescribe technical field values to respect. Thus the confusions of   engineers relying solely on API when writing a specification. Since design engineers rarely take on the reponsability of the trench stability, specialty contractors should be allowed to make their own decision at the proper times with respect to the   viscosity, the slurry being in fact one of their tools. In any case, the use of bentonite slurry usually requires the removal of suspended solids by appropriate means upon the completion of the excavation. This can be a lengthy task and a difficult one at times if the viscosity has reached a point where pumping is almost impossible, generally caused by some form of flocculation or excessive gelling.

DEFINITION OF A BIO-POLYMER TRENCHING FLUID:

CHALLENGE:

Can a fluid stabilize the walls of a trenched excavation by forming a cake with the suspended fines while allowing the granular fraction to settle continuously during the course of the excavation and to be removed by the excavating tool? Can this fluid keep its characteristics   within a narrow band throughout the process, maintaining its viscosity by being chemically neutral in the presence of calcium. Can the desanding operation be eliminated altogether? Can a fluid drain fast enough from spoil materials to load dump trucks at full capacity? Can a trenching fluid be reused any number of times until the end of the project, and then be disposed of legally in the sanitary sewer system after proper preparation, the product being entirely biodegradable?

ANSWER:

Such a fluid exists in the form of a synthetic low molecular weight cellulosic polymer formulation combined with a colloidal mineral suspension . This fluid, after penetrating porous formations, forms a thin low permeability cake membrane capable of maintaining a substantial head over the ground water table (54 ft or 17 m. at L.A. Union Station [note 1]).

Despite the cake formation capability, the trenching fluid   has little or no gel strength so that all suspended solids finally segregate and is thus self-cleaning. The new trenching fluid's chemistry is such that common salts present in the ground, the   ground water quality   or cement   will have no effect on the slurry properties throughout the construction process.

In addition, the polymer slurry contains an additive preventing the swelling of clayey soils. This reduces the weakening of clayey trench walls, limits the amount of clay dispersing in the slurry which reduces the potential for gel formation . In addition, the metallic surfaces, such as the shells of the grab, remain free from sticky clay.

The trenching fluid can be reused as many times as necessary, allowing for time or centrifugation to eliminate undesirable fines. This   limits the need for slurry disposal to the last few panels. After separation of the non-acqueous phase and neutralization of the liquid pH, the slurry can be released to the the environment without harm.

ACQUIRED EXPERIENCE WITH SYNTHETIC BIO-POLYMERS:

The material used is a synthetic cellulosic derivative which combines an antiswelling agent, a biodegradation inhibitor and a pH booster base.

1) VISCOSIFICATION:
Easily dispersed in fresh water at a rate of 1 to 2 thousandths by weight of water, the viscosification occurs within minutes with gentle agitation. Sprinkling over a water spray   or using a flash mixer are the prefered mixing methods. By comparison, a natural gum bio-polymer requires 5 to 8 thousandths to produce the same viscosity; in the case of bentonite, it is 40 to 60 thousandths by weight of water.

Given the extremely small quantity of synthetic bio-polymer used, the mixing water mineralization can affect substantially the viscosity for a given amount of polymer. Trial mixes with local water are necessary to establish the polymer's site specific performance. This writer has observed a variation from 32 to 40 Marsh seconds at 2 thousandths proportioning using tap and bottled water respectively.

However, by modifying the polymer content, trenching fluids can be prepared with almost any kind of water (fig.1).

A synthetic bio-polymer was used in 1990 at the Boston Harbour cleanup project on Deer Island where the only water for slurry preparation was either waste water in the process of being treated or sea water. Sea water was chosen as a more stable source for trenching panels 120 Ft (36m.) deep in clayey glacial till [note 2]. A 50% increase in polymer content was required to produce the same viscosity obtained with fresh water. A year later, with fresh water available, a second   shaft was constructed on Deer Island by an other contractor but at a normal proportioning rate[note 3].

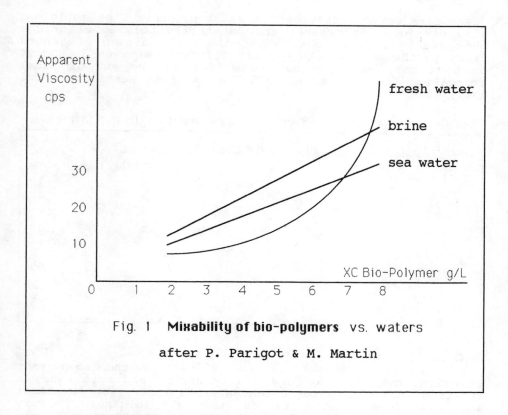

Fig. 1 **Mixability of bio-polymers** vs. waters

after P. Parigot & M. Martin

As a new preparation, the slurry is a purely viscous fluid. A working slurry carrying fines in a dynamic mode will have a viscosity of only one or two seconds higher. Only when the fines amount is in excess (cake thicker than 4 mm.) will the viscosity become linked to the solid content(fig 2).
The desirable starting viscosity is between 32 and 35 Marsh seconds and a working range of 34 to 38 seconds seem to satisfy most cases.

2) FILTRATION:
Such a slurry, in its polymer plus water form, has a total water loss when tested as per API 13B but can in fact be a perfectly workable slurry This is due to the low molecular weight of the polymer . Heavy molecular weight polymers such as the natural gums or the non-biodegradable polyacrylamide drilling polymer types have a better intrinsic filtration characteristic and will glaze over a porous medium or screen. The apparent inconvenience of the lighter weight polymer

disappears very quickly once a small percentage of colloidal size particles is present and permit the polymer to bridge over (table 1). In fact, with only the addition of trench fines to the polymer slurry, API filtrates between 15 and 20 cc have been measured by the writer at the end of panel excavation (test panel #3, 325 7th. street, Washington D.C. 1989).

Table 1. Filtrate of polymer slurry with colloid addition

Base slurry: 1 kg of bio-polymer per m3 of water						
				(after M.M. Jannaire)		
% addition of bentonite	0	.5	1	1.5	2	3
viscosity in Marsh seconds	30.1	31.6	36.7	35.7	42.9	49.1
apparent viscosity cp	6	7.5	10	12	13.5	16
API filtrate cm3	total	38	28.5	23.4	20.2	16.5

3) CAKE:

A small amount of colloidal fines allow the bio-polymer to bridge over and to form a very strong and thin cake, a fraction of a millimeter thick. Whereas filtration is almost solely an economical criterion, the cake thickness is very much a technical criterion; a cake maximum thickness is rarely specified except in some European countries. The French standard is that cakes thicker than 5mm.(3/16 inch) force the slurry to be discarded or regenerated. Thick cakes are generally caused by non plastic fines like silts or by flocculated bentonite. Thick cakes can be the source of defects in a diaphragm wall such as exposed rebars. Although the problem is identical with any slurry, in the case of a purely viscous polymer slurry, the remedy is simpler since, over time, all fines will settle. If time or storage are not available, centrifugation of the slurry is very effective and regeneration is always possible.

4) pH:

The pH of potable city water is generally about neutral with a tendency to be acidic in the North East, probably due to the acidity of rain water. This is sporadically compensated by base introduction at the filtration plant giving variable pH readings up to 9 as in Washington D.C.

Bacteriological development will occur best on the slightly acidic side, at pH values between 6 and 7. At a pH above 9 no bacteria multiplication will occur. Values above 10 are considered toxic by water regulating authorities (and the reason why used cement contaminated bentonite slurries do create a disposal problem at pH up to 12) [3].

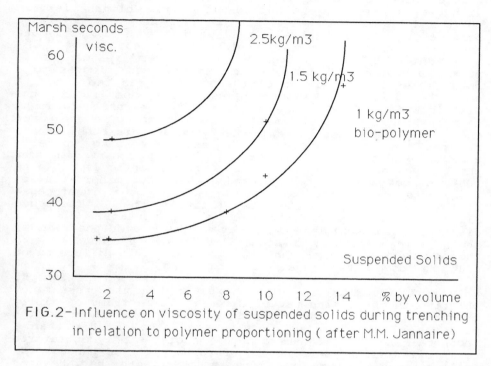

FIG.2-Influence on viscosity of suspended solids during trenching in relation to polymer proportioning (after M.M. Jannaire)

The bactericide incorporated in the bio-polymer formula will protect the slurry for a relatively short time which is adequate for deep french drain type work. For diaphragm wall construction, where the slurry is meant to be recycled for weeks, the pH should be maintained above 9. This requires the addition of soda ash to the new slurry at the beginning of the work, up to the point where enough calcium from the concrete provides enough alkali to run the pH eventually up to 12.

On a recent project in Washington D.C. as part of the redevelopment of the World Bank headquarters, the writer tested slurry recovered from a tieback reservation, two months after installation of the pannel: viscosity 32 Marsh seconds,filtrate 25 cc, cake .3mm, pH 11. Beside the intrinsic biodegradability of the bio-polymer slurry, a high pH eliminates the obvious concern for the practitioner. pH reduction is eventually easily achieved with an acid.

5) EROSION:

Like all organic polymers used for drilling muds, biodegradable or not, chlorine has a destructive effect on the polymer chains. The phenomenon consists in the rupture of the sugar links holding the chains of monomers together, and reverting to smaller chains or to monomers. It is a water well driller practice to destroy the natural gum drilling slurry with Clorox prior to the well development. Chlorine is very toxic and its use in the drilling industry has been tolerated because of the small scale, localised nature of the work, and regularly overlooked by most regulatory agencies.

Chlorine is used massively in water treatment as a potent bactericide but removed later in the process to a potable level by addition of thiosulfates and the likes. A small and variable amount of chlorine remains in the distribution system for water "quality". The residual amount is much higher in the USA where "germs" used to be the worst enemy compared to Europe where heavy metals are considered a greater health hazard. To the extent of the writer's experience in the North East, the difference in performance of the bio-polymer on the two sides of the Atlantic is close to 100%, based on tap water. Although the water mineralization has a substantial role, chlorine appears to be a bigger cause of lower yields and shorter useful life in the US. The added difficulty for the practitioner is the variability in the distribution of chlorine in a water system over the time of the day: in Baltimore, in August 1988 , at a hydrant close to the John Hopkins Medical Center, a polymer yield difference of 100% was noted between 7 am and 11 am.

Aside from lower performance, over time and at high pH, a loss of viscosity can only be explained by the presence of chlorine in the mixing water. Given the time frame of slurry trenched projects, the polymer erosion problem due to the presence of chlorine is more an economical rather than a technical one. The mechanical erosion of the polymer refered to in oil drilling as a result of turbulent flow through the drill bit and the pump impellers is not a factor her. Neither is temperature within normal ambient conditions.

US APPLICATIONS TO DATE

As stated above, the US applications for the synthetic biodegradable polymer in slurry trenched excavations has involved mainly two types of work: narrow deep french drains and structural diaphragm walls.

DEEP FRENCH DRAINS:

A technique more and more appealing to ground water remediation engineerswhich consists in switching from a multiple extraction well system to a single linear drain structure with very few collection points. This method is particularly well suited for saturated low permeability soils.

Whether the intent is extraction or recharge, the advantages of a linear system over a puntual one are obvious , either from a hydrogeologic or a maintenance standpoint.

It can be expected that the soils are water bearing and that shoring and dewatering would be required to install a conventional french drain. Dewatering in a contaminated environment is problematic and onerous since the extracted water must be treated, often before any onsite treatment facility exists. It is possible to excavate a continuous trench under biodegradable slurry as narrow as the equipment permits, 18 to 36 inches wide depending on depth. The soils are generally sufficiently rich in fines to trench with pure bio-polymer slurry and to maintain a head over the water table. At many locations of the New Jersey corridor, the water table is very close to the surface and head conditions are often minimal. The length of the open trench varies with depth but are shorter than would be the case for a slurry trenched cutoff wall since the pea gravel filter backfill slope stabilizes at 1V in 4H compared to soil bentonite backfill slope which can do to 1V in 10H or more.

The typical sequence of operation is as follows: 1) trenching to full depth in one pass and grade the trench bottom as necessary, 2) installing a coarse gravel bedding with the same equipment, 3) lowering a 4 to 6 inch diameter flexible perforated or slotted drain pipe (properly ballasted) into position on the bedding, 4) backfilling with clean filter gravel, either dumping through the slurry if the gradation is more or less uniform or unloading at the top of the slope in the soil bentonite backfilling manner if there is concern for segregation.

Once the crews are trained and synchronized, the rate of progress is imcomparably faster than any other method except the deep plow technique which can be used for shallow drains. The more contaminated, the more mechanized the operation can be, resulting in less exposure to the workers in comparison to a conventional construction approach.

A number of conceptual points should be stressed since the transition from a french drain installed in the dry and one under slurry is not obvious to all engineers: a typical french drain design includes today a filter fabric at the interface between the soil and the stone backfill. This design attributes all the filtering power to the filter fabric and the stone backkfill is just an open porosity and a conduit. In the case of a slurried drain where a polymer/colloid/fines cake is formed on the trench walls, entrapping the cake between the soil and the filter fabric, the filter fabric will remain at least partially if not totally clogged at the time of attempting to develop the drain. Although the polymer is biodegradable over the short or medium term, the fines will remain trapped. A filter fabric around the drain pipe is also not desirable when constructing under slurry: a polymer slurry has no means of suspending fines in a static conditions and in the course of the trenching operation and drain pipe placement a deposit of loose fines will accumulate at the bottom of the trench. This sludge-like deposit will fill the openings of the filter gravel, possibly a few feet above the drain pipe.

After a while, the sludge may consolidate and allow for a reopening of the pores thus allowing the drain to be developed. The slot opening size in the drain pipe should be a multiple of the largest fine that may settle out of the slurry in order that all fines may be removed during the development process. It is this writer's view that drain development be part of the installation procedure for two reasons:

The first reason is to assure that the drainage be uniform and the drawdown or recharge level constant. One should be aware of the pitfall of thinking that the potential yield of the drain is way in excess of the on site treatment capacity and therefore good development way be a waste of money. The advantage of the drain over the well is to exercise a constant gradient potentially over the entire drain length. Good development is the condition to achieve this result.

The second reason is that if the bio-polymer slurry and the cake matter are removed early enough from the drain before biodegradation occurs, no bacteriological infestation of the ground can occur. This latter concern is one of the reasons why gum based natural bio-polymers have been banned in certain states like New Jersey or Michigan or certain European countries. Upon extraction, the slurry is either recycled for further trenches or stored to biodegrade and settle its fines, or for future treatment if contaminated during the trenching process. From a client and public standpoint, the biodegradation in open air of a synthetic bio-polymer is much less injurious to the olfactory nerves than gum based natural polymers; construction inspectors exposed to both types of products have voiced their preference!

Biodegradation may take place at different times even at the same site: a number of drain trenches were installed on the grounds of a pharmaceutical company in New Jersey (Fig.3); the slurry bio-degraded overnight when crossing a sodded area while it took four days to degrade at trench location through a cleared area. After bio-degradation, BOD counts are low enough to allow discharge in the sewerif no contaminants are present. Leachate collection of petroleum products recovery drain projects in california and at various locations on the eastern seaboard have confirmed the merits of this construction method.

Fig.3 Drain construction in N.J.

STRUCTURAL DIAPHRAGM WALLS:

The cost of disposing spent slurries and trench excavation spoils in Europe, where land for public discharge is even scarcer than it is in the US, has forced slurry wall contractors to look at other alternatives. The departure from well honed practices based on bentonite slurry to support the trench walls and the change to a synthetic biodegradable polymer based slurry is being encouraged for very practical reasons which are familiar to all diaphragm wall practitioners.

Handling, storage and processing of bagged bentonite requires space, labor, powerful mixing pumps and dust masks. Typically, the storage and handling requirement for the polymer is about 30 times less.

Mixing polymer and water can be performed directly with the water supply, without any pump. One labor can mix 25 to 40 m^3 (30 to 50 CY) per hour, handling a mere 50 to 80 kg (110-176 lbs) of polymer. Pumping is required if additived are needed. A recirculation pump is used to homogenize the mix. The slurry plant must be managed by a qualified and experienced laborer.

Since the polymer slurry is not thixotropic, pumping through the lines is much easier and easy on the pumps as well. In the experience of this writer, 3 inch slurry lines are quite sufficient compared to the 4 inch lines or larger normally used with bentonite slurry.

When the slurry storage tanks stand upright, an entire site can be gravity fed and the line pump is eliminated.

The abrasivity of bentonite slurry with its suspended sand is a well known fact and wear of clamshell cables and pins and bushings enter in the cost of doing the work. With polymer slurry, the sand fraction is settling during the trenching process, the slurry in the panel is much cleaner, hence gentler on the equipment.

With its lubricating properties, a polymer slurry will prevent sticky soils from adhering to metals and in particular to the jaws of the clamshell, a vexing problem when using pure bentonite slurry in trenching very easy and very sticky clays. By the same process, the potential for suctioning in clays is vastly reduced, which may permit excavation of very soft clays such as bay muds.

Unlike the soupy aspect of trench spoils excavated under bentonite slurry, materials excavated under a polymer slurry will drain readily if granular in nature and develop a much greater angle of repose (Fig.4).

This is a significant advantage for the cleanliness of the site and for the excavating contractor in charge of hauling and disposing these materials. Excavated materials can be loaded directly in a dump truck and hauled directly to the dump site in full loads and at regular dumping fees (Fig.5).

Fig.4 Free draining trench spoils

Fig.5 Direct loaded dump truck

Since the slurry has no gel strength, should a slurry loss be observed, the most expeditious way to stop the loss is to dump fine sand or previously excavated fine soils which will fall readily at the loss zone and contribute the missing fines. This will permit the resumption of trenching without having lost control of the slurry viscosity. This simple slurry loss control method is not possible with bentonite slurries where fine sand would "float" and the addition of cement or other plugging agents would affect the slurry quality to the point that it may be detrimental to the endproduct.

Once excavated, a panel is left to rest to allow for the fines to settle to the bottom. All coarse sand will have been removed during the excavation process. The time required varies according to depth, viscosity and slurry weight. A satisfactory sequence is to allow a full day between the day when trenching is completed and the day when the panel is poured. A bottom cleanup with a toothless clamshell at 12 hours intervals during that time will generally be all that is required. If end bearing is a design concern, air lifting or pumping the bottom prior to pouring will complete this procedure. If in fact too many silt size fines have accumulated in the slurry and a longer settling time would be required, it is more judicious to store this otherwise good slurry in settling tanks and use newer slurry in the panel. The traditional desanding and recycling operation are therefore eliminated along with all the work it comprises.

A mechanical approach to accelerate the settlement of extra fines is to use a battery of desilting cones or a centrifuge machine recycling the stock of used slurry at the plant. With proper timing and periodic cutting of used slurry with new, the synthetic biodegradable polymer slurry can be carried out throughout the construction of the wall and the need for disposal may be limited ideally to the volume corresponding to the last panel.

To the practitioner, a most attractive feature of this technology is the absence of slurry flocculation [3] when it comes in contact with calcium, either from the concrete of previously poured panels or from fresh concrete falling , unavoidably, through the slurry during a tremie pour operation. The polymer slurry will not be affected and when displaced by the concrete during the pour, it can be pumped back in its entirety to the storage tanks with no particular effort on the part of the pump (Fig.6).

Because of this chemical neutrality, the slurry concrete interface is very clear and there is no contaminated concrete. Provisions for chipping down excess concrete contaminated are not necessary (Fig.7). This of particular interest in case of panels cast low under the guide walls. With a clean slurry maintaining a low viscosity throughout the pour, and with good quality and good service provided by the concrete supplier, the cleanliness between panels can be remarkable. The absence of a bentonite cake behind the wall destroys the myth that the latter provides added watertightness to the wall when bentonite slurry is used. Nothing is more watertight than good quality concrete.

Fig.6 Pumping slurry to the last drop

Fig.7 Clean top of wall   Fig.8 Exposed wall in Arlington

As can be observed in Fig.8, once the wall is exposed, things do not look different. At close range, the interface between granular soils and the concrete comprises a hardened cake matter, much harder than what can be observed when bentonite is used. This difference could improve skin friction in the case of load bearing elements using slurry techniques.

CONCLUSIONS:

The double cornered panel at the World Bank Headquarters project site(Fig.9) demonstrates that a light weight synthetic biodegradable slurry can assure the stability of a slurried trench excavation, even in coarse granular soils, successfully. The use of this new slurry provides a simplification of the slurry wall construction process. This does not mean that slurry quality control process can be relaxed. On the contrary, this writer has found that a high degree of involvement on the part of a slurry technician is required to monitor the use of the different losses of slurry. This is important both technically and economically. Ultimately, the total cost of the polymer used on a project will depend on a large extent to the judicious usage of the various lots of slurry by the slurry specialist.

All aspects of site cleanliness are largely improved following the switch from bentonite based to synthetic polymer slurry. This cleanliness extends to the dump as well, eliminating the trails of unwanted mud and the mixing with dry materials before landfilling. Disposal of relatively minor quantities of leftover slurry is very economical with different methods possible according to specific site conditions and availability of time:

1- pH correction, natural biodegradation, seperation of clear water and solid with time and final discharge of the biodegraded slurry to the sanitary sewer.

2- pH neutralization by a strong acid which also breaks down the polymer causing the fines to settle faster which expedites the release of the water fration.

3- pH neutralization and centrifugation with mechanical separation between liquid and solid phases.

4- pH neutralization and instantaneous separation of phase by addition of an "anti" polymer solution and separation through a filtering belt.

Since the slurry is entirely biodegradable, it is not necessary to achieve biodegradion prior to discharge. Coordination with local water authorities should be routine practice.

Although the environmental benefits of the synthetic biodegradable polymer slurry are a clear step forward for the slurry trenching construction techniques, it ia at the operational level, from the practitioner's standpoint that the writer welcomes this new technology. Working cleaner, more economically and getting a good or better an endproduct while having an easier time at it, this can be called progress.

* * * * * * * *

Notes:

1. Case International test panel #23 Union Station ,Los Angeles Metro, 1991 .
2. Nicholson Construction, access shaft main outfall tunnel, Boston Harbour cleanup project, Deer Island,1991
3. ICOS Boston, Nut Island to Deer Island feed tunnel, Boston Harbour cleanup project, 1991

References:

[1] Parigo P.et Martin M., Boues au Biopolymere, Paris,France
    Forages No.47   4/1970.
[2] M.M. Jannaire, Les Boues de forage,Paris , France
    Travaux 8/1990
[3] Rogers W.F., Composition and properties of oil well
    drilling fluids, Gulf Publish.Co. Houston,TX 1953

Acknowledgements:
     The writer is particularly appreciative of the
confidence shown by Alan G. Hobelman, V.P. Foundations
Depnt.of the George Hyman Construction Co., Behtesda, MD, for
allowing the use of synthetic biodegradable polymer on his
full scale exposed foundation diaphragm walls projects. These
projects were the first biodegradable applications in North
America for structural construction. The writer wishes also to
recognize Maurice Marie Jannaire of Geothermie Sondage
Petrole, Lyon, France, as the leading pioner in the
development of polymer compounds for geotechnical engineering
specific applications.

Fig.9   The World Bank Headquarters   project,Washington.D.C.

Hsai-Yang Fang[1], Sibel Pamukcu[1] and Ronald C. Chaney[3]

SOIL-POLLUTION EFFECTS ON GEOTEXTILE COMPOSITE WALLS

REFERENCE: Fang, H. Y., Pamukcu, S., and Chaney, R. C., "Soil-Pollution Effects on Geotextile Composite Walls," Slurry Walls: Design, Construction, and Quality Control, ASTM STP 1129, David B. Paul, Richard R. Davidson, and Nicholas J. Cavalli, Eds., American Society for Testing and Materials, Philadelphia, 1992.

ABSTRACT: For designing or selecting proper types or porosity of the geotextile to be used in a composite wall, it is necessary to know the grain size distribution of the surrounding soil under consideration. This determination becomes especially critical when the engineered facility is exposed to various biological and chemical stresses overtime. A series of laboratory investigations were conducted to examine the effects of pore fluid pH, soil adsorption of particulate matter and also particle volume change on the grain size distribution of soils.The results showed that the particle size distribution curve shifted to finer scales as water pH increased for non-dispersive clays. For a dispersive clay, the trend of the particle size distribution curve was opposite, shifting to the finer sizes with decrease in water pH. Surrounding water pH was also found to correlate with volume change of soil particles and soil matrix which subsequently would affect particle size distribution.

KEY WORDS: Soil pollution, grain size distribution, soil/ geotextile compatibility, pore water pH, soil volume change

INTRODUCTION

Composite walls or liners engineered for drainage, filtration, erosion control or liquid barrier functions are expected to perform under adverse effects of changing physical and chemical environment. In systems for which the environment stays more or less constant, or for which the extent of changing conditions can be estimated with some degree of accuracy, long-term compatibility of different components of a composite system can be assured over the life time of the engineered system. In reality, this may be a relatively complex task.

---

[1] Professor and Assistant Professor, respectively, Department of Civil Engineering, Lehigh University, Bethlehem, Pa, 18015

[2] Professor, Department of Environmental Resources Engineering of Humboldt State University, Arcata, Ca, 95570

Some of the common factors in design of composite systems, such as a soil/geotextile system that serve filtration or drainage functions are the permeabilities of the soil and the geotextile and the retention of soil by the geotextile. There are well established methods to measure or predict these characteristics and design composite systems the components of which are compatible overtime. There has been a number of case studies (Giroud, 1984) that show good performances of existing engineered facilities. However, there is much room for research when longer term performances are to be estimated under possible changes in soil environment such as changes in the pore fluid chemistry, availability of water, biological activity, etc. These types of activities have been shown to influence soil physical and chemical parameters significantly over time, especially in the fine size ranges. Physical or chemical changes in the soil component of a composite system will alter the designed compatibility of soil with adjacent geotextile and may ultimately cause the cease of the function of the system. The physical and chemical changes may also take place in the geotextile component as well.

In this paper some of the process that may result in the incompatibility of soil and geotextiles are discussed. Although, one can conceptualize numerous processes in a complex soil-water system, the following were selected to highlight their particular significance with respect to geotextile composite walls or liners. They are:

1.   Soil-pollutant interactions
2.   Particle volume change
3.   Adsorption processes (bacteria/suspended matter)

The probable effects of these processes on the stability of composite systems are discussed based on the synthesis of available data and background information.

BACKGROUND

Use of geotextile composite systems in construction have expanded significantly over the past 15 years. Major uses of these systems can be categorized as (Koerner, 1990):

1. Separation of dissimilar materials
2. Reinforcement of weak soils and other materials
3. Filtration (Cross-Plane Flow)
4. Drainage (In-Plane Flow)
5. Moisture Barrier

One of the most critical parameters in the design of composite systems with geotextiles is the permeability. When the composite system is intended for the function of filtration or drainage, the geotextile component must be permeable enough not to slow down the flow of water, yet its openings small enough not to allow movement of soil particles. To satisfy these conditions, the geotextile and the soil components need be compatible, that is the soil particles should not clog or wash through the geotextile liner. In the past it has been shown that for

either cohesionless sands and/or silts, gap graded particle size
distributions and high hydraulic gradients are major causes of clogging
as well as other conditions such as blocking, arching and the formation
of upstream soil filters (Koerner, 1990, 1991).

A number of approaches has been developed to help select the
appropriate geotextiles that are compatible with soil found at a project
site. These approaches utilize the apparent opening size (AOS) or 95%
'retained on' a US Standard sieve opening size referred to as the O_{95} of
the geotextile. The soil properties that are used in the compatibility
analysis are either D_{50} (particle size corresponding to 50% finer), or
D_{85} (particle size corresponding to 85% finer), and C_u (D_{60}/D_{10}) the
coefficient of uniformity. Carroll (1983) recommended that:

$$O_{95} < (2 \text{ or } 3) \ D_{85} \qquad\qquad (1)$$

Giroud (1982) recommended a more conservative approach in which a linear
coefficient of uniformity, r, derived from the central linear part of a
gradation curve. This retention criteria for geotextile filters is shown
in Figure 1, in which C_u ($= /D_{100}/D_0$) is defined different than C_u ($=
D_{60}/D_{10}$).

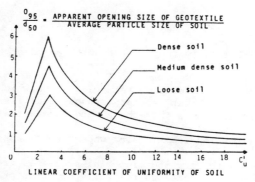

$$\frac{O_{95}}{d_{50}} = \frac{\text{APPARENT OPENING SIZE OF GEOTEXTILE}}{\text{AVERAGE PARTICLE SIZE OF SOIL}}$$

Dense soil

Medium dense soil

Loose soil

LINEAR COEFFICIENT OF UNIFORMITY OF SOIL

(a)   Retention criteria based C_u'

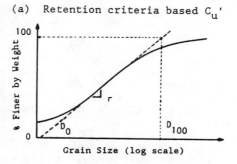

(b) Determination of C_u' ($= D_{100}/D_0$)

Figure 1. Retention Criteria for Geotextile Filter (after Giroud, 1982)

Soils are environmentally active materials, especially when they contain appreciable amount of fines. This is because, soil clays react to physico-chemical changes in the environment in a way that influence their physical properties. These changes can range from sudden loading of the soil with caustic chemicals to slow biological processes due to the presence of microbial communities. When considering long-term compatibility of the components of a composite system such as a retaining wall or a barrier wall that utilize geotextiles in their functions, it is necessary to look at the consequences of environmental impact on all the components. A number of studies have been conducted to evaluate environmental compatibility and durability of geotextile materials, which include studies on their resistance to chemicals, bacteria, temperature, light, weather and burial deterioration (Fang et al., 1984). Formalized tests have been developed by the American Society for Testing and Materials (ASTM) for most of these evaluations. However, there has been relatively little work on environmental durability and stability of soil geotextile composites in general. The study reported here looks at this aspect specifically applied to the interaction of soil and geotextile components in a composite system.

INVESTIGATION

Pollution Process

In general, soil pollution comes from three major sources. These are:

a.   Direct or indirect effects of rain: acid rain which percolates into the ground or rain water that leaches through landfills into the ground;
b.   Pollutants infiltrating into the ground from surface spills or waste containing lagoons;
c.   Pollutants migrating from leaking underground tanks.

Physico-chemical, weathering and microbial processes are all factors that contribute in some degree to the soil pollution process. In all of these the major controlling factors are heat, organic matter/bacteria, amount of clay size material, quantity of percolating water and also the type and concentration of the chemicals in polluted water. The chemical processes that cause the physical changes in clay minerals are: hydrolysis, carbonation, oxidation and solution (Fang, 1987, 1989). Chemical and bacterial processes can change soil properties significantly. For example, decomposition in landfills tend to increase the surrounding ground temperature. When the temperature is high, the sulfate concentrations rise. Bacteria may also flourish under these conditions and oxidize hydrogen sulfide into sulfuric acid creating a corrosive environment.

When soil interacts with water, a number of forces and their subsequent stresses are produced as listed in Figure 2. The magnitude of these forces are influenced by the degree of pollution in soil water systems (Fang, 1989). The interaction between soil mineralogy, pore water chemistry and precipitation is presented in Figure 3. Soil

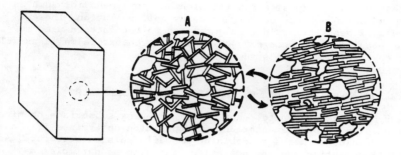

Environmental Forces in Soil-Water-Air Systems	Factors Effecting Soil Structure Arrangement
. Heat of wetting force . Kinetic dispersive force . Electro-motive force . Electro-magnetic force . Water-vapor force	. Ion exchange reaction . Redox reaction . Polarization . Proton migration

Figure 2. Possible Environmental Forces Effects on Soil/Water Systems

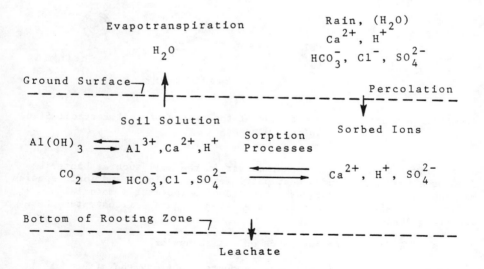

Figure 3. Soil-Water Interaction and Interaction of Rainfall,
          Percolation,

properties such as grain size distribution and soil behavior such as swelling and shrinkage can be influenced by soil pollution. These properties and behavior are directly related to the factors used to determine stability and integrity of composite geotextile walls as well as other engineered earthen structures.

Effects of Soil Pollution on Geosynthetic Composite Systems

Clays have been shown to react to the changing subsurface chemical environment. The pH of the water during deposition determines if the clay will develop either a flocculated or deflocculated structure. As a result of flocculation and agglomeration, the size of particles may appear to have increased. The swelling or shrinking of diffuse double layer, or adsorption of organic or inorganic substances onto the clay surfaces could change the 'apparent' particle size. Therefore, one can expect that as pH changes soil particle sizes might change over time.

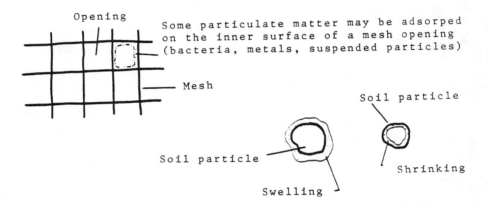

Figure 4. Schematic Representation of the Effect of Soil Particle Size or Pollutants on Mesh Openings

Furthermore, pollutants or other matter in the soil such as bacteria - dead or alive -, suspended dust particles and colloids and ionic species may accumulate inside the mesh openings of a geotextile material reducing the effective area for water flow. Figure 4 illustrates these occurrences conceptually.

A.   Effect of Porewater pH on Soil Behavior

A number of experiments were conducted to study the effect of porewater pH on gradation and particle size. In general, low pH causes the diffuse double layer of clays to compress which results in flocculation and higher rate of settlement of clay suspensions (Tuncan and Pamukcu, 1992). This compression is a result of increased concentration of H^+ ions as pH reduces. H^+ is good cation exchanger, thus will occupy exchange sites and cause the release of cations (Mg, Al, Fe, and others) from clay surfaces, increasing the electrolyte concentration in the pore fluid. The increased electrolyte concentration, in turn, reduces the repulsion forces between clay particles promoting flocculation. At high pH conditions, the diffuse double layers are thick and repulsion between particles is strong. The settlement rates in such systems are slower, but the resulting mass is denser as opposed to the more open structure formed by flocculated clay.

The standard hydrometer analysis was modified to study the sedimentation process of a soil/water slurry. In these tests, the hydrometer analysis was conducted following the ASTM method for Particle Size Analysis of Soils (D-422) except that the demineralized water in the jar was replaced with waters of different pH. The results of these tests conducted using different soil types are shown in Figures 5 and 6. The results pertain to single tests using the passing No. 200 sieve size portion of the same soil type in waters of varying pH.

The effect pH has on the grain size distribution of material finer than the No. 200 sieve is shown in Figure 5. A review of Figure 5 shows that as the pH increases the gradation curve is shifted in the direction of smaller particle sizes. This is probably because the increasing pH of the solution promoted the deflocculation of the clay. This in turn resulted in slower settling rates and the shift of the gradation curve toward the smaller particle sizes.

Results of similar tests on a dispersive clay are shown in Figure 6. A review of Figure 6 shows that the opposite of what was observed for Bethlehem silty clay (Figure 5) occurs for this dispersive clay. In this case, the increasing pH probably resulted in shorter settling times which in turn shifted the gradation curves in the direction of larger particle sizes. Similar observations were made with dispersive clays by Statton and Mitchell (1972), in which they showed that dispersive behavior of a clay shale material was suppressed between pH 8.9 and 11.1. Their results also showed decreased dispersive behavior of clay at sufficiently low pH of 3.2. This does not agree with the finding in this work where the 'apparent' particle size decreases with decreasing pH, as evidenced by the shift of the gradation curve to right for solution pH values of 2 and 3. This may be attributed to the dissolution of clay at low pH or changes in surface charge characteristics for the particular clay tested. Nevertheless, the change in 'apparent' particle size distribution with surrounding solution pH is observed in both Figures 5 and 6.

As the gradation and particle size distribution change so does the values of D_{10}, D_{50}, D_{85} and the uniformity coefficient C_u. These are critical soil parameters used in determining the soil and geotextile compatibility in designing composite systems as discussed earlier. The laboratory data shows that in non-dispersive soils, D_{10} and D_{60} decrease with increasing pH. However, since change in the D_{10} is often larger than the change in D_{60}, the uniformity coefficient, C_u, increases with

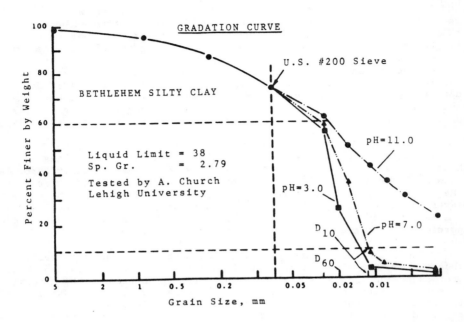

Figure 5. Grain Size Distribution - Hydrometer Test on Bethlehem Silty Clay Using Water of Varying pH

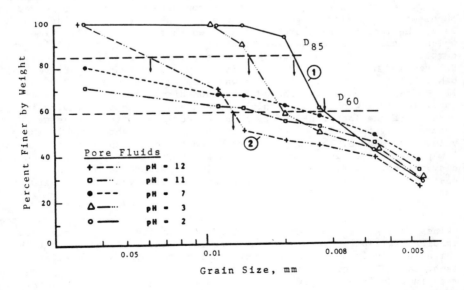

Figure 6. Grain Size Distribution - Hydrometer Test on Dispersive Clay Using Water of Varying pH

increasing pH (see Figure 5). In dispersive clays the reverse of this condition takes place, for which the increasing pH increases the 'apparent' particle size. The change in D_{60} is larger than the change in D_{10}, therefore the uniformity coefficient decrease consistently with increasing pH.

B.   Effect of Soil Particle Volume Change (Swelling/Shrinking)

When water is added to dry clay, its particle volume increases as water molecules move into the interlayer space between sheets. This phenomena is called the 'swelling' of clays. As water is removed from the soil, by drying or other means, part of the interlayer water may move out into the pore space thus creating 'shrinkage' of the particle. These processes are spontaneous when the environmental conditions favor a decrease in the free energy or an increase in the entropy of the soil-water system. The rate of swelling and also the magnitude of swelling pressure are directly proportional to the available free energy. The rate of swelling is also controlled by availability of water and the resistance of the soil particle system to conduction of this water in the matrix. The severity and extent of swelling and shrinkage of different types of clays when treated with fluids of different chemical compositions can be observed from their cracking pattern upon drying (Fang, 1987).

Figure 7 shows the effect of pH on the volume change behavior (swelling and shrinking) of different types of soils. Bentonite (Na-montmorillonite), being a highly active clay, shows the largest volume change among the three types of clays tested, as expected. What is interesting to note is the systematic increase in volume change of all the clays (bentonite, illite and muscovite) as the pH of their pore fluid increases. When the clays are air dried as opposed to oven drying, the excessive volume change occurs at low pH values as well as high pH values. The increase in volume of the compact clay system can be explained by the swelling of the particle itself, by swelling of the double layer and also by dispersion or deflocculation of the clay. Since there is a combination of factors, it is difficult to interpret what exactly might happen to the 'apparent' particle size as measured in the hydrometer analysis, for instance. Particle swelling would increase the 'apparent' particle size, however, deflocculation would decrease it. In either case, it is clear that pH of the environment and the rate of water supply or loss influence the volume of a clay system either at the particle level or at the overall matrix level. Figure 8 shows a conceptual illustration of the general range of moisture contents at which polluted waters would affect the volume change behavior of soil matrices.

C.   Effect of Adsorbed Bacteria or Suspended Particles

Fine soil particles have a tendency to adhere to other solids in the ground such as geotextiles. In addition, bacteria, suspended matter, colloids and various ionic species in the pore water of a polluted soil will also have a tendency to adhere and accumulate on a geotextile mesh

as well as on soil particles. This concentration of materials on a
surface is called 'adsorption'. In order for the adsorption to be
appreciable, it is necessary that the adsorbent have a large surface
area. Therefore, fine soil with large surface area, such as clay
materials, would have higher adsorption capacity than granular soil.
Fine mesh of geotextiles may also provide sufficient surface area for
appreciable adsorption of particulate matter. Suspended particles or
dust can be key factors in the transport of pollution in water, soil-
water systems and also in air (Fang, 1989).

Bacteria and suspended particles can be adsorbed onto the soil
particles or on the surfaces of geotextile mesh. The accumulation of
these materials on the mesh openings would eventually result in clogging
of the openings as illustrated in the conceptual drawing in Figure 4.

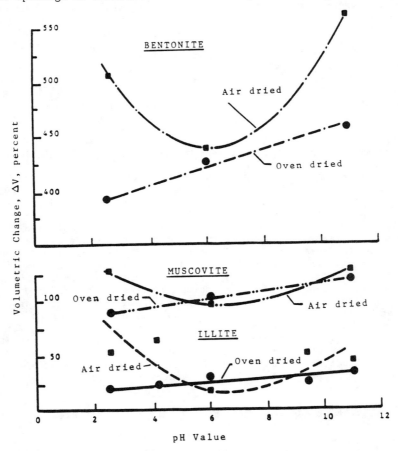

Figure 7. Effect of pH Values on Volumetric Changes of Some Clay
           Minerals (after Fang et al., 1984)

Bacteria affects soil behavior directly. Most aerobic bacteria exist at a shallow depth below the ground surface and above the groundwater table in the A-horizon, which consists of dark colored organic matter and humic substances. The rate and degree of most bacterial activity depends on the availability of nutrients, micro-organic types, substrata composition and temperature. Flooding, fluctuating water table or increasing the ground temperature will accelerate the aerobic process. In contrast, anaerobic bacteria exist primarily below the groundwater table and their activities are slower. Various bacterial activities in the soil may change the characteristics of pore water or soil structure over time. Bacteria can change a weak acid into a strong acid, such as by oxidizing hydrogen sulfide to sulfuric acid under aerobic conditions, which is often the condition in landfills and polluted soils above the groundwater table. The sulfuric acid in the ground then creates a low pH and also corrosive environment which would effect the underground structures as well as soil itself as discussed earlier.

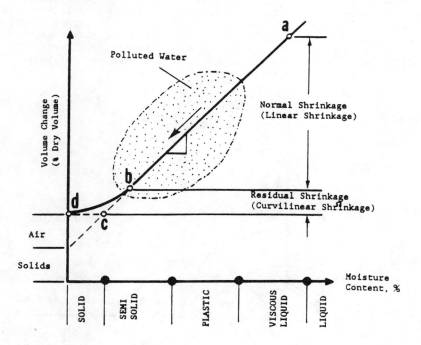

Figure 8. Schematic Presentation of Volume Change and Soil Consistency

Long-Term Integrity of Geosynthetic Composite Walls Near Polluted Sites

Slurry walls and clay liners are commonly used for hazardous and toxic waste control and storage systems. When using geotextiles in these facilities, certain attention must be paid to the long-term interaction of the soil and geotextile components. To asses the long-term integrity of these systems in a polluted environment, the behavior of the contaminated water and the resulting stresses around the vicinity of the facility need to be evaluated.

Figure 9 shows schematically the interaction of chemical and biological activities that might take place near a composite wall. Water existing in the soil-water system can be divided into two groups. One is the free water and the other is the bonded water. The forces affecting the free water are gravity and capillary tension. In contrast, the bonded water is the water in the diffuse double layer, which can be referred to as hydration water, osmotic water or the oriented water. The bonded water is strongly influenced by the local environment, especially in polluted soil-water systems. The environmental forces or stresses developing in the vicinity of a structure are caused mainly by the changes indicated in Figure 9. These stresses may play a significant role in assessing the long-term stability and integrity of composite geotextile walls as well as the mechanical loads such as surcharge, lateral earth pressure or construction activities.

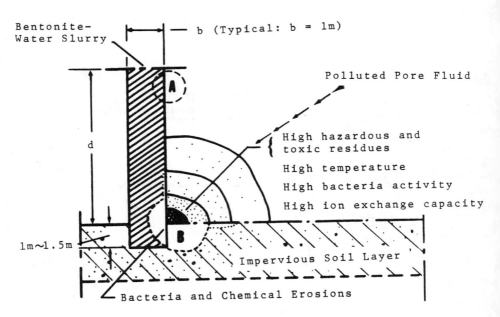

Figure 9. Schematic Presentation of Possible Interaction of a Barrier System with Polluted Environment

CONCLUSIONS

The use of geotextiles and geotextile composites in design of various earth structures have increased significantly over the past 15 years. There has been little work on the environmental durability and stability of soil-geotextile composites with respect to soil pollution, in general. Soil pollution is often the result of one or a combination of the following mechanisms: (a) direct or indirect effects of rain, (b) pollutants infiltrating into the ground, (c) pollutants migrating from leaking underground tanks. Physico-chemical, weathering and microbial processes are all factors that contribute to some degree to the soil pollution process. In all of these the major controlling factors are heat, organic matter/bacteria, amount of clay size material, quantity and chemistry of the percolating water.

The study reported here looked at the following: (a) the effect of porewater pH on soil gradation behavior, (b) the swelling and shrinkage of soils as a function of porewater pH and mineralogy, (c) the potential effect of the accumulation of fine grained material on mesh openings and also bacterial activity in soil-geotextile composites. The following conclusions were reached:

1.   One of the more general effects of porewater pH on soil behavior can be characterized as either flocculation or dispersion of the particles finer than No. 200 sieve size. This influences the soil gradation by creating flocs or dispersed colloids. The variation in the gradation of the surrounding soil, in turn, affects the performance of geotextile composites designed for drainage and filtering.

2.   The severity and extent of swelling and/or shrinkage of clays is dependent on the mineralogy of the clay particles and the pore water chemistry. Results were shown for three clays (bentonite, illite, and muscovite) which indicated that with changing pH of the pore water, the volume change response of the clay changes.

3.   Fine particles such as bacteria, suspended matter, colloids, clays and various ionic species in the pore water of a polluted soil have a tendency to adhere and accumulate on a geotextile mesh. The resulting accumulation decreases the ability of the geotextile to transmit leachate either in-plane or normal to the plane of the material. Various bacterial activities in the soil may change the characteristics and chemistry of the pore water and also the soil structure over time, which in turn would affect the performance of soil-geotextile composites.

ACKNOWLEDGMENTS

The authors would like to acknowledge with appreciation the help of Sarah A. Halley and Craig H. Benson who conducted some of the tests the results of which are reported here.

REFERENCES

Carroll, R.G., Jr., (1983), "Geotextile Filter Criteria", TRR 916, Engineering Fabrics in Transportation Construction, TRB, Washington, D.C., pp. 46-53.

Fang, H.Y., Evans, J.C. and Kugelman, I.J. (1984), "Solid and Liquid Waste Control Techniques," Chapter 10, Solid and Liquid Wastes: Management, Methods and Socioeconomic Considerations, Majurdam and Miller, eds., The Pennsylvania Academy of Science, pp. 104-118.

Fang, H.Y. (1987) "Soil-Pollutant Interaction Effects on the Soil Behavior and the Stability of Foundation Structures", Environmental Geotechnics and Problematic Soils and Rocks, Balkema, Rotterdam, pp. 155-163.

Fang, H.Y. (1989), "Particle Theory: A Unified Approach for Analyzing Soil Behavior", Proc. of the 2nd International Symposium on Environmental Geotechnology, Envo Publishing Co, Bethlehem, Pa, v.1, pp. 167-194.

Giroud, J.P. (1984) Geotextiles and Geomembranes Definitions, Properties and Design: Selected Papers, Revisions and Comments, 4th ed., Industrial Fabrics Association International, St. Paul, Minnesota, 404 p.

Giroud, J.P., (1982) "Filter Criteria for Geotextiles", Proc. of the Second International Conference on Geotextiles, Las Vegas, Nev., v. 1, pp. 103-108.

Koerner, R.M. (1990), Designing with Geosynthetics, 2nd ed., Prentice Hall, Inc., N.J., 652 p.

Koerner, R.M (1991), "Geosynthetics in Geotechnical Engineering", Chapter 22, Foundation Engineering Handbook, 2nd ed. Van Nostrand Reinhold Co., N.Y. pp. 796-813.

Reuss, J.O. (1978), "Simulation of Nutrient Loss from Soils Due to Rainfall Acidity ", EPA Report No. 600/3-78-053.

Statton, C.T. and Mitchell, J.K. (1977), "Influence of Eroding Solution Composition on Dispersive Behavior of a Compacted Clay Shale", ASTM STP 623, Dispersive Clays, Related Piping and Erosion In Geotechnical Projects, Sherard and Decker, eds., American Society for Testing and Materials, Philadelphia, Pa, pp. 398-407.

Tuncan, A. and Pamukcu S. (1992), "Geotechnical Properties of Petroleum and Sludge Contaminated Marine Sediments", Proc. of the Second International Offshore and Polar Engineering Conference, ISOPE-92, The Int. Soc. of Offshore and Polar Eng., San Fransisco, Ca., (in print)

R. Gary Garvin, Joseph F. Boward

USING SLURRY WALLS TO PROTECT AN HISTORIC BUILDING: A CASE STUDY

REFERENCE: Garvin, R. G., Boward, J. F., "Using Slurry Walls
to Protect an Historic Building: A Case Study", Slurry Walls:
Design, Construction, and Quality Control, ASTM STP 1129,
David B. Paul, Richard R. Davidson, and Nicholas J. Cavalli,
Eds., American Society for Testing and Materials, Philadel-
phia, 1992.

ABSTRACT: Slurry Wall construction was used in the construction of a five-level underground parking structure adjacent to
a settlement-sensitive historic building. The slurry wall
minimized ground disturbances and maintained groundwater
levels in the soil supporting the building. Employed for both
temporary and permanent excavation support, the slurry wall
was designed as the permanent perimeter foundation wall of the
parking structure. Geotechnical instrumentation was installed
to monitor ground movements during excavating operations and
construction. Groundwater levels were also monitored to
evaluate the performance of the wall in minimizing groundwater
drawdown in critical areas. The instrumentation data confirmed that the wall performed as intended; it successfully
supported the excavation and new building without disturbing
the historic structure.

KEYWORDS: slurry walls, excavation support, ground anchors,
geotechnical instrumentation, inclinometers, piezometers

Slurry wall construction, unique to Southwestern Pennsylvania, was
successfully used to facilitate the construction of a five-level
underground parking structure in the City of Pittsburgh's urban
university area.

Because of the urgent need for parking space and the lack of
available sites in the relatively congested Oakland area of Pittsburgh, it was decided to construct a totally underground parking
structure below the two-acre lawn area in front of Allegheny County's
historic Soldiers' and Sailors' Memorial Building. The cut and cover
project preserved the open and desirable green area of the memorial
grounds.

Garvin and Boward are Principal Engineer and Project Engineer,
respectively, of Engineering Mechanics, Inc., Pittsburgh, PA 15205.

The garage site is bounded on three sides by city streets and on the fourth side by the Memorial Building (see Fig. 1). The ground surface falls about 7 m (22 ft) in elevation from the building first floor entrance level to the level of Fifth Avenue, a distance of 91.5 m (300 ft). The parking structure design required that the excavation extend an average of 9.2 m (30 ft) below the street levels and about 8.0 m (26 ft) below the building foundations. The slurry wall was located 7.3 m (24 ft) from the front wall of the building.

Geotechnical engineering evaluations provided excavation support design parameters and identified special design considerations. Of primary concern was minimizing ground disturbances while maintaining groundwater levels in the soil supporting the historic building. Slurry wall (cast-in-place concrete diaphragm wall) construction was chosen to minimize groundwater draw-down outside the excavation and because the walls could be designed as part of the permanent parking structure. Ground anchors provided temporary lateral support for the wall; permanent support was accomplished internally in the design of the parking structure. The construction of 345 m (1130 ft) of slurry wall about the perimeter of the site and the installation of 180 ground anchors were accomplished during Sept., 1989, thru Feb., 1990, and the parking structure was opened for use in Jan., 1991.

Geotechnical instrumentation was installed along the building side of the excavation to monitor ground movements in response to horizontal deflections of the slurry wall during excavating operations and wall construction. Groundwater levels were also monitored to evaluate the performance of the wall in maintaining groundwater levels in critical areas. This paper presents a summary of the field measurements and describes the successful performance of the slurry wall.

GEOLOGIC AND SUBSURFACE CONDITIONS

The soil mantle in the garage site varies from 7.0 m (23 ft) to 13.4 m (44 ft) in thickness; it is generally composed of stratified alluvial soils - varying mixtures of silt, sandy silt, silty clay, sand, gravel and rock fragments - overlying bedrock. Standard penetration test "N" values generally range from 4 to 45 throughout the soil mantle, although some localized higher values were encountered in the coarse-grained soils immediately overlying bedrock. The lower one-third of the soil mantle is generally composed of fine to medium sand with some gravel and boulders.

The bedrock surface falls about 1 m (3 ft) in elevation from the building north wall to its lowest elevation along Fifth Avenue on the south side of the site. To a depth of about 11 m (35 ft) below its surface (the limits of the test borings), the horizontally layered bedrock is composed of 6.1 m (20 ft) of hard interbedded siltstone and sandstone and 4.6 m (15 ft) of comparatively soft claystone. The sedimentary bedrock layers are units of the Casselman Formation of the Conemaugh Group, Pennsylvanian System.

Zones of perched water were encountered in the normally consolidated silty soils atop layers of relatively impervious silty clay

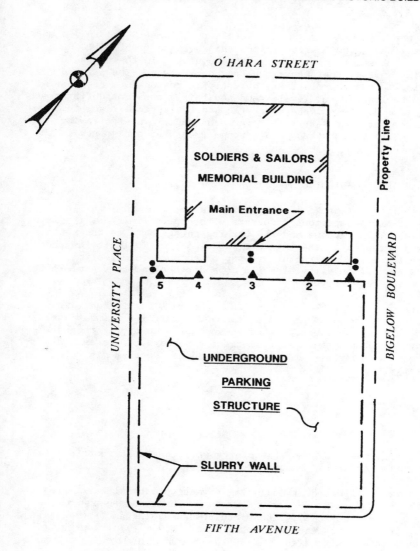

O'HARA STREET

Property Line

SOLDIERS & SAILORS
MEMORIAL BUILDING

Main Entrance

UNIVERSITY PLACE

BIGELOW BOULEVARD

5   4   3   2   1

UNDERGROUND

PARKING

STRUCTURE

SLURRY WALL

FIFTH AVENUE

SCALE :

```
0        25 m        50 m
|----|----|----|----|
0    50 ft       150 ft
        100 ft
```

LEGEND :

▲ : INCLINOMETER

● : PIEZOMETER

FIG. 1 -- Site plan.

throughout the soil mantle. Such levels were 5.5 m (18 ft) to 7.3 m
(24 ft) below the ground surface along the building front wall. A
lower, more consistent water table was encountered in the coarse-
grained soils several feet above the bedrock surface. The perched
water levels fluctuated relatively abruptly in response to precipitation while the lower water levels remained fairly constant during the
monitoring period. Beyond the site, the bedrock surface rises to the
northwest such that the water table is recharged by waters flowing
south through the sand layers, and through fractures and joints in the
underlying bedrock.

PROTECTING EXISTING BUILDING

The Memorial Building, constructed between 1908 and 1910, is a
massive, four-story sandstone structure with ornate finishes; its main
entrance faces Fifth Avenue and the parking garage site to the south.
The building includes a basement level about 6.1 m (20 ft) below the
first floor level. The structure is supported on spread footing
foundations bearing on alluvial soils at a depth of about 6.4 m (21 ft)
below the first floor level.

Because of its age and construction, the building is considered to
be sensitive to even minor ground settlements under its foundations.
Perched water zones were encountered in the soil supporting the building foundations. Removing water from these perched water zones would
increase effective stresses in the soils inducing settlements which
would distress the building.

SLURRY WALL DESIGN

Lateral Pressures

To minimize the height of the slurry wall, the upper portion of
the soil mantle was sloped where possible (see Fig. 2).

The slurry wall was designed using an active lateral earth pressure coefficient, K_a, of 0.35 and an effective soil shear strength
friction angle, ϕ', of 28.8°. The earth pressure diagram (Fig. 2) was
developed using a generalized soil profile of: 5.2 m (17 ft) of silt
and clay at a total unit weight, γ, of 2083 kg/m³ (130 lb/ft³); 5.2 m
(17 ft) of sand at a unit weight of 1923 kg/m³ (120 lb/ft³); and a
permanent water table level at 1.5 m (5 ft) above the bedrock surface.
The lateral pressures also included a surcharge loading from the sloped
soil mantle above the slurry wall: no building surcharge was included.

Foundation Design

All vertical loads were transferred to bedrock which was assigned
an allowable design bearing capacity of 2394 kPA (50 ksf). It was
assumed that the slurry wall would not settle as all loads were transferred to the hard bedrock. The slurry wall design called for a
minimum penetration into bedrock of 0.3 m (1 ft). Where the garage
floor level extended below the bedrock surface, the slurry wall was

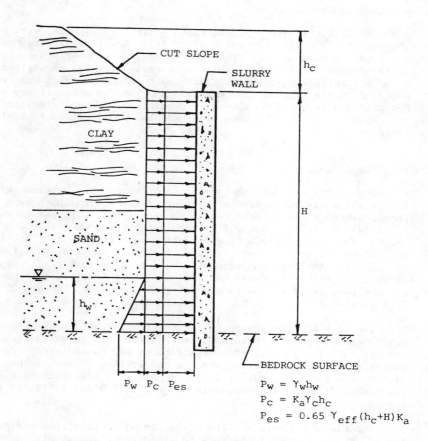

$P_w = \gamma_w h_w$

$P_c = K_a \gamma_c h_c$

$P_{es} = 0.65 \, \gamma_{eff} (h_c + H) K_a$

FIG. 2 -- Lateral soil pressures
based on simplified
subsurface profile.

continued into bedrock 0.3 m (1 ft) below the planned floor subgrade level.

Where additional lateral restraint was required at the base of the wall, primarily along the building side of the excavation, toe ties were installed vertically into bedrock below the slurry wall. Each panel contained three toe ties consisting of No. 18 reinforcing bars embedded 3 m (10 ft) into rock. The toe ties were not prestressed.

Slurry Wall Construction

The wall trench was excavated in sections or panels, with panel lengths of 7.3 m (24 ft) to 7.6 m (25 ft). Steel pipes were used as end forms between panels. The soil excavation was performed with cable-operated clam buckets while rock excavation was accomplished using a free-falling chisel. Fractured rock and sediment was "vacuumed" from the bottoms of the panels and the bentonite slurry was desanded and returned to the panel excavation. Ground vibrations from the chiseling operations were minor and had no effect on the existing building.

Structural Design

The slurry wall was designed to span vertically between garage floors which assumed complete transfer of loads from the ground anchors, although the anchors remain in place. The wall panels vary from 9.4 m (31 ft) to 11.6 m (38 ft) in height and the wall is 0.6 m (2 ft) thick. Horizontal reinforcing for all panels consisted of No. 7 bars on 30.5 cm (12 in.) centers for both the front and back wall faces. Vertical reinforcing consisted of: No. 7 bars on 30.5 cm (12 in.) centers for all front faces; No. 11 bars on 25.4 cm (10 in.) centers for the back faces of the panels along the building; and No. 11 bars on 35.6 cm (14 in.) centers for the back faces of all other panels.

Tie-back anchors were utilized for temporary lateral support during construction. These entailed two rows of tie-backs with two anchors each for a total of four tie-backs per panel, except for the corner panels where internal bracing was utilized. Each anchor consisted of 4 to 10 strands of 1862 MPa (270 ksi) yield strength steel. The anchor design loads ranged from 102 kN (23 kips) to 721 kN (162 kips).

The tie-backs were drilled at 30° to 45° angles from horizontal and all were anchored in bedrock to minimize potential soil creep. The bonded lengths ranged from 3.0 m (10 ft) to 6.1 m (20 ft) with total anchor lengths ranging from 9.1 m (30 ft) to 21.3 m (70 ft). Fourteen of the tie-backs were performance tested to 150% of their design load. All other tie-backs were proof-tested during installation to at least 133% of their design load and all were locked off at 110% of their design load. The tie-back capacity was based on a design bond stress of 689 kPa (100 psi) average stress about the 11.4-cm (4.5 in)-dia drill hole in rock.

A cap wall was constructed atop the slurry wall, which supports the perimeter roof and floor loads, to raise it to the roof level. The interior roof and floor loads are supported on interior columns with spread footing foundations bearing on bedrock. Upon completion of the garage structure, an average of about 1 m (3 ft) of soil was placed on the roof to re-establish the lawn and landscaping.

INSTRUMENTATION AND MEASUREMENTS

A total of six piezometers were installed at two levels near the center and front corners of the building (see Fig. 1) to monitor water levels in the soil mantle. The shallower piezometers measured the perched water levels to a depth of 3 m (10 ft) below the building foundations while the deeper piezometers measured water levels in the sand layer immediately above bedrock.

To monitor movements of the ground in response to deflections of the slurry wall during excavation and construction, inclinometers were installed at five locations along the front of the building (see Fig. 1). The inclinometers extended from the top of the slurry wall to 1.5 m (5 ft) into bedrock. They were installed through the soil mantle about 0.6 m (2 ft) behind the wall after the guide wall was constructed, but before the slurry wall excavation.

The initial piezometer and inclinometer data were obtained prior to the slurry wall and tie-back anchor construction. The piezometers and inclinometers were then monitored twice a week during the three-month period required to complete the slurry wall construction, site excavation, and ground anchor installation. The building itself was monitored for settlements with survey measurements.

MEASUREMENTS/OBSERVATIONS

Graphs of the data for Inclinometers 2 and 3 (see Fig. 1) are presented and discussed herein. The types of movements observed and the graph shapes are similar for all slope indicators.

The inclinometer graphs indicate ground movements at six stages of the slurry wall construction and site excavation:

Stage 1 - prior to the slurry wall excavation;

Stage 2 - site excavation to a depth of 3 m (10 ft) or 0.6 m (2 ft) below top anchor row;

Stage 3 - installation and stressing of the top row of ground anchors;

Stage 4 - excavation to a depth of 7.6 m (25 ft) or 0.6 m (2 ft) below bottom anchor row;

Stage 5 - installation and stressing of bottom row of ground anchors; and

Stage 6 - completion of site excavation to floor subgrade level at or below bedrock surface.

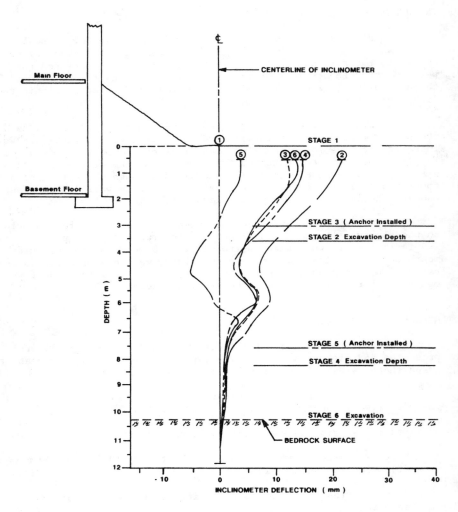

FIG. 3 -- Inclinometer 3 data graphs.

The graph for Inclinometer 3 (Fig. 3) near the center of the wall indicates the greatest wall movement: 21.3 mm (0.84 in.) at the top of the wall was observed at Stage 2 as the wall cantilevered above the excavation. The subsequent anchor installations and excavations caused the inclinometer to fluctuate. The permanent inclinometer deflection indicated by the graph of Stage 6 represents essentially the final deflection through the subsequent construction period. The graphs indicate distortion of the inclinometer casing between depths of 5.2 m (17 ft) and 8.2 m (27 ft) caused by its close proximity to the slurry wall excavating operations.

Ground movement graphs for Inclinometer 2 (Fig. 4), midway between the center of the wall and the corner, are similar to those for Inclinometer 3, although the maximum movement was 10.2 mm (0.4 in.) at Stage 2.

The ground movements at the corners of the wall as indicated by Inclinometers 1 and 5 are negligible - generally less than 2 mm (0.1 in.) at any of the stages - as expected for the comparatively rigid slurry wall corner configuration.

Although a maximum ground movement of 21.3 mm (0.84 in.) was observed at the top of the wall at Inclinometer 3, the movement at the foundation level, and below, is generally less than 10 mm (0.39 in.). At Inclinometer 2, movements at the foundation level are generally less than 5 mm (0.2 in.). It is expected that the ground movements diminished with distance from the slurry wall to the face of the building.

Survey measurements on the building indicated no settlement of the building.

Piezometer readings were obtained during the course of the project to evaluate the impact of construction on the water levels behind the slurry wall. It is noteworthy that 1990 was the wettest year on record in the Pittsburgh area with 132.7 cm (52.24 in.) of precipitation. In all piezometers, the water levels fluctuated over a range of 0.6 m (2 ft) in response to precipitation.

Water leakage occurred through the slurry wall at panel joints and through openings for the ground anchors. Although the rate of water leakage was not quantified with measurements, it was relatively minor and was easily sealed prior to completion of the parking structure. Excavations for column footings inside the garage area generally extended below the bottom of the slurry wall. Water flowed into these excavations through fractures and joints in the bedrock. Although relatively minor, the quantity of water seeping into the excavation was sufficient to warrant the design and installation of a sub-floor water collection and permanent sump system in the parking garage. In some places, the footing excavations extended 3 m (10 ft) below the surface of the water table in the coarse alluvial soils immediately overlying bedrock. Despite periodic water pumping from the excavation, the piezometer readings indicated that this lower water table behind the slurry wall remained relatively constant, primarily due to recharge from southward flows of subsurface waters through water-bearing zones which rise to the north. Field observations and measurements indicated that pumping water from the relatively coarse-grained alluvium overly-

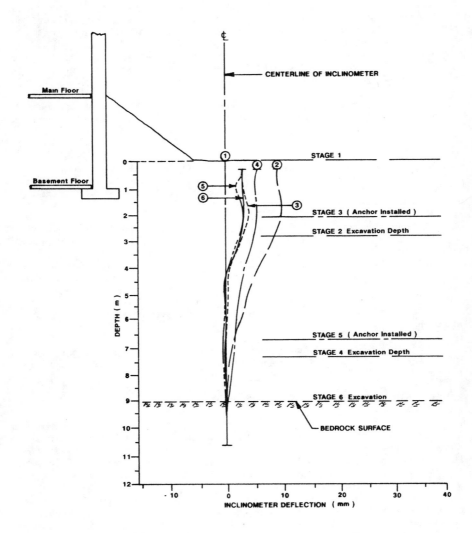

FIG. 4 -- Inclinometer 2 data graphs.

ing bedrock was not detrimental to the building. More importantly, the perched water tables were sufficiently maintained to avert consolidation of the building subgrade.

CONCLUSIONS

In summary, conclusions regarding slurry wall construction and performance at the site are as follows:

The slurry wall performed as expected in providing temporary support of the excavation as well as becoming the permanent wall of the garage structure.

The Memorial Building was protected as no building settlements or other distresses were observed.

Although groundwater seepage was encountered, the slurry wall adequately controlled groundwater to facilitate the work inside the wall and to maintain adequate water levels outside the site.

The soil, rock and groundwater conditions at this site were favorable for the use of conventional slurry wall techniques and equipment.

Slurry wall construction was economically feasible because the temporary wall became part of the permanent structure.

Conventional soldier beam and lagging excavation support would have required extensive measures to control groundwater.

Lateral restraint of the slurry wall was successfully provided by the ground anchors.

ACKNOWLEDGEMENTS

The project was managed and constructed by NADCO Construction Inc. The slurry wall and tie-backs anchors were designed and installed by Nicholson Construction Company. Tasso Katselas Associates provided the architectural design.

Sin F. Chan[1] and Teck F. Yap[2]

EFFECTS OF CONSTRUCTION OF A DIAPHRAGM WALL VERY CLOSE TO A MASONRY
BUILDING

REFERENCE: Chan, S. F. and Yap, T. F., "Effects of Construction of a
Diaphragm Wall Very Close to a Masonry Building", Slurry Walls: Design,
Construction and Quality Control, ASTM STP 1129, David B. Paul, Richard
R. Davidson and Nicholas J. Cavalli, Eds., American Society for Testing
and Materials, Philadelphia, 1992.

ABSTRACT: Observations were made to study the settlement behavior of
an old 4 story masonry building during the construction of a 25m deep
diaphragm wall. The adjacent building, which was only 1.2m to 1.5m
from the wall, was supported on shallow footings founded on weak
deposits of loose sand and soft clay. A preliminary assessment before
construction in the critical area indicated that settlement would be
excessive if conventional construction procedures were followed. This
led to the adoption of several settlement control measures in the
construction process. It was found that these measures were effective
in restricting the average settlement of the adjacent building to only
7.2mm and there was no visible sign of cracking.

KEYWORDS: diaphragm wall, construction, control measures, building,
settlement.

INTRODUCTION

The historic Raffles Hotel is a famous landmark in Singapore. It
is approximately 100 years old and consists of a number of buildings
up to 4 stories high. Recently an ambitious extension program was
implemented which called for the construction of new buildings. An
important feature of the program was that the existing buildings should
be preserved.

---

[1] Technical Director of Pilecon Engineering Bhd., 12 Lg. Taman Pantai
6, 59100 Kuala Lumpur, Malaysia;

[2] Marketing and Contracts Manager, Bachy Soletanche (M) Sdn Bhd.,
B18, Lg. Rahim Kajai 14, 60000 Kuala Lumpur, Malaysia.

The existing buildings were supported on shallow footings founded on weak soil deposits. The new buildings were provided with underground car parking facilities. This involved the construction of a deep diaphragm wall very close to an existing 4 story masonry building. There was grave concern for the safety of this old structure since it was 1.2m to 1.5m away from the diaphgram wall. This Paper describes how the construction of the diaphragm wall was managed and the resulting settlement behavior of the adjacent building.

The process of construction of a diaphragm wall can cause settlement of the adjacent ground and buildings. This is because excavation of the deep trench causes a release of the in-situ stresses in the surrounding ground thereby leading to horizontal and vertical ground movements. This release of ground stresses is partly alleviated by the use of the stabilizing bentonite slurry. Nevertheless, the magnitude of settlement in a given case is dependent on a number of factors. From an examination of these factors it is possible to adopt strategies which will minimize the resulting settlement. This Paper highlights the measures which were taken in order to control the settlement of the adjacent building to within permissible limits.

Apart from settlement due to the construction of the diaphragm wall itself, the excavation of the ground in front of the completed diaphragm wall, e.g. for basement construction, gives rise to further settlement. This other category of settlement is a function of the sequence of excavation, stiffness and levels of the struts or ground anchors, stiffness of the wall and ground properties. However, this other type of settlement is outside the scope of the present Paper.

SUBSURFACE CONDITIONS

The subsurface conditions were generally poor, with weak materials extending from the ground surface to a depth of about 20m. A subsurface profile of the site together with geotechnical properties of the soil are shown in Fig. 1.

The top stratum, which was 5m thick, was a loose sand. Beneath this were three weak strata of recent marine origin which were part of the Marine Member of the Kallang Formation of Singapore. The first of the three strata was a 3m thick, soft marine clay which was underlain by 6m of loose sand. Below this was another soft marine clay deposit 6m thick.

Firm materials were only encountered below 20m depth in the form of a very thick deposit of Bouldery Clay. The Bouldery Clay consisted of abundant sandstone boulders embedded in a hard silty clay matrix with SPT values exceeding 50 blows/0.3m. At this site the boulders, which had a range of sizes up to 1.5m across, were

very hard and usually required chiselling for penetration, except
near the top of the deposit where the boulders were weathered to
form residual soils. In the weathered zone of approximately 2m to
3m thick the SPT values were generally between 20 to 50 blows/0.3m.

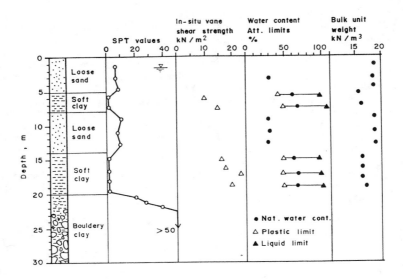

Fig. 1 -- Subsurface Profile.

The thicknesses of the upper weak strata varied across the
project site. However, the subsurface conditions shown in Fig. 1
were representative of the critical area which was the subject of
this Paper.

ADJACENT MAIN BUILDING

A layout of the diaphragm wall and the existing buildings is
shown in Fig. 2. It can be seen that the diaphragm wall was located
close to four existing buildings but the most critical was the Main
Building.

The Main Building was a 4 story masonry structure with a thick
external wall which was situated only 1.2m to 1.5m from the
diaphragm wall. A plan view of the diaphragm wall in relation to
the Main Building is shown in Fig. 3. A photograph of the external
wall of the Main Building during excavation of the slurry trench is

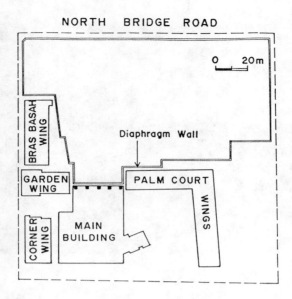

Fig. 2 -- Raffles Hotel, Singapore.

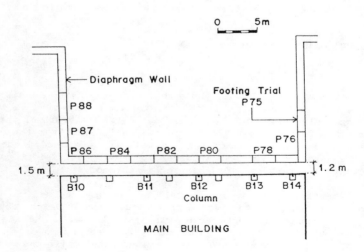

Fig. 3 -- Diaphragm wall adjacent to
Main Building.

Fig. 4 -- Main Building during diaphragm wall construction

shown in Fig. 4. The external wall comprised of a number of 600mm x 600mm brick columns, connected by beams at the floor levels. The wall panels between columns consisted of either 300mm thick brick walls or timber cladding. The external wall was connected to the rest of the building by timber beams and planks forming the floors.

CONSTRUCTION OF DIAPHRAGM WALL

Description of Wall

The diaphragm wall, which had a thickness of 800mm, consisted of a series of vertical panels with a minimum length of 2.8m in the horizontal direction, see Fig. 3 and Table 1. The depth of the wall varied from 20m at Panel P77 to 25m at Panel P86. From the design standpoint it was necessary for the wall to be embedded about 5m into the hard Bouldery Clay in order to provide sufficient passive resistance and vertical load bearing resistance.

The vertical joints between wall panels were formed using the patented CWS Bachy System with a centre bulb rubber water stop. In each joint the rubber water stop was installed with the aid of a robust steel stop end form. This steel form served to protect the water stop and the concrete of the previous panel while the next one was being excavated. The reinforcement cages were detailed to ensure easy flow during tremie concreting.

TABLE 1 -- Panel details

Panel No.	Panel length, m	Excavation date	Concreting date
P77	2.8	day 22	day 23
P78	2.8	day 24 to 26	day 26
P79	4.1	day 40 to 41	day 42
P80	2.8	day 20	day 21
P81	2.8	day 28	day 29
P82	2.8	day 30 to 34	day 35
P83	2.8	day 15 to 16	day 16
P84	2.8	day 17	day 18
P85	2.8	day 37 to 38	day 39
P86	2.8	day 22 to 24	day 24

Construction Procedure

The first stage was the construction of a pair of parallel reinforced concrete guide walls, for guiding the slurry trench excavation. As usual the diaphragm wall was constructed in a series of short panels. For a typical panel, excavation of the trench was carried out using a line grab mounted on a crawler crane, see Fig. 4. Bentonite slurry was used as the stabilizing medium at all stages of excavation. Except in the upper weathered zone, penetration into the Bouldery Clay usually required chiselling using a 5000kg tool.

Upon completion of excavation for a typical panel, the slurry was recycled or replaced so as to attain the desired properties for concreting. The reinforcement cage was then lowered into the trench. This was followed by tremie concreting in one continuous operation from bottom to top of the diaphragm wall panel. The above procedure was repeated for other panels.

Table 1 shows the length and sequence of construction of each panel in the critical area near to the Main Building.

Settlement Control Measures

In general, the settlement of the surrounding ground and adjacent buildings during the process of construction of a diaphragm wall is governed by several factors. By identifying and controlling these factors, it is feasible to minimize the settlement. The settlement control measures adopted were as follows:

Head of slurry: Since the head of the bentonite slurry had a predominant effect on settlement, the resulting settlement of the building was reduced by raising the slurry level up to 0.5m above existing ground level. This was implemented by raising the level of the guide walls correspondingly.

Length of panel: The horizontal deformation of the ground towards the excavated trench, and hence the resulting settlement, would increase rapidly with increasing length of panel. Therefore, in order to reduce settlement, the length of each panel was kept to a minimum. As shown in Table 1, all the panels except one were limited to a length of 2.8m which corresponded to the width of the excavation tool. The single long panel, 4.1m, was the final closure panel for the diaphragm wall adjacent to the Main Building. Under normal circumstances it is common to adopt a panel length of 6m.

Construction time: Since ground deformation arising from trench excavation was time dependent, the total construction time of each panel was kept to a minimum. This was the period from the beginning of trench excavation to final concreting of the panel. This control measure involved working extended hours.

Arrangement of panel layout: For a panel of given length, ground settlement near the centre of the panel would be greater than the settlement near the ends of the panels. Thus, it was advantageous to plan the length and layout of panels, see Fig. 3, such that each existing masonry column was located near one end of a panel. It should be noted that the loads of the adjacent Main Building were concentrated at the columns only.

Number of panels under construction: The number of panels being constructed simultaneously at any time should be minimized. In general, in the critical area only one panel was constructed at any time and no trench excavation work was carried out near a newly completed panel unless 12 hours had elapsed. As shown in Table 1, the only exception to the above guideline was the case of panels P77 and P86 which were located at opposite ends of the diaphragm wall.

Preliminary Observations and Trials

As shown in Fig, 1, apart from the Main Building, three other existing buildings were also located near the diaphragm wall. Earlier on in the project, the settlement of these other buildings was monitored during the construction of the diaphragm wall. The results showed that the buildings within 2.4m to 4.0m from the diaphragm wall had settled from 7.5mm to 15mm in ground conditions similar to those of the Main Building. Furthermore, it was found that diaphragm wall construction had an appreciable effect on settlement of a nearby building up to a limiting distance of 12m. No special precautions were taken in the wall construction except that each panel length was restricted to 2.8m in the vicinity of buildings. However, these three buildings, mainly of timber construction, were lighter than the masonry Main Building. Since the Main Building was also nearer to the diaphragm wall, i.e. 1.2m to 1.5m away, its settlement would be expected to be larger unless special settlement control measures were adopted.

In view of the historic importance of the existing buildings, it was considered prudent to conduct a full-scale trial using the adopted control measures before diaphragm wall construction could proceed in the critical area adjacent to the Main Building. The location of the trial is shown in Fig. 3. The trial was conducted by using concrete blocks of approximately the same weight as a typical column load and stacking them on the ground at a distance of 1.2m from the diaphragm wall, see Fig 5. Precise levelling measurement showed that the construction of the adjacent diaphragm wall Panel P75 resulted in an average settlement of the blocks of 3.2mm. This value was considered satisfactory, indicating that the expected settlement of the Main Building would be small.

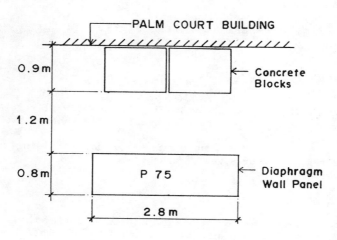

Fig. 5 -- Preliminary trial.

SETTLEMENT OF MAIN BUILDING

Instrumentation

The settlement of the Main Building and other buildings affected by diaphragm wall construction was measured by means of precise levelling using a Kern GK-2A automatic level and a precision Invar staff. For this purpose each of the columns to be monitored was mounted with a special BRE levelling station of the type designed by the Building Research Establishment of the United Kingdom (Cheney 1974). The details are shown in Fig. 6.

The   BRE levelling station comprised of a 25mm diameter stainless steel socket grouted in a horizontal hole drilled into the column. During monitoring, a rigid short levelling plug with a spherical end was securely fixed into the socket for receiving the Invar staff. When not in use, the socket was protected with a detachable cover which was flushed with the surface of the column.

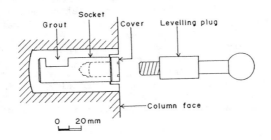

Fig. 6 -- BRE levelling station (after Cheney 1974).

The five columns, B10 to B14, of the Main Building chosen for settlement monitoring are shown in Fig. 3. Settlement readings were taken at various stages of the construction of diaphragm wall.

Apart from settlement monitoring, the Main Building was also inspected regularly for signs of cracking.

Settlement Behavior

The settlement behavior of the Main Building during the process of construction of the diaphragm wall was found to be complex. In order to facilitate understanding of the behavior, firstly the settlement of a typical column, B12, at various stages of construction will be presented. This will be followed by a general presentation of the overall behavior of all the columns which were monitored.

The effect of excavation of a typical panel is illustrated in Fig. 7 which shows the settlement of Column B12 due to the excavation of Panel P80. This panel was 1.33m away from the column which was located at one end of the former, see Fig. 7. It can be seen that the column settled progressively up to 0.6mm as the excavation depth increased from 0 to 22.5m. Chiselling of a further 2.5m through the hard unweathered Bouldery Clay caused the settlement to be doubled to 1.2mm. The effect of concreting of the panel was small compared with that of excavation.

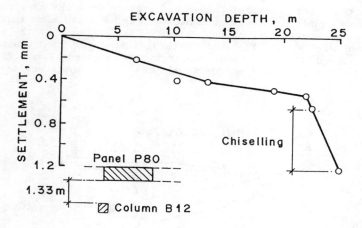

Fig. 7 -- Settlement of Column B12
due to excavation of
Panel P80.

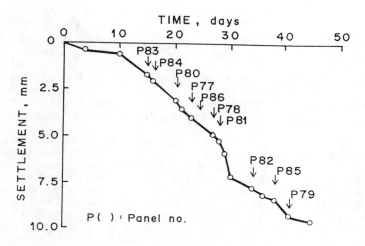

Fig. 8 -- Settlement of Column B12 due to
excavation of various panels.

The total settlement of Column B12 arising from the construction of various panels nearby is presented in Fig. 8 which also indicates the time of construction of each panel. The locations of the panels are shown in Fig. 3. The most striking feature of the results was that, although the settlement caused by the adjacent Panel P80 was small, the total settlement due to all the other panels was several

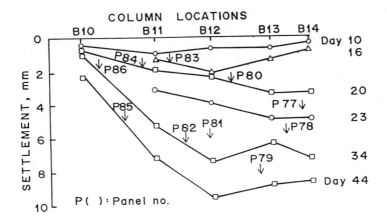

Fig. 9 -- Settlement of Main Building.

times larger. This was because each of the other panels had a significant influence on the settlement of Column B12. The total settlement at the end of construction of the whole diaphragm wall was 9.5mm. It should be noted that out of this amount the initial settlement of about 1.0mm before Day 15 was due to construction of diaphragm wall panels just outside the critical area, e.g. P88.

The settlement pattern of the Main Building is shown in Fig. 9. The location and approximate date of construction of each panel are also indicated. The results showed that all the columns settled progressively by different amounts as the various panels were constructed in turn. However, the total settlement at the end of diaphragm wall construction was small, with an average settlement of 7.2mm and a maximum settlement of 9.5mm occuring at Column B12. This was also the column with the heaviest load. The differential settlement and angular distortion between adjacent columns were only a fraction of the permissible limits usually accepted for masonry structures (Bjerrum 1963, Sowers 1962). Visual inspection of the building showed that there was no sign of cracking. The response of the Main Building as a result of the construction of the diaphragm wall was therefore considered satisfactory.

CONCLUDING REMARKS

Observations were made concerning the settlement of an old 4 story masonry building during the construction of a 25m deep diaphragm wall. The building, which was 1.2m to 1.5m away from the wall, was supported on shallow footings founded on weak deposits of loose sand and soft clay.

Preliminary observations in the early stage of the project indicated that the settlement of the adjacent building arising from wall construction would be unacceptable. This led to the adoption of certain special measures in the wall construction process. These included raising of slurry level, limitation of panel length, rearrangement of panel layout and reduction in construction time.

The observed settlement behavior of the adjacent building was complex. It was found that by adopting the above settlement control measures the average settlement of the adjacent building was limited to only 7.2mm. There was also no visible sign of cracking.

REFERENCES

Bjerrum, L., 1963. Discussion to European Conference on Soil Mechanics and Foundation Engineering, Wiesbaden, Vol. III, pp. 135.

Cheney, J.E., 1974, "Techniques and Equipment Using the Surveyor's Level for Accurate Measurement of Building Movements," Proceedings, Symposium on Field Instrumentation in Geotechnical Engineering, British Geotechnical Society, Butterworths, London, pp. 85-99.

Sowers, G. F., 1962, "Shallow Foundations," Foundation Engineering, G. A. Leonards, Ed., McGraw-Hill, New York, pp. 525.

Kris Ramachandra and Calvin H. Swan

DESIGN AND CONSTRUCTION OF CEMENT-BENTONITE CUTOFF WALL FOR
S.A. MURRAY JR. HYDROELECTRIC STATION

REFERENCE: Ramachandra, K., and Swan, C., "Design and Construction of Cement-Bentonite Cutoff Wall for S. A. Murray Jr. Hydroelectric Station," Slurry Walls: Design, Construction and Quality Control, ASTM STP 1129, David B. Paul, Richard R. Davidson, and Nicholas J. Cavalli, Eds., American Society for Testing and Materials, Philadelphia, 1992.

ABSTRACT: The Sidney A. Murray Jr. Hydroelectric Station is the largest, low-head run-of-river hydroelectric facility in the United States. Located near Vidalia, Louisiana, the plant generates 192 MW of electric power from eight 24 MW units. The powerplant structure and abutment dams are subjected to differential hydraulic heads of up to 8m (26 ft) under the project flood conditions and up to 12m (39 ft) under extreme, emergency conditions. Plastic concrete cutoff was installed utilizing cement-bentonite mixes placed by the slurry trench method to control seepage and uplift under the structures. This paper presents design concepts, mix design, field installation procedures and test data of the cores from the installed cutoff. Permeability, Modulus of Elasticity and Pinhole erosion criteria were used as the main control parameters for acceptance of the work.

KEYWORDS: Slurry Walls, Cement-Bentonite, Cutoff, Seepage, Erosion Resistance

INTRODUCTION

The power plant, a run-of-river hydroelectric plant, is located at the U.S. Army Corps of Engineers Old River Control Project in the state of Louisiana. The plant, consisting of a preassembled plant structure (PPS), a draft tube extension and a foundation mat, is located approximately 610m (2,000 ft) north of the U.S. Army Corps of Engineers (USACOE) Old River Control Overbank Structure and 1,402m (4,600 ft) from the right bank of the Mississippi River (Fig. 1). The other structures complementing the power plant consist of abutment dams forming a connection between the PPS and the mainline levees, and the training walls bordering the transition of the intake channel to the power plant and the tailrace.

K. Ramachandra, P.E., is a consulting civil engineer with Ebasco Services Inc., 2 World Trade Center, New York, NY 10048; C. Swan, P.G., is an associate consulting geologist with Ebasco Services Inc., 2211 West Meadow View, Greensboro, NC 27407.

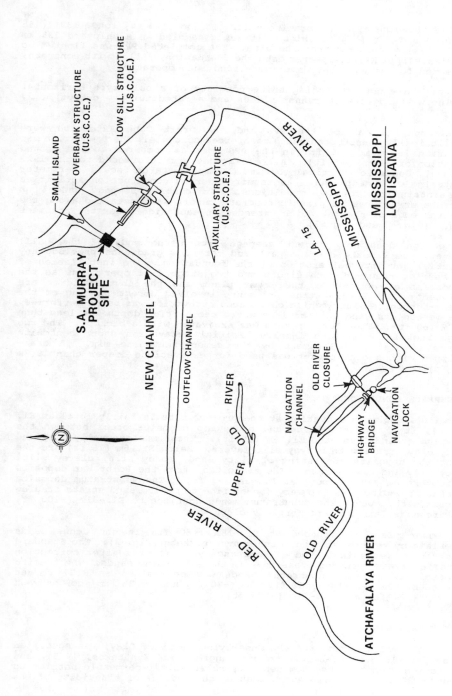

FIGURE 1 -- Location Plan

The PPS, housing eight generating units, is 44m (144 ft) long, 139m (456 ft) wide and 38m (124 ft) high. It was assembled in a shipyard 335 km (208 miles) downstream from the site. The completed PPS was floated up the Mississippi River, lowered onto the foundation, filled with concrete, connected to the abutment dams and placed into operation.

Each of the eight generating units consists of a bulb type horizontal turbine with adjustable runner blades and a rated turbine output of 24 MW.

The foundation mat of the PPS and the Draft Tube Extension were monolithically constructed using reinforced concrete. The foundation mat elevation is -18m (-60 ft) in the PPS area as compared to the ground elevation of +14m (+45 ft). All elevations are referenced to the 1929 National Geodetic Vertical Datum (NGVD). Large scale perimeter dewatering with deep wells was required during construction activities to maintain dry working conditions. To control seepage under the concrete structures, a plastic concrete cutoff was installed along the upstream edge of the mat which extended on each side under the abutment dams. (Fig. 2 and Fig. 3).

The design does not prevent seepage around the ends of the wall. However, the lengthy seepage path and very low gradients preclude any potential for internal erosion of the foundation. The installation of the barrier required both single and two stage fill operations as the foundation elevations of the power plant and the abutment dams are different. The single stage procedure involved direct pumping of the cement-bentonite slurry while continuous excavation was being performed. This method was used in locations where the barrier depth was less than 18.3m (60 ft). The slurry trench was excavated with a backhoe. The two stage backfill operation involved initial excavation under bentonite slurry and later replacement by the cement-bentonite mix. A crane equipped with a clam bucket was used for excavations deeper than 18.3m (60 ft).

SUBSURFACE CONDITIONS

The existing ground elevation at the project site is fairly level at El. 18m (45 ft). Natural levee and backswamp deposits occur between the existing ground level and El. 6m (15 ft). These are generally clay and silty clay strata with clayey silt layers. Below El. 6m (15 ft) are the Point Bar deposits consisting of silty sand, sandy silt, clayey silt, silty clay and clay strata. The transition from the Point Bar deposits to substratum sands occurs at El.-1m (-3 ft). The substratum deposits consist of medium dense to very dense, fine to medium sand strata grading coarser with depth. The substratum sands continue to El.-31m (-103 ft) and are underlain by hard Tertiary clays.

The power plant is founded at El.-18m (-60 ft) in the dense sands underlain by very dense sands with gravel pockets (Fig. 3). The Standard Penetration Tests indicated a resistance value of 48, after correction for effective overburden pressures, in the substratum sands. The in-situ permeability of the substratum sands was determined as 0.07 cm/sec between El.-1m (-3 ft) and El.-21m (-70 ft) and 0.28 cm/sec between El.-21m (-70 ft) and El.-31m (-103 ft).

DESIGN CRITERIA

The cutoff wall, keyed into the underlying Tertiary Clay, was specified to be plastic, cement-bentonite with aggregates (Xanthakos, 1979), and to provide a continuous, homogeneous, relatively impermeable barrier to groundwater seepage while approximating the modulus of elasticity of the

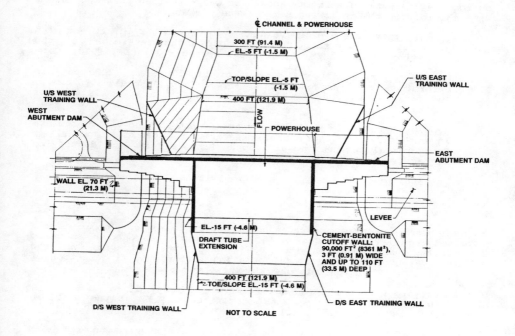

FIGURE 2 -- Site plan showing cutoff wall

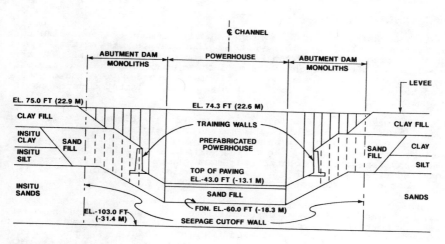

FIGURE 3 -- Foundation profile looking downstream

surrounding in-situ substratum sands. It was specified that the cutoff wall should meet the following performance criteria:

Permeability: The average value not to exceed 1 X 10^{-6} cm/sec with no value greater than 5 X 10^{-6} cm/sec as determined by the procedures given in EM 1110-2-1906, Appendix 7 (ACOE, 1970).

Modulus of Elasticity: A minimum of 13,790 kN/m^2 (2000 psi) as determined by the procedure in EM 1110-2-1906, Appendix 10 (ibid.), and measured as a secant modulus at 5% strain after 28 days of curing.

Erosion Resistance: Maximum consistent with the above requirements as determined by the method presented in the ASCE Journal of Geotechnical Engineering Division, "Pinhole Test for Identifying Dispersive Soils" (Sherard et al, 1976).

Continuity: Continuous installation without voids or breaks.

DESIGN MIX

Murray Powerhouse Constructors, subcontractors to Ebasco Services Inc., retained the services of Geocon Inc. as a specialist subcontractor to install the cutoff at the site. STS Consultants Ltd. performed the laboratory studies on behalf of Geocon Inc. before the finalization of the field mix. The materials used in these studies were:

Bentonite: From the Federal Bentonite Company of Belle Fourche, South Dakota complying with Specification 13A of the American Petroleum Institute (1990).

Cement: Type I Portland Cement meeting the requirements of ASTM Standard Specification C 150 (ASTM, 1989). A cement retarder marked HR-7 furnished by Halliburton Services of Houston, Texas was also used.

Water: Obtained from dewatering wells at the site.

Aggregate: Fine to medium sand.

The mixes were formulated by adding a specific amount of bentonite to a predetermined volume of site water. The mixture was agitated in a mechanical mixer at 10,000 rpm for a 20-minute period. The mix was then allowed to hydrate overnight. The mixing was continued the next day when the proper amount of cement, sand and cement retarder were added to the bentonite-water mixture. The total mix was then agitated for a period of 20 minutes.

The slurry was then poured into a 50.8 mm (2 in.) diameter by 101.6 mm (4 in.) high plastic mold. The molds, containing the slurry, were positioned on porous stones with filter paper to allow for drainage of the slurry specimens during the curing period. The cylinders were stored in an environmentally controlled room where the temperature was maintained at 23°C (73.4°F ± 3°) and the humidity maintained at 97.5% ± 2.5%. Most of the specimens were allowed to cure for 14 days.

The cured specimens were placed and sealed in a triaxial compression cell. Test specimens were saturated using backpressure by simultaneously increasing both the confining and backpressure in small increments. Test specimen saturation was considered complete when a Skempton's pore pressure parameter B of 0.95 or greater was achieved. Following the full saturation, a hydraulic conductivity test was performed. Permeant flow was initiated through the bottom of the test specimen and exited the top of the test specimen, collecting in a capillary burette. Permeant volume versus time measurements were then recorded and the hydraulic conductivity was determined.

The finalized mixes meeting the specification requirements were:

TABLE 1 -- Finalized mixes

Mix	Cement kg/m^3 (lbs/cyd)	Bentonite kg/m^3 (lbs/cyd)	Sand kg/m^3 (lbs/cyd)	Water kg/m^3 (lbs/cyd)	Total kg/m^3 (lbs/cyd)
13A	192.8 (325) (15.9%)	73.2 (123.3) (6%)	60.9 (102.7) (5%)	890 (1500.1) (73.1%)	1216.9 (2051.1) (100%)
14A	207.6 (350.0) (16.96%)	73.5 (123.9) (6%)	61.2 (103.2) (5%)	882 (1486.7) (72.04%)	1224.3 (2063.8) (100%)

The field mix was essentially an average of the mixes 13A and 14A. Field testing was limited to the quality assurance and control of the field mix specified above.

EXCAVATING EQUIPMENT AND BATCHING PROCEDURES

Excavating Equipment

The slurry trench was excavated with a Link Belt LS7400A extended arm backhoe, equipped with a 0.91m (36 in.) wide rockbucket. The backhoe when fully extended was capable of excavating to depths of 18.3m (60 ft).

Excavation below 18.3m (60 ft) was performed with a Manitowok 4000 crane equipped with a 13,600 kg (15 ton) slurry trench clam bucket capable of excavating 0.91m (36 in.) wide slots 3.05m (10 ft) long.

Bentonite Slurry Batching

Bentonite slurry was produced by metering water from the dewatering wells into a five cubic yard colloidal mixer. Bentonite was added to the mixer with a volumetric screw auger controlled by an electric rheostat, which allowed a precise amount of bentonite to be added. Mixing continued sufficiently to completely disperse the bentonite and produce a stable, homogeneous, colloidal suspension of bentonite slurry. The slurry was then pumped to either the trench, cement-bentonite (C/B) mixer or 76.46 m^3 (100 cubic yards) hydration tank as required. Hydration tanks were equipped with circulating pumps to reactivate bentonite slurry prior to transfer of the slurry to the cement-bentonite mixer for the single stage construction.

Cement/Bentonite Slurry Batching

To produce C/B slurry, the previously prepared bentonite slurry was metered through a venturi mixer where cement was added from an overhead silo. The cement was batched through a rotary valve controlled by an electric rheostat. The resulting cement-bentonite slurry then flowed into an adjacent five cubic yard colloidal mixer where further mixing provided a homogeneous product with cement particles fully dispersed.

Once fully mixed, the cement-bentonite slurry was transferred directly to the trench.

Sand Aggregate Additions

Sand aggregate was provided in the trench through spillage from the backhoe during excavations. While careful equipment operation by experienced operators could maintain the sand content within the specified 5 to 15% range, sand contents as high as 30% were measured. When excesses occurred while excavating under the bentonite slurry, centrifugal desanding equipment was used to reduce the sand content to the specified 15%. When excesses occurred while excavating under the cement-bentonite slurry, removal of the sand with desanding equipment was no longer feasible due to presence of cement. The excessive sand laden slurry was bailed out with a backhoe bucket, loaded into trucks and hauled to waste. The bailed slurry was immediately replaced with cement-bentonite slurry without sand. Through dilution, the sand content was eventually reduced to meet the specified limits.

Admixture Additions

Addition of HR-7 retarder, a proprietary admixture produced by Halliburton Co., at a controlled rate of 1.5 kg/m^3 (2.5 lbs per cubic yard) was accomplished to improve and extend the workability of the relatively viscous C/B mixes. The retarder was added systematically at the C/B mixer by a laborer using a calibrated container and time clock.

INSTALLATION PROCEDURES

Two Stage C/B Transfer

During the two stage transfers, the previously batched and appropriately desanded bentonite slurry was pumped in batches from the trench to the mixing plant for addition of cement and HR-7 retarder. This pumping resulted in a drop of only a few inches in the slurry level within the trench and did not affect the trench stability. After thorough blending and mixing to fully disperse the cement particles, the resulting homogeneous C/B mixture was pumped back to the trench and placed from the bottom up by tremie.

The tremie system consisted of a valved header at grade level which distributed the C/B mix to seven 101.6 mm (4 in.) diameter tremie pipe strings located on 3.05m (10 ft) centers along the line of the trench. Each tremie string consisted of a series of 1.5m to 6.1m (5 to 20 ft) long pipe sections which were quick-coupled together to extend to the trench bottom. Accurate measurements of the pipe lengths in each string were made and recorded to assist in an appropriate, later, removal of the pipe sections as the C/B slurry rose.

During the C/B transfer, frequent depth measurements with a weighted line were made at each tremie station to chart the level of the rising C/B mix. Header valves were adjusted as appropriate by the header operator to maintain the top of C/B essentially level and keep tremie pipes as vertical as possible. As the C/B level in the trench rose, tremie pipe lengths were individually removed as appropriate to maintain a minimum of 1.5m (5 ft) of embedment in the rising slurry. This prevented contact of the raw C/B mix with the bentonite slurry and avoided incorporation of bentonite floc within the completed wall.

C/B in the top 0.61m to 0.91m (2 to 3 ft) of panels placed by the tremie, which had become contaminated by the creation of bentonite floc at the C/B-bentonite interface, were not used in the final construction. The contaminated material was either removed by excavation and replaced with fresh C/B or the wall was overbuilt sufficiently so that the removal was accomplished during excavation to the final grade.

Single Stage C/B Transfer

Single stage C/B transfers involved direct pumping of the C/B slurry to the trench while continuous excavation was being performed. Unlike the two stage method where bentonite slurry was the supporting medium during excavations, the C/B slurry provided this support while also becoming the final wall. The single stage method eliminated joints and was the much preferred method when site conditions permitted its use.

After the initial set, the top of the completed single stage walls usually showed subsidence depressions and related cracking which sometimes extended below the final grade. At these locations the disturbed C/B was removed by excavation and replaced with fresh material. In practice, most panels were overbuilt sufficiently so that the final grade excavation removed the deficient material and bottomed in sound, undisturbed C/B.

Joints Between Wall Panels

Slurry trench cutoff walls were constructed by the alternate panel method for the two stage work and both the alternate panel and continuous excavation methods for the single stage work. Each panel was tied together to the next panel by over-excavating a minimum of 0.91m (3 ft) into the adjacent or underlying previously constructed panels. Assurance of a continuous water tight barrier through joint locations was provided by close inspection supported by appropriate depth measurements and ground surveys to verify overlap and alignment of the panels.

Embedment in Tertiary Clay

The C/B cutoff walls were constructed through the substratum sands to key a minimum of 0.31m (1 ft) into the underlying Tertiary Clay as specified. To provide verification of the minimum embedment, cuttings from the trench bottom were obtained by the excavating equipment (backhoe or clam) on 3.05m (10 ft) centers along the line of the trench. The cuttings were visually inspected and sampled to document that the full length of the cutoff wall met the top of Tertiary Clay. Additional excavations were performed where cuttings were not definitive. Upon verification of the top of Tertiary Clay by the contractor and the owner's engineering representative, depth measurements of the trench bottom were made and recorded. Additional excavations were then performed and a second round of depth measurements taken to verify that embedment in the Tertiary strata was a minimum of 0.31m (1 ft). During the course of the work, actual embedment was in the range of 0.61m to 3.05m (2 to 10 ft). Upon attainment of the final embedment depth, a second round of cuttings inspection and sampling was performed. All samples were retained and stored on the site.

Accumulated Sediment Removal

Sand, gravel or other sediments which accumulated on the trench bottom prior to the C/B transfer were removed by clam or airlift as required to ensure a positive cutoff at the trench bottom. At most locations the subcontractor purposely extended excavations in excess of the required 0.31m (1 ft) into the Tertiary Clay so that small sediment accumulations, if they did occur, would not compromise the integrity of the wall. The additional embedment also tended to accommodate fluctuating changes in the top of Tertiary Clay.

QUALITY CONTROL PROGRAM

The field quality control program for the cutoff wall construction is
illustrated in the following table.

**TABLE 2 -- Field quality control program
for cutoff wall**

SUBJECT	STANDARD	TYPE OF TEST	FREQUENCY	SPECIFIED VALUES
Water	–	pH Total hardness	Per water source or as changes occur	As required to properly hydrate bentonite with approved additives
Additives	–	Certificate of compliance	One per truckload	As approved by Engineer
Bentonite	API STD 13A	Certificate of compliance	One per truckload	Premium grade Sodium cation Montmorill-onite
Cement	ASTM C 150	Certificate of compliance	One per truckload	Portland, Type I
Bentonite Slurry	API RP 13B	Viscosity Gelation Density pH Filtrate loss	One set per shift	MF=34 to 90 sec. Gel=MF ±5 sec. Specific Gravity 1.025 to 1.360 pH = 8 Loss 5 to 30 mL
C-B Slurry	API RP 13B	Viscosity Unit Weight C/W Ratio Overbreak (one-stage only) Sand content	5 sets per shift	MF 40 sec Unit Wt 75 to 100 pcf C/W = 0.17 to 0.24 O.B. = 1.3 to 2.5 S.C. = 5 to 15%
	ASTM C 143	Workability (Slump)		6 in. min

MF = Marsh Funnel Viscosity

HR 7 Retarder was used in all C/B mixes at a measured rate of 1.5 kg/m^3
(2.5 lb per cubic yard).

VERIFICATION OF COMPLETED WORK

Verification of the completed work to assure that the cutoff wall met the specified requirements was provided in the following ways:

- Core drilling and sampling
- Inspection of the exposed wall surface
- Laboratory testing of cores and cylinders

Core Drilling and Sampling

To verify the continuity and integrity of the cutoff wall, a series of borings were drilled in the completed panels. They consisted of continuous 0.61m (2 ft) long pushed shelby tube samplings at intervals along the line of the wall. The samplings were spaced to provide representative information on wall homogeneity and embedment depths into Tertiary Clay. The recovered 76.2 mm (3 in.) diameter samples were tested with a pocket penetrometer and closely inspected for homogeneity, tightness, open cracks and/or joints or other defects that would indicate other than essential water tightness and strength.

Any panels found deficient were re-excavated, replaced and redrilled to verify compliance.

The resulting 700+ shelby tube samples were sealed in cellophane and tin foil, placed in styrofoam containers and stored on site for later inspection and/or testing. The final round of core drilling included over 228.6 linear meters (750 linear feet) of C/B core, providing a good representation of the vertical dimension of the completed wall. The final core samples verified the essential tightness and homogeneity of the completed wall and did not identify any feature that would detract from its use as a seepage cutoff wall.

Inspection of Completed Wall Surfaces

Upon completion of final excavations to foundation grade for the Powerhouse, Draft Tube Extension and Abutment Dams, the freshly trimmed C/B wall top was inspected for deficiencies. Further close inspection accompanied the cutting and cleanup of the 0.61m (2 ft) deep slot in which the stainless steel water stop was installed to provide tie-in between the wall and the overlying structures. In all cases, as with the final round of borings, the observed wall surfaces were essentially tight, homogeneous and free of significant defects that would detract from the intended use as a cutoff wall. Over 487.7 linear meters (1600 linear feet) of completed wall were inspected.

Laboratory Testing of Cores and Cylinders

Laboratory testing was performed on both test cylinders made at the time of placement and core samples obtained from the verification borings. Tests performed included permeability, modulus of elasticity and erosion resistance. Results of the testing are discussed in the summary below.

SUMMARY OF TESTING

Permeability

Effective permeability was measured at the expected actual overburden pressure, or 192 kN/m^2 (2 TSF). The average permeability of 18 samples analyzed is 1.45×10^{-6} cm/sec as compared to the specification requirement of an average 1×10^{-6} cm/sec. The highest permeability measured was 5.6×10^{-6} cm/sec as against the specification requirement of "no value greater than 5×10^{-6} cm/sec". The slight excess measured is marginal and can be ignored considering the visual inspection of over 228.6 linear meters (750 linear feet) of cores which has demonstrated the integrity of the slurry wall.

Modulus of Elasticity

The average modulus of elasticity of 18 samples analyzed is 36,722 kN/m^2 (5,326 psi) as compared to the specification requirement of a minimum of 13,790 kN/m^2 (2000 psi) which approximated the surrounding soil properties. All the tested samples showed a secant modulus at 0.5% strain above the minimum requirement.

Erosion Resistance

The wall was determined to be erosion resistant based on pinhole erosion tests performed on the undisturbed samples taken from the installed wall. The laboratory test results proved that the barrier materials are nondispersive under the design hydraulic gradients.

CONCLUSION

As the intent of the specifications was satisfied, the cutoff wall was considered acceptable. Results of periodic monitoring of the piezometers indicate that the underseepage barriers are performing as designed.

REFERENCES

American Petroleum Institute, 1990, Specification for Drilling Fluid Materials, API Specification 13A.

American Society for Testing and Materials, 1989, Standard Specification for Portland Cement, C150-89.

Corps of Engineers, U.S. Army, 1970, Engineering Manual for Laboratory Soils Testing, EM 1110-2-1906.

Sherard, J.L., Dunnigan, L.P., Decker, R.S. and Steele, E.F., 1976, "Pinhole Test for Identifying Dispersive Soils," Proc. ASCE Journal of Geotechnical Engineering Div., Vol. 102, No. GT1, January, pp. 69-85.

Xanthakos, Petros P., 1979, Slurry Walls, McGraw-Hill.

Douglas G. Gifford[1] and James R. Wheeler[2]

CONCRETE SLURRY WALL FOR TEMPORARY AND PERMANENT FOUNDATION WALL AT
GALLERY AT HARBORPLACE - BALTIMORE, MARYLAND

REFERENCE: Gifford, D. G., and Wheeler, J. R., "Concrete Slurry
Wall for Temporary and Permanent Foundation Wall at Gallery at Harborplace - Baltimore, Maryland," Slurry Walls: Design, Construction,
and Quality Control, ASTM STP 1129, David B. Paul, Richard R. Davidson,
and Nicholas J. Cavalli, Eds., American Society for Testing and Materials, Philadelphia, 1992.

ABSTRACT: The selection and installation of a concrete diaphragm
wall by the slurry trench process simplified construction and provided
high quality underground space for a 5-level garage in Baltimore, Maryland. The tieback supported wall retained the adjacent streets and
utilities with surface settlement ranging from 0.5 to 0.75 in. (12.7 to
19.1 mm). Groundwater levels were maintained and seepage into the
excavation was reduced to about 5 gallons per minute (0.32 L/s).
Geotechnical instrumentation data confirmed satisfactory performance of
the wall and tieback system; instrumentation was also key during assessment and resolution of construction problems which led to additional
lateral displacement of the wall.

KEYWORDS: slurry wall, tiebacks, instrumentation, seepage, settlement, lateral earth pressures

BACKGROUND

Selection of a lateral support system for a deep excavation in an
urban area requires consideration of design and construction constraints as well as an evaluation of impacts and risks associated with
undertaking the work. During the design phase, the owner and design

[1]Vice President, Haley & Aldrich, Inc., 58 Charles Street,
Cambridge, MA 02141.

[2]Senior Engineer, Haley & Aldrich, Inc., 58 Charles Street,
Cambridge, MA 02141.

team, including the general contractor evaluated alternate foundation
and lateral support schemes for a 4-level, 1 155 car underground garage
to be located along Pratt Street in Baltimore, Maryland. The block
square site, 320 x 370 ft (97.5 x 112.8 m), shown on the site plan,
Fig. 1, was only one block from Baltimore's Inner Harbor. The project
would ultimately be developed into quality retail, hotel and office
space including a 28-story office tower above a portion of the site.
In all aspects, quality of the finished project was a major consideration and goal. A concrete diaphragm wall constructed by the slurry
trench method (slurry wall) was selected and installed [1].

Design and construction concerns for the excavation and foundation systems centered on the ability to complete a 50 ft (15.2 m) deep
excavation, 40 ft (12.2 m) below the groundwater (harbor) level. The
system had to provide maximum floor space by building to property lines
while minimizing impacts on adjacent streets, preserving utilities,
maintaining traffic and preserving groundwater levels.

Subsurface soils encountered at the site illustrated in Fig. 2
included approximately 12 to 23 ft (3.7 to 7.0 m) of miscellaneous FILL
overlying naturally deposited soils. Within the limits of the site,
the fill layer also included a strata of naturally deposited organic
sediments (oysterbeds and organic silt) up to 11 ft (3.4 m) in thickness. This strata was deposited within the limits of the colonial
harbor slips. Beneath the fill, a layer of very dense gravelly SAND
was encountered which in turn was underlain by residual soils comprised
of very stiff low plasticity SILT and clayey SILT. The residual soil

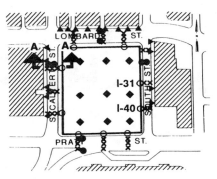

Legend:

●   Observation well

◆   Piezometer

○   Instrumented panel

×   Surface settlement points

▲   Building settlement points

FIG. 1--Site location and instrumentation plan.

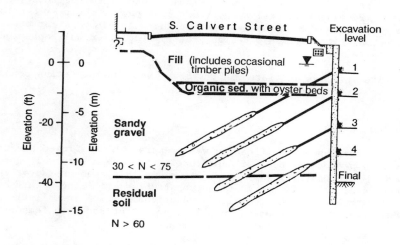

FIG. 2--Typical cross section.

was formed by the in-place weathering of the underlying schist bedrock. Competent bedrock was encountered well below the proposed basement level [2].

Protection of the bearing capacity of the residual soils at the foundation level was required to allow construction of the mat and spread footing foundations. Testing of the residual/weathered rock before and during construction confirmed that unconfined or exposed material would rapidly absorb water and would, within minutes, transform a stiff competent bearing soil into a soft, saturated "mud". Approximately one quarter of the site included the buried remnants of a former colonial harbor slip. The timber structures comprising the slip and the loose soils and voids around the structure provided a direct hydraulic link to the Inner Harbor less than 300 ft (91.4 m) away. Protection of the bearing soil was required during construction either by a seepage barrier or a very effective, reliable dewatering system. Also, long term groundwater control required a decision to either waterproof the entire basement and design for hydrostatic uplift or reduce groundwater seepage and underdrain the structure.

Alternate foundation and lateral support systems were evaluated. A slurry wall was finally selected as the temporary and permanent wall, acting as a seepage cutoff and allowing the use of permanent underdrains and greater use of spread footings, thereby reducing the need for a mat foundation to the area occupied only by the tower. Higher bearing capacities, up to 14 kips per square foot (669 kPa) were used in design since subgrade disturbance would not be a construction concern [2]. The wall also supported perimeter vertical loads from the

ground surface deck, but otherwise was separated from the interior
framing. Permanent lateral support was provided by the post tensioned
garage floor slabs which butted against the wall but were not doweled
into the wall itself. This design greatly simplified wall construction
and installation.

Site work was initiated in November 1984 and foundation construction completed in January 1986.

SELECTION OF EQUIPMENT

A performance specification was prepared which allowed the Contractor to propose methods of construction for the slurry wall and
tiebacks. The contract was awarded to a specialty subcontractor who
selected a slurry wall system to be constructed utilizing a self-boring
excavating tool, the "Hydrofraise". A unique tieback installation
procedure was developed using the "lost point" method with temporary
casing driven by a vibratory impact hammer.

The counter rotating cutting wheels of the Hydrofraise, shown in
Fig. 3, were ideally suited to the excavation of sands, gravels and the
residual soil (weathered schist). With the exception of occasional

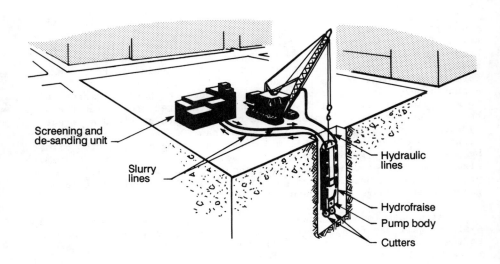

FIG. 3--Concrete diaphragm (slurry) wall
construction utilizing "hydrofraise" excavating tool.

jamming from cobbles, the equipment routinely excavated an 18.25 x 2.0 x 56 ft (5.6 x 0.6 x 17.1 m) panel in 6 to 8 hours.

The innovative tieback installation equipment worked effectively in the upper dense sand but had difficulty penetrating the residual soils. Ultimately, a redesign was required in the lower two levels of support, switching from tiebacks to rakers at portions of the lowermost support level along the Pratt Street perimeter wall. .The switch was prompted by the construction schedule. Tieback installation, including extended time required to drive casing, complete multiple stage regrouting, together with reduced load capacity were factors forcing the change to rakers.

CONSTRUCTABILITY

The Hydrofraise excavating equipment was uniquely suited to the project and met all expectations for excavation of the slurry trench while maintaining a neat site work area. A pre-trenching operation was completed to remove remnants of previously demolished buildings. Trenching was completed in short stretches, about 25 to 30 ft (7.6 to 9.1 m), using a backhoe. After removal of obstructions, the trench was immediately backfilled with compacted clay. Concrete guidewalls were formed providing horizontal and vertical control for the excavation. The 48 ft (14.6 m) high, 8 ft (2.4 m) wide and 2 ft (0.6 m) thick unit weighed approximately 16 tons (14.5 t). Hanging by cables from a crane, cutting wheels churned into the ground between the guide walls. The verticality of the cutter was continuously and remotely monitored in two axes. Like a giant "plumb bob" the unit maintained verticality tolerances well within the 2 percent tolerance allowed for installation.

Broken cobbles, gravel, sand, silt and clay were suspended in a bentonite slurry which was pumped by the Hydrofraise cutter to a centrally located, electrically powered desanding unit which included a cyclone and vibratory screen. The bentonite slurry was recovered while the screened sand and gravel stockpiles, essentially free of bentonite, were removed. Field tests were completed to check the slurry for specific gravity, sand content, filtration properties, and pH. Values were consistent with those suggested by Xanthakos [3]. With the exception of several broken slurry pipes which sprayed adjacent streets, the process was exceptionally quiet, neat and orderly. Joints between panels were watertight, due to the interlocking pattern created as the cutter teeth carved vertical grooves in the edges of adjacent recently constructed panels.

The tieback equipment was assembled specifically for the project and utilized an ICE vibratory hammer to drive a continuous 4-in. (101 mm) O.D. pipe casing fitted with a disposable or "lost" drive point. Tieback tendons consisting of 4 to 6 multistrand cables (58 kip (258 kN) guaranteed ultimate strength) were inserted into the casing and temporarily anchored by drive points at the top and bottom of the casing. Prestressing of the cables then allowed the casing to be

driven, carrying the cables and drive point into the ground displacing
the sand. For the upper ties, shown in Fig. 2, a "one-shot" grouting
process was used as the temporary casing was removed. Tieback
capacities ranging from 130 to 250 kips (578 to 1 112 kN) were developed. Preliminary field tests on several vertical anchors were successful, but gave no indication of the subsequent adhesion limitations of
the bond length in the residual soil.

For the lower two levels of tiebacks, the socket length of the
inclined tiebacks encountered residual soils and weathered schist, and
driving of the casing became more time consuming. A wash water jet
installed at the tip did little to increase production rate. Increasing vibratory impact resulted in more equipment failures while tieback
tests failed at 50 to 75 percent of design capacity. Regrouting of
tiebacks failed to reestablish load capacity and the tieback design was
reevaluated. Fortunately groundwater levels observed from the start of
construction, were somewhat lower than design values, reducing actual
design loading on the tiebacks. This allowed tieback installation to
proceed with reduced capacity and some of the lowest level tiebacks
were replaced with inclined rakers.

GEOTECHNICAL INSTRUMENTATION PERFORMANCE DATA

A system of geotechnical instrumentation comprised of surface and
building settlement reference points (60 total), eight observation
wells, nine piezometers, and nine instrumented slurry wall panels including slope inclinometers and tieback load cells was installed to
document the performance of the foundation system throughout construction. The instrumentation layout and typical instrumented section are

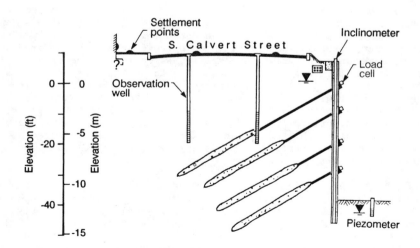

FIG. 4--Typical instrumented cross section.

shown in Figs. 1 and 4, respectively. The following sections provide a
brief description of data available which documented design and construction performance.

Typical Wall Deflection

Each excavation cycle involved dewatering inside the slurry wall
barrier, excavating, installing and tensioning of the tiebacks. The
wall deflections were monitored, and ranged from 0.25 to 0.75 in. (6.4
to 19.1 mm). Typical wall deflection data are illustrated in Fig. 5.
No additional deflection of the wall was measured during removal of the
tiebacks and rakers as load was transferred to the garage floor slabs.

Overpressurizing of Tiebacks

In an attempt to develop design load capacity, selected third
level tiebacks along South Street were regrouted several times. Grout
volumes pumped into the tube-a-machettes exceeded the theoretical grout
"take" volume by a factor of 50 at grout pressures up to 500 psi
(3.44 MPa). Careful, simultaneous monitoring of the wall and tieback
load cells confirmed that excess grout flowed behind the wall, deflect-
ing the entire wall into the excavation. Monitoring of deflections
before, during and after grouting confirmed that the wall had moved
temporarily almost another 0.5 in. (12.7 mm) into the excavation for a
total displacement of about one inch (25.4 mm) following the grouting.
Plots of inclinometer displacement data included in Fig. 6 illustrate
the wall behavior during the over grouting events. The inclinometer
data were also confirmed by independent readings obtained by optical
offset surveys.

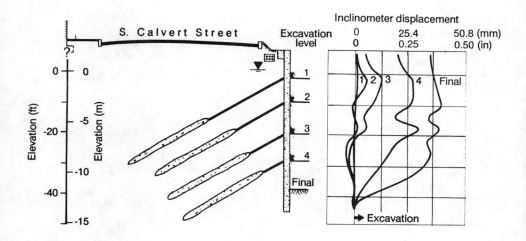

FIG. 5--Typical slurry wall displacement after excavating
and tensioning tiebacks at each excavation level, as noted.

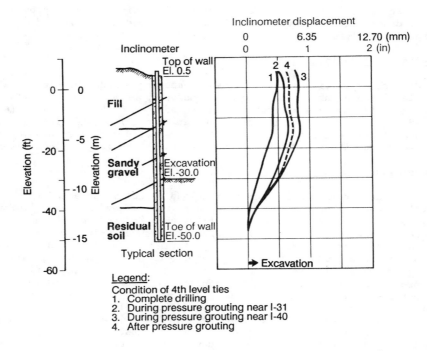

FIG. 6--South St. slurry wall displacement measured
during overgrouting events.

Prestressing loads in the tiebacks forced the fluid grout back
into the sand and ultimately returned the wall to within 0.5 in.
(12.7 mm) of its original location. Precise instrumentation and rapid
interpretation of data confirmed the suspected problem and resulted in
a major reduction in allowable grout volumes during subsequent staged
regrouting of tiebacks.

Dewatering

Because the slurry wall was excavated into the very low permeability residual soil, dewatering of the excavation was reduced essentially
to removal of rainfall and leakage through the tieback ports in the
slurry wall. Temporary pumping was accomplished from one or more of
four temporary wells located on the site. The wells were drilled
through the sand and following the initial few weeks of pumping, required daily monitoring to prevent the submersible pumps from running
dry.

Excessive leakage through the tieback sleeves penetrating through
the concrete diaphragm wall immediately following tieback installation
was controlled by forcing a pipe cylinder, the "bazooka", over the ends
of the cables and injecting sodium silicate/cement grout. The bazooka

was temporarily left in place until the seepage was under control. In several cases water flows exceeding 30 to 50 gallons per minute (gpm) (1.9 to 3.2 L/s) were encountered and controlled. After sealing the tieback holes, the measured total pumping rate at the end of general site excavation and foundation construction was about 5 gpm (0.32 L/s).

Surface Settlement

Groundwater levels adjacent to the project were maintained within several feet of the normal levels throughout the project. This elimi- nated the risk of potential damage to adjacent streets and utilities due to settlement caused by lowering of the groundwater levels. Major utilities surrounding the site included an 11 ft (3.35 m) diameter outfall under Pratt St., a 30 in. (762 mm) diameter high pressure water main on South St. and a relocated phone and electrical duct bank on South Calvert St. During construction, settlement points established in the streets and on adjacent structures were routinely surveyed.

Typical settlements monitored throughout construction, shown in Fig. 7, ranged from 0.25 to 0.50 in. (6.4 to 12.7 mm) with a maximum observed settlement of 0.88 in. (22.4 mm) observed along a short por- tion of South St. This minor settlement problem beneath the South St. pavement (caused by the pretrenching operation) was quickly repaired

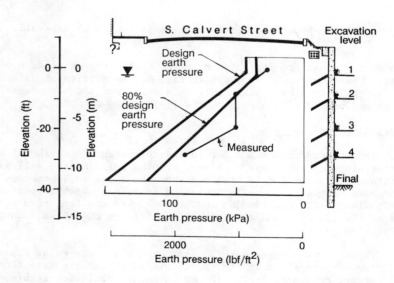

FIG. 7--Typical settlement data during staged excavation versus horizontal offset from slurry wall.

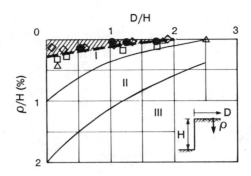

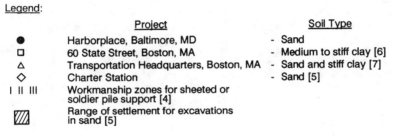

Legend:

	Project	Soil Type
●	Harborplace, Baltimore, MD	- Sand
□	60 State Street, Boston, MA	- Medium to stiff clay [6]
△	Transportation Headquarters, Boston, MA	- Sand and stiff clay [7]
◇	Charter Station	- Sand [5]
I II III	Workmanship zones for sheeted or soldier pile support [4]	
▨	Range of settlement for excavations in sand [5]	

FIG. 8--Summary of soil settlements behind slurry wall.

by injecting grout from the tieback plant. When expressed as a percentage of excavation depth, as shown in Fig. 8, the settlement data compare favorably to other slurry wall excavation projects completed in sand or medium to stiff clay deposits [4-7].

Lateral Earth Pressures

Tieback performance and lateral earth pressure behavior of the concrete diaphragm wall was evaluated at nine instrumented wall panels utilizing displacement data obtained from the slope inclinometers and hollow core tieback load cells installed at each tieback support level. The load cells provided an indication as to the long term performance of the tiebacks and redistribution of loads on the wall during construction.

Typical load changes vs. time and excavation stages at upper level tiebacks are shown in Fig. 9. Typically, tiebacks were tensioned to 80 percent of design load. The measurements confirmed stable, satisfactory performance of the tiebacks during periods of non-excavation. Decreases in the tieback loads result from redistribution of load as lower level ties were tensioned.

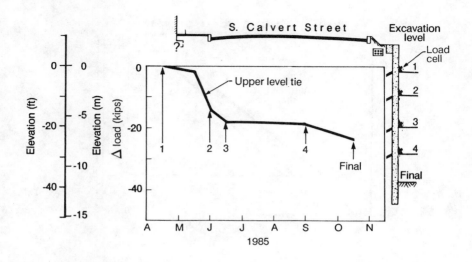

FIG. 9--Upper level tieback load cell data showing
load changes with time and excavation level.

Total lateral pressure data obtained from the tieback load cells
are shown on Fig. 10 compared to envelopes representing 80 and 100
percent of the permanent design pressures. Selection of the design
earth pressure required consideration of allowable lateral movement of
the slurry wall. The design required that wall movements be re-
strained; therefore, the restraining force to be applied to the wall
must be twice the active earth pressure force [8]. Consequently, the
design earth and water pressure for the project was computed as

$$P_d = 2K_a \gamma_b D + \gamma_w H = 34D + \gamma_w H$$

(1)

where

P_d = Horizontal Earth Pressure (lbf/ft^2; 1 lbf/ft^2=47.88 Pa)

D   = Depth below Ground Surface (ft; 1 ft = 0.3048 m)

γ_w = 62.4 (lbf/ft^3; 1 lbf/ft^3 = 16.02 kgf/m^3)

H   = Depth below groundwater level (ft)

K_a = 0.33 = coefficient of active earth pressure

γ_b = 52 (lbf/ft^3)

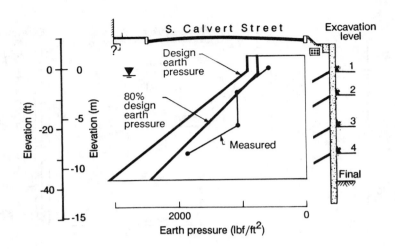

FIG. 10--Design earth pressure envelopes versus
measured earth pressure data.

Total pressure envelopes include earth pressures plus hydrostatic
and surcharge pressures. Final loads measured at each of the tieback
levels to the design envelopes indicated a satisfactory correlation
between the measured total pressures and the design total pressure
envelope.

CONCLUSIONS

Selection of a slurry wall for temporary and permanent support of the
five level deep parking structure simplified construction operations
and provided the desired high-quality underground space. The relatively watertight wall reduced long term groundwater seepage to 5 gpm
(0.32 L/s) and allowed construction to proceed systematically with a
minimum of dewatering. Geotechnical instrumentation, including displacement and settlement measurements, confirmed the overall satisfactory performance of the wall. At the same time, the instrumentation data
was critical when evaluating and resolving construction problems related to tieback grouting operations.

ACKNOWLEDGEMENTS

The project was undertaken by the Baltimore Center Associates, Ltd.
Partnership with architectural and structural design provided by

Zeidler Roberts Partnership and Quinn Dressel Associates, respectively. HCB Contractors was general contractor and construction manager while Recosol, a joint venture of The Reinforced Earth Company and Soletanche was the specialty contractor for slurry wall/tieback construction.

REFERENCES

[1]   Bordenaro, Michael J., "Gallery at Harborplace Exhibits Function Through Facade," in Building Design and Construction, Vol. 30, No. 3, March 1989, pp. 62-66.

[2]   "Report on Subsurface Investigations and Foundation Recommendations - Proposed Gallery at Harborplace," prepared by Haley & Aldrich, Inc. for the Rose Company, Columbia, MD, 27 June 1984.

[3]   Xanthakos, Petros P., "Underground Construction in Fluid Trenches," National Education Seminar, University of Illinois at Chicago Circle, April 1974.

[4]   Peck, R. B., "Deep Excavations and Tunneling in Soft Ground," in State-of-the-Art Volume, 7th International Conference of Soil Mechanics and Foundation Engineering, Mexico City, 1969, pp. 225-290.

[5]   Clough, G. Wayne and O'Rourke, Thomas D., "Construction Induced Movement of Insitu Walls," in Proceedings of ASCE Conference on Design and Performance of Earth Retaining Structures, Cornell University, Ithaca, New York, June 1990.

[6]   Johnson, E. B., Gifford, D. G., and Haley, M. X. "Behavior of Shallow Footings Near a Diaphragm Wall," Preprint 3112, ASCE Fall Convention, San Francisco, California, October 1977.

[7]   Gifford, D. G., Wheeler, J. R., and Howard, A. L. "Summary Instrumentation Report, Transportation Building, Park Plaza, Boston, Massachusetts," prepared for Goody, Clancy & Associates for submittal to Massachusetts Department of Capital Planning and Operations, March 1983.

[8]   Sandhu, B. S., "Earth Pressure on Walls Due to Surcharge," Civil Engineering, ASCE, Vol. 44, No. 12, pp. 68-70, December 1974.

Ernest Winter, T.Skep Nordmark, and Gilbert Tallard

SLURRY WALL PERFORMANCE ADJACENT TO HISTORIC CHURCH

REFERENCE: Winter, E., Nordmark, T. S., and Tallard, G., "Slurry Wall Performance Adjacent to Historic Church", Slurry Walls: Design, Construction, and Quality Control, ASTM STP 1129, David B. Paul, Richard R.Davidson, and Nicholas J. Cavalli, Eds., American Society for Testing and Materials, Philadelphia, 1992.

ABSTRACT: Underpinning and conventional sheeting and shoring using soldier beams and wood lagging was substituted with a slurry wall adjacent to a historic Washington, D.C. church. This church was badly damaged in 1970 due to ground movement from a building excavation to the west. Understandably there was concern regarding a proposed new excavation on the east side for an office building planned only a few metres away. The church hired consultants to review all design and construction measurement data independently. This paper presents the measurement data on the slurry wall from readings on slope inclinometers embedded in the wall, survey of surface points and observations on the church itself. Readings at the various stages of construction are shown. The work was completed without any significant movement or damage to the church.

KEYWORDS: Slurry wall, excavation support, wall movements, inclinometer measurements.

INTRODUCTION: Excavation adjacent to the Church of the Epiphany at 1317 G Street in Northwest, Washington, D.C. created special problems. Previous building excavation experience using sheeting and shoring on the west side of the church, where a deep basement was excavated in 1970, caused considerable ground movement and damage to the church. In order to avoid similar problems in 1987, when another building with several basements was planned on the east side of the church, a careful evaluation was made of available excavation support methods. It was considered that a concrete diaphragm slurry wall system would meet the requirements of limiting horizontal and vertical movements adjacent to the excavation. In addition the slurry wall could be developed as a basement wall. Delay of excavation associated with this construction was minimized by installing the caisson foundations while the slurry wall was built.

Messr. Winter and Nordmark are Principal and Associate of Schnabel Engineering Associates., 10215 Fernwood Road., Bethesda Md; Mr. Tallard is owner of Envirotrench, Pelham, NY.

SITE CONDITIONS: Lower floor grade for the new building was about El 10, or about 10 metres (30 feet) below site grades. The church parish house at the north end had no basement, and the floor grade was at about El 42 with footings adjacent to the new construction at about El 39. These footings were about 2 metres (6 ft) from the proposed excavation. At the south end the church had a basement at about El 34 and was about 10.7 metres (35 feet) from the new building. However, this part of the church was older and could have been founded on stone footings. The Church building and the layout of the new building including the location of observation points is shown on Figure 1.

Test borings indicated about 3 metres (10 feet) of fill, underlain by Pleistocene Terrace sands and clay to about 15 to 21 metres (50 to 70 feet) depth. Some of the clay layers were relatively soft, and the new structure was accordingly designed for caisson foundations drilled through the Terrace layers into Cretaceous Age very compact clayey sands. This stratum was also scheduled to support the loads of the slurry wall. The profile through two adjacent borings is shown on Figure 2.

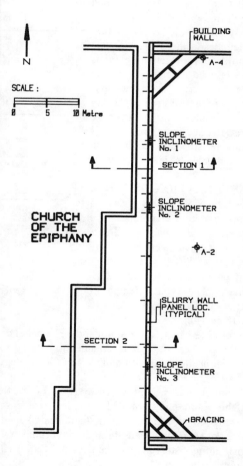

DESIGN CONSIDERATIONS:
The design loads on the slurry wall ranged from 766 to 1000 newtons per metre (16 to 21 kips/lft) from dead and live loads of the new structure and tieback loads. The slurry wall was designed for bearing in the Cretaceous compact sand to match caisson grades and limit differential settlement. The allowable bearing capacity of this soil was 1437 $N/m2$ (15 tsf). For economy only alternate primary panels at the north end, and portions of the larger panels at the south end, were lowered to the Cretaceous soils for bearing.

For the temporary excavation support condition, the slurry wall was designed using a trapezoidal soil pressure distribution with maximum lateral pressure of 0.24 γ H (25H (psf)), where γ = soil unit weight and

Figure 1. Location Plan

H = height of cut. This pressure includes a 20% increase over normally anticipated soil pressures to allow for horizontal and vertical stresses from church foundations as calculated using Westergard distribution, and to reduce soil movements. The design was based on a computer program RIDO. The RIDO program was developed by Professor Rober Fages in the early 1970's. The program calculates the elastoplastic equilibrium of retaining walls and is used extensively by the French slurry wall industry. The program has the capability of considering surcharge loadings, various soil characteristics and variations in groundwater table.

INSTALLATION DETAILS: The slurry wall was a cast in place concrete diaphragm type installed in panels. Joints between panels were formed by a steel end form (Stop end). All panels were 0.61 m (2 ft) thick. The typical length of panels was 2.4 to 3 metres (8 to 10 feet) at the north end and 7 metres (23 feet) at the south end. The panel depth varied between 13.7 to 24 m (45 to 80 ft) where the panels extended to bearing soils. Shorter panels extended 10.7 m (35 ft) at the south end and to 9 m (30 ft) depth at the north end.

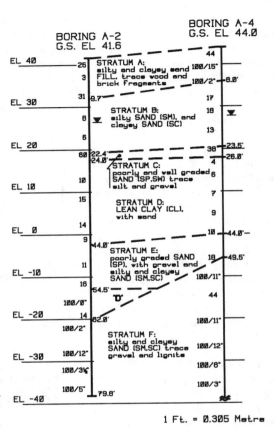

Figure 2. Typical Soil Section

Lateral support was provided by two rows of tiebacks at the north end and one row at the south end, installed into the terrace sand and clays. The tiebacks were prestressed to 120 percent of their design load and locked in at 90 percent. The tiebacks were installed through preformed holes in the wall, which consisted of positioning a steel pipe at the tieback locations.Typical design sections are shown on Figures 3 and 4.

The wall was installed during a time period of about one month. Slope inclinometer casings were embedded into the walls for observation of displacements.

OBSERVATIONS: Observations and measurements of wall movements were evaluated from the slope inclinometer readings taken in the casings installed in the wall, from survey measurements at the top of the wall, and from data on observation points installed on the church building. In order to illustrate the shape of wall deflections we have included the displacement curves at the three inclinometer locations for typical dates. On these plots, shown in Figure 5a through 5c, the horizontal displacements are plotted along the slope inclinometer pipe indicating movements towards the excavation.

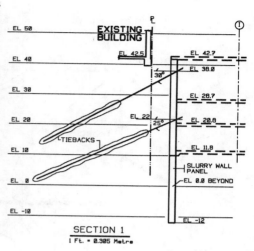

Figure 3. Typical Design Section

At the dates marked on the selected curves, displacements corresponding to the initial, intermediate and maximum excavations are shown. These curves typically indicate a bowing out of the wall with the maximum movement near the lower third of the excavation height, and displacements typically in the range of 7.6 to 12.7 mm (0.3 to 0.5 in). Inclinometer 3 showed some initial movement at the top of wall. This may be due to the use of only one tieback in this section.

On Figure 6a through 6c the displacements are plotted against time, showing the same points in view of the excavation sequence. A review of Plots 5 and 6 indicate the majority of the movements occurring during the lower portion of the excavation, generally below 5

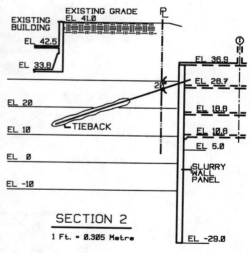

Figure 4. Typical Design Section

metre depth. At Inclinometer 3 large movements were noted at the top of the wall prior to October 30 and an upper tieback in this area was added. In general, only minor movements were noted after completion of the excavation at Inclinometers 1 and 2. At Inclinometer 3 movements were noted indicating a possible relaxing of the tiebacks.

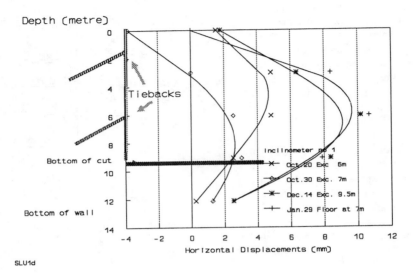

Figure 5a.

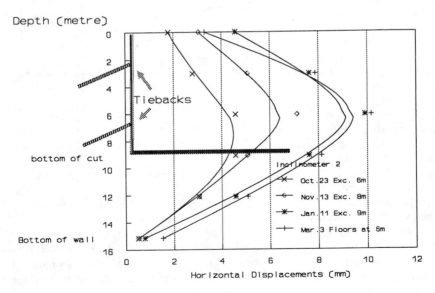

Figure 5b.

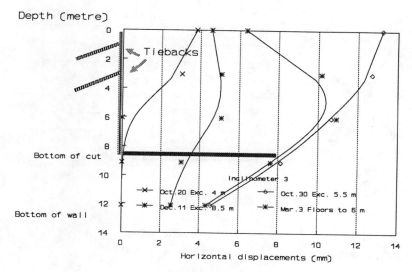

Figure 5c.

Displacements on points installed on the Church walls adjacent to the excavation were minimal. During the installation of the slurry wall measured horizontal movements were 2 to 3 mm or less, and during excavation 1 to 2 mm or less. Towards the center of the Church some crack monitors showed horizontal movements up to 6 mm, still well within the range of acceptable values.

ANALYSIS OF DATA: The displacements adjacent to walls supporting excavations depend on various factors, including quality of workmanship and installation methods. Any movements accordingly reflect to a certain degree the quality of installation.   Any conclusions made regarding soil behavior from movements will be influenced by these factors. With this in mind a comparison was made between the movement measured on this project and "typical" movements that could be expected based on published observation data.(FHWA-RD-75-128. 1976)

The data available on wall movements is generally grouped by soil types in the literature. The retained soil on this site was generally a clay and silt over the major portion of the wall height. The performance of this system was accordingly analyzed in comparison to walls supporting fine grained soils.

The normalized horizontal movements of the wall typically ranged between 0.1 to 0.15 percent of the height, which is an acceptable low value for the system. The majority of comparable retaining systems measure in the 0.2 to 0.3 percent range in the literature.

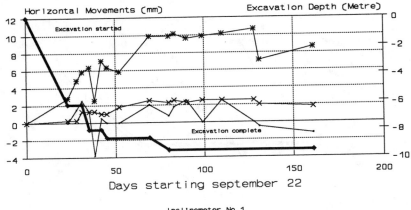

Figure 6a.

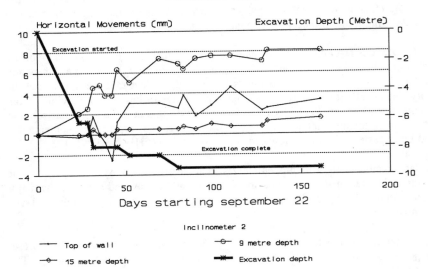

Figure 6b.

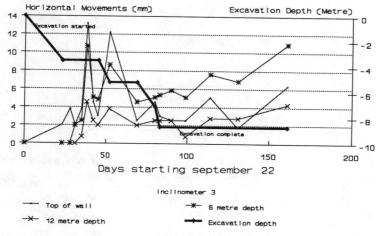

Figure 6c.

Measurements made at a distance from the wall indicate movements that may have been transferred to the church. These movements included horizontal displacements not exceeding about 6 mm.

The shape of the wall deflections would indicate a flexible wall deformation, with most of the movements occurring in the mid portion of the wall. Considering the small magnitude of these movements however, it is not conclusive whether the wall behaved as a rigid or flexible structure.

CONCLUSIONS: The results of measurements and observations show that the slurry wall construction can be expected to support excavations with very minor displacements. Consequently adjacent structures at close distances are well protected against detrimental movements. The wall under observation provided protection against horizontal movements, and none of the measured values were in excess of 0.15 percent of the wall height.

ACKNOWLEDGEMENTS: The authors gratefully acknowledge the help and cooperation of the George Hyman Co., builder of the slurry wall, and in particular the assistance given by Alan G. Hobelman and his department for making measurement and construction data available.

REFERENCES:
FHWA-RD-75-128 April 1976, "Lateral Support Systems and Underpinning". Final Report April 1976 Vol.I, Federal Highway Administration, Offices of Research and Development. Washington DC. 20590

Raj P. Khera[1] and Ramnarayan K. Tirumala[2]

MATERIALS FOR SLURRY WALLS IN WASTE CHEMICALS

REFERENCE: Khera, R. P., Tirumala, R. K., "Materials for Slurry Walls in Waste Chemicals", Slurry Walls: Design, Construction, and Quality Control, ASTM STP 1129, David B. Paul, Richard R. Davidson, and Nicholas J Cavalli, Eds., American Society for Testing and Materials, Philadelphia, 1992.

ABSTRACT: The majority of test data indicate that the hydraulic conductivity of soil-sodium bentonite mixtures increases several folds with many of the chemicals found at waste disposal sites. This investigation is on mixtures consisting of calcium bentonites from four different sources, cement, slag, and fly ash using flexible wall permeameter. The mix with calcium bentonite from Greece yielded hydraulic conductivity values which were equal to or lower than 10^{-7} cm/s. With water and organic chemicals (aniline 5,000 ppm, phenol 5,000 ppm, toluene 500 ppm) the soil mix showed a decrease in hydraulic conductivity. Over a 40 day period the hydraulic conductivity decreased from about 10^{-7} cm/s to 10^{-9} cm/s. The rate of decrease in hydraulic conductivity with phenol was somewhat slower. The hydraulic conductivity did not increase with time with any of the chemicals.

KEYWORDS: slurry wall, calcium bentonite, sodium bentonite, hydraulic conductivity, flexible wall permeameter, fly ash, slag, cement

Relatively impervious barriers are built around hazardous waste sites to prevent contamination of soils and ground water by waste chemicals and leachate. The most widely used technique for such construction is the slurry wall method. The two common types of cut-off walls are the soil bentonite and cement bentonite walls. In a soil bentonite wall (SB) backfill materials consisting of sodium bentonite and soils displace bentonite slurry and form the impervious barrier.

[1]Professor, Department of Civil and Environmental Engineering, New Jersey Institute of Technology, 323 Dr. Martin Luther King Blvd., Newark, NJ 07102.

[2]Staff engineer, Dames & Moore, 12 Commerce Drive, Cranford, NJ 07016.

In a cement bentonite wall (CB) the slurry is composed of bentonite and cement which is left in place to act as "impervious" barrier. CB walls are constructed in a single operation, require less working area, and have a shorter construction duration when compared with SB walls. The low value of hydraulic conductivity of both types of walls is to a large extent due to the presence of sodium bentonite in the mix. The bentonite-cement mixes currently used in SB walls yield a hydraulic conductivity of about 10^{-6} cm/s which is an order of magnitude higher than that considered acceptable for such structures. The higher hydraulic conductivity may be partly due to calcium in cement replacing some of sodium in bentonite.

The majority of test data indicate that the hydraulic conductivity of soil sodium bentonite mixtures increases several fold in the presence of many organic waste chemicals. In an ordinary sodium bentonite organic compounds with individual concentrations less than 75 ppm caused an increase in hydraulic conductivity of more than three times. With the same permeant the hydraulic conductivity was more than five and half times [1] for a contaminant resistant bentonite. Hydraulic conductivity of soil-sodium bentonite backfill material increased by a factor of 5 to 10 when permeated with sodium hydroxide [2], whereas the same permeant lowered hydraulic conductivity of magnesium montmorillonite 13 fold [3].

Sodium is an externally adsorbed ion in bentonite. It balances the charge deficiency caused by isomorphous substitution of some of the alumina by magnesium. An externally adsorbed ion can be replaced by other ions with greater replacing power. For example, calcium ion which has an higher replacing power than sodium can readily replace a sodium ion. Similarly, sodium ions can be replaced by organics. The properties of a clay which has undergone an ionic exchange can differ substantially from the original clay. The soils which realize their low hydraulic conductivity from an abundance of monovalent ions are most likely to exhibit increased hydraulic conductivity when these ions are replaced by higher valence ions.

The hydraulic conductivity of specimens containing sodium bentonite, cement and slag was reported [4] to increase from 1.5×10^{-7} cm/s to 10^{-6} cm/s in two months with a reconstituted leachate. When calcium bentonite was used the hydraulic conductivity showed a decrease from 1.5×10^{-8} cm/s to 10^{-10} cm/s in the same period. The water absorption capacity of sodium bentonite was more than four times that of calcium bentonite but it occurred only in a narrow range of pH. As the pH deviated from 8 the water absorption capacity declined rapidly reaching about the same value as that of calcium bentonite. The greater resistance of calcium bentonite to chemicals may be partly due to the fact that its water absorption capacity is essentially constant in the entire pH spectrum. The negative consequence of lower water absorption capacity of calcium bentonite is that 3 to 4 times more of calcium bentonite is required for a comparable adjustment in hydraulic conductivity and gel strength.

MATERIALS TESTED

Various materials, their sources, and the symbols used in specimen designations are shown in Table 1.

Table 1 -- Materials and their sources

Material	Symbol	Source
Calcium bentonite	A	American Colloids Company, USA
Sodium bentonite cs 200	O	
Calcium bentonite	I	AIMCOR, USA
Calcium bentonite from Greece	G	IKO Industriekohle GmbH & CO, Marl, Germany
Tixoton CV 15 - a Na_2CO_3 treated calcium bentonite	T	SÜD-Chemie, AG, Munich Germany
Type A Portland cement	C	Lehigh Cement Co., USA
Slag	L	Blue Circle Atlantic of Atlanta, GA, USA
Fly ash - from Hudson	H	Public Service Electric & Gas,
- from Mercer	M	Newark, NJ, USA
Sand passing No. 40 sieve	S	Shortcrete, USA

PERMEANTS

Permeants and their concentrations are given in Table 2. These concentrations are within their water solubility limits.

Table 2 -- Permeants for hydraulic conductivity tests

Chemical	Symbol	Concentration, ppm
Water	W	
Aniline	A	5,000
Phenol	P	5,000
Toluene	T	500

SAMPLE PREPARATION

Bentonite was mixed with water and left overnight for hydration. Cement, slag, and fly ash were added to the hydrated bentonite, as needed, and mixed in a mechanical blender. The moisture content at this stage was about 32 percent. The mixture was then poured into cylindrical molds about 70 mm in diameter. The height of specimens ranged between 25 mm and 60 mm. The molds containing the mixes were stored in a humid room for curing. After seven days the specimen were extruded from the molds, wrapped in wet paper towels, sealed in zip-lock bags, and left in the humid room till used. See Table 3 for composition of test specimens.

EXPERIMENTAL PROCEDURE

The testing equipment consisted of a compressed air pressurizing system, permeant interface devices, and flexible wall stainless steel hydraulic conductivity cells.

A test specimen is mounted between saturated porous stones and covered with filter papers. A plastic film is wrapped around the soil specimen and sealed to the top and bottom end platens previously coated with silicon grease. A rubber membrane was slipped over it and sealed at both ends with rubber 'O' rings. The plastic film protects the rubber membrane from chemical attack.

The cell is filled with deaired water. All the drainage lines are flushed with the permeant and the connections checked for leakage. A water head of about two meters is maintained at the bottom of the sample and a suction at the top until bubbles stop passing through the suction tube.

The specimen is subjected to a cell pressure of 50 psi (345 kPa) and a back pressure of 42 psi (290 kPa) till the volume of the cell and the sample attain steady values for at least six hours. The hydraulic conductivity tests were conducted with hydraulic gradients of 20 to 60.

Table 3 -- Design mixes for test specimens

Name	Design mix
Calcium bentonite from American Colloid	
AC	12% bentonite + 15% Cement
ACL	12% bentonite + 15% Cement:sLag (1:1)
A12C4H	12% bentonite + 12% Cement + 4% fly ash (Hudson)
ACL3	12% bentonite + 15% Cement:sLag (1:3)
A12CL4M	12% bentonite + 12% Cement:sLag (1:1) + 4% Mercer fly ash
Calcium bentonite from AIMCOR	
IC	12% bentonite + 15% Cement
ICL	12% bentonite + 15% Cement:sLag (1:1)
I12CL4H	12% bentonite + 12% Cement:sLag (1:1) + 4% Hudson fly ash
Calcium bentonite from Greece [G]	
GC	15% bentonite + 15% Cement
GCL	15% bentonite + 15% Cement:sLag (1:1)
Tixoton CV 15 from Germany treated with Na_2CO_3	
TC	12% bentonite + 15% Cement
TCL	12% bentonite + 15% Cement:sLag (1:1)

RESULTS AND DISCUSSION

A typical cumulative time versus cumulative flow curve is shown in Fig. 1. A change in slope of this curve indicates a change in hydraulic conductivity and a constant slope indicates a steady value. For most of the specimens the hydraulic conductivity continued to decrease with time. Since the emphasis was only on those mixes which would yield the acceptable hydraulic conductivity value of 10^{-7} cm/s, tests on specimen which showed very high or very low hydraulic conductivity were terminated early. The results of hydraulic conductivity tests are presented in Table 4.

Table 4. — Hydraulic conductivity of specimen at the end of testing

Specimen No.	Permeant	Concentration, ppm	hydraulic conductivity cm/s
AC-8W	water		1.8×10^{-6}
AC-8P	phenol	5,000	3.2×10^{-6}
AC-9T	toluene	500	2.2×10^{-6}
A12C4H-8W	water		1.3×10^{-5}
A12C4H-8P	phenol	5,000	1.0×10^{-6}
ACL-1W	water		1.5×10^{-6}
ACL3-W	water		3.8×10^{-7}
A12C4M-W	water		3.3×10^{-7}
IC-1W	water		6.5×10^{-6}
ICL-W	water		1.9×10^{-5}
GC-2W	water		2.3×10^{-6}
GCL-1W	water		5.0×10^{-9}
GCL-2P	phenol	5,000	4.0×10^{-8}
GCL-1A	aniline	5,000	5.0×10^{-10}
TC-1W	water		4.0×10^{-7}
TCL-1W	water		7.0×10^{-7}

Bentonite and Cement Specimen

The final values of hydraulic conductivity (k) of test specimens AC-8W, IC-1W, GC-2W and TC-1W were 1.8×10^{-6} cm/s, 6.5×10^{-6} cm/s, 2.3×10^{-6} cm/s, and 4×10^{-7} cm/s, respectively. These specimens contained cement and bentonite and were permeated with water. The lower value of hydraulic conductivity for Tixoton may be attributed to the abundance of sodium ions due to the treatment with sodium carbonate resulting in a very high water absorption capacity [5]. Note that none of these hydraulic conductivity values are suitable for containment structures.

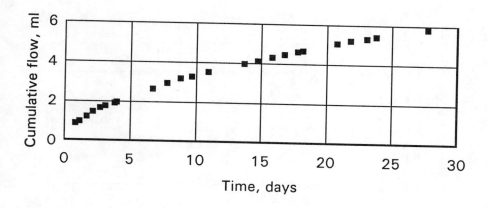

Fig. 1 Typical cumulative time versus cumulative flow curve

Bentonite, Cement, and Slag Specimen

The results of hydraulic conductivity tests where half the cement was replaced by slag are presented in Fig. 2. The final hydraulic conductivity values for ACL-1W, ICL-1W, TCL-1W and GCL-1W, are 1.5×10^{-6}, 1.9×10^{-5} cm/s, 7×10^{-7} cm/s, and 5×10^{-9} cm/s, respectively. The first three specimens, when compared with the corresponding specimens without slag, AC-8W, IC-1W, and TC-1W, show an increase in hydraulic conductivity of 10% to 300%. Though these hydraulic conductivity values show a decreasing trend with time, they are higher than 1×10^{-7} cm/s and, therefore, the tests were terminated as soon as these trends were established. The exception is test GCL-1W which contained calcium bentonite from Greece and showed the most dramatic decrease in hydraulic conductivity with the addition of slag. Its hydraulic conductivity value of 4×10^{-8} cm/s (Fig. 2) at the end of four days when compared with the hydraulic conductivity value of 2.3×10^{-6} cm/s for the same period of time for specimen GC-2W has decreased by almost two orders of magnitude. It is also evident from Fig. 2 that the hydraulic conductivity continued to decrease with time and reached a value of 5×10^{-9} cm/s after about 38 days when the test was terminated.

Proportions of Slag and Cement

The proportion of cement to slag was 1:3 in specimen ACL3-W. It showed a hydraulic conductivity of 3.8×10^{-7} cm/s which is about four times lower than ACL-1W which had a hydraulic conductivity of 1.5×10^{-6} cm/s. The hydraulic conductivity of this bentonite increased with the addition of smaller proportions of slag but it decreased with higher proportions of slag. Since only one set of comparative data is available any conclusion that hydraulic conductivity decreases with an increase in slag content cannot be supported.

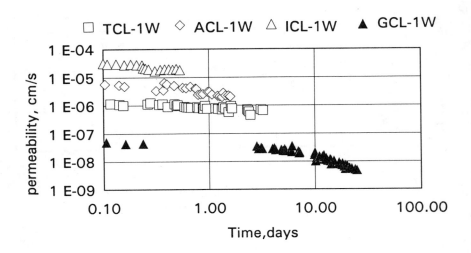

Fig. 2 Hydraulic conductivity of specimens containing cement and slag with water

Effect of Fly Ash on Hydraulic conductivity

Comparing test AC-8W (k = 1.8×10^{-6} cm/s) which had no fly ash with test A12C4H-8W (k = 1.3×10^{-5} cm/s) which contained 4% fly ash from the Hudson generating station an increase in hydraulic conductivity of almost one order of magnitude is evident. On the other hand when ACL-1W (k = 1.5×10^{-6} cm/s) is compared with A12CL4M-W (k = 3.3×10^{-7} cm/s) which contained fly ash from Mercer a five fold decrease in hydraulic conductivity is observed. Thus no general statement can be made regarding the contribution of fly ash in reducing the hydraulic conductivity of soil mix. When using fly ash to replace some of the cement it must be evaluated for its effect on the hydraulic conductivity. The influence of fly ash on such factors as mix strength and curing time were not studied.

Effect of Chemicals on Hydraulic conductivity

Observe from Table 4 that of the materials tested only the slag-calcium bentonite mixture had hydraulic conductivity values are in the range of 1×10^{-7} cm/s or less. The results of hydraulic conductivity tests for this soil mixture are shown in Fig. 3.

As indicated by test GCL-1W the hydraulic conductivity decreased with time from a starting value of about 10^{-7} cm/s to 5×10^{-9} cm/s during the testing period of 38 days. The initial values of hydraulic conductivity with 5000 ppm aniline are much lower than the initial values with water. This is due to the fact that at the end of the test with water aniline replaced water as the permeant. However, the hydraulic conductivity continues to decline at about the same rate as that of water. Test specimen GCL-2P where phenol was used right from the start the initial hydraulic conductivity is essentially the same as that with water (GCL-1W). And the hydraulic conductivity continued to decrease with time though somewhat slower than with water.

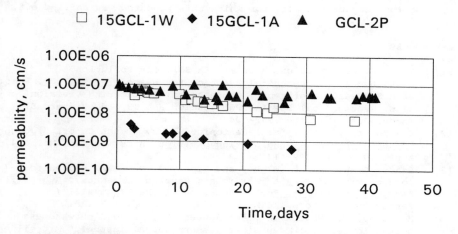

Fig. 3 Effect of permeants and time on hydraulic conductivity of calcium bentonite from Greece

All of the data show that the hydraulic conductivity values decrease with time for both the chemicals and water. In all instances these values are well within the acceptable value of 10^{-7} cm/s.

CONCLUSIONS

The hydraulic conductivity tests on specimens prepared with calcium bentonite and cement indicate that their suitability for slurry wall depends on various components of the mixture.

1. Partial replacement of cement with slag lowered the hydraulic conductivity for calcium bentonite from Greece to values less than 1×10^{-7} cm/s. For the other calcium bentonites there was some increase in hydraulic conductivity and these values were greater than 1×10^{-7} cm/s.

2. Addition of fly ash from the Hudson generating station increased the hydraulic conductivity by almost one order of magnitude whereas fly ash from Mercer decreased it by more than five fold. Irrespective of the source of fly ash the values of hydraulic conductivity were all greater than 1×10^{-7} cm/s

3. The hydraulic conductivity of all calcium bentonite specimens decreased with continued permeation regardless of whether the permeant was water or an organic chemical. Only the mixtures containing calcium bentonite from Greece yielded hydraulic conductivity values less than 1×10^{-7} cm/s

ACKNOWLEDGMENTS

The authors acknowledge the Industry/University Cooperative Center for Research in Hazardous and Toxic Substances at NJIT, which provided funding for Project Site 16, for which this research was carried out.

REFERENCES

[1]   Ryan, C. R., "Vertical Barriers in Soil for Pollution Containment," Geotechnical Practice for Waste Disposal '87, Proc. of a Specialty Conference, Geotechnical Engineering Division, ASCE, Geotechnical Special Publication No. 13, Ed. Richard D. Woods, June 1987, pp. 182-204.

[2]   D'Appolonia, D. J., "Soil-Bentonite Slurry Trench Cutoff," Journal of the Geotechnical Engineering Division, ASCE, V. 106, No. GT4, April 1980, pp. 399-417.

[3]   Lentz, R. W., Horst, W. D., and Uppot, J. O., "The Hydraulic conductivity of Clay to Acidic and Caustic Permeants," Hydraulic Barriers in Soil and Rocks, Johnson / Frobel / Cavalli / Pettersson, Editors, ASTM, STP 874, 1985, pp. 127-139.

[4]   Hermanns, R., Meseck, H., and Reuter, E., "Sind Dichtwandmassen beständig gegenüber den Sickerwässern aus Altlasten?," Mitteilung des Instituts für Grundbau und Bodenmechanik, TU Braunschweig, Heft Nr. 23, Ed. H. Meseck, Dichtwände und Dichtsohlen, Braunschweig, Federal Republic Germany, June 1987, pp. 113-154.

[5]   Tirumala, R. K., " Calcium Bentonite in Containment Structure," Masters Thesis, NJIT, Newark, NJ 1989.

[6]   Khera, R. P., "New Materials for Slurry Wall Containment Structures," Research Report, NSF Industry/University Cooperative Research Center, NJIT, Newark, NJ, July 1990.

Mario Manassero and Claudio Viola

INNOVATIVE ASPECTS OF LEACHATE CONTAINMENT WITH COMPOSITE SLURRY
WALLS: A CASE HISTORY

REFERENCE: Manassero, M., Viola, C., "Innovative Aspects of Leachate Containment with Composite Slurry Walls: A Case History",
Slurry Walls: Design, Construction and Quality Control, ASTM STP
1129, David B. Paul, Richard R. Davidson and Nicholas J. Cavalli,
EDS, American Society for Testing and Materials, Philadelphia,
1992.

ABSTRACT: The main technological and construction features of a
composite cement-bentonite slurry wall carried out for containment of subsoil pollution due to a chemical plant located in
the northern part of Italy, are presented.
The subsoil profile shows a high permeability sand and gravel
layer, 3 to 15 m thick, underlined by a natural low permeability
stratum of overconsolidated and cemented clay, more than 150 m
thick.
The solution adopted for remedial works was aimed to gain advantage from subsoil conditions which were nearly ideal for cut-off
barrier effectiveness.
Design approach, preliminary and final checks are also described
in the paper.

KEYWORDS: waste, leachate containment, composite slurry walls,
lab tests, field tests, permeability, case history, drainage

FOREWORD

The 100 year old "ACNA" Organic Chemical Plant, located in the
Italian region of Liguria, gained nationwide notoriety in 1989 due to
its sudden closing down, in the wake of serious pollution of the
adjacent Bormida River.
Under pressure from the workers' unions concerned with the
potential loss of over 700 jobs and, on the other side, of
environmentalists and farmers protesting for a definite shut-down, a
crash cleanup program was implemented by the ACNA management which
eventually led, in a few months' time, to the reopening of the plant
under officially certified safe conditions.

Dr. Manassero is head of the environmental engineering section at
Studio Geotecnico Italiano, Via Ripamonti, 89 - 20141 Milano, Italy;
Mr. Viola is senior geologist, also at Studio Geotecnico Italiano.

The requirement for an absolutely fail-safe solution and working under the public spotlight were an uncomfortable environment for designers and contractors; however the result was innovative, effective and, most important, passed stringent tests without any problem.

1. GEOLOGICAL OUTLINE OF THE SITE

The plant is built on the right bank of the Bormida River, on an alluvial deposit of sand and gravel in silty-sandy matrix with occasional cobbles and boulders. The alluvial deposits rest on a marl bedrock (Fig. 1).

During the 100 plus years of operative life, sludges were deposited over, and partly mixed with, the superficial deposits thus creating a polluted layer 3 to 12 m thick.

A comprehensive site investigation, with borings ranging from 30 m to 170 m below g.ℓ. supplemented by test pits and geophysical measurements concluded the following main aspects:

— the thickness of the polluted alluvial deposits was between 3 and 12 m; permeability ranged from 10^{-2} to 10^{-4} cm/s;
— the marl bedrock showed no sign of pollution; it is over 150 m thick, with permeability less than 10^{-7} cm/s;
— the top of the marl is flat, slightly dipping towards the river, with no significant discontinuities;
— the polluted water table within the alluvial deposits is between 0.5 and 4.0 m thick, depending on the marl bedrock level, on river level and on rainfall;
— the groundwater flow is towards the river.

2. BASIC DESIGN PRINCIPLES

The local geological conditions pointed to a design approach that could take advantage of the very high impermeability of the marl bedrock.

A containment system was therefore developed, based on two ideas:

a) a vertical containment barrier, well keyed into the marl and surrounding all portions of the plant area located downstream in respect to groundwater flow (see Fig. 2);
b) a dewatering system capable of lowering the water table inside the plant area.

As shown in Fig. 3, the system is well suited to oppose the migration of pollutants towards the river, combining:

— a positive gradient from the outside towards the inside of the area (on the average $50 \div 100$ cm difference in piezometric head is kept);

— a virtually impermeable containment barrier constructed with a composite cement-bentonite slurry wall and a high density poliethylene (HDPE) geomembrane.

The composite slurry wall was designed to comply with Italian and international standards on permeability relevant to side and bottom impermeabilization of toxic waste landfills.

Solutions were inspired by state-of-the-art papers, such as [1], [2], [3], [4], [5].

The containment system was completed by a series of drainage trenches, equipped with automatic pumps and alarms (Fig. 4).

Referring to a standard year as far as rainfall is concerned, the water removed by the whole drainage system ranges on the average between 60 to 80 m^3/h. The polluted water is treated "in house" by a biochemical treatment plant also used for water coming from production activities. The full capacity of the water treatment plant is 450 m^3/h; the total cost of treatment is about $2 \div 3$ U.S. $ per m^3 of leachate.

3.   DETAIL OF THE COMPOSITE SLURRY WALL

The vertical barrier consists of a cement-bentonite slurry wall containing an HDPE geomembrane (Fig. 5). This solution was selected to minimize horizontal permeability and as an added defense against chemical agression of the wall itself. The detail of joints between the HDPE panels inside the slurry wall is shown in Fig. 6.

The reference migration time by advection for a polluted particle to cross the barrier horizontally was estimated as suggested by the proposed Italian Regulations for the sides of new landfills (i.e. thickness of the barrier divided by apparent seepage velocity) and by assuming conservatively 1 m hydraulic gradient between the inside and the outside of the barrier. The global hydraulic conductivity of the composite slurry wall was evaluated according to indications from laboratory permeability tests on jointed systems performed by Cortlever [6].

Considering a spacing between the joints of 2.5 m and the geomembrane panels practically impermeable, an equivalent global permeability of $2\text{x}10^{-10}$ m/s ($2\text{x}10^{-8}$ cm/s) has been assessed and used for the calculation of migration time through the slurry wall, that must be longer than 50 [years] to comply with the above mentioned Italian Regulations:

$$t_1 = \frac{s^2}{K_d \, \Delta H} \approx \frac{0.6^2}{2\text{x}10^{-10} \cdot 1} = 1.8\text{x}10^9 \text{ [s]} \approx 57 \text{ [years]} > 50 \text{ [years]}$$

where:

s   = slurry wall thickness

K_d = slurry wall hydraulic conductivity

ΔH = piezometric head difference through the slurry wall.

The depth of embedment of the barrier inside the marl bedrock was evaluated by imposing the reference migration time (t_2), for a hypothetical polluted particle seeping around the key of the barrier, without crossing the HDPE geomembrane, to be three times the value of t_1 assessed before (i.e. ~150 [years] as stated by the proposed Italian Regulations for the bottom sealing system of new landfills) therefore:

$$t_2 = \frac{4\,\ell^2}{K_b\,\Delta H} = \frac{4 \times 1.5^2}{1.5 \times 10^{-9} \times 1} = 6.0 \times 10^9 \ [s] \approx 190 \ [years] > 150 \ [years]$$

being:

K_b = conservative vertical permeability of the natural bedrock

ℓ = embedment of the slurry wall into the bedrock.

Results of these calculations pointed to an embedment of 1.5 m; a value of 2 m was actually adopted for added safety.

Construction was carried out according to the following steps:

a) a first cement-bentonite slurry wall, 120 cm thick, was built with conventional clamshell equipment down to the base of the alluvial deposit. This first operation allowed to remove the large boulders occasionally present at the base of the deposit;

b) after setting of the 120 cm thick slurry wall mixture, a series of 60 cm diameter borings were made inside the first slurry wall, at 1.5 ÷ 2.0 m spacings; the borings reached 2.0 m inside the marl and were drilled without using any fluid or casing. This decreased the duration of drilling operations into the marl, compared with more conventional working procedures;

c) the final cement-bentonite mixture was then cast by tremie and finally the material between the drill-holes excavated by conventional clamshell equipment; in this way a second 60 cm thick slurry wall embedded 2 m into the bedrock was obtained;

d) before setting of the mixture, the interconnected HDPE panels were lowered by a counterweighted steel frame into position at the center of the slurry wall and then suspended by steel bars crossing the head of the HDPE panels and resting at ground level.

The resulting slurry wall was extremely precise and well constructed, thanks to having been poured in a perfectly regular and stable trench.

4. SUITABILITY AND FINAL CHECKS

Before starting the actual construction, an optimum cement-bentonite slurry mixture was researched in the lab, in order to minimize hydraulic conductivity and to check the chemical compatibility of the mixture with the leachate to be contained. A series of permeability tests with different contents of basic elements of the mixture and at different curing times has been carried out. Permeability values of cement-bentonite slurries are highly influenced by curing time. The chart in Fig. 7 compares measured permeability with that of similarly composed slurries. A good correlation of results can be observed, which also testifies to the quality of the slurry mixture adopted.
According to [8], [9] and [10] observed permeability values tend to stabilize to an upper boundary of about 1×10^{-7} cm/s after curing time ranging between 4 months and 3 years.

Referring to chemical compatibility checks, the following basic test procedure has been carried out:
— long term permeability tests in triaxial cell on hardened mixtures using the leachate which is to be contained instead of water as permeant; almost 3 pore volumes went through the sample;
— long term permeability tests using higher concentrations of the main components found in the leachate (i.e. chlorinated solvents, sulfonic acid, sulfonic salt, naphtene);
— the same procedures have been performed on slurry samples, mixed with leachate instead of water or cured in a sandy bed saturated by the leachate;
— stress-strain tests on samples, following the permeability tests.

Final results show that the curing time, the hydraulic conductivity, the stress-strain behaviour of the mixture are not affected significatively by the chemical components of the leachate to be contained.
A careful quality control program was implemented during construction testing consistency, viscosity and cement-bentonite ratio of the mixture.
20 samples were collected for every 100 m^3 of slurry, for compression and permeability lab tests at 7, 14 and 28 days curing time.

Test results were analyzed statistically; some brief comments are given here, in particular concerning lab permeability determinations on 360 samples after 28 days of curing:

— The graph in Fig. 8 shows a good correlation between the frequency distribution of the examined samples and that of a "normal" frequency, in logarithmic scale.

— It is therefore possible to refer to a "normal" distribution in logarithmic scale for the statistical evaluation of permeability of cement-bentonite mixtures.
This approach is commonly used for permeability evaluations of natural and/or compacted fine-grained soils [7].
— Referring to the logarithmic scale, the average of permeability tests results is 1.4×10^{-6} cm/s while 95% of results are lower than 5.6×10^{-6} cm/s.

Functional checks at completion of the work were as follows:
— general test of the inside drainage and leachate extraction system;
— water table measurements in piezometers, both on the inside and on the outside of the barrier;
— in-situ permeability tests inside trial panels close to the slurry wall, at the wall-marl interface and inside the marl bedrock.

The groundwater table elevation was always higher on the outside than on the inside, which indicates that the internal drainage system and the barrier are functioning as intended.
After the slurry wall construction, in-situ tests were carried out inside "ad hoc" trial panels without geomembrane constructed at the same time, in the same conditions and close to the true cutoff wall.
Setups of these in situ tests are shown in Figs.9 and 10.
Along the whole perimeter of the slurry wall, a total of 32 in situ tests of this type have been performed, comprising tests inside the slurry wall, at the interface with the bedrock and inside the bedrock.

The average values of the three series of tests are:

TABLE 1 -- "In situ" tests results on slurry wall and bedrock

	number of test n [-]	average permeability value K [cm/s]
inside the slurry wall	12	1×10^{-7}
interface with the bedrock	11	1×10^{-6}
inside the bedrock	9	1×10^{-8}

Permeability of the slurry mixture measured in situ after about 3 months' curing is well in accordance with the values charted in Fig.7.
The permeability at the interface between diaphragm and bedrock is the highest, probably due to unavoidable sedimentation problems of

sandy material at the bottom of the excavation. In any case the value is still completely acceptable, considering that the design approach does not take into account the contribution of the bottom to the cut-off wall performance.

The bedrock permeability tests performed in this phase confirm the results from the site investigation phase prior to the design and construction phases.

5. FINAL CONSIDERATIONS

— In order to defend the environment from pollution originating in the subsoil of the ACNA Plant, the most advanced operative techniques were adopted referring in particular to a composite slurry cut-off wall.

— Suitability laboratory tests on the cement-bentonite mixture to be adopted have been carried out to check hydraulic conductivity and the chemical compatibility with the leachate to be contained. No significant reactions have been noticed also after observation periods of one year.

— A high density poliethylene (HDPE) geomembrane was inserted into the slurry wall, forming a composite sealing system to decrease the global permeability of the barrier and to increase safety against chemical agression. The chemical compatibility of HDPE with the pollutant produced by the chemical plant had already been proved before the project, having HDPE geomembranes been used for lining lagoon impoundments inside the plant. The HDPE geomembrane, after more than fifteen years at direct contact with liquids with high concentrations of pollutants performs quite faultlessly.

— "In situ" permeability tests carried out after construction of the cut-off wall are in very good agreement with suitability laboratory tests and with literature data referred to similar cement-bentonite mixtures.

— Thickness, composition and embedment of the cutoff wall have been developed on the basis of the new Italian regulation proposals for sealing systems of toxic waste landfills.

— The reclamation system is completed by drainage trenches for lowering the inside water table in respect to the outside groundwater and river levels. The pumped leachate is conveyed to the treatment plant which already serves the chemical industrial activities.

— The reclamation system will be further implemented by a comprehensive monitoring network.

— The first laboratory data coming from the monitoring of groundwater quality are definitely encouraging: the concentration of pollutants in the groundwater outside the barrier shows a decrease of one order of magnitude in one year.

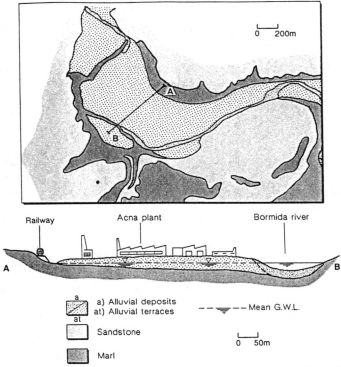

FIG. 1 -- Geological map and profile before construction of the barrier.

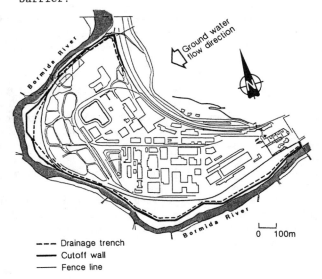

FIG. 2 -- Plan view of the alignment of the slurry wall and drainage trench systems.

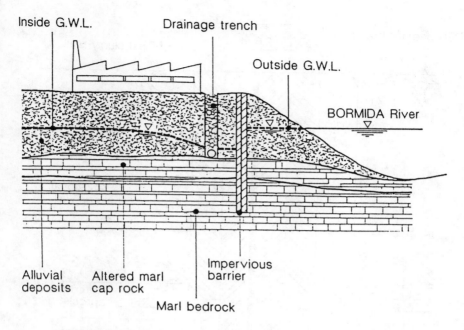

FIG. 3 -- Basic outline of the system.

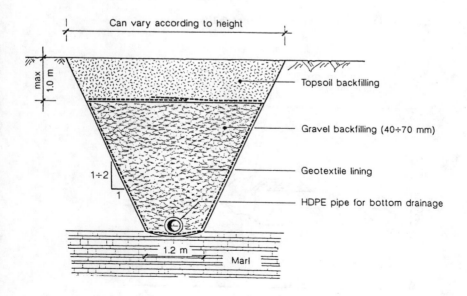

FIG. 4 -- Vertical cross-section of the drainage trench.

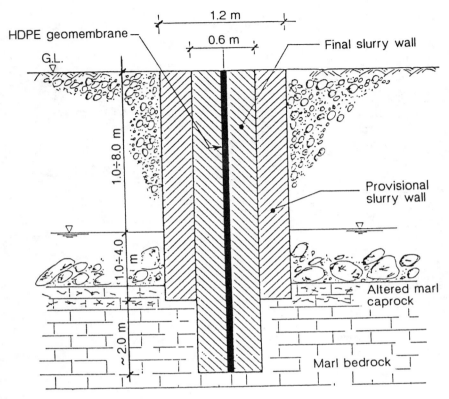

FIG. 5 -- Detail of the barrier (vertical section).

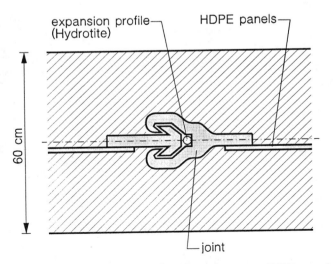

FIG. 6 -- Horizontal section of joints between HDPE panels.

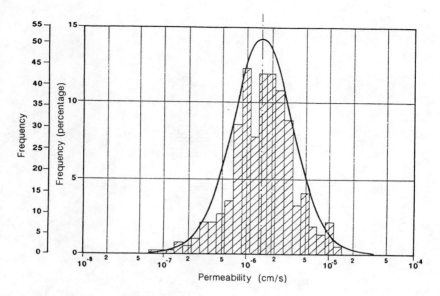

FIG. 7 -- Permeability of cement-bentonite slurries as a function of
          curing time.

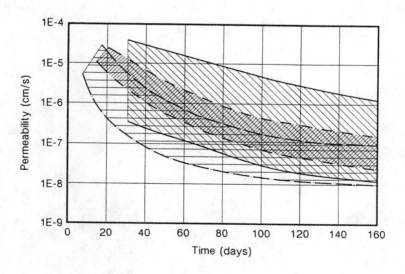

FIG. 8 -- Frequency vs. permeability (in logarithmic scale) of
           cement-bentonite slurry after 28 days curing compared to
           a "normal" distribution curve.

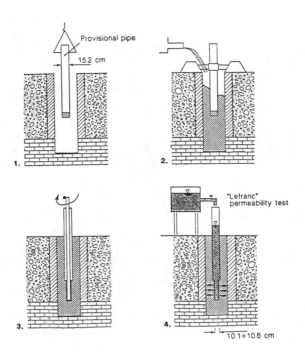

FIG. 9 -- In-situ permeability test inside the slurry wall.

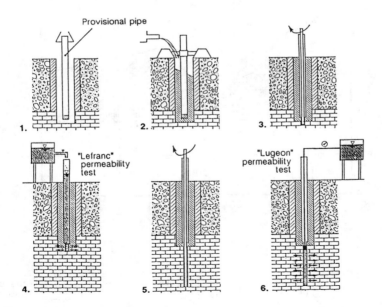

FIG.10 -- In-situ permeability test at the slurry wall bedrock
           interface (step 4) and inside the bedrock (step 6).

REFERENCES

[1] U.S. Environmental Protection Agency (1984). Slurry Trench Construction for Pollution Migration Control — Handbook EPA Cincinnati. OH.

[2] Ryan, C.R. (1987). Vertical Barriers in Soil for Pollution Containment. Specialty Conference on Geotechnical Practice for Waste Disposal. University of Michigan.

[3] Meseck, H. (1987). Dichtwande und Dichtsohlen — Fachseminar, June 2-3, Stadthalle Braunschweig, Techische Universitat Brounschweig.

[4] Meseck, H. and Hollstegge, W. (1989). Case History on the Construction of Cut-Off Wall Diaphragm Wall Method. Proceedings of the Twelfth International Conference on Soil Mechanics and Foundation Engineering - Rio de Janeiro, A.A. Balkema Rotterdam pp.1503-1506 Vol.III.

[5] Daniel, D.E. (1988). Short Course on Waste Disposal, Studio Geotecnico Italiano, Milano.

[6] Cortlever, N.G. (1988). Geolock. Geotechnics Amsterdam. Holland.

[7] Olson, R.E. and Daniel D.E. (1979). Field and Laboratory Measurement of the Permeability of Saturated and Partially Saturated Fine-Grained Soils — Geotechnical Engineering Report GR80-5, Department of Civil Engineering, University of Texas.

[8] Schweitzer, F. (1989). Strength and Permeability of Single-Phase Diaphragm Walls — Proceedings of the Twelfth International Conference on Soil Mechanics and Foundation Engineering Rio de Janeiro, A.A., Balkema Rotterdam, pp. 1515-1518, Vol.III.

[9] Neff, H.K. (1990). Workshop for preparation of Geotechnics of Landfills and Contaminated Land Technical Recommendations — Bochum University, Bochum.

[10] Manassero, M. (1990). Seminary on Impervious Barriers for Leachate Containment — Italian Electricity Board Research Center ENEL — CRIS Milan.

David A. Schoenwolf[1] and Daniel J. Dobbels[2]

UNDERREAMED DRILLED SHAFTS INSTALLED USING SLURRY METHODS

REFERENCE: Schoenwolf, D. A., Dobbels, D. J., "Underreamed
Drilled Shafts Installed Using Slurry Methods," Slurry Walls: Design, Construction, and Quality Control, ASTM STP 1129, David B. Paul,
Richard R. Davidson, and Nicholas J. Cavalli, Eds., American Society
for Testing and Materials, Philadelphia, 1992.

ABSTRACT: This paper presents a case history on the use of end-
bearing, underreamed drilled shaft foundations installed using slurry
methods to support a 21-story building in Boston, Massachusetts. Factors leading to the selection of drilled shaft foundations for the
project, design criteria, results of a pre-construction testing program
as well as production foundation installation and quality control procedures are presented. Data on performance of the foundation system
through the completion of construction and comments regarding the general applicability of underreamed drilled shafts installed using slurry
methods are also presented.

KEYWORDS: underreamed drilled shafts, bentonite slurry, foundations, design, construction

---

The 101 Arch Street building is a 21-story office tower located
adjacent to the financial and retail districts of downtown Boston,
Massachusetts. The building consists of 35 300 square meters (380 000
square feet) of first-class office space and 3 700 square meters
(40 000 square feet) of retail space. Special features include direct
access to an adjacent subway station via the concourse level. The
building is owned by Metropolitan Life Insurance Company.

The superstructure has a reinforced concrete frame with shear
walls in the central core. Typical interior column design loads ranged

---

[1]Vice President, Haley & Aldrich, Inc., 4909 Cordell Ave.,
Bethesda, MD 20814.

[2]Senior Engineer, Haley & Aldrich, Inc., 58 Charles Street,
Cambridge, MA 02141.

from approximately 4.4 to 17.8 MN (1 000 to 4 000 kips), exterior column design loads ranged from approximately 2.9 to 13.3 MN (650 to 3 000
kips) and shear wall design loads in the core area were approximately
3.6 MN/m (250 kips/ft). The lowest level floor slab was constructed at
El. 2.9 m (9.5 ft). Foundation construction for the tower was completed in the spring of 1986 and the tower was topped out in the summer of
1987.

SITE CONDITIONS

The 101 Arch Street building is bordered by city streets on two
sides, an alley on the third, and existing buildings on the fourth
side. Figure 1 shows the 101 Arch Street building in plan relative to
surrounding streets and structures. Figure 2 shows a typical cross
section of the building and adjacent structures. A subway station,

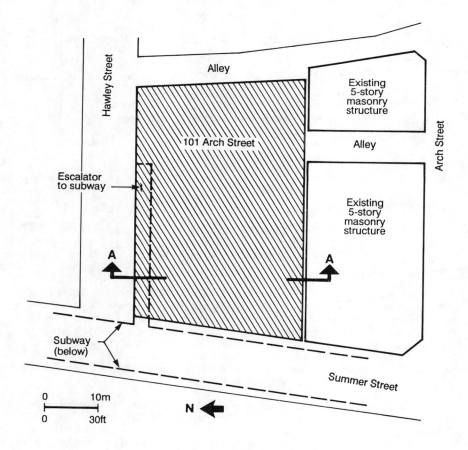

FIG. 1--Site Plan.

constructed in the early 1900's, is present below Summer Street on the west side of the building. An entrance to the subway station and associated escalatorway exists on the north side of the building. The building cantilevers out over the escalatorway as shown in Figure 2. The escalatorway had significant impacts to both the design and construction of the foundation system for the building. Five-story masonry bearing wall structures with one basement level constructed in the late 1800's abut the structure to the south. These structures are founded on spread-footing foundations bearing at shallow depths below the lowest level floor slabs.

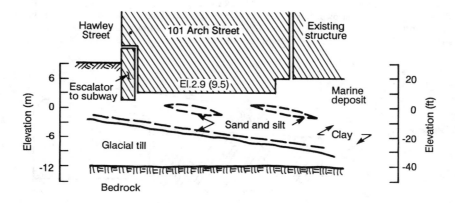

FIG. 2--Section A-A.

SUBSURFACE CONDITIONS

A typical subsurface profile for the site is presented in Figure 2. A deposit of marine soils exists immediately below the lowest level floor slab. Underlying the marine deposit is glacial till and bedrock.

The marine deposit is described as a soft to very stiff silty clay interbedded with layers and lenses of medium dense to very dense fine sand to fine sandy silt. The layers and lenses of fine sand and fine sandy silt are typically 0.9 to 1.2 m (3 to 4 ft) thick; however, the layers can be up to 4.6 m (15 ft) thick. A continuous layer of fine sand is present immediately above the glacial till. The total thickness of the marine deposit below the lowest level floor slab ranges from approximately 7.6 to 12.2 m (25 to 40 ft).

The glacial till is described as a very dense silty coarse to fine sand with some gravel, to hard silt with little coarse to fine sand and gravel. Cobbles and boulders are present throughout the deposit. The thickness of the glacial till ranges from approximately 3.0 to 7.6 m (10 to 25 ft).

The bedrock at the site consists of highly to completely weathered argillite. Past experience with argillite with this weathering profile in the Boston area indicated that this material generally behaves as a hard silt; however, its properties are quite variable locally. The depth to bedrock below the lowest level floor slab elevation is approximately 15.2 m (50 ft).

Groundwater levels at the site at the time of construction were typically several feet below the proposed lowest level floor slab elevation.

FOUNDATION ALTERNATIVES

Several different foundation system alternatives were evaluated during the design phase of the project: reinforced concrete mat, driven piles, and drilled shafts. Initial consideration was given to a reinforced concrete mat foundation bearing on the marine deposit since it was judged that such a system would be the most cost-effective. The key to the feasibility of a mat foundation was the anticipated post-construction settlement due to consolidation of the underlying marine deposit. The critical area, in terms of settlement, was adjacent to the escalatorway where contact stresses at the base of the mat would be highest due to the presence of columns supporting the portion of the superstructure which cantilevers over the escalatorway. The estimated settlement of a mat foundation in this area was judged to be unacceptable. In addition, with such heavy column loads on the edge of the mat, the top of the mat would have been in tension, inconsistent with typical mat designs. Therefore, the mat foundation alternative was eliminated.

Driven pile foundations deriving their support in end-bearing in the glacial till were considered to be the second most cost-effective foundation type. However, for typical pile design capacities in the Boston area, the required number of piles would have resulted in unacceptable disturbance to adjacent structures in terms of excessive vibrations, potential heave and subsequent recompression of the marine deposit.

Drilled shaft (pier) foundations were then evaluated. Consideration was given to straight-shaft and underreamed piers deriving their support in end-bearing on the glacial till. Because of the presence of cobbles and boulders in the glacial till, the feasibility of fully penetrating the glacial till with standard drilled shaft equipment without significant delays during construction was questionable. In addition, because the bedrock was of very poor quality, the allowable bearing pressure in the glacial till was determined to be greater than that for the bedrock. For these reasons, underreamed drilled shaft foundations bearing on the glacial till were considered the most appropriate foundation system for the structure. A presumptive allowable bearing pressure of 2.1 MN/m^2 (22 tons/ft^2), which is more than twice the presumptive bearing pressure provided in the applicable building code at the time of design, was selected. This relatively high

bearing pressure was based on recent experience with similar soil types
in the Boston area. A full scale load test was performed on a proto-
type drilled shaft to verify the presumptive allowable bearing pressure.

It was recognized during design that the key to successful construction of drilled shaft foundations was control of groundwater inflow and seepage pressures in the glacial till during construction.
The presence of a layer of fine sand on top of the glacial till and the
granular nature of the glacial till precluded groundwater control by
means of open pumping from the bottom of the drilled shafts as they
were constructed. Predrainage of the glacial till prior to drilled
shaft construction was considered the preferred groundwater control
alternative. A second alternative--the use of bentonite slurry to
stabilize the excavation in lieu of dewatering, which had been used
previously for several straight-sided drilled shaft projects in the
Boston area--was also considered acceptable. During the design phase,
it was envisioned that bentonite slurry, if used, would be used in
conjunction with straight-sided drilled shafts.

PRE-CONSTRUCTION TEST PROGRAM

Background

A drilled shaft test program was developed such that prospective
contractors could submit proposals to do the work in accordance with
minimum design criteria established by the design team. These criteria
included allowable bearing pressures in the glacial till and bedrock,
allowable side resistance in the glacial till, and performance requirements for groundwater control measures. Prospective contractors were
allowed flexibility to propose their own installation methods and procedures.

Proposals were received from two contractors. One proposed a
somewhat conventional approach consisting of pre-drainage of the glacial till and overlying fine sand and installation of underreamed
drilled shafts in the dry. A second contractor proposed a unique approach: underreamed drilled shafts bearing at the top of glacial till,
installed using bentonite slurry. Both proposals were economically
competitive; however, neither the design team nor the second contractor
had previous experience with the installation of underreamed drilled
shafts using slurry.

The use of bentonite slurry for end-bearing foundation elements,
including end-bearing concrete diaphragm walls constructed by the slurry trench method and straight-sided drilled shafts, had been in practice in the Boston area prior to the 101 Arch Street project. However,
no documentation of the successful use of bentonite slurry for underreamed drilled shaft construction in the United States could be found.
Specific concerns with this approach included verification of the shaft
bearing area, assurance that the entire bearing area was in glacial
till, and cleanliness of the bearing surface prior to concreting.

Although it was believed that adequate means could be developed to address these concerns, it was the design team's opinion that there was less risk associated with the conventional approach. Since there was no economic penalty associated with the conventional approach, it was selected initially.

However, during the test program, the contractor's dewatering system was not able to the lower the piezometric head in the glacial till to a level equal to or below the proposed drilled shaft bearing elevation. The contractor made several attempts at drilled shaft installation, but in each attempt, the glacial till bearing surface became disturbed and unstable as a result of excessive seepage pressures. Due to schedule constraints, it was decided to abandon the attempts at conventional construction rather than to install additional dewatering wells. The second contractor was requested to install a test shaft using the bentonite slurry/underreamed drilled shaft approach.

Drilling Procedures

The test program consisted of installing a shaft with a 69 cm (27 in.) diameter shaft underreamed to 107 cm (42 in.) at the base and two reaction piers with 91 cm (36 in.) diameter shafts underreamed to 244 cm (96 in.) at the base. The generalized load test setup is shown on Figure 3. Drilling was conducted using a truck-mounted Williams LDH

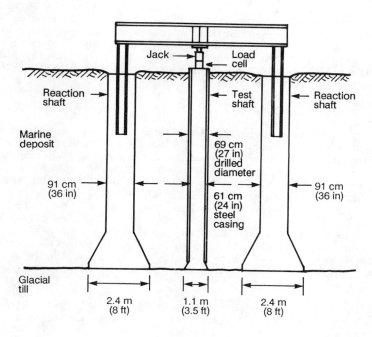

FIG. 3--Load test set-up.

80 T drill rig. Drilling of each shaft began with the installation of a 4.6 m (15 ft) long starter casing to a depth of approximately 4 m (13 ft). Once the starter casing was installed, bentonite slurry with a bentonite concentration of 3.5 percent by weight, which had been pre-mixed and allowed to hydrate for 24 hours, was introduced into the excavation. After the slurry was added, drilling continued to the top of the glacial till stratum. Additional slurry was added as necessary to maintain a 1.5 m (5 ft) head of slurry above the groundwater level. The depth at which glacial till was encountered in the shaft was marked by a very dramatic increase in drilling resistance and the presence of glacial till in the drilling spoil.

After drilling was completed to the top of the glacial till, the bottoms of the shafts were underreamed using standard underreaming buckets. The diameters of the underreams for the reaction shafts were estimated by measuring the travel of the kelly bar as the wings of the underreaming bucket were opened at the bottom of the shaft and then measuring the distance between wings when the kelly bar traveled the same amount with the bucket resting on the ground surface. The diameter of the underream for the test shaft was determined in a similar manner except that stops were welded to the underreaming bucket to ensure the maximum possible underream would be no greater than 107 cm (42 in.).

A 61 cm (24 in.) outside diameter steel casing was installed in the test shaft after completion of underreaming. The casing was suspended in the shaft such that its bottom was approximately 10 cm (4 in.) above the top of the underream. The slurry-filled annulus was intended to serve as a bond breaker to minimize the load transfer above the underream during load testing. Two steel conduits were welded diametrically opposite each other on the inside of the casing and extended its full length. The conduits were used as part of the internal instrumentation described below.

<u>Bottom Cleaning and Concreting</u>

Upon completion of casing installation for the test shaft and underreaming of the reaction shafts, cleaning of the bottom of the shafts and the slurry was performed. This was accomplished by means of an airlift and a desanding unit as shown in Figure 4. The airlift served the dual purpose of (1) providing a means of bringing contaminated slurry at the bottom of the shaft to the surface so that it could be desanded and (2) removing the spoil at the bottom of the shaft. A unique feature of the airlift pipe was the addition of a 90-degree elbow at the bottom that was used to direct the suction action into the underreamed portion of the drilled shaft. The elbow attachment extended approximately 10 cm (4 in.) laterally from the outside face of the airlift pipe. The general sequence of the bottom cleaning activities was as follows:

1.   Sweep the airlift pipe, without the 90-degree elbow, across the bottom of the drilled shaft until large size particles were no longer emitted from the desander.

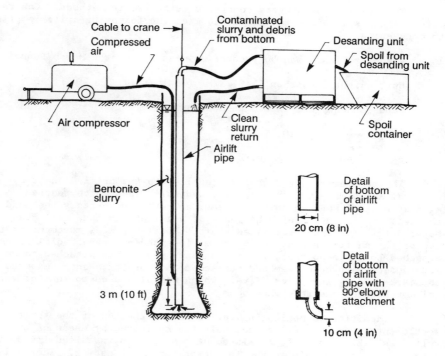

FIG. 4--Bottom cleaning and desanding.

2.   Sweep the airlift pipe around the perimeter of the shaft with the
      90-degree elbow attached and directed into the underream until
      large size particles were no longer emitted from the desander.

3.   Sound the bottom of the shaft by allowing the airlift pipe to
      free-fall from a height of approximately 15 to 30 cm (6 to
      12 in.) above the bottom of the shaft. The purpose of the sound-
      ing was to determine if any loose or soft material remained on
      the bottom.

4.   Continue airlifting and desanding operations until the sand con-
      tent of the slurry was less than 5 percent by volume.

     In addition to taking soundings with the airlift pipe, soundings
were also conducted using a 44.5 N (10 lbs) weight attached to the
bottom of a tape measure. Soundings were taken at frequent intervals
before, during and after bottom cleaning operations. The soundings
taken before bottom cleaning were used to develop a "feel" for the
action of the weighted tape in an unclean excavation. This assisted
the construction monitoring personnel in making judgements as to the
cleanliness of the bottom after cleaning and again prior to concreting.

The drilled shafts were concreted using tremie methods. Contract specifications required the slurry to meet the following criteria prior to concreting:

1.   Viscosity less than 50 seconds as measured by the Marsh Funnel.

2.   Unit weight less than 11.8 kN/m^3 (75 lb/ft^3).

3.   Sand content less than 5 percent by volume.

4.   pH between 7 and 10.

Load Test Procedures and Results

The compression test load was applied to the drilled shaft by means of a 4.4 MN (500 ton) capacity hydraulic jack which reacted against a steel beam spanning between the reaction shafts. The load on the test shaft was measured by means of a calibrated load cell placed between the jack and the drilled shaft. Total vertical movement at the top of the shaft was measured by three independent means: dial gauges attached to an independent reference beam, piano wire attached to an independent reference beam and stretched in front of a scale mounted on the jack, and by an optical level, which was also used to monitor vertical movement of the reference beams.

In addition to monitoring settlement at the top of the shaft, settlement at the bottom of the shaft was monitored by means of two telltales. Each telltale consisted of a steel rod installed inside the steel conduits attached to the inside of the steel casing. The telltale rods were free to move vertically inside the steel conduits. The vertical movements of the top of the telltale rods were monitored with dial gauges attached to a reference beam.

The test pier was loaded to twice the design load in steps of approximately 25 percent of the presumptive design load. The presumptive design load was equal to 2.1 MN/m^2 (22 tons/ft^2) on the bearing area of 0.9 m^2 (9.6 ft^2) or 1.9 MN (211 tons). The load settlement curve for the bottom of the pier and the duration of each load increment is presented in Figure 5. Comparison of the theoretical elastic compression of the shaft with measured movements indicated that 100 percent of the test load applied at the top of the shaft was transferred to the bearing surface.

Evaluation of the load settlement curve indicated that excessive settlement of the test shaft occurred when the applied load exceeded approximately 2.8 MN (317 tons) or 3.2 MN/m^2 (33 tons/ft^2) on the bearing area, which was less than twice the presumptive design load. These results led to the conclusion that the presumptive design load of 2.1 MN/m^2 (22 tons/ft^2) was overly optimistic and the design load would have to be reduced for the production drilled shafts. Settlement analyses were conducted based on settlement parameters back-calculated from the load test results. Based on these analyses, an allowable

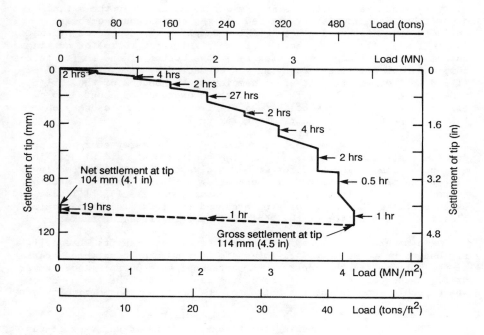

FIG. 5--Load test results.

bearing pressure of 1.6 MN/m^2 (17 tons/ft^2) was selected for design of the production shafts.

INSTALLATION OF PRODUCTION DRILLED SHAFTS

After completion of detailed design of drilled shafts using parameters developed from the load test data, installation of production drilled shafts using slurry methods began.

Eighty-six drilled shafts were installed between January and April 1986. They ranged in size from 0.61 m (2 ft) diameter straight-sided shafts to 2.4 m (8 ft) diameter shafts with 3.8 m (12.5 ft) diameter underreams. Two drill rigs were used: a truck-mounted Williams LDH for the smaller shafts, and a crawler-crane mounted rig for the larger shafts.

Production shafts were constructed using the same general installation and quality control procedures as those used during the test program; however, several additional quality control measures were implemented during production work. These measures included taking samples at the bottom of the shafts and comparing the theoretical and actual rise of concrete as the concreting operations were under way.

The purpose of bottom sampling was to ensure that the marine deposit had been adequately removed and the shafts would be bearing entirely on undisturbed glacial till. Sampling was conducted at the completion of airlifting because of the significant volume of cuttings and disturbed soil that were present at the bottom of the shafts at the completion of drilling. Sampling was conducted by attaching a 3.5 cm (1-3/8 in.) diameter split-spoon sampler to the bottom of the airlift pipe and letting the pipe free fall from a distance of about 30.5 cm (12 in.) from the bottom of the shaft. Two to six samples were obtained in each drilled shaft, depending on the shaft diameter.

Results of bottom sampling conducted in the early stages of production installation indicated that the contractors' initial drilling and bottom cleaning procedures were not always effective in removing all of the marine deposit from the bearing surface. This was attributed to (a) insufficient shaft depth to assure that glacial till was exposed across the entire bearing area and (b) insufficient mechanical cleaning of the bottom of the shaft with the underreaming bucket.

On several occasions, for the larger diameter shafts, the drill rig had to be re-mobilized to the shaft to remove unacceptable material at the bottom. As the contractors' personnel gained experience, their drilling and bottom cleaning procedures improved and the frequency of unacceptable material at the bottom of the shaft decreased significantly.

The purpose of comparing the theoretical and actual rise of concrete as the concreting operations were under way was to ensure that no significant sloughing of the underream or the sides of the drilled

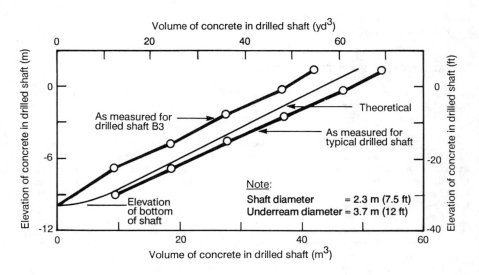

FIG. 6--Plot of rise in concrete vs. volume of concrete.

shaft occurred after completion of airlifting. The general procedure included plotting the theoretical rise in the concrete versus the volume of concrete placed, and superimposing on this a plot of measured rise of concrete versus volume of concrete placed. Measured rise exceeding theoretical rise indicates that sloughing from the sides of the shaft or collapse of the underream had occurred prior to concreting. Plots of this type were completed for each drilled shaft at the time that concreting operations were under way. A typical plot is presented in Figure 6.

Production drilled shaft installation generally proceeded without significant technical problems except for two drilled shafts located at the western end of the escalatorway. For both these shafts, it was observed that the measured rise of concrete exceeded the theoretical rise. An example is shown in Figure 6. Although this observation was made at the beginning of the concreting process, the contractor elected to complete concreting and evaluate the cause of the discrepancy at a later date. The results of core borings through these drilled shafts indicated that the concrete in the shafts was of good quality; however, a 30 cm (12 in.) thick layer of loose fine sand was encountered below the shaft and above the glacial till. The results of test borings adjacent to the shafts indicated that the underreams for both shafts were filled with loose, disturbed soil.

The exact reason for the presence of disturbed soil at the bottom of the shafts and in the underreams could not be determined. Quality control checks prior to concreting indicated that the bottoms of the shafts were clean at that time. Possible explanations include collapse of the underreams during the initial stages of concreting and sloughing of the shaft below the bottom of the starter casing when the concrete trucks backed up to the shaft. The drilled shafts were abandoned after evaluation of several remedial alternatives and replacement shafts were successfully installed.

PERFORMANCE DATA

Long term settlement monitoring of selected internal columns and the corners of the shear walls had been planned. However, data were collected only up to the time that the 14th story was completed (i.e. approximately two-thirds of the total dead load) due to the inadvertent destruction of the settlement monitoring pins by the General Contractor during cleaning operations. Settlement measured in the final data set ranged from approximately 8 to 13 mm (0.3 to 0.5 in.), depending on column location. Corresponding predicted settlement was 13 mm (0.5 in.) or less. No settlement-related distress has been observed in the structure to date.

CONCLUDING COMMENTS

A unique combination of subsurface soil and rock conditions, structural requirements, considerations for impacts to adjacent struc

tures, and the willingness on the part of the owner and the design and
construction teams to use innovative methods resulted in the unprecedented use of underreamed drilled shafts for the 101 Arch Street
project. The risks associated with this foundation type were judged to
be relatively high during the design stage. Although the project was
completed successfully, experience gained during construction served to
confirm initial judgements.

During construction, there was total cooperation between the
design and construction teams. Problems that did arise during construction were resolved with input from all parties. If adversarial relationships had developed, it is doubtful that the project could have
been successfully completed.

The 101 Arch Street project demonstrated that underreamed drilled
shafts installed using slurry methods can be a technically feasible
foundation alternative. Due to the inherent risks involved, however,
it is the authors' opinion that this alternative should only be considered after eliminating other potentially viable foundation systems. If
underreamed drilled shafts installed using slurry methods are used as
the foundation for a building, an extensive field monitoring program
should be implemented during construction. Constructing end-bearing
foundation elements under slurry is equivalent to "working blind", and
without a competent field representative and cooperative foundation
contractor, soil behavior inconsistent with design concepts could result from initially undetected problems.

Edmund G. Johnson, Keith E. Johnson, and Chris M. Erikson

DEEP FOUNDATION ELEMENTS INSTALLED BY SLURRY WALL TECHNIQUES

REFERENCE: Johnson, E. G., Johnson, K. E., and
Erikson, C. M., "Deep Foundation Elements Installed
by Slurry Wall Techniques," Slurry Walls: Design.
Construction, and Quality Control, ASTM STP 1129,
David B. Paul, Richard R. Davidson, and Nicholas J.
Cavalli, Eds., American Society for Testing and
Materials, Philadelphia, 1992.

ABSTRACT: Deep foundation units, installed using
slurry wall techniques, are generally referred to
as Barrettes or Load Bearing Elements (LBEs). This
paper reviews examples and applications of this
foundation type, and describes two case studies in
which these units were utilized in Boston.

Current design issues and construction installation
details are presented. The design discussion
focuses on the selection of foundation type and
load transfer into the bearing stratum. Issues
related to construction include excavation
equipment and stabilization, bottom cleanup,
installation of reinforcement, tremie concrete
placement, and quality control during installation.
For both case studies, the LBEs were installed for
projects constructed by the "up/down" method, which
is described in the paper. Although there are some
unique advantages when used with this construction
method, the selection of LBEs should be considered
for conventional construction as well.

KEYWORDS: deep foundations, load bearing elements,
barrettes, up/down construction, slurry foundations.

Mr. E. Johnson is a Principal and Messrs. K. Johnson and
C. Erikson are Senior Engineers at Haley & Aldrich, Inc.,
Geotechnical Engineers and Environmental Consultants, 58
Charles St., Cambridge, MA 02141.

INTRODUCTION

At urban sites, where deep foundation piers must be advanced throug
unstable soils or where high seepage pressures are anticipated, a
deep dewatering is not feasible, installation procedures similar
those used for slurry walls are often utilized. In Boston there ha
been several projects wherein this procedure has been used to stabili
drilled shaft excavations in locations where excavation "in-the-dr
would have otherwise been impractical or uneconomical. In each cas
the circular hole was advanced under slurry and the spoil removed
rotary drilling tools attached to rigid stems.

In two recent deep foundation projects (1988 and 1990) alterna
excavation procedures were utilized very effectively. Cable-hu
clamshell type digging buckets advanced through soil and rock
slurry-filled excavations, followed by placement of tremie concret
using essentially the same procedures as for traditional slurry wa
panels. At these sites, the selection of this method was driven by t
fact that the equipment had already been mobilized for installation
perimeter slurry walls.

The method has been initially developed in Europe; the foundati
units are generally referred to as Barrettes (as installed
Soletanche) or Load Bearing Elements (as installed by ICOS). For th
paper, the latter will be used.

After   a   discussion   of   pertinent   design   and   constructi
considerations for this foundation type and items to consider in t
selection process, two case studies are presented. For both of the
projects the "up/down" construction method was used, and therefc
presented certain constraints to LBE installation. However, there a
certain additional advantages to the LBE method, as described herei
which should apply to conventional construction situations as well.

The "up/down" construction method involves: 1) the construction
a reinforced concrete slurry wall around the perimeter of the baseme
space, 2) the installation of interior columns and foundation suppo
from the ground surface, 3) the placement of the ground floor sl
which braces the wall, and 4) general excavation below the sl
followed by slab placement and mining in sequence below each successi
floor to the deepest level. This permits the erection of
superstructure to proceed upward before the deep excavation
completed.

DESIGN CONSIDERATIONS

The current design practice for LBEs, as employed in the Boston projects, is primarily based on empirical or semi-empirical methods. The LBEs typically derive support in the deep glaciomarine or glacial till soils, as well as bedrock, similar to deep drilled shafts. LBE design parameters are generally based on presumptive stresses (end bearing and friction) that local drilled shaft experience has found satisfactory from observed performance, with modifications based on field or laboratory data. Field load tests may also be performed to establish design criteria.

As with the design of drilled shafts, the LBE design process involves three integral parts: 1) an appropriate subsurface exploration and field testing program, 2) determination of compatible design parameters and, 3) provisions for field modifications if necessary during construction.

Subsurface Exploration and Field Testing Program

A thorough subsurface exploration program is required prior to LBE construction to determine the depth, quality and properties of the supporting soil and rock. Soil or bedrock conditions which may lead to installation problems should also be assessed. In particular, the investigations should determine the presence or extent of the following:

a) Urban fill, soft organic soils, highly pervious granular soils or artesian groundwater conditions, which may reduce the effectiveness of the bentonite slurry to maintain trench stability.

b) Existence of boulders and the quality of bedrock which may influence the productivity of the LBE excavation equipment for LBEs installed in these strata.

Laboratory testing of glacial soils to aid in the selection of design parameters for LBEs, should include: Standard Penetration Tests (SPT "N" Values), grain size analyses and Atterberg limits. Tests on rock cores generally include unconfined compression tests and point load tests. In the field, Menard pressuremeter tests are very useful, in both soil and low-strength rock.   Hardness, weathering and fracturing of rock core samples should also be evaluated.

Field load tests may also be performed to establish design parameters. Load tests are generally conducted when: 1) subsurface investigations indicate significantly different conditions than those used to establish presumptive design parameters or, 2) design modifications, based on load test results, would result in substantial foundation cost savings. To reduce costs, load tests may be performed on small diameter shafts as opposed to a full scale test of an LBE. Specific installation procedures for those foundations which are to be load tested should be well documented to provide useful information for test evaluations. When performed prior to bidding, such data are of great value to prospective bidders.

Design Parameters

Analyses to calculate allowable skin friction and end bearing values and to estimate settlement generally involve conventional geotechnical techniques used in drilled shaft design. The determination of limit pressures and pressuremeter moduli from in-situ pressuremeter testing are used extensively to estimate design parameters (Briaud, et al. 1985; Briaud 1987). Typical allowable skin friction and end bearing values are presented in the two case studies.

Since frictional resistance is developed at much smaller displacements than for end bearing support, appropriate safety factors need to be selected to deal with differences in deformation behavior (Osterberg and Gill 1973; Kienberger 1975; Pells and Turner 1979). To account for this "strain compatibility" and to limit settlements, LBEs presented in the case studies were generally designed to support 20-40% of the applied load in end bearing and 60-80% of the load in friction.

Review of existing load test data by Tamaro (1987) and Xanthakos (1979) indicate that no conclusive evidence exists to suggest that the load-transfer characteristics of deep foundations installed under slurry substantially differ from those constructed in the dry. However, the method and quality of excavation, bottom cleaning and concreting can greatly influence the as-built load-transfer performance.

Design parameters generated from in-situ and laboratory testing should be adjusted based on anticipated installation techniques and field conditions. In the selection of design parameters, the potential effects of installation difficulties such as extended exposure of the open slurry-filled trench and inadequate cleanup of the bearing surface prior to concreting must be considered. Further judgement in the selection of design parameters is influenced by the variability of the subsurface conditions.

Field Modifications to Design During Construction

The subsurface conditions encountered during construction will greatly influence the contractor's construction scheme. Tentative procedures should be discussed and adopted to handle variable ground conditions. Since LBE design is partially qualitative and involves considerable judgement, a qualified field representative of the geotechnical engineer must be at the site to observe, monitor and verify that bearing soils or other subsurface conditions are consistent with the assumptions made during design. The representative must communicate field conditions immediately to the designer if modifications to LBE bearing area or depth are required based on actual conditions encountered. It is critical that the field representative monitor the properties of the slurry, procedures for base cleaning and concrete placement. Deficiencies in any of these areas can result in lower LBE capacity than anticipated in design.

INSTALLATION OF LOAD BEARING ELEMENTS

General

Load bearing elements (LBEs) are installed using the full array of slurry wall excavation equipment, including reverse circulating rotary cutting heads or clam shell buckets. The installation procedures for LBEs are similar to a slurry wall panel, with increased emphasis on alignment, slurry control and reinforcing consistent with the load carrying function of the LBE. The following factors are critical to a successful LBE installation:

- o proper quality control of the slurry material
- o accurate alignment of the unit during excavation
- o effective cleanup of bearing surfaces
- o configuration and installation of the reinforcing
- o accurate alignment and location of column steel (up/down method)
- o placement of tremie concrete and a well designed concrete mix
- o backfill treatment above concreted section (up/down method)

These factors are discussed in the following sections. References regarding LBE or slurry foundation construction include: Xanthakos (1979), Ramasuamy and Pertusier (1984), Reese and Tucker (1985), Tamaro (1987) and Johnson and Johnson (1990). Figure 1 illustrates the significant stages of LBE installation for the up/down construction method.

Typical Construction Procedure

1. Construct a concrete guide wall at ground surface which establishes the desired cross section of the LBE.
2. Fill the partially excavated hole with slurry pumped from the storage tanks. Maintain the level of the slurry to within 1 m of the top of the guide wall, adding slurry as necessary during excavation.
3. Excavate the LBE to the required depth using excavation tools, buckets and chisels, as required.
4. Remove as much loose material as possible from the bottom of the hole with the excavation bucket.
5. Insert airlift pipe and begin bottom cleaning and desanding operation. Airlift pipe should initially be approximately 3 m from the bottom of the hole and advanced downward as desanding proceeds to avoid clogging the equipment.
6. Perform tests to determine quality of slurry.
7. Sound bottom of hole with airlift pipe or weighted tape to determine that all soft or disturbed materials have been removed.

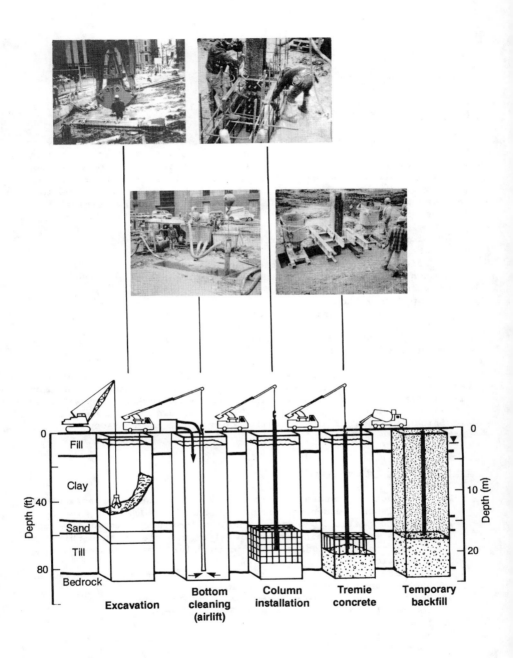

FIGURE 1 -- Up/Down LBE Construction Sequence

8. Place reinforcing cage (and column if required).
9. Place concrete by tremie method to the desired cutoff grade (for up/down construction this would be below the lowest floor level).
10. Backfill excavated trench above concrete cutoff level (up/down method only).

Cleaning and desanding may be necessary during excavation if sandy soils are encountered. In this case continuous reverse circulating slurry may be used in conjunction with the excavation buckets.

Guide Wall Construction

Pre-excavation of the LBE area is sometimes required to remove near surface below-grade obstructions. The excavated area should be backfilled with compacted fill material or lean concrete to preclude loss of ground during LBE excavation. The bulk lean concrete can be formed to serve as the guide wall.

Guide walls are useful to maintain alignment of the units at ground surface and are used to secure reinforcing and column steel. Typically the outer wall of the guide wall is formed against the soil. The inner walls are formed to the shape of the LBE unit. The walls should be of sufficient thickness and depth to provide firm bearing and to preclude undermining of the wall. The guide walls should be at least 15 cm higher than the adjacent ground surface to prevent soil and contaminated slurry from flowing into the excavation.

Alignment Of Units

Typically, criteria for alignment and location of LBEs are more stringent than those for the standard slurry wall or circular foundation units, given the concern for eccentric loading on single or multiple linear elements, and the installation of columns associated with "up-down" construction. Typical tolerance for slurry wall alignment may vary from 3 to 6 in. from the as-designed location. Tolerances for LBE excavations associated with "up-down" construction may range from 1 to 3 in.

Alignment is a concern especially for cable-hung equipment, which relies on the mass of the excavation bucket to maintain proper verticality. The location can be influenced by non-homogenous soils and the presence of cobbles or boulders.

Cables should be checked at ground surface for alignment, with the bucket at the bottom of the hole, using a long carpenter's level, plumb bob or optical instrument at least once for every 4.5 m of depth as the excavation advances.

If alignment appears to be a problem it may be necessary to increase the size or shape of the excavation. A linear element may be widened by placing steel plates on the buckets. Alignment may also be corrected with angled digging teeth.

Bottom Cleaning And Desanding

After excavation and bottom mucking by mechanical means is completed, the slurry must be circulated and desanded to maintain uniformity and remove coarse and suspended material throughout the depth of the hole. It is especially important that heavy materials at the bottom of the excavation be removed to insure adequate end bearing capacity.

The slurry desanding and bottom cleaning are accomplished by means of a desander and an airlift. The airlift serves the dual purpose of: 1) circulating the slurry throughout the depth of the excavation, and 2) removing drilling spoil remaining at the bottom of the hole. The airlift usually consists of a 15 to 20 cm diameter steel pipe suspended by a cable attached to a crane to enable the pipe to be moved up and down in the excavation. Compressed air is introduced at a point approximately 3 m from the bottom of the open pipe.

At the surface, the slurry is passed through a desanding unit usually consisting of vibrating screens or a rotating centrifuge (cyclone) to separate the solid particles from the slurry. The cleaned slurry is returned to the excavation, completing the circulation procedure.

Desanding and bottom cleaning operations generally are completed in approximately 3 to 4 hours time depending on the size of the excavation, type of soil excavated and efficiency of the desanding equipment. Operations are continued until no large size particles or excavation spoil are discharged from the desander.

Reinforcing And Structural Column (Up/Down Method)

The steel reinforcing cage is constructed at ground surface in the shape of the unit. The reinforcing cage is partially lowered into the slurry filled excavation and secured to the top of the guide wall. The bottom end of the steel column (containing shear studs), is lowered into the reinforcing cage and rigidly secured to the cage before lowering to the bottom of the excavation as a single unit.

The reinforcing cage and steel column must be constructed to allow free flow of concrete and prevent creation of voids. A minimum of 7.5 cm of concrete cover is required between the reinforcing and the sides of the excavation. More cover allows for column plumbness despite minor deviations in the excavated trench.

Concrete Placement

The slurry-filled excavation should be concreted as soon as possible after airlifting, desanding and testing of the slurry to avoid build-up of filter cake on the sides of the excavation, degradation (increased viscosity) of the slurry mixture, resedimentation or loss of ground into the excavation.

Concrete is placed by tremie methods, either by gravity flow or by pumping, in such a manner that the concrete adequately displaces the slurry from the bottom upward, rising uniformly to the cutoff elevation, such that intermixing of the concrete and slurry does not occur. The bottom of the tremie pipe should be maintained a minimum of 3 m below the top of the concrete at all times during the placement. In linear elements longer than 2 to 3 m in plan dimension, or in multiple linear elements it may be necessary to employ two or more tremie pipes to maintain uniform rise of concrete and prevent slurry inclusions from developing caused by concrete displacing slurry in a horizontal direction rather than in a vertical direction. The top of the concrete is sounded with a weighted tape and documented to determine the volume of the completed hole and to maintain embedment of the tremie pipe. The theoretical volume is compared with the actual to determine loss of ground occurrence, before or during concreting.

The concrete must have good flow characteristics with a slump of 18 to 22 cm, to create scour at the sides of the excavation and insure slurry displacement. Vibration of the concrete is not recommended due to the high slump of the mixture.

Backfill Placement Within Trench (Up/Down Method)

As part of the up/down construction technique, backfill material is placed within the trench above the cutoff level of the concrete. The backfill is placed from the top of the concreted section of the LBE to approximately the underside of the guide wall. In the two Boston case studies, a cement/bentonite mixture was used as backfill. Other projects have used granular fill for this purpose.

The selection of backfill type is an important consideration. If backfilled with weak materials, the installation of LBEs located in close proximity to in-place slurry walls may create a reduction in the passive soil resistance necessary to control lateral wall movements. Also, the type and stiffness of the backfill material will effect the unsupported length of building columns during the up/down excavation sequence. The point of fixity of the column during the temporary construction stage is directly influenced by the backfill type and placement method. The type of backfill material selected will also effect dewatering efforts and groundwater flow during the up/down excavation sequence.

Field Monitoring

With the use of slurry, direct observation of the bottom conditions is not possible. Indirect observation methods are sometimes employed. For large projects an inspection device as described in Holden (1984) may be justified.

Typically, bottom cleanliness is determined by "feeling" the bottom with a weighted tape or neutral buoyancy probe after airlifting. Feeling the airlift pipe bouncing off the bottom during cleaning is also useful. The bottom can also be "tested" and sampled by attaching a split spoon sampler to the side of the airlift pipe with a special side adapter and then lifting and dropping the pipe a known distance. The penetration is noted and the recovered sample observed (ADSC 1989).

COSTS AND PRODUCTION RATES

The type of subsurface materials to be excavated most greatly influences both the costs and production rate of LBE installation. Other factors such as site access and required support equipment also effect LBE installation costs. In Boston, soil conditions vary from soft to stiff blue clay which excavates easily, to more difficult glacial till with boulders and bedrock.

Costs for recent LBEs constructed in the Boston area on up/down projects using cable-hung clam buckets have generally ranged from $325 to $375/m^2 for easily excavatable soils and from $485 to $540/m^2 for more difficult subsurface conditions. Production rates vary from about 2.5 to 7.0 m^2/hour. Cost and production rates indicated are for wall surface area, assuming a typical 0.6 to 1.0 m wide digging bucket (ICOS 1991).

Another important cost factor involves the slurry type used during LBE excavation. Historically, a bentonite slurry has been used on previous slurry wall and recent LBE projects in the Boston area. However, with the enactment of new regulations regarding disposal of sedimented (used) slurry, removal costs have become a significant cost component of the LBE construction process. Polymer slurries, which minimize disposal quantities, are quickly becoming more popular due to their cost effectiveness. When polymer slurries are used, the unit costs may be reduced by approximately 5 to 10 percent (ICOS 1991).

ADVANTAGES

LBEs are an effective high capacity foundation type that may be installed to offset adverse subsurface conditions such as unstable soils or relatively high seepage pressures and where deep dewatering is not practical.

The various sizes and shapes available for LBE units can be an advantage over circular shaped foundation units especially in urban areas where site constraints are an issue. Typically, LBEs offer more load carrying capability per unit area than piles and can develop significant moment capacity.

LBEs are often selected on projects which require slurry wall construction because LBEs are installed using the same equipment, thus avoiding mobilizing other equipment for foundation installation. Coordination and scheduling of operations may also be improved if the same subcontractor installs the wall and the foundation units.

LBEs installed using cable hung equipment can be excavated to greater depths than caissons using conventional Kelly bars. LBEs have been installed to depths exceeding 60 m (Davidson 1987). However, clamshell and chisel equipment is limited for excavation in harder rock materials.

CASE STUDIES

125 Summer Street

125 Summer Street is a 23-story office tower in downtown Boston. Five levels of underground parking were constructed below the building in 1988 inside a perimeter concrete diaphragm wall (slurry wall) using the "up/down" technique. The slurry wall technology was also used to construct load bearing elements (LBEs) which were combined in different shapes to form the foundations. The use of the same equipment for slurry wall panels and the LBEs was considered a significant advantage by the Contractor, Turner Construction Company, because it made it easier for simultaneous construction of slurry wall panels and LBEs within a congested site. We believe that this project is the first in the U.S. to utilize LBEs in conjunction with "up/down" construction.

Table 1 describes typical LBEs sizes which were combined to form cross-shaped or linear elements. The column loads at the perimeter of the building were supported by the perimeter slurry wall. Some exterior columns were supported on T shaped elements installed perpendicular to the perimeter slurry wall. LBEs bear in the glacial till or rock at depths ranging from 16.5 to 21 m below ground surface. A typical LBE installation is shown in section in Figure 2. As shown in Table 1 loading for the 28 LBEs ranged from 2300 kN to 27,300 kN. Heavier loaded LBEs (greater than about 18,000 kN) were socketed into rock a depth of 1 to 3 m below the top of rock. Other LBEs with loading less than 18,000 kN were terminated in the glacial till a minimum of 4.5 m below the lowest level floor.

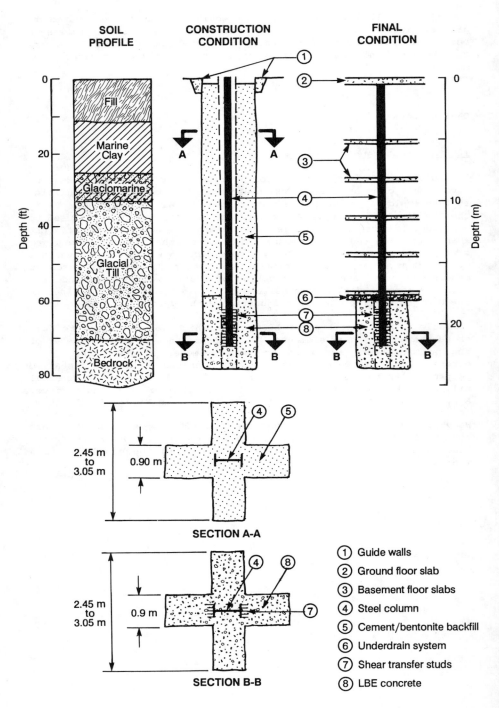

SOIL PROFILE

CONSTRUCTION CONDITION

FINAL CONDITION

SECTION A-A

2.45 m to 3.05 m

0.90 m

SECTION B-B

2.45 m to 3.05 m

0.9 m

① Guide walls
② Ground floor slab
③ Basement floor slabs
④ Steel column
⑤ Cement/bentonite backfill
⑥ Underdrain system
⑦ Shear transfer studs
⑧ LBE concrete

FIGURE 2 -- 125 Summer Street: LBE Section Details

TABLE 1 -- 125 Summer Street: Design Summary

Column loads	2,300 kN to 27,300 kN	
Recommended allowable designs values	Skin friction	Glacial till 170 kPa Bedrock 620 kPa
	End bearing	Glacial till 1,900 kPa Bedrock 2,850 kPa
LBE sizes	Cross	0.90 m x 2.45 m and 0.90 m x 3.05 m
	Linear	0.90 m x 2.45 m, 0.90 m x 3.05 m and 0.90 m x 6.50 m
Bearing strata	Glacial till	Very stiff (dense), gray clayey SILT, some to little fine SAND, some to little GRAVEL, trace coarse to medium SAND, trace CLAY (well bonded in-situ)
	Bedrock	Very soft to moderately hard, completely to moderately weathered, extremely to slightly fractured, gray APHANITIC ARGILLITE, joints close, open to tight, smooth to rough, planar to irregular with occasional clay seams

1 m = 3.28 ft   1 kN = 0.22 kips   1 kPa = 0.021 kips/ft^2

The LBEs were designed to support the entire column load by a combination of end-bearing and side friction. Based on the assumed natural load distribution of the element which would occur in the field and the characteristics of the soil and rock bearing material, it was determined that LBEs should be designed with approximately 65% of the load supported by side friction with the remaining 35% supported by end-bearing. Rock core borings indicated that the rock was extremely to moderately fractured and contained zones of completely weathered rock. A greater portion of the load was designed to be supported by side friction to offset the potential for excessive settlement due to inadequate bottom clean-up and the potential for encountering weathered rock at the bearing elevation. It was also reasoned that units designed with approximately the same ratio between side friction and end-bearing would exhibit similar strain characteristics thereby reducing differential settlement between columns.

Static load tests were performed on smaller circular augered units to confirm design values for side friction in the glacial till and the rock. The values selected for design are given in Table 1.

As installed column alignment was generally within 0.2 cm of the proposal location. The maximum out of location at the lowest level floor was 1.2 cm. Settlement of columns were measured during steel erection. The settlement of LBE units were less than one centimeter under about 80% of design load.

Post Office Square Garage

The Post Office Square Garage Project is located in downtown Boston and extends seven levels below grade for parking, with no above-grade structure. A public park was constructed above the roof slab at ground level, covering the approximately 6,700 m² site. The project was built using the up/down construction method and included the installation of 101 LBEs excavated from 24 to 29 m below ground surface (Figure 3). Site demolition began in October 1988; garage construction was completed in August 1990.

Selection of LBEs for foundation support did not occur until during the construction phase of the project. Initially, caissons installed "in-the-dry" were specified for foundation support. However, since several column locations were in close proximity to the slurry wall, there was concern for potential disturbance or loss-of-ground associated with conventional caisson installations which could result in unacceptable wall movements. Inasmuch as the equipment necessary to install the LBEs was already mobilized, and production rates for the walls were better than expected, this type was favored. In addition, flow of construction equipment within the site was harmonized by the presence of one foundation subcontractor.

TABLE 2 -- Post Office Square Garage: Design Summary

Column loads	6,200 kN to 13,800 kN		
Recommended allowable designs values	Skin friction	Glacial till Bedrock	190 kPa 190 kPa Upper 4.5 m 290 kPa Lower 4.5 m
	End bearing	Glacial till Bedrock	765 kPa 1,435 kPa
LBE sizes	Linear	0.90 m x 3.05 m and 0.90 m x 3.95 m	
Bearing strata	Glacial till	Hard gray clayey to gravely SILT to a very dense gray-brown silty coarse to fine SAND, "N" values ranged from 40 to 200+	
	Bedrock	Fine grained ARGILLITE and coarse to fine grained SANDSTONE. Weathering varied from complete to slight. Recoveries ranged from 0 to 100%. RQD values ranged from 0 to 35%. Split spoon samples were able to be recovered in several borings.	

1 m = 3.28 ft   1 kN = 0.22 kips   1 kPa = 0.021 kips/ft²

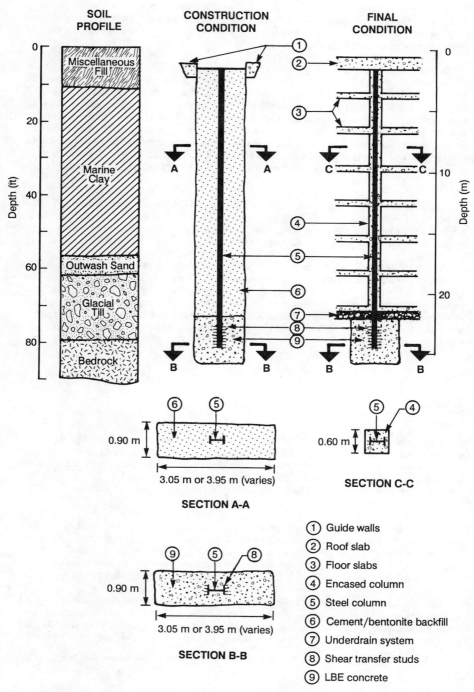

FIGURE 3 -- Post Office Square Garage: LBE Section Details

The recommended allowable design values presented in Table 2 were selected based on both the results of pressuremeter testing conducted during site exploration phases and presumptive stresses from local experience and load tests results.

A cement/bentonite slurry mixture consisting of 10 bags of Portland Type II cement (427 N per bag) to 3 m³ of bentonite slurry was used to backfill the LBE trench at the project. The "cement/water" ratio of the backfill ranged from approximately 0.10 to 0.20. The objective of the material was to create an impervious backfill of low strength which could readily be excavated away from the steel columns during subsequent excavation. In addition, the impervious backfill would minimize any upward groundwater seepage along the columns which could accumulate at the subgrade surface causing difficulties in excavation production.

Laboratory and in-situ field strength tests performed on the backfill indicated undrained shear strength generally ranging from approximately 4.7 to 23.8 kPa. No significant trend in strength with depth was observed from the test results.

During subsequent stages of construction, wall movements were closely monitored with inclinometers. At certain locations where the LBEs were located 3.5 m from the wall, and oriented parallel to it, greater inward wall movements of 20 to 25 percent were observed as compared to other areas. It is generally concluded that the use of a stiffer backfill material would have been more effective in controlling wall movements.

SUMMARY

The design of LBEs is generally similar to conventional drilled shaft design techniques. Laboratory and in-situ testing results are used to modify or confirm presumptive design parameters typically used in the Boston area. Considerable judgement is required in anticipating the influence of installation details on the selection of design parameters.

Installation of LBEs can generally be conducted with standard slurry wall equipment. Particular attention is required during construction to maintain proper trench alignment and insure thorough bottom cleaning. When the "up-down" construction method is used, specialized techniques are required for column installation and backfilling.

Use of LBEs are most effective in instances where deep dewatering is not practical or unstable soils exist. Due to improved coordination, scheduling and lower mobilization costs, LBEs are often selected as the preferred foundation type on projects which also require slurry wall construction.

The two case studies which are presented illustrate how LBE foundations were effectively utilized for "up-down" construction projects in Boston.

REFERENCES

ADSC, 1989, The Joint Caisson/Drilled Shaft Committee of the International Association of Foundation Drilling and the DFI, Deep Foundation Institute "Drilled Shaft Inspector's Manual," First Edition.

Briaud, J.L., Tucker, L., Olsen, R., August 1985, _Pressuremeter And Foundation Design_, Vol. I., Notes from Short Course, Texas A&M University.

Briaud, J.L., December 1987, _The Pressuremeter_, Notes from Short Course, Texas A&M University.

Davidson, R., 1987, "Foundation Innovations Cut Costs," _Civil Engineering_, pp. 54-56.

Holden, J.C., 1984, "Construction of Bored Piles in Weathered Rocks," Technical Report No. 69, Road Construction Authority of Victoria.

ICOS Corporation of America - Boston Office, 1991, Mr. Nino Catalano, Personnel Communication.

Johnson, E.G., Johnson, K.E., Spring 1990, "Foundation Piers," Notes from M.I.T. Geo-Construction Course, Session No. 5.

Kienberger, H., 1975, "Diaphragm Walls as Load Bearing Foundations," _Proceedings_, Conference on Diaphragm Walls and Anchorages, Institution of Civil Engineers, Paper 3, London, U.K., pp. 19-21.

Osterberg, J.O., and Gill, S.A., 1973, "Load Transfer Mechanism for Piers Socketed in Hard Soils or Rock," _Proceedings of the 9th Canadian Symposium on Rock Mechanics_, Montreal, Quebec.

Pells, P.J.N., and Turner, R.N., August 1979, "Elastic Solutions for the Design and Analysis of Rock-Socketed Piles," _Canadian Geotechnical Journal_, Vol. 16, No. 3.

Ramasuamy, F. and Pertusier, E.M., 1984, "Construction of Barrettes for High-Rise Foundations," International Conference on Tall Buildings, Singapore, pp. 455-462.

Reese, L.C., Tucker, K.L., 1985, "Bentonite Slurry in Constructing Drilled Piers," _Drilled Piers and Caissons II_, Proceedings of Geotechnical Engineering Division of ASCE, ASCE Convention, Denver, Colorado.

Tamaro, G.J., November 1987, "Load Bearing Elements Constructed Using Bentonite Slurry Techniques," <u>Foundation Problems in the New York/Metropolitan Area</u>, ASCE Seminar, New York, New York.

Xanthakos, P.P., 1979 <u>Slurry Walls</u>, McGraw-Hill, New York.

Roy A. Bell and John L. Sisley   [1]

QUALITY CONTROL OF SLURRY CUTOFF WALL INSTALLATIONS

REFERENCE: Bell, R.A. and Sisley, J.L., "Quality Control of Slurry Cutoff Wall Installations," Slurry Walls: Design, Construction and Quality Control, ASTM STP 1129, David B. Paul, Richard R. Davidson, and Nicholas J. Cavalli, Eds., American Society for Testing and Materials, Philadelphia, 1992.

ABSTRACT: A predominantly sandy levee embankment along an 18 km portion of the Sacramento River had a history of heavy seepage during river flood stages. A seepage cutoff wall keyed into clayey layers in the foundation soils was chosen by the U.S. Army Corps of Engineers to remedy the seepage problems. A test cutoff program utilizing 4 different methods (backhoe, trencher, mix-in-place and vibrated beam) of installing a cement-bentonite cutoff wall was undertaken as a performance type of contract to evaluate the methods and results of installing cutoffs with specified minimum width, depth, strength, and maximum hydraulic conductivity. This was followed by a Phase I contract to install 3.2 km of cutoff wall (27,870 m^2) with essentially the same performance type specification as used in the test program. The quality control programs involved sampling and molding specimens of cutoff wall materials and sampling of the hardened materials with drilled borings, in situ packer permeability testing, and numerous sampling methods. Test results raised questions of the representativeness and degrees of disturbance caused by the various sampling and testing methods and they indicated the cutoff walls did not always meet the required minimum unconfined compressive strength of 103 kPa or the maximum hydraulic conductivity of 1×10^{-6} cm/sec. The paper presents the test results and discusses the quality control methods, procedures and problems encountered in both the test program and Phase I contract.

KEYWORDS: Slurry walls, quality control, testing, inspection, mix-in-place, vibrated beam, trencher, backhoe, slurry strength, slurry hydraulic conductivity.

This paper is based on experiences in planning and carrying out quality control (Q.C.) inspection and testing on seepage cutoff wall installations in a predominantly sandy levee along the Sacramento River, Sacramento, California (Fig. 1). The Q.C. programs were on two U.S. Army Corps of Engineers (C.O.E.) projects; a test installation, and an approximately 3.2 km long seepage cutoff wall.

The fact that the cutoff walls were always hidden from view, even during installation, and their effectiveness can only be proven during a major flood, which may not occur until years after installation, makes the Q.C. program and Q.C. record the primary means of evaluating how well the installations fulfilled the design requirements. The Q.C. test results from parts of these projects indicated the cutoff wall material may not have always met the design requirements. This lead to questions about the representativeness, of sampling and testing procedures and the uniformity of slurry batches, and those questions lead to other questions concerning the precision of batching and slurry metering equipment, and what different properties the cutoff materials have when mixed and cured in the cutoff wall compared to laboratory mixes.

[1]   Mr. Bell is a principal geotechnical engineer at Roger Foott Associates, Inc., 530 Howard Street, 4th Floor, San Francisco, CA 94105; Mr. Sisley is a civil engineer at the U.S. Army Corps of Engineers, Sacramento District, Valley Resident Office, 2021 Jefferson Blvd., West Sacramento, CA 95691

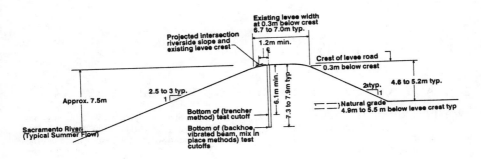

Fig. 1 -- Test cutoff wall installation typical levee cross -section

In the following text the four trial cutoff wall installations are described and the results of the Q.C. tests are presented. The paper concludes with a list of Q.C. requirements considered by the authors to be appropriate for the types of installations described.

Four methods of cutoff wall installations were selected for trial application. The first was a conventional backhoe trench, excavated using a slurry backfill to support the excavation and capable of hardening into a suitably strong and impermeable wall. The second method was the use of vertical mix-in-place equipment, whereby the slurry was mixed into natural soil to form a low permeability material. The third method was based on land drain installation technology whereby a trenching machine was modified to work with a slurry backfill and install the wall using a continuous excavation/backfill process. The fourth method was the use of a vibrated beam, in which a wide flange beam section was vibrated into the ground and slurry was injected as the beam was withdrawn, leaving the cutoff wall in place. In all cases the cutoff was achieved by introducing a low permeability cement bentonite slurry into the ground, forming a relatively impermeable barrier down through the sandy levee and connected into the less permeable underlying strata.

The trial installation called for construction of discrete 76 m lengths of cutoff using each installation technique. All the cutoffs penetrated 7.6 m below the levee crest, except for the trencher method which penetrated 6.1 m below the crest of the levee. In the 3.2 km long cutoff project, penetration varied from 6.9 m to 9.1 m and all other features were essentially the same as subsequently described for the mix-in-place trial installation.

The trial program was performed within a 800 m long segment of levee. The slurry plant used for all trial cutoff installations was located from about 150 m to 640 m away from the cutoff installations. In the 3.2 km long project the slurry plant was moved from time to time to be within 1000 m of cutoff installation.

During each cutoff installation, samples of the cutoff wall materials were obtained from between 3 m and 6 m below the top of levee. Specimens were cast from these samples, cured in a moist environment for various periods of time and then tested to evaluate the unconfined compressive strength and permeability of the trial cutoff walls within 28 days after cutoff installation. Undisturbed Shelby tube or NX core samples obtained from depths of 3 to 4.6 m were tested in unconfined compression for strength and in triaxial apparatus for permeability. The boreholes were also used to conduct in-situ packer permeability tests within the bottom 1 to 1.5 m of each hole. Vertical guidepipes installed in each cutoff prior to setup of the cutoff materials were used to center the borings in the cutoff wall. Similar boring and testing was also performed in the 3.2 km long project.

BACKHOE INSTALLATION

The backhoe trench was excavated with a Caterpillar 235 backhoe fitted with a 0.6 m wide bucket which cut a trench about 0.76 m wide. The excavated materials were placed directly into 90 kN, 2 axle dump trucks located directly behind the backhoe, and hauled to the spoil area. During excavation the trench was kept filled to within 0.6 m of the working platform with cement-bentonite slurry composed of 19% type II Portland cement and 6% Wyoming bentonite by weight of water, giving a slurry density of 11.3 kN/m^3.

At the beginning of trench excavation, problems were encountered in delivery of slurry from the mixing plant to the cutoff trench, a distance of about 640 m. The slurry delivery system required 1 to 2 hours to get into operation each morning and a similar amount of time to flush and clean out at the end of the day. It appeared that the flushing processes caused significant dilution of slurry in the cutoff wall. Probably as a result, the initial backhoe cutoff did not meet the specified minimum 14 day, 103 kPa unconfined compressive strength.

Upon completion of the other test cutoff installations the initial backhoe wall was removed and replaced with another cement bentonite wall using essentially the same installation methods and procedures, but with better control of slurry placement and a somewhat faster rate of slurry delivery.

MIX-IN-PLACE INSTALLATION

The mix-in-place cutoff wall was installed with the GeoCon deep soil mixing (DSM) machine. The machine consists of 4 intertwining hollow stem augers 0.91 m in diameter with their stems 0.69 m on centers, and is capable of reaching more than 30 m. The augers along with their hydraulic power unit were mounted on a Manitowoc 4100 crane with tracks that covered the entire width of the top of levee. The mix-in-place installation also used a Cat 235 backhoe to dig a starter trench and reservoir, build slurry contaminant berms along the sides of the top of levee, and remove excess soil slurry mix and pile it over the top of the previously completed installation.

The installation procedure consisted of pumping a predetermined amount of slurry through the hollow stem augers as they were rotated and penetrated into the ground. Upon reaching design depth the augers and mixing paddles on the drill shafts were rotated for a few minutes until the soil and slurry were uniformly and thoroughly mixed. The augers were then withdrawn. The crane was then moved along the levee until the trailing end auger was aligned with the completed hole from the leading end auger of the previous insertion. The procedure was then repeated. For each insertion of the augers, the trial cutoff was thus advanced 2 m, equivalent to about 15.2 m^2 of 7.6 m deep cutoff wall face and about 12.9 m^3 of soil slurry mixture. Time from one insertion to the next varied from 10 to 35 min, with most between 15 and 20 min.

The initial portion of DSM wall was installed using the same cement-bentonite slurry mixture as used in the backhoe cutoff. The last 10.4 to 10.7 m used a recently developed product consisting of 40% type II Portland cement, 40% slag, 20% gypsum (A patented mixture called the Chiyoda Thoroughbred Gypsum Method, CTG).

The test results from the trial installation indicated the soil/cement-bentonite slurry mix was capable of meeting and exceeding strength and permeability requirements while the soil/CTG slurry mix greatly exceeded both requirements. On the 3.2 km project, which used a cement-bentonite slurry, problems in meeting the specified properties were not resolved at the time of preparing this paper and therefore specific results are not presented. The fact that problems occurred has helped illustrate the importance of a well run Q.C. program and helped to identify some important Q.C. features recommended in this paper.

TRENCHER

Trenching machines are specially built for installing flexible pipe and granular backfill for subdrains. The test installation machine was modified for the cutoff installation by sealing off the pipe and gravel chute and attaching rubber belting along its trailing edge to form a shield between the cutting teeth and the slurry filled trench. The cutting teeth were set at a width of 0.41 m, which resulted in a trench width of about 0.46 m. With the boom in the vertical position, the maximum depth of trench below the working platform was 5.8 m. Slurry was placed at least 0.3 m above the working platform between spoil piles which formed on both sides of the trench.

The same cement-bentonite slurry mix as used in the backhoe and mix-in-place cutoffs was used to fill the trench behind the trenching machine. In an attempt to accommodate a faster digging rate, the slurry plant was operated in the continuous mode rather than the batch mode used during the other methods. With the continuous slurry plant and the narrower and shallower trench, the plant appeared capable of keeping up with the machine, although quality control testing of the slurry was less accurate. The trencher trial cutoff was finished before a smooth continuous operation was established.

VIBRATED BEAM

The vibrated beam method was performed with a 0.76 m web and 0.27 m wideflange beam, fitted with grout pipes and a built up width of 0.15 to 0.18 m near the tip. The beam was vibrated into the levee, initially with a MKT-V14 vibrator, but a MKT-V16 was used for most of the installation. The vibrated beam equipment was mounted on the same Manitowoc 4100 previously used for the DSM method. Most of the insertions overlapped the previous insertions by about 0.15 to 0.25 m. A reservoir trench and berms were constructed with the Cat 235 backhoe prior to beam installation. A cement-bentonite slurry consisting of 6% bentonite and 25% type II Portland cement by weight of water resulting in a 11.8 kN/m^3 mix was used for the vibrated beam cutoff wall. Difficulty was experienced in forming a 0.15 m wide slot without caving or squeezing in the previously installed slot below depths of 4.6 to 6.1 m.

During the installation of the vibrated beam cutoff the time to penetrate/withdraw the beam and the quantity of grout pumped was recorded. Total quantities of materials used were also reported. The theoretical volume of the cutoff wall was 1.16 m^3/m of wall, plus penetration of slurry into the soils adjacent to the wall. The average volume of slurry pumped was about 1.9 m^3/m of wall, although a large portion of the slurry was lost in the reservoir trench and spoil pile, in addition to wall penetration.

SLURRY EVALUATION

The specifications required the cutoff wall material to have a permeability no greater than 1x10^{-6} cm/sec for cutoffs at least 0.3 m wide and 5x10^{-7} cm/sec for the minimum 0.15 m wide vibrated beam wall. In the test program, a minimum unconfined compressive strength of 103 kPa was required to provide a material at least as strong as the insitu levee and foundation soils and thus avoid weakening the levee. In the trial program the cutoff material was required to achieve this minimum strength within 14 days. A maximum compressive strength of 1.03 MPa was used in the trial program to avoid excessively expensive materials that would not be economical in a larger installation.

The design slurry mixes selected by the Contractor and used in the trial installations were as follows:

Backhoe
Initial: 19% cement, 6% bentonite by weight of water, design density 11.3 kN/m^3.

Reconstructed: 25% cement, 6% bentonite by weight of water, design density 11.8 kN/m^3.
Mix-in-Place
Cement-bentonite*: same as initial backhoe with target volume equal to 50% of the neat volume of cutoff wall.

CTG: 20% gypsum, 40% slag, 40% cement, 80% water by weight of total solids. Target 15% CTG solids by weight of saturated soils within neat in-situ volume of cutoff wall.
Trencher: Same as initial backhoe.*

Vibrated beam: Same as reconstructed backhoe.*
*Indicates some fluidifier (Chrome Free Desco) was added.
The trial program slurry plant consisted of two 3.8 kL high speed mixing tanks, one for mixing bentonite/slag-gypsum with water, the other to mix cement into the mixture from the first mixing tank; two 75 kL holding tanks for bentonite-water slurry; a 580 kN cement silo; water supply pumped from river; pelletized bentonite in 0.45 kN bags, gypsum in 0.45 kN bags, slag in 17.8 kN bags; pumps, valves, and

flow meters. Q.C. testing and monitoring included checking the material quantity usage, the slurry density and viscosity. Plastic pipe of 0.15 m diameter was used to transport slurry from plant to cutoff wall. A third 3.8 kL high speed mixer was used along the 0.15 m distribution pipeline.

The bentonite-water slurry was initially mixed at 6% bentonite by weight of water giving a slurry density of 10 kN/m^3 and a marsh funnel of 38 s. The 19% cement mixture is equivalent to 0.544 kN bentonite, 1.72 kN cement and 9.05 kN water per m^3 of slurry. The 25% cement mixture is equivalent to 0.534 kN bentonite 2.25 kN cement and 9.01 kN water per m^3 of slurry.

In the CTG slurry mix, the first step combined 2 parts slag to 1 part gypsum by weight with water for a slurry density of 11.94 kN/m^3 to which another 2 parts of cement were added for a slurry density of 13.83 kN/m^3. This is equivalent to 1.54 kN gypsum, 3.08 kN slag, 3.08 kN cement and 6.13 kN water per m^3 of slurry.

The backhoe method mixes some soil with the slurry during the digging process. No special effort was made to introduce soil into the slurry, but it occurs as the bucket is sloshed in the trench and as slurry drains from the bucket prior to being placed in the dump trucks. Quality control is primarily at the slurry plant and by sampling the backfill mixture beyond the zone of agitation by the backhoe. Laboratory test results, summarized in Figure 2, show wall densities in the initial backhoe trench from

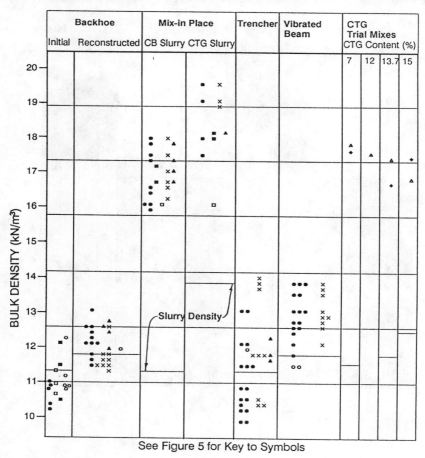

See Figure 5 for Key to Symbols

Fig. 2 -- Cutoff wall density test results

10.53 to 12.26 kN/m^3 with many results lower than the design slurry density of 11.32 kN/m^3. The loss in density is believed to have resulted from dilution by wash water. In the reconstructed backhoe wall the densities were from 11.32 to 13.04, with average core sample density about 11.9 kN/m^3.

The higher densities were a result of the increased percentage of cement, the result of some loss of water by bleeding into the soils at the sides of the trench, and the inclusion of some soil particles. Soil water may also combine with the mix. Some of the water in the mix combines chemically with the cement, perhaps up to 20% by weight of cement when fully hardened. For these reasons the composition of the materials in the backhoe cutoff wall is somewhat different to the mix at the slurry plant. With the exception of the dilution problems, the other factors would be expected to improve strength and reduce permeability. Similar changes in composition occur in the other methods as described below. The estimated composition of each mix is given in Figure 3.

The composition of the soil slurry mixture in the mix-in-place method was estimated by assuming the volume of affected in-situ soil was combined with the target of 50% by volume of slurry. The resulting composition is a function of insitu soil density, amount of spoil and final density of the soil slurry mixture. The computed composition roughly checks with the total quantities of materials used, the amount of spoil, and estimates of overbreak/penetration into the soil formation. Quality control measurements should, at a minimum, include slurry quantities used per volume of soil penetrated for

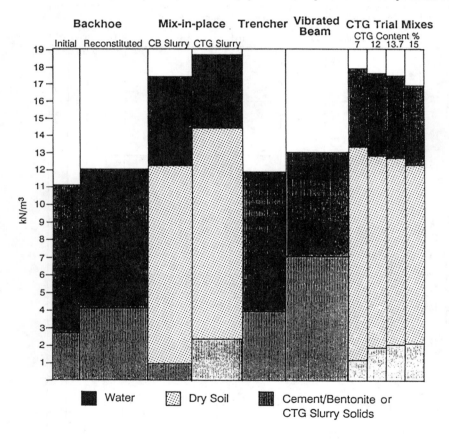

Fig 3. -- Average composition of hardened cutoff wall

each penetration of the augers, times during penetration, mixing and withdrawal. The uniformity and thoroughness of mixing is primarily a function of the operator's skills and care. With constant flow to the augers, constant rates of rotation and penetration, a subjective appraisal of uniformity is possible.

The trencher method allowed practically no mixing of soil with slurry in the cutoff wall. Considerable amounts of slurry were mixed with the cuttings, but most ended up in the spoil pile rather than in the wall. The quantities of materials used indicated the probability that a large amount of slurry penetrated the trench walls; a significant amount was mixed with soil and become spoil, and further amounts of excess slurry were placed along the top of cutoff wall and later removed during reconstruction of the levee roadway.

Quality control testing and monitoring was essentially the same as for the backhoe method.

In the vibrated beam method, very little soil gets mixed with the slurry. Depressions that formed within a few hours after placement in the top of the slurry filled slot indicated some slurry or bleed water soaked into the sides of the trench. This was also readily apparent in the trencher method wall. Considerable additional amounts of slurry were wasted in the trial because the pumping rates greatly exceeded the rate of wall formation. Quality control monitoring, in addition to slurry sampling and testing involved probing the slot for conformance to minimum wall width.

Strength and permeability test results are summarized in Figures 4 and 5. They show a wide scatter of results, with some tests on each of the cement-bentonite installations not meeting the specified requirements. With the exception of the initial backhoe installation, most of the cement bentonite strength test results are well above the minimum requirements. Less than half of the cement-bentonite permeability test results met the project specification. The fact that the backhoe and mix-in-place walls are wider than specified would indicate the overall effectiveness of these cutoffs should be about the same as the specified 0.3 m wide wall. All of the low strength and two of the highest permeability test results from the trencher installation were located at the end of an experimental segment at the beginning of the test section. By excluding these tests and allowing for the wider than minimum cutoff walls, the remainder of test results indicate the trencher cutoff wall comes very close to being equivalent to the specified seepage barrier.

All of the strength and permeability tests on the CTG mixes met minimum requirements, but most exceeded the specified maximum strength, indicating that a mix with a smaller percentage of CTG materials would have been more appropriate. Both the cement-bentonite slurry and CTG slurry when mixed with soil produced equal or superior strength and somewhat lower permeability than the similar cement-bentonite slurry mixes without soil.

Because of the highly superior strength and impermeability developed by the CTG mix, a laboratory experimental program was performed to explore the potential for use of thinner slurry mixes and smaller amounts of CTG ingredients. Even the lowest amount tested (7% CTG by saturated in-situ soil density) exceeded the project specifications, indicating a more economical mix should be possible with CTG slurry than with cement-bentonite slurry.

RECOMMENDATIONS FOR QUALITY CONTROL OF CUTOFF WALL INSTALLATIONS

In preparing the Q.C. inspection and testing requirements for a seepage cutoff wall performance contract the designer should bear in mind that the effectiveness and cost of a cutoff wall will be the combined result of factors related to both wall installation details and the slurry used in the construction.

The first step in developing cutoff wall performance specifications is to establish the depth and "effective impermeability" required for the cutoff. Both these factors depend on what the cutoff is intended to achieve in terms of limiting seepage flows and/or controlling seepage pressures. They require that the design establish these requirements and then determine the depth of penetration and effective impermeability required to achieve them.

The strength requirements of the cutoff material must also be defined by the debility requirements. Consideration of the slow strength gain properties of some slurries will probably be important to site safety, including the potential for loss of slurry through holes, cracks, or buried pipes, and the ability to rebuild a trafficable crest roadway.

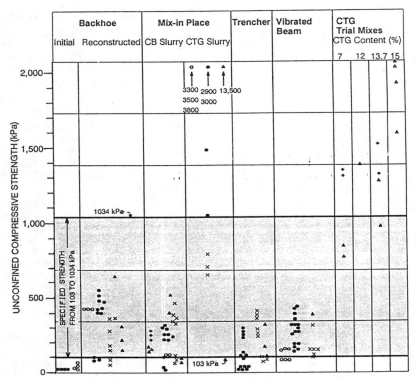

See Figure 5 for Key to Symbols

**Fig. 4 -- Cutoff wall unconfined compressive strength
test results**

The contractor should have an incentive to economize the slurry mix, and it may be necessary to allow sufficient time in the contract for trial mixes to be developed. A carefully developed laboratory mix design should be proven with regard to strength and permeability requirements by means of sampling and testing of field installations. It is recommended these proof tests be conducted during the initial portion of installation and thereafter whenever there are changes in the mix design.

To adequately perform the Q.C. functions requires the Q.C. engineer to have a thorough understanding of the construction methods, slurry mix formulations, and measurement devices. The engineer needs to know the work plan and schedule in order to be at the right place at the right time. The engineer should have a good understanding of sampling and testing procedures, and must thoroughly understand the technical requirements of the contract.

The following list and comments are offered as a guide of the Q.C. portions of technical specification for cutoff wall projects.

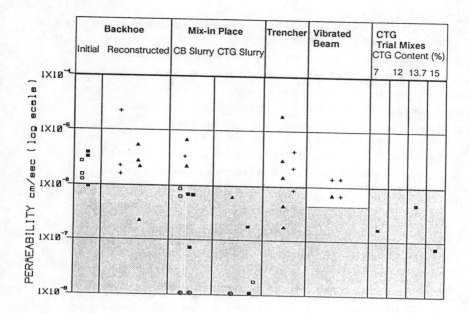

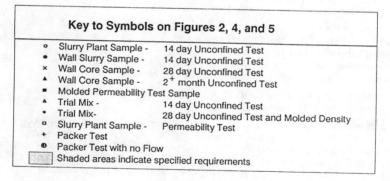

Fig. 5 -- Cutoff wall permeability test results

Q.C. of Slurry Mix

1. Check the calibration of all measuring devices.

2. Measure and record quantities of each ingredient as metered by the batch plant.

3. Compare batch measurement totals with material inventory usage. Record comparisons each shift or more frequently. Investigate disparities.

4. Measure and record specific gravity of each slurry mix component.

5. Measure and record viscosity/slump as appropriate.

6. Document observations and comments on sequence of combining ingredients and thoroughness of mixing. Record times when changes are observed.

Q.C. During Slurry Placement

1. Record time elapsed between batching and placement in wall, rate of slurry delivery and indicate location (station) in wall where batches are placed.

2. Measure and record depth, width, and wall continuity at frequent intervals.

3. Measure and record depth to top of backfill at time of placement and after set up.

4. Document observations and comments on caving, squeezing or other ground movements.

5. Obtain samples of slurry backfill prior to setup from mid to lower portions of wall.

6. Mold slurry samples for laboratory testing. Avoid excessive mixing. For slurries that shrink or bleed, molds should be more than 2 diameters long.

7. Store and transport samples to avoid vibration and exposure to excessive heat or cold.

8. Install guide casings for subsequent drilling and sampling in deep or narrow walls.

Q.C. During and After Setup/Hardening

1. Visually inspect backfilled trench for indications of variability, cracking, excessive drying, contamination, dilution, bleeding, subsidence, disturbance etc., until material has hardened and cover is in place.

2. Observe installation of construction joints at shift start-up and after delays during installation.

3. Drill and sample cutoff materials for visual inspection and laboratory testing. Use drilling and sampling methods compatible with wall strength and sensitivity to minimize sample disturbance.

Note: By specifying in detail the drilling, sampling and testing methods, controversy as to the representativeness of results can be minimized because the minimum acceptable results apply only to those obtained by the specified methods. The methods used can also be improper or controversial, particularly in weak or fragile materials. Therefore all details of drilling, sampling, sample handling, transport and storage must be carefully evaluated in the Q.C. program, particularly when results indicate marginal or inadequate strength or hydraulic conductivity.

4. Packer tests performed on the trial cutoff walls were not completely successful. In narrow walls and in weak materials their results are questionable.

Q.C. During Laboratory Testing

1. Moisture content and dry density results from molded and core samples are useful in evaluating wall uniformity and changes that occur in the mix after batching.

2. Unconfined compressive strength tests were considered appropriate for evaluating wall strengths on the C.O.E. projects.

3. The measurement of hydraulic conductivity of nearly impermeable materials requires quality apparatus, skillful care in sample preparation, testing, recording and presenting results. ASTM test method D5084 for measurement of hydraulic conductivity of saturated porous materials using a flexible wall permeameter was being balloted by Committee D18 at the time of these projects. Now that it has become a standard, it would provide an appropriate test for the types of cutoff materials used in the projects described in this paper.

Q.C. of Other Aspects

Besides inspection and testing of the cutoff wall installation and materials there are likely to be other Q.C. functions than the ones discussed in this paper. For example, on the C.O.E. projects, environmental and safety concerns were specified to be part of the Q.C. program. Obstructions, pipe and utility crossings, levee roadway restoration required Q.C. to assure the completed project satisfied the designer's intent.

Dale L. Roberts and Da-Min Ho

CONSTRUCTION OF DIAPHRAGM WALL AT WELLS DAM EAST EMBANKMENT

REFERENCE: Roberts, D. L., and Ho, D. M., "Construction of Diaphragm Wall at Wells Dam East Embankment," Slurry Walls: Design, Construction, and Quality Control, ASTM STP 1129, David B. Paul, Richard R. Davidson, and Nicholas J. Cavalli, Eds., American Society for Testing and Materials, Philadelphia, 1992.

ABSTRACT: A concrete diaphragm wall was constructed at the Wells Dam east embankment to cutoff seepage. Sinkholes were observed on the embankment crest in early 1990, more than 20 years after the construction of the embankment dam. After extensive investigations a diaphragm wall was adopted to positively cutoff seepage and to stop internal erosion.

The wall was excavated in vertical panels with clam shell bucket through the embankment core and riverbed deposits overlying bedrock to a maximum depth of 70 m (230 ft). A total of 11,600 sq m (125,000 sq ft) of diaphragm wall was constructed. The success of the wall was evaluated based on core drilling, water tests, piezometer data and geophysical survey after the construction.

This paper presents a brief description of the project and sinkhole investigations, with the main emphasis placed on the construction of the concrete diaphragm wall, including procedure, quality control and verification, and difficulties.

KEYWORDS: Embankment dam, sinkhole, internal erosion, concrete diaphragm wall, geophysical investigation.

Messrs. Roberts and Ho are Supervising Geologist and Senior Soils Engineer , respectively of Bechtel Corp., 50 Beale Street, San Francisco, Ca. 94119

INTRODUCTION

The Wells hydroelectric power station is located on the Columbia River near Azwell, Washington about 180 km (110 miles) east of Seattle and 180 km (110 miles) west of Spokane in Douglas County, Washington.

The Wells Project consists of the hydrocombine, east and west embankments, fish passages and propagation facilities. A project layout is shown on Fig. 1.   The embankments extend from the hydrocombine to the abutments. The east embankment which spans across the original river channel, is about 300 m (1000 ft) long, 50 m (160 ft) above riverbed and 70 m (230 ft) above the bedrock at the maximum section.   Extensive exploration at the embankment site indicated that the riverbed deposits were relatively impervious and a cutoff to the relatively deep bedrock would not be necessary.

Construction of the embankments began in the fall of 1963 and completed in January 1969.   The east embankment consists of a central core flanked with granular shells. A typical section of east embankment is shown on Fig. 2. The embankment dam was constructed on the dense riverbed deposits.   The core below Elev. 220 (723 in ft) was placed underwater with clamshell after the construction of the upstream and downstream turning dikes.   Conventional placement and compaction in dry conditions was used for the core above Elev. 220 (723 in ft) (Burke 1971).

Two small sinkholes were noticed in the dam in 1967 and in 1974.   At the time their significance was not cause for concern as it was thought their occurrence was due to consolidation of the underwater placed core.   After years of operation without incident, a new sinkhole was discovered on the crest of the east embankment in early 1990 when the road pavement over a sinkhole collapsed under the weight of a moving truck.

A comprehensive investigation program was carried out to investigate the extent and the cause of the sinkhole. As a result, a positive cutoff wall through the east embankment dam extending to bedrock was recommended and adopted by the Public Utility District No. 1 of Douglas County.   The construction of the diaphragm wall began July, 1990 and completed February, 1991.

INVESTIGATION

Extensive investigations were carried out soon after the sinkhole was discovered to investigate its extent and cause and to determine the most appropriate corrective measures for ensuring continued safety and functioning of the dam.

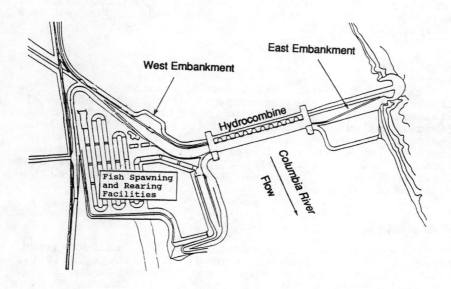

FIGURE 1
PROJECT LAYOUT

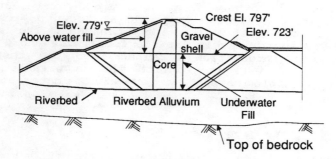

FIGURE 2
TYPICAL SECTION OF EAST EMBANKMENT

Investigations consisted of review and analysis of available data from construction records and performance monitoring, formulation of scenarios as to the cause of sinkhole, test pit excavation, geophysical surveys, and bathymetric inspection.

Data Review

Piezometer and settlement records since the construction of the embankment were reviewed. All piezometers in and below the downstream shell and its foundation indicated safe conditions. The data did not indicate unusual pattern of piezometer pressure distribution and/or unusual settlement conditions. Although one core piezometer closely followed the head water and another core piezometer closely followed the fluctuation of the tailwater.

Geophysical Surveys

The geophysical self-potential surveys included ground penetrating radar (NORCAL Geophysical Consultants 1990), self-potential, and electric resistivity (Corwin 1990). The self-potential (SP) and electric resistivity, which provided the most useful data, identified anomalous flow patterns. The SP data indicated the presence of a significant seepage concentration within the embankment between Sta. 52+00 and Sta. 54+00 and no deeper than Elev. 216 to 220 m (710 to 720 in ft). This concentration of flow was in the same area as the 1990 sinkhole.

Test Pits

To complement other investigations, several test pits were excavated in April — May 1990 at known or possible sinkholes on the crest of the east embankment. The largest sinkhole was approximately 3 m (10 feet) wide and 6 m (20 feet) deep. Information obtained from the test pit excavations appeared to confirm the occurrence of a classical sinkhole caused by removal of material from below.

Bathymetric Inspection

Bathymetric inspection of the reservoir bottom upstream included taking TV pictures of a depression by a remote operated vehicle and inspection by a hard hat diver (Williamson and Associates 1990).

Conclusion from Investigation

Other than the streaming potential survey (SP), the findings of other geophysical methods were non-conclusive in that no indications of other sinkholes or possible core or foundation material loss were found. The streaming potential survey did indicate the occurrence of seepage in the vicinity of the known sinkhole. The seepage passing through the embankment and/or its foundation in the area of sinkhole was cause for concern. Any loss of materials from the core was critical to the integrity of the embankment. A deep diaphragm cutoff wall was therefore adopted as the remedial measure.

Before construction of the cutoff wall, six exploratory slurry inflow test holes along the upstream crest at the locations of the proposed diaphragm wall were completed. Significant slurry loss occurred at several elevations in the inflow test hole nearest to the large sinkhole at Sta.52+40. Five pairs of piezometers, one in the wet placed fill and one in the in situ river alluvium immediately downstream of the core were also completed. In several nearby piezometers the water levels were higher than normal.

DIAPHRAGM WALL CONSTRUCTION

General

The construction of the diaphragm wall began July 1990 and was completed February 1991. The Contractor was Bencor-Petrifond Joint Venture of Houston, Texas. Bencor-Petrifond worked 10 hours a day for six days week initially; night shift for trench excavation was added later. Other work activities including concrete backfill was done on day-shift only. The contractor's work force consisted of 24 manual and 5 non-manual. Bechtel Corp., the Construction Manager, had a staff of four, which included a site construction manager, two geologists and one soils engineer.

Major construction equipment employed during construction included the following:

    Link Belt LS 218 crane (2) with clam shell buckets
    Link Belt cherry picker
    Manitowoc 4000 crane
    Komatsu excavator
    Dump trucks
    Compressors
    Bentonite slurry mixers
    Concrete batch plant
    Transit concrete mixers

Safety Concerns

The normal pool level at Elev. 238 (780 in ft) and full hydroelectric power production with head difference about 21 m (70 ft) were to be maintained throughout the wall construction. Several safety measures regarding the stability of the dam were stipulated in the specification: no more than 4 primary or secondary panels were allowed to be excavated simultaneously; the maximum length for primary or secondary panel was not to exceed 3.6 m (12 ft) unless approved; excavation of an adjacent panel was not allowed until its concrete strength reached at least 4800 kPa (700 psi). The slurry loss in the panel was monitored 24-hours a day throughout the construction.

Design Layout

The general layout of the diaphragm wall construction at Wells dam east embankment is shown on Fig. 3. The diaphragm wall is located near the upstream edge of the embankment to leave as much of the core as possible downstream of the wall (see detail in Fig. 3). Construction activities such as excavation, installation and removal of joint pipes, concrete placement, and carrying waste to the disposal area, etc. were carried out on the downstream side of the wall. Pipelines for bentonite slurry, air-lift, and water were laid along a small existing berm on the upstream side of the wall.

Two bentonite slurry holding ponds were located on the east abutment of the dam. One pond was for fresh mixed slurry and another for returned slurry from airlift desanding operation and slurry from the trench as it was displaced by the tremie concrete. The concrete batch plant was located west of the hydrocombine, about 0.8 km (one half mile) away from the construction site.

Sequence of Construction

Construction began with preparation of a 18 m (60 ft) wide work platform by removing 1.8 m (6 ft) from the embankment crest and the construction of a guide walls. The concrete guide walls were reinforced, built at grade and straddled the alignment of the wall. The guide walls serve several functions: 1) to control the alignment and grade of the trench; 2) to support the trench walls from heavy construction surcharge; and 3) to protect the sides from erosion and washout during the up and down operation of clam bucket and chisel.

Excavation of diaphragm wall panels began after the completion of the guide walls. Clam bucket excavation started with three test panels. The purpose of the test panels was to verify the method, equipment and execution of

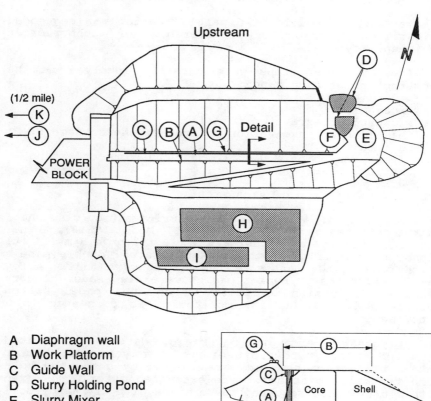

A Diaphragm wall
B Work Platform
C Guide Wall
D Slurry Holding Pond
E Slurry Mixer
F Desander
G Slurry/Airlift Pipelines
H Slurry & Waste Disposal Area
I Stockpile for Material Removed
   from Embankment Crest
J Batch Plant
K Mechanical Shop

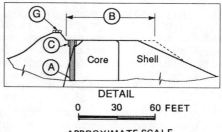

DETAIL

0   30   60 FEET

APPROXIMATE SCALE

FIGURE 3
DIAPHRAGM WALL CONSTRUCTION LAYOUT

diaphragm wall construction. All test panels were primary panels with joint pipes at both ends. The use of the joint pipe forms a concave vertical panel joint to ensure the continuity of the paneled wall to full depth. The primary panel was followed by secondary adjacent panel with a joint pipe at only one end. The panel location was sequenced primarily to minimize interference of construction equipment movement.

The following steps were normally involved in the construction of each panel:

o Excavation
o Disposal of excavated materials
o Chiseling and excavation to prepare the surface of bedrock
o Slurry desanding and bottom cleanup for concreting
o Concrete placement

A brief description of each step follows:

Excavation. Excavation was carried out by clam shell bucket operated by a crane (LINKBELT, Model LS218). Panel length initially was either 3.6 m (12 ft) or 4.3 m (14 ft) depend on the width of the bucket. Later, double panels which require two passes of the bucket were made. A few panels wider than 2 bucket passes were also made. A more detailed discussion of panel excavation, panel bottom verification, and quality monitoring is presented in a later section.

Disposal of excavated materials. Materials excavated from the trench were first dropped from the clam bucket into a collection-box, and transferred by a backhoe to a dump truck for disposal. The excavated materials, mixed with slurry, were required to be mixed with dry sandy soil obtained from the east river bank to improve stability as they were stockpiled in the permanent disposal area.

Chiseling. Heavy chiseling was required to break the boulders and to loosen the dense soil deposits encountered in riverbed during excavation. Chiseling was also used to prepare the bottom of the panel for concreting when bedrock was encountered. Although the chiseling was essential to the completion of the trench excavation, its effectiveness was found to be quite limited in breaking the sound, hard fresh granitic bedrock and in loosening the dense sandy and silty alluvial deposits. Fortunately extensive chiseling was not required.

Preparation for concreting.   Preparation for
concreting began after the final depth of excavation was
approved.   The preparation included lowering of joint
pipe(s) at the end(s) of the panel, airlifting to remove
loose debris, installation of tremie pipes, checking slurry
in the panel for its density and sand content.

Concrete placement.   Ingredients for concrete were
batched in the batch plant, then transported and mixed in
the transit trucks.   Each truck normally carried 5.4 cu m
(7 cu yds) of concrete.   Concrete was placed by tremie
method.   As the concrete was placed, the displaced slurry
was pumped out and discharged to the slurry holding pond on
the east bank.   During the placement of concrete, the level
of the concrete was periodically checked by sounding and
the bottom of the tremie pipe was generally buried in 3 to
6 m (10 to 20 ft) of concrete.

Lifting of the joint pipe(s) began 4 to 5 hours after
the placement of concrete and the concrete had somewhat
hardened in the initial set but before a strong bond
between the concrete and the pipe developed.

Quality Control

Trench quality such as verticality, continuity, and
width were monitored during excavation.   Width was
controlled by the pre-constructed guide wall.   Continuity
of the panel wall was achieved by using joint pipe between
panels.   Verticality of the panel was normally well within
the tolerance of one percent of wall depth.   On a few
occasions, when the wall appeared to be out of plumb, a
special triming tool was used to correct the plumbness.
For all panels excavated, most of the panels deviated less
than 0.5 percent, the maximum deviation was 0.79 percent.

Materials

Materials involved in the diaphragm wall construction
included concrete, bentonite slurry and soils.   Concrete
was used to backfill the trench, slurry was used to
maintain the stability of the excavated panels, and soils
were removed during excavation.   These materials are
briefly discussed in this section.

Concrete.   After trials with several different
concrete mixes, most of the diaphragm wall was constructed
as an unreinforced concrete wall with 28-day compressive
strength of about 14,000 kPa (2000 psi).

The concrete mix was designed to have high workability
so that the fresh concrete fed through the tremie pipes
would flow readily into the concrete already placed and
forced the previously placed concrete upward.   The slump

was measured in the range from 20 to 24 cm (8 to 9.5 inches) with a water-cement ratio between 0.52 to 0.55. The ratio of coarse aggregate to fine aggregate averaged 51 to 49. The combined gradations of the coarse and the fine aggregate resulted a well-graded and self-filtering material. Type II cement was used and flyash was used as pozzolanic material. The admixtures used included air-entrainment and water reducing agent.

Concrete was batched in the batch plant, then mixed and transported to the construction site by transit-mix trucks. The concrete was placed in the panel by the tremie method.

Quality control testing for the concrete included field tests such as slump, air content, temperature and unit weight for fresh concrete, and laboratory compressive tests of concrete cylinders for hardened concrete.

<u>Bentonite Slurry</u>. Bentonite slurry used during the wall construction was mixed with 180 to 230 kg (400 to 500 lbs) of powdered bentonite in 1.9 cu m (500 gallons) of water. The slurry was stored in the slurry holding pond, located on the east abutment. The quality of the freshly mixed slurry was monitored daily. Testing for quality included viscosity with Marsh Funnel, viscosimeter, density and pH. Occasionally, additional tests such as apparent viscosity, plastic viscosity and gel strength were performed. The wall construction contractor was responsible for maintaining the quality of the bentonite slurry.

The quality of the bentonite slurry in the trench, such as density, sand content and pH value, were monitored within two hours prior to the beginning of concrete placement to ensure that the slurry in the trench would be successfully displaced by tremie concrete. The density was generally in the range of 1120 to 1200 kg/cu m (70 to 75 lbs per cu ft), sand content was in the range of 2 to 5 percent, and pH was in the range of 9 to 11.

<u>Soils</u>. Soil samples were obtained during panel excavation. Gradation tests were made on all samples. Only a few samples were selected for testing of natural moisture content and unit weight, and Atterberg Limits. By comparison to the gradation test results made 20 years ago during dam construction, it was possible to determine whether the soil gradation had changed. Additionally, the gradation of the riverbed deposits was closely examined. In general, all embankment fills were mixtures of silt, sand and gravel. During the construction of the dam, the core material was prepared by blending silt and sandy gravel. The product was slightly gap-graded, lacking of medium to coarse sand sizes. This was more noticeable for the embankment fill placed under water.

The gradation of embankment soils recovered from the zone placed under water showed considerably less fines than the soils placed during construction. This was an indication that some fines in the embankment might have been washed away due to internal erosion over the years.

The riverbed alluvial deposits were generally dense, "till-like" material, difficult to excavate. Based on test results of two relatively undisturbed samples, one was identified as silty sand with some gravel and another as gravelly sand with some silt. Both samples were densely packed with in situ dry densities of 90 and 95 percent of the maximum dry density determined in accordance with ASTM Tests for Moisture-Density Relations of Soils and Soil-Aggregate Mixtures using 10-lb (4.54 kg) Rammer and 18-in (457 mm) Drop (D 1557), respectively.

CONSTRUCTION RELATED PROBLEMS

Slow Progress in Alluvium

The embankment core materials consisting of predominantly silty sand and gravel were ideally suited to clam bucket excavation. Excavation progress was rapid without difficulty until the alluvial foundation materials were encountered at an approximate depth of 44 m (145 feet). As indicated on Figure 4, there is a considerable thickness of alluvial materials overlying bedrock for over one-half of the wall length. These very dense "till like" materials consist chiefly of gravelly silty sand and sandy gravel. The gravel content was generally less than 40%. Clam bucket excavation of these dense materials was difficult and slow. For many panels, excavation progress was less than 3 m (10 feet) in a 10 hour shift compared to 23 to 30 m (75 to 100 feet) per shift in the overlying embankment core materials. Loosening of these materials by chiseling was not always effective.

Preparation of Bedrock Surface

Approaching bedrock, progress of clam bucket excavation aided by chiseling became less and less. The granitic bedrock surface across individual panel bottom consisted of bedrock highs and lows filled with dense alluvial materials. To prepare the panel bottom for concrete placement on relatively sound rock chiseling was specified to remove weathered and friable material. Chisel passes across the panel bottom alternated with clam bucket clean-out were continued until noticeable angular, fractured granite rock fragments appeared in the bucket discharge. Once the bedrock highs were reduced by chiseling, additional chiseling produced little or no penetration. Further chiseling tended to form a protective cushion layer

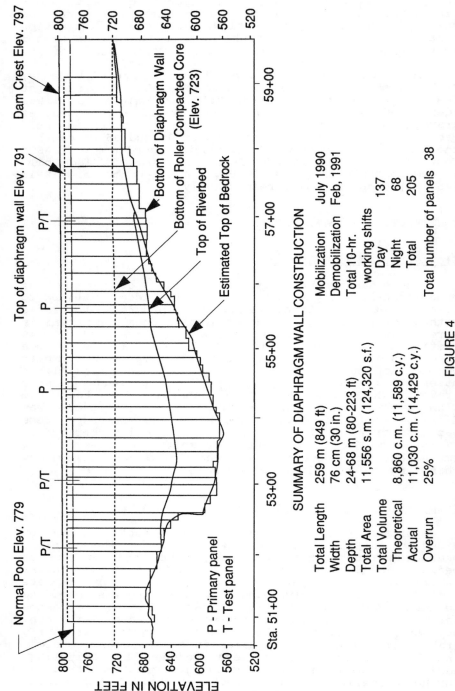

SUMMARY OF DIAPHRAGM WALL CONSTRUCTION

Total Length	259 m (849 ft)	
Width	76 cm (30 in.)	
Depth	24-68 m (80-223 ft)	
Total Area	11,556 s.m. (124,320 s.f.)	
Total Volume		
Theoretical	8,860 c.m. (11,589 c.y.)	
Actual	11,030 c.m. (14,429 c.y.)	
Overrun	25%	

Mobilization	July 1990
Demobilization	Feb, 1991
Total 10-hr.	
working shifts	
Day	137
Night	68
Total	205
Total number of panels	38

FIGURE 4

DIAPHRAGM WALL PROFILE AND SUMMARY OF CONSTRUCTION STATISTICS

over the panel bottom diminishing the effectiveness of chiseling and the final clam bucket clean-out. The air lift clean-out used was not capable of lifting gravel size larger than approximately one inch.

For the deeper panels establishing a continuous bedrock surface the length of panel bottom was difficult to accomplish with any degree of certainty. The unconfined compressive strength of the granitic bedrock in excess 140,000 kPa (20,000 psi) caused chisel edges to readily blunt, resulted in the chisel becoming more a compaction tool rather than the break-up or rock fracturing tool intended.

Based on bottom materials recovered after chiseling, areas of bedrock however large or small, were judged to be at the bottom of every panel. For those panels excavated in embankment core materials (less than 38 m (125 feet) deep) establishing and preparing the bedrock surface was done with more certainty. Quality verification core borings confirmed panel bottom materials to consist of a thin interface zone of densified alluvial materials with intervening rock projections. It was concluded that these materials at the interface, where present, together with sound bedrock provided a satisfactory foundation for the diaphragm wall.

Slurry Losses

Other than normal addition of one to two feet of slurry, rapid slurry loss occurred on three occasions. The largest loss occurred at a depth of 42 m (138 feet) in a panel upstream of the sinkhole at Sta. 52+40. At this location the slurry surface subsided 6 m (20 feet) within 20 minutes. Corrective action, included the addition of bentonite, straw, and partial backfilling of the panel. These actions, which took seven hours, abated the slurry loss and clam bucket excavation was resumed. Moderate slurry losses of 1.2 to 1.5 m (4 to 5 feet) occurred in two other panels at depths of 40 and 50 m (131 and 166 feet). Slurry was added to re-establish the normal levels and no further losses were experienced.

Equipment Downtime

Downtime that occurred during construction was largely due to equipment failures. One to two hours were regularly lost when a clam bucket closing cable was snapped or ripping tooth on the clamshell bucket was broken. Nearly two weeks were lost retrieving a stuck clam bucket from a depth of 65 m (212 feet). After numerous unsuccessful attempts, the clam bucket was finally retrieved by a specially designed hook welded to the end of a joint pipe. Other significant downtimes were due to damage to a digging crane boom and for another crane a broken swing gear. On each occasion nearly two weeks excavation time for one crane was lost.

Weather Related Problems

Over half of the wall was constructed during the cold winter months of December, January and February with frequent sub-zero temperatures. The clam bucket excavation was not greatly affected by low temperatures. However, difficulties were experienced with the operation of the concrete batch plant, slurry lines, pumps and water lines. The delays at the concrete batch plant were caused by freezing aggregates and freezing water lines. Stoppages due to freezing temperature were corrected after the batch plant subcontractor completed winterization measures. Protection of the slurry lines and pumps located on the embankment crest against freezing was never done. The Contractor relied on gravity drainage and blowing of the pipe lines. This approach was largely ineffective and frequently resulted in one to two hours of loss time each morning to thaw pipes.

VERIFICATION OF WALL QUALITY

The completed diaphragm wall with a summary of construction statistics is shown on Fig. 4. Width and depth of individual panels are shown, and test and primary panels are indicated.

Core Drilling and Water Test

Core borings, NX sizes, were required to verify the quality of the diaphragm wall concrete and the continuity of the panel joints. The specification required one boring for every 15 linear meters (50 feet) of completed wall and one additional boring at each pre-production test panel. A core recovery of 95% was required for each core run in concrete for the full panel depth. Due to panel inclination, maintaining core hole verticality alignment within the concrete panel the full depth, particularly the deeper panels, was not always successful. Fifteen of the 27 core holes exited the panel walls before reaching the panel bottom. Replacement core holes for those prematurely exiting the panel were drilled at most locations.

In the first few holes cored intervals of less than 95 percent of the specified recovery were encountered causing some initial concern. Core recovery in subsequent holes was vastly improved by delaying panel coring to allow the concrete to attain higher strength, usually two to three weeks. With few exceptions, core recovery of 95 percent or more was achieved below the upper five feet of most holes.

Slurry contamination and less consolidation generally in the upper five feet weakened the concrete causing raveling and resulting in lower core recovery. In general, panel joints were either in close contact or were separated by thin slurry interface. Completed core holes were tested for water loss and then tremie backfilled with grout. Cores were logged, photographed, and sampled for compressive strength testing.

Piezometer Readings

At the completion of the wall, all the piezometers in the downstream shell which showed residual heads of approximately 35 percent before wall construction now show readings close to tailbay level. This was an indication of the benefit of the wall in reducing seepage.   The foundation piezometers in the in situ riverbed dense material still showed some 13 to 23 percent residual head.

Geophysical Survey

The post-remediation self-potential (SP) data indicated no evidence of concentrated seepage flow through the embankment. It was concluded that the concrete wall had effectively blocked essentially all seepage flow through the embankment (Corwin 1991).

POST-CONSTRUCTION MONITORING

Post-construction monitoring will include piezometric levels, settlement and movement of the embankment crest by surface monuments, and lateral movement of the embankment by inclinometers.

ACKNOWLEDGMENTS

Appreciation is expressed to Ken Pflueger, Chief Engineer, PUD No.1 of Douglas County, WA. for permission to use acquired construction data from this project. Also, the writers thank Chris Gardner, the Project Manager for Bechtel Civil, Inc. for his critical review of the paper. Technical supports throughout the project from the writers' colleagues, Richard Kulesza and Peter Yen, are gratefully acknowledged.

REFERENCES

Burke, H. H., March 1971, "Soils Engineering for Wells
   Project," Journal of the Power Division, American
   Society of Civil Engineers, Vol. 97, No. PO2,
   pp. 317-333.

Corwin, R. F., August 8, 1990, "Direct-Current
   Electrical Resistivity Investigation, East
   Embankment, Wells Dam, Douglas County Public District
   No. 1, Washington," report submitted to Bechtel
   Corp.

Corwin, R. F., March 1991, "Evaluation of Effects of
   Cutoff Wall Construction on Seepage Flow Using
   Self-Potential Data, East Embankment, Wells Dam,
   Douglas County Public Utility District No. 1,
   Washington", report submitted to Bechtel Corp.

NORCAL Geophysical Consultants, Inc., April 1990,
   "Ground Penetration Radar Survey Wells Dam, Douglas
   County, Washington," report submitted to Bechtel
   Corp.

Williamson and Associates, Inc., March 1990, "Results
   of the Geophysical and ROV Surveys at Wells Dam,
   Columbia River, Washington," report submitted to
   Bechtel Corp.

Eugene D. Erwin[1] and Joe M. Glenn[2]

PLASTIC CONCRETE SLURRY WALL FOR WISTER DAM

REFERENCE: Erwin, E. D., and Glenn, J. M., "Plastic Concrete Slurry Wall for Wister Dam", Slurry Walls: Design, Construction, and Quality Control, ASTM STP 1129, David B. Paul, Richard R. Davidson, and Nicholas J. Cavalli, Eds., American Society for Testing and Materials, Philadelphia, 1992.

ABSTRACT: After near failure in 1949 by piping through the embankment, Wister Dam operated with no serious leakage problems to actively threaten the safety of the embankment. However, investigations revealed horizontal and vertical cracking that, combined with the dispersive clay embankment material and lack of sand filter, made the potential for a piping failure too great to ignore. Significant underseepage occurred at modest pool differences through preferred seepage paths that appeared to be cracks resulting from differential settlement. Emergency repairs performed in 1949 and 1950 apparently hydrofractured the embankment. To minimize the potential for a piping failure of the dam a sand filter was constructed in the downstream embankment and a plastic concrete slurry wall cutoff was constructed along an upstream berm. A method for determination of maximum safe panel length for the slurry wall was devised and a plastic concrete mix design was developed to increase the ability of the wall to yield or deform.

KEYWORDS: piping, hydrofracturing, dispersive clay, slurry wall, plastic concrete

GENERAL

Construction History

Wister Dam was constructed by Tulsa District, U.S. Army Corps of Engineers, between April 1946 and May 1949, on the Poteau River, in

[1]Mr. Erwin is a Civil Engineer in the Dam Safety Section, Geotechnical Branch, Tulsa District, US Army Corps of Engineers, PO Box 61, Tulsa, OK 74121.

[2]Mr. Glenn is Chief of the Dam Safety Section, Geotechnical Branch, Tulsa District, US Army Corps of Engineers, PO Box 61, Tulsa, OK 74121.

eastern Oklahoma. The project consists of an earthfill embankment 1737
meters (5700 feet) long, an earthfill dike 731 meters (2400 feet) long,
a gated outlet works conduit, and an uncontrolled spillway. The 30
meter (98 feet) high embankment is essentially a homogeneous impervious
fill, with upstream and downstream waste fill berms constructed of
shale. The foundation consists of approximately 9 meters (30 feet) of
alluvial material, underlain by sandstone and shale, dipping
approximately 25 degrees toward the left abutment. Figure 1 shows the
general plan of the project. Figure 2 shows the typical cross section
of the embankment as originally constructed.

Seepage Problem During Construction

     In January 1949 heavy rainfall over the watershed caused the
reservoir to fill prematurely to elevation 150.5m (493.8 feet), even
though the outlet works gates were wide open. The embankment was
essentially complete at that time, but impoundment had not begun.
Between 30 January and 3 February 1949, seeps were observed in the
downstream slope of the embankment from station 32.3m (1+06) to 438.89m
(14+40), with a maximum discharge of 0.566 m³/s (20 cfs). Field
inspection and borings showed that piping was occurring through the
embankment, starting at about elevation 147.82m (485 feet) upstream and
emerging at about elevation 144.77m (475 feet) downstream. Remedial
work was begun in February and continued until the work was
substantially completed in September 1949.

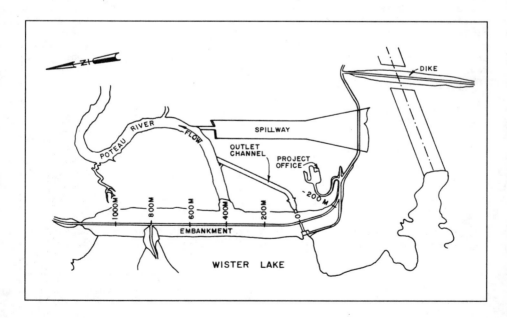

Figure 1 -- General Plan

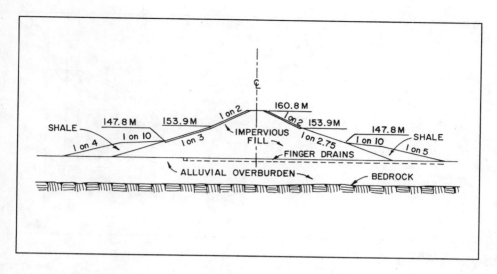

Figure 2 -- Typical Section of Original Embankment

Remedial work   Remedial work consisted of cement grouting in the embankment and foundation, mud grouting in the embankment, installation of a steel sheet pile cutoff wall through the closure section of the embankment, and construction of a sand filter and toe drain system over a 152.4 meter (500 foot) length of the downstream toe and foundation.

The cement grouting operation resulted in 3,167 sacks of cement and 1.27 cubic meters (46 cubic feet) of mud being placed in the upstream embankment at locations where drill water was lost. All water losses occurred between stations 57.91m (1+90) and 426.7m (14+00), and all but four of the water losses were between elevation 137.15m (450.0) and 144.77m (475.0). A total of 4,475 sacks of cement were placed in the rock foundation, to a depth of approximately 9 meters (30 feet). The cement grout placed in the embankment was believed to be only a temporary filling, but the grout placed in the rock was believed to form a relatively tight foundation within the top 9 meters (30 feet).

The mud grouting operation resulted in 910 cubic meters (32,140 cubic feet) of mud grout being placed along the centerline of the embankment. This operation was eventually suspended due to the amount of cracks being generated in the embankment crest.

The sheet pile cutoff wall was installed along the upstream berm of the embankment between the north edge of the intake structure and station 344.4m (11+30), mostly on a line 35.65 meters (117 feet) upstream of the center-line. An impervious cap was placed over the sheet pile wall, as shown in Figure 3.

The waste fill berm and foundation overburden were excavated to rock along the downstream toe of the embankment from station 262.1m (8+60) to 414.5m (13+60), and a filter blanket and perforated drain were

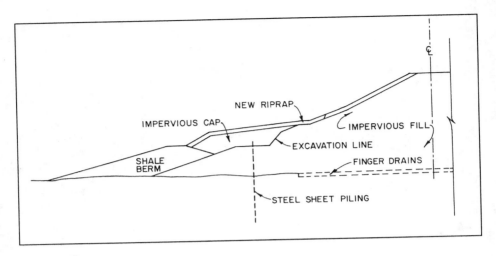

Figure 3 -- Steel Sheet Piling Cutoff

installed to collect and drain seepage through this area. As a
contingency plan a channel was excavated upstream and downstream of the
earthfill dike, with provision to breach the dike if necessary to
prevent failure of the main embankment if the seepage could not be
controlled. The remedial measures were completed in September 1949,
except for drilling for record samples. Borings were completed in May
1950, and storage of water in the reservoir began in June 1950.

     A Board of Consultants determined that the cause of the seepage
through the embankment was cracking due to differential settlement. It
was also later discovered that some of the soil used in the embankment
construction was dispersive, in accordance with the definition and test
methods recommended by Sherard (Sherard et al. 1972), in papers
presented at the ASTM Conference on the Performance of Earth and Earth-
Supported Structures, 1972 [1],[2]. Erosion of the downstream
embankment slopes has been a constant maintenance problem since the
project was put into operation.

BASIS FOR REHABILITATION

     Although the project had operated for the last 35 years with no
major problems, the continued subsurface erosion of the downstream slope
and the high phreatic surface within the embankment, coupled with the
lack of any second line of defense against piping failure, led to a
special investigation of the seepage potential of the embankment. The
dispersive tendencies of the embankment soils were verified by
laboratory tests. Borings showed some vertical cracks and many
laminations or weak horizontal seams, both in the embankment and in the
foundation materials. Figure 4 shows the location of borings along the
proposed alignment of the slurry wall cutoff.

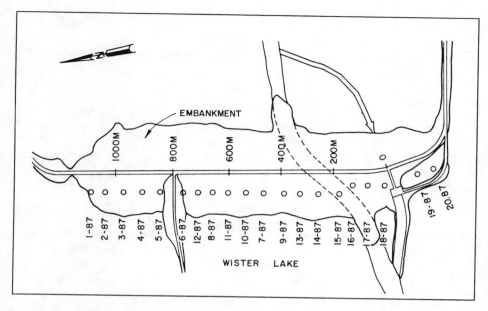

Figure 4 -- Location of Borings

A review of the reports of the remedial work showed that the sheet pile wall had many windows between the bottom of the sheet piles and the rock foundation. The bottom of some of the sheets were as much as 4.6 meters (15 feet) higher than the bottom of the adjacent sheets. The mud grouting operation resulted in extensive cracking of the embankment, causing the grouting to be stopped, even though relatively large takes were still occurring. These cracks left little doubt that the embankment had been hydrofractured by the grouting operation, although only gravity pressure was reportedly used.

There was a great deal of evidence to show that cracking was widespread throughout the embankment and foundation overburden, and that much of the material was susceptible to dispersive erosion. The combination of cracking and dispersive material, with the utter lack of a secondary line of defense such as a sand filter blanket, made the possibility of a piping failure too great to ignore.

A downstream filter blanket, with a toe drain system, and a positive cutoff through the embankment and foundation overburden materials were considered necessary to mitigate the risk of a piping failure of the embankment. Because of the widespread dispersive tendency of the clayey soils in the area it was also considered necessary to treat the outer zone of soil with lime to stop subsurface erosion. The positive cutoff selected for use was a slurry wall of plastic concrete, constructed along an upstream berm. Figure 5 shows a typical section of the downstream repair. Figure 6 shows sections through the upstream slurry wall.

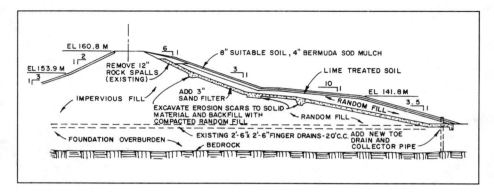

Figure 5 -- Downstream Repair Section

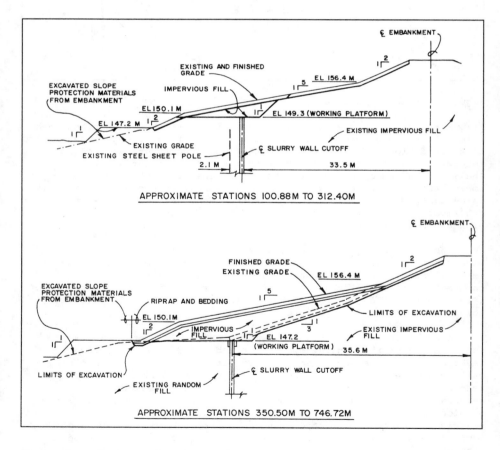

Figure 6 -- Upstream Repair Sections

DESIGN CONSIDERATIONS

Selection of Alignment for Slurry Wall

The upstream slurry wall was designed by Tulsa District personnel, since there did not appear to be any complicated or unusual construction problems that would require specialized expertise or justify soliciting proposals from specialty contractors. The upstream alignment of the slurry wall was selected, over a centerline alignment, because at the upstream alignment a working platform could be provided relatively easily and inexpensively, whereas a centerline alignment would have required lowering the crest and rerouting traffic from the state highway on the crest. Lowering the crest would have been not only more expensive, but would have made the embankment more vulnerable to overtopping during construction. The upstream alignment places the cutoff upstream of the foundation finger drains and coincides more closely with the grout curtain alignment in the foundation rock.

Slurry Wall Design Details

The slurry wall was designed to be seated 1.52 meters (5 feet) into the foundation rock, and to be constructed of plastic concrete. Based on a report by Tamaro[4], the plastic concrete was desired to have an unconfined compressive strength at 90 days of from 36.6 to 73.1 kg/cm^2 (500 to 1000 psi), which was expected to result in a Modulus of Elasticity (Tangent Modulus) of about 117,000 to 168,000 kg/cm^2 (1,600,000 to 2,300,000 psi). Mix design tests were performed by the Southwestern Division Laboratory of the US Army Corps of engineers. The tests were performed at cementitious material contents of 163 and 217 kg/cubic meter (300 and 400 pounds per cubic yard), and with varying proportions of Portland cement, bentonite, and flyash. The mix selected for use consisted of 190 kg of cementitious material per cubic meter of plastic concrete (350 pounds per cubic yard), of which 70 percent was Portland cement, 20 percent was flyash, and 10 percent was bentonite, by weight. This mixture was selected for use because the 163 kg/cubic meter (300 pounds/cubic yard) cementitious content mix did not give unconfined compression test results that were uniformly above the desired minimum of 36.6 kg/cm^2 (500 psi), and the 217 kg/cubic meter (400 pounds/cubic yard) cementitious content mix was generally well above the desired maximum of 73.1 kg/cm^2 (1000 psi).

DETERMINATION OF MAXIMUM PANEL LENGTH

Soil Strength Testing

Triaxial compression tests of undisturbed samples showed that large portions of the embankment and foundation had relatively low shear strength. Standard Penetration Test results generally agreed with the laboratory shear tests, confirming the presence of zones of low strength. Figure 7 shows the strength distribution of the soil along the alignment of the slurry wall cutoff, as represented by contours of the Standard Penetration Test blow count.

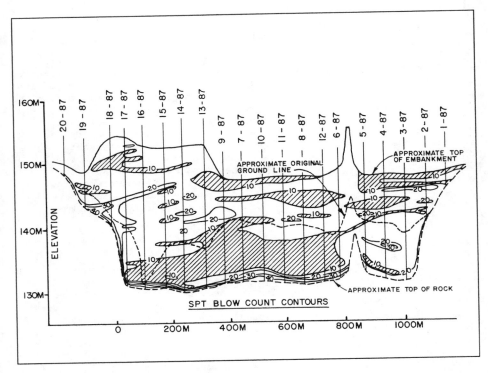

Figure 7 -- Distribution of Soil Strength

Stability Analyses

Conventional circular arc stability analyses of the embankment indicated a safety factor of less than one for a continuous trench, verifying the need for excavation of panels of some finite length.

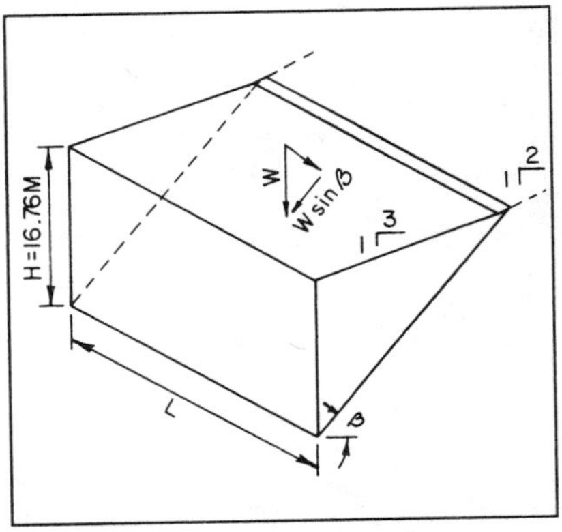

A three-dimensional wedge analysis was developed, so that end effects of panels of finite length could be incorporated into the stability analysis procedure. Figure 8 shows the generalized failure wedge for failure along a single plane. This wedge was evaluated for angles of 40, 50, 60, and 70 degrees from horizontal, and for lengths varying from 1.52 meters to 152.4 meters (5 to 500 feet). For each length analyzed, a curve was plotted of failure surface angle versus factor of safety. For analysis of stability of the

Figure 8 -- Failure Wedge

portion of the embankment between about station 374.89m (12+30) and 740.63m (24+30) and station 801.58m (26+30) and 1045.41m (34+30), Figure 9 shows the selection of the design shear strength used.   Figure 10

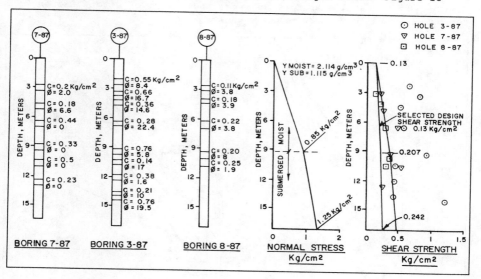

Figure 9 -- Selection of Design Shear Strengths

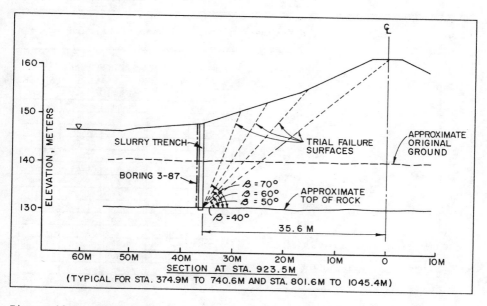

Figure 10 -- Embankment Section and Trial Failure Surface

shows the embankment section and trial failure surfaces analyzed.
Figure 11 shows the prisms whose volumes represent the shear strength on
the ends and along the base of the failure wedge. Figure 12 is a
summary of the trial stability analyses and a plot of safety factor
versus trial failure surface slope angle.

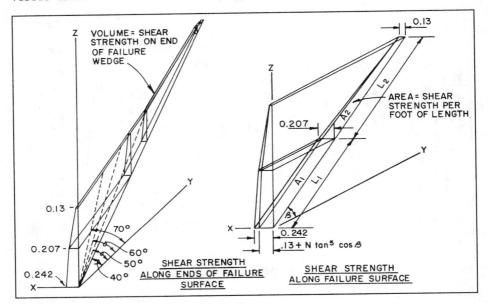

Figure 11 -- Shear Strength Prisms for Ends and Base of Failure Wedge

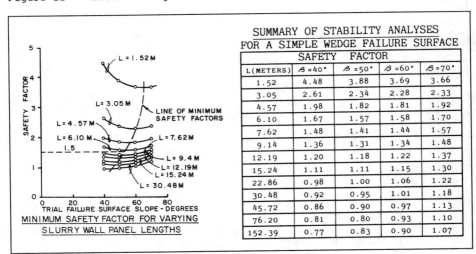

SUMMARY OF STABILITY ANALYSES FOR A SIMPLE WEDGE FAILURE SURFACE

L(METERS)	β =40°	β =50°	β =60°	β =70°
1.52	4.48	3.88	3.69	3.66
3.05	2.61	2.34	2.28	2.33
4.57	1.98	1.82	1.81	1.92
6.10	1.67	1.57	1.58	1.70
7.62	1.48	1.41	1.44	1.57
9.14	1.36	1.31	1.34	1.48
12.19	1.20	1.18	1.22	1.37
15.24	1.11	1.11	1.15	1.30
22.86	0.98	1.00	1.06	1.22
30.48	0.92	0.95	1.01	1.18
45.72	0.86	0.90	0.97	1.13
76.20	0.81	0.80	0.93	1.10
152.39	0.77	0.83	0.90	1.07

Figure 12 -- Summary of Trial Stability Analyses

A similar analysis was performed for the portion of the embankment between station 76.2m (2+50) and 350.5m (11+50). From these analyses a maximum length of panel of 7.61 meters (25 feet) was selected, for which a minimum safety factor of about 1.3 could be expected. A more complete description of the stability analyses is given in Design Memorandum No. 1, Wister Dam [3].

PLASTIC CONCRETE MIX DESIGN

Initial Mix Design Considerations

Conventional Portland cement concrete was initially believed to be the material best suited for the construction of the slurry wall cutoff primarily because of the impermeable nature and low compressibility of the material, as well as the fact that the strength would permit excavation without damage to panels already in place. However, the possibility of cracks or construction joints allowing concentrated seepage flow to pass through the cutoff was considered to be a liability.

A cement-bentonite backfill was considered, and it was felt that if a mixture of cement, bentonite, and inert filler material could be designed that would be somewhat plastic, rather than rigid or brittle, that it might be better than concrete as a cutoff wall material. It would have to be relatively impervious, sufficiently incompressible to prevent creep of embankment materials, plastic enough to deform without cracking, but strong enough to stand vertically when adjacent panels were excavated.

A plastic concrete described by Tamaro [4] appeared to have the properties desired for the cutoff wall at Wister. This mix was expected to have a slump of about 20 cm (8 inches), to be very workable, to have a compressive strength of 36.6-73.1 kg/cm^2 (500-1000 psi) at 28 days, and a permeability of about 1x10^{-7} cm per second. A similar mix was selected for further design studies at the Corps of Engineers Southwestern Division Laboratory.

Laboratory Mix Design Studies

The Laboratory performed mix design studies using rounded gravel coarse aggregate, river sand, Portland cement, bentonite, and flyash. All mixes used 55 percent coarse aggregate and 45 percent sand. Mixes of cement, flyash, and bentonite in the proportions of 100-0-0, 90-0-10, 85-0-15, 80-0-20, and 70-20-10 were tested for cementitious material weights of 163 and 217 kg per cubic meter (300 and 400 pounds per cubic yard). The unconfined compressive strength, Tangent Modulus (initial), Secant Modulus (at ultimate load), and percent strain at ultimate load were determined for curing periods of 3-days, 7-days, 28-days, and 90-days for each mix.

The mix consisting of 70 percent cement, 20 percent flyash, and 10 percent bentonite appeared to have the properties of strength and

elasticity desired for the plastic concrete slurry wall. A plot of
compressive strength versus time is shown in Figure 13. The interpolated values for compressive strength for a mix containing 190 kg per
cubic meter (350 pounds per cubic yard) are also shown on Figure 13. For
the desired strength range of 36.6 to 73.1 kg/cm^2 (500 to 1000 psi) at
90 days the interpolated values appeared to be the best mix, and this
cement factor was specified for construction of the slurry wall.

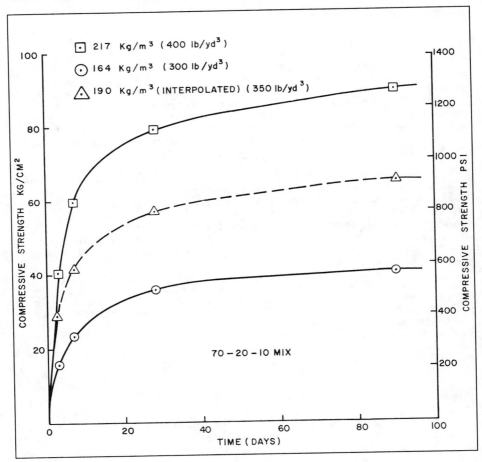

Figure 13 -- Compressive Strength vs. Time

Figure 14 shows the plots of Tangent Modulus versus curing time
for the 163 and 217 kg (300 and 400 pounds) of cementitious material
mixes, with the interpolated values for a mix containing 190 kg (350
pounds) of cementitious material. For the specified cement factor a
Tangent Modulus, E_t, of about 138,000 kg/cm^2 (1,900,000 psi) was
anticipated for the 90-day cure. This compares with a value of 371,200

kg/cm² (5,280,000 psi) for the conventional concrete mix cured to 90 days.

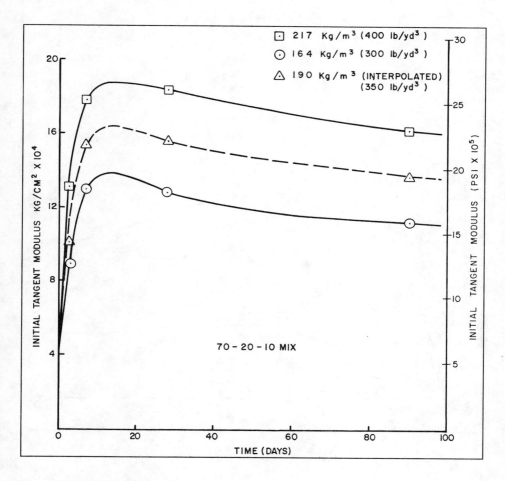

Figure 14 -- Tangent Modulus vs. Curing Time

Figure 15 shows the plots of Secant Modulus versus curing time for the 163 and 217 kg per cubic meter (300 and 400 pounds per cubic yard) cement factors. The interpolated values for a cement factor of 190 kg per cubic meter (350 pounds per cubic yard) are also shown. For this cement factor a Secant Modulus of about 62,000 kg/cm² (850,000 psi) was anticipated for the 90-day cure. This compares with a value of 153,200 kg/cm² (2,180,000 psi) for the conventional concrete mix cured to 90 days.

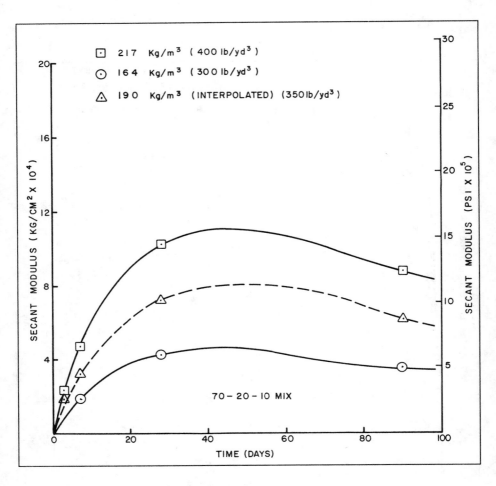

Figure 15 -- Secant Modulus vs. Curing Time

Determination of Job Mix

    The specifications for the slurry wall contract required the
contractor to perform mix design tests using the actual materials to be
used in the construction. The specifications required the use of
natural rounded gravel for the coarse aggregate and river sand for the
fine aggregate, and that the sand should be at least 45 percent of the
total aggregate. For bidding purposes the cement content was specified
to be 190 kg/m^3 (350 pounds per cubic yard), and the proportioning to be
70 percent Portland cement, 20 percent flyash, and 10 percent bentonite,
by weight. The mix selected for use is shown in Table 1 below.

This mix had a slump of 20 cm (7.8 inches) and a 28-day compressive strength of 42 kg/cm^2 (598 psi). Based on these tests the mix was approved for the plastic concrete slurry wall.

TABLE 1 -- Selected Mix Design for Plastic Concrete

Material	Weight As Mixed		Weight SSD	
	kg/m^3	(lbs/yd^3)	kg/m^3	(lbs/yd^3)
Cement	133	245	133	245
Flyash	38	70	38	70
Bentonite	19	35	19	35
Coarse Aggregate	1008	1859	1008	1859
Fine Aggregate	727	1340	706	1301
Water	190	350	208	383

CONSTRUCTION OF THE CUTOFF WALL

Contract Summary

The contract was awarded to Bauer of America Corporation on 20 February 1990, for a contract amount of $5,080,000.00. Because of high pool levels in the spring of 1990 it was 27 July 1990 when the first panel was placed. Since that time the contractor proceeded, with no major difficulties, to complete placement of the 326 panels on 19 January 1991.

Construction Procedures

The contractor used a special cutting device to excavate the panels. The cutter consisted of a heavy steel frame approximately 11 meters (35 feet) high, with four cutting wheels driven by individual hydraulic motors, and a discharge pump and discharge line to remove the cuttings. The cutter was suspended from a crane, whose operator also operated the cutter. An inclinometer system provided continuous information to the operator, which enabled him to maintain the verticality of the excavation to a tolerance of less than 1-inch for each 10-feet of depth, and provided a computer printout of the data.

The cutter excavated a slot 2.2 meters (7.2 feet) by 0.61 meters (2 feet) in each pass. Primary panels were constructed 5.5 meters (18 feet) long by making a vertical pass at each end of the panel and then by removing the material between the passes. A distance of 2 meters (6.56 feet) was left between primary panels. After the primary panels had been backfilled and had gained sufficient strength, the secondary panel was excavated, cutting away some of the concrete from each primary panel to ensure a tight joint against sound concrete.

The slurry containing the cuttings was pumped to the desanding plant, where two screens removed the cuttings and sand size particles from the slurry, allowing it to be reused. When the panel excavation was completed, the slurry in the excavation was replaced with fresh slurry so that there would be no problem with settling of suspended materials from the excavation.

The primary panels were backfilled, using two tremie pipes and transit mix trucks. The secondary panels were backfilled using only one tremie pipe. The plastic concrete was batched at the job site by a subcontractor.

Concrete guide walls 90 cm (36 inches) deep by 30 cm (12 inches) wide were used to maintain alignment and stability of the top of the excavation. The cutter has a frame that fits on top of the guide walls to properly position the cutter for location and verticality. Pre-excavation was done with a backhoe or a special clam shell bucket the same width and thickness as the cutter. The cutter needs to be about 4.5 meters (15 feet) deep when it begins excavation to cut evenly and to properly remove cuttings. However, pre-excavation can be done to within about 1.5 to 3 meters (5 to 10 feet) of rock to speed up the excavation process. Shallow panels, 4.5 meters (15 feet) or less, were excavated with a backhoe.

After the first panel was placed on 27 July 90 the contractor placed 930 square meters (10,000 square feet) of slurry wall in the next 20 days, after which he maintained a fairly constant rate of about 120 square meters (1300 square feet) per day. The contractor worked two shifts per day for six days per week on excavation of the slurry wall panels, and one shift per day for six days per week backfilling the excavated panels with the plastic concrete.

The contract unit price per square meter of slurry wall was $143.71 ($13.35 per square foot), which included all excavation of the slurry wall and backfilling with the plastic concrete. The total cost for the 20,065 square meters (216,000 square feet) of slurry wall was $2,883,600. The bulk of the remainder of the $5,080,000 was to remove existing riprap from the embankment, prepare the work platform, and to add an impervious fill cap and new riprap protection stone.

AS-CONSTRUCTED DATA FOR THE WALL

The primary quality assurance testing of the plastic concrete was for slump and compressive strength. A total of 126 sets of concrete cylinders were cast during the placement of the plastic concrete slurry wall, and cured in water tanks at the site. The slump varied from 14 to 21.6 centimeters (5.5 to 8.5 inches), with 87 of the 126 batches tested ranging between 17.8 and 20.3 centimeters (7 and 8 inches).

A temporary testing laboratory was set up at the site for performing the unconfined compression testing of the concrete cylinders. Some of the sets of test cylinders were tested after 3-day, 7-day, 28-day, 90-day, 6-month, and 1-year curing times, but all of the sets were tested at 90-day curing time. Table 2 below summarizes the results of the unconfined compressive strength testing of the plastic concrete.

TABLE 2 -- Summary of Compressive Strength Tests

Curing Time	Number of Tests	Compressive Strength (kg/cm^2)
3 Days	68	22.67
7 Days	93	28.62
28 Days	96	43.90
90 Days	252	66.39

CONCLUSIONS AND RECOMMENDATIONS

Although the average 90-day compressive strength was within the desired range there were 93 of the 252 tests that exceeded the desired maximum strength of 70 kg/cm^2 (1000 psi). For the slurry wall to be as plastic as desired the cement factor should have been less, probably about 163 kg/m^3 (300 pounds per cubic yard).

No severe problems of workability were observed for the range of slump specified; however, the minimum specified slump should be closer to the desired 20 centimeters (8 inches). This should eliminate some of the higher values of compressive strength, and the resulting higher values for the Modulus of Elasticity.

The bentonite was batched dry into the transit mix trucks. It is likely that if prehydrated bentonite slurry were used, instead of the dry bentonite, better mixing and more uniform results would be obtained.

REFERENCES

[1] Sherard, J.L., Decker, R.S., and Ryker, N.L., Proceedings, Conference on the Performance of Earth and Earth-Supported Structures, American Society of Civil Engineers, Vol. 1, June 1972, pp. 589-626.

[2] Sherard, J.L., Decker, R.S., and Ryker, N.L., Proceedings, Conference on the Performance of Earth and Earth-Supported Structures, American Society of Civil Engineers, Vol 1, June 1972, pp. 653-689.

[3] US Army Corps of Engineers, Tulsa District, Wister Dam, Poteau River, Oklahoma, Design Memorandum No. 1, Embankment Rehabilitation, June 1988

[4] Tamaro, George J., "Plastic Concrete Cutoff Walls," Proceedings of REMR Workshop on New Remedial Seepage Control Methods for Embankment Dams and Soil Foundations, 21-22 October 1986, US Army Engineer Waterways Experiment Station, Vicksburg, MS

Seepage Cutoffs

Richard R. Davidson[1], Garet Denise[2], Brent Findlay[3], and Richard B. Robertson[4]

DESIGN AND CONSTRUCTION OF A PLASTIC CONCRETE CUTOFF WALL FOR THE ISLAND COPPER MINE

REFERENCE: Davidson, R.R., Denise, G., Findlay, B., and Robertson, R.B., "Design and Construction of a Plastic Concrete Cutoff Wall for the Island Copper Mine," Slurry Walls: Design, Construction and Quality Control, ASTM STP 1129, David B. Paul, Richard R. Davidson and Nicholas J. Cavalli, Eds., American Society for Testing and Materials, Philadelphia, 1992.

ABSTRACT: A plastic concrete slurry wall was constructed at the Island Copper Mine on Vancouver Island to prevent excessive seepage from the ocean into a large copper mine open pit during a south wall push-back which would lead to pit slope stability problems and flooding. An unusually low strength plastic concrete was chosen as a backfill to sustain relatively large deformations without cracking and to resist erosion if a crack should develop. Very difficult construction problems were successfully surmounted including excavation through a loose, pervious mine rock waste dump and embedding the toe of the wall into a very hard glacial till. Pit slope excavation has been completed through the cutoff soils without problem.

KEYWORDS: Slurry wall, mine, open pit, slope stability, seepage, bentonite, plastic concrete, copper, glacial till, finite element analysis, clamshell.

INTRODUCTION

The Island Copper Mine is a 90,000 tpd (ore and waste) open pit mine operated by BHP-Utah Mines, Ltd. on the northern end of Vancouver Island in British Columbia, Canada. Started in 1971, the mine is situated on the north shoreline of an arm of Rupert Inlet which is connected to the Pacific Ocean (Figure 1). The open pit is currently about 3500 feet (1167 m) wide, 7500 feet (2286 m) long, and 850 feet (260 m) deep. Original plans called for the mine to extend to a depth of 1000 feet (305 m). Once this depth was attained, it would not have been possible to mine deeper to extract more ore with the current pit slope configuration, and mining operations would cease (Figure 2).

There is, however, an economically recoverable body of ore in and behind the south pit wall, under the original shoreline. Waste rock from the mining operations has been disposed by dumping into the inlet, moving the shoreline out from its original location by as much as 3,000 feet (914 m). The south wall of the mine pit is located such that a narrow rim

[1] Senior Associate, Woodward-Clyde Consultants, 4582 South Ulster Street Pkwy., Suite 1000, Denver, Colorado 80237

[2] Senior Staff Engineer, Woodward-Clyde Consultants, 4582 South Ulster Street Parkway, Suite 1000, Denver, Colorado 80237

[3] Mine Maintenance General Foreman, BHP-Utah Mines, Ltd., Island Copper Mine, Port Hardy, British Columbia

[4] Engineering Manager, BHP-Utah Mines, Ltd, Island Copper Mine, Port Hardy, British Columbia

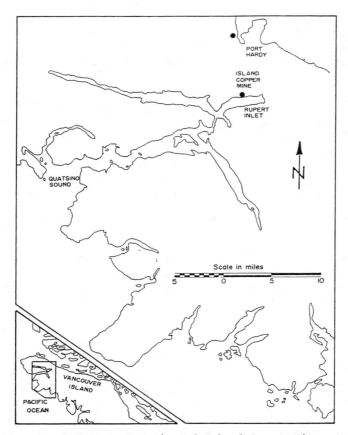

FIG. 1 -- Location of Island Copper Mine

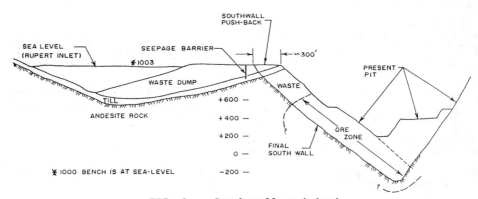

FIG. 2 -- South wall push-back

of rock and clay fill form a natural seepage barrier. Extracting the additional ore body by moving back the south pit wall would allow seepage through the highly pervious waste dump material and flood the pit. Increasing the steepness of the south pit wall was not feasible either, due to pit slope stability problems which had already been manifested in the form of pit slope movements.

With the possibility of running out of ore and shutting down the mine, the mine operators sought a method of controlling the seepage which would be created by a push-back of the south wall. Construction of a grout curtain or slurry wall seepage barrier were both viewed as possible solutions. Faced with a very difficult engineering task, the mine operators sought the advice of several engineering consultants and specialty contractors at a two-day round table discussion. Each participant was asked to alternately argue for or against both grouting or slurry walls. Due to the high heads involved (up to 100 feet [30.5 m] across the barrier) and the large displacements expected in the loose dump material, the mine operators chose to construct a slurry wall seepage barrier.

BARRIER WALL DESIGN

Configuration

The alignment selected for the seepage barrier wall was configured to accommodate a push-back of the south pit wall of about 300 feet (91.5 m). This will result in the recovery of approximately 83 million tonnes of mill feed and extend the life of the mine about 4 years. This will also extend the mine to a depth of 1200 feet (366 m) below sea level, making it the lowest point on the face of the earth.

The wall alignment has an average depth of 90 to 100 feet (27.5 to 30.5 m) in its central portion, with the deepest panel being 105 feet (32 m). The wall has a length of 4100 feet (1250 m) and an area of 300,000 ft^2 (27,870 m^2). Approximately 15 percent of the wall length is founded on bedrock. The remainder of the wall was excavated a minimum of 8 feet (2.4 m) into glacial till for embedment.

Site Conditions

The mine is excavated in bedded and massive tuffs and formational breccias. The actual ore body is a quartz-feldspar porphyry dyke. The bedrock surface topography has largely been created by glaciation, and dips gently into Rupert Inlet. A near-vertical fault, the End-Creek fault, is oriented NW-SE through the pit and intersects the south wall push-back.

Overlying the bedrock is a glacial till, about 30-50 feet (9-15 m) thick, and dipping into Rupert Inlet with the bedrock surface (Figure 3). The till is generally well graded from clay and silt through gravel sizes, very dense, and with a relatively low permeability. However, some outwash lenses with higher permeability exist within the till. These outwash zones are not predictable, and are difficult to locate. Portions of the top of the till from the last glacial retreat are loose and not over-consolidated, but still relatively well graded. Overlying the till is a silty sand beach material, characterized by the presence of shell fragments. The beach deposits were generally 5 to 10 feet (1.5 to 3 m) thick over the main portion of the wall, but up to 50 feet (15 m) thick in the western portion of the wall. At some locations, a mantel of coarse-grained (sand) fluvial deposits overlays the till deposits with a general thickness of 5 to 10 feet (1.5 to 3 m), but up to 30 feet (9 m) deep in the western portions of the wall. The mine waste rock dump completes the stratigraphy. The dump consists of a loose, highly permeable random matrix of material ranging from clay size particles to boulders several

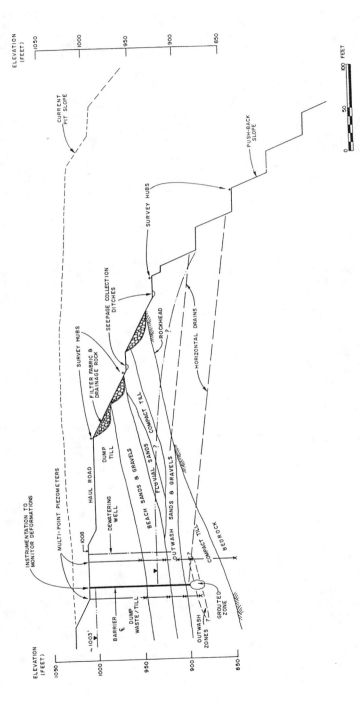

FIG. 3 -- Seepage barrier wall section

feet (meters) in diameter. Rumors circulated from the early days of mine operation of 150-ton haul trucks leaving the pit loaded with single boulders; a formidable obstacle to any type of construction! The dump materials range up to 70 to 80 feet (21 to 24 m) deep in the central portions of the wall alignment, and taper off toward the ends. The stratigraphy along the wall alignment is shown in profile in Figure 4.

Seepage Barrier Wall Analysis

Deformation analysis - - The two most significant design criteria for the slurry wall were the ability of the slurry wall backfill material to deform without cracking and to resist erosion if it did crack. It was recognized that as the pit slope was dewatered and excavated, and a hydraulic head of up to 100 feet (30 m) was applied across the wall, significant deformations would occur in the waste rock dump materials through which most of the wall would be constructed. A finite element soil-structure interaction analysis was performed to evaluate the magnitude of these deformations and the resulting stresses and strains in the slurry wall backfill material. The analysis was performed using the program "SOIL-STRUCT" which uses a hyperbolic stress-strain model for the soil materials.

Since one of the more important input parameters to this analysis would be the modulus of the loose waste rock dump, a settlement test pad was constructed and instrumented. The settlement test pad was constructed by building up additional mine waste rock on top of the dump materials to a height of about 50 feet (15 m) and 60 feet (18 m) square on top and then monitoring the resulting settlement. This resulted in a settlement of 0.4 to 0.7 feet (0.12 to 0.2 m), from which an elastic modulus of about 300 to 700 kips/ft^2 (14 to 33 MPa) was estimated for the dump materials. Properties for the other materials were estimated from pressuremeter testing and laboratory triaxial testing.

With these geotechnical parameters, the finite element analysis was carried out for two critical slope sections at stations 26+50 and 27+50 using property values to represent a range of slurry wall backfill materials from strong plastic concrete to a cement-bentonite mix. The finite element mesh used to represent the wall section in the areas of deeper dump deposits (27+50) is shown in Figure 5. For a low-strength backfill, deflections ranging from 0.6 to 2 inches (1.5 to 5 cm) and settlement of less than ½ inch (1 cm) were predicted at the top of the wall due to dewatering and slope excavation (Figure 6). This analysis indicated that a low modulus backfill would not tend to crack, whereas a stiffer backfill material would develop tensile stresses and tend to crack near the contact with the till. The goal of the backfill mix design program was to match the backfill material stiffness to that of the surrounding soil mass, and achieve a low permeability and high resistance to erosion.

Seepage Analysis -- A seepage analysis was performed to evaluate the quantity of water that would flow under the wall and the potential for piping of the glacial till material. A flow net analysis estimated the overall seepage for the wall to be between 70 and 700 imperial gallons/min (igpm) (0.3 to 3.2 m^3/min). Piping was evaluated using filter criteria for the till and outwash zones, and resulted in the requirement of 8 feet (2.4 m) of embedment into the till, with a minimum of 3 feet (0.9 m) of the embedment being low permeability till. The thickness of the wall was chosen to be 30 inches (76 cm) based on precedent in the industry and a minimum requirement of 24 inches (61 cm) of continuity between adjacent panels.

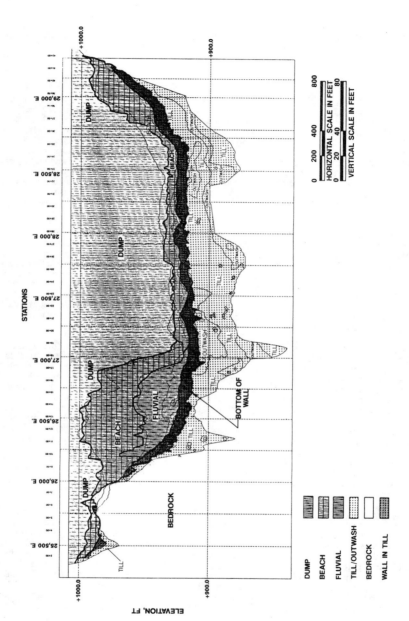

FIG. 4 -- Stratigraphic section along slurry wall

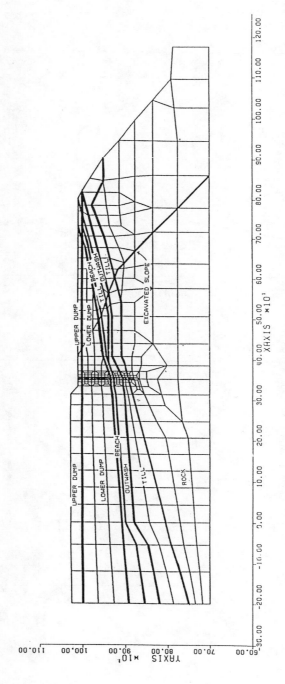

FIG. 5 -- Finite element analysis mesh

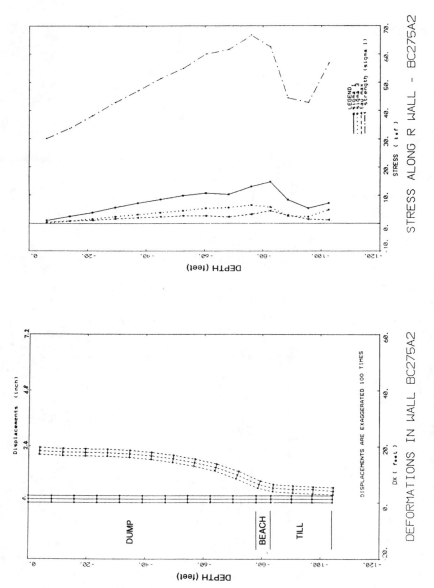

FIG. 6 -- FEM predictions of wall behavior after excavation
          Case BC 275A2 - Section 27,500, plastic concrete

Backfill Mix Design

To achieve the best combination of properties, a wide range of backfill mixes were tested in the laboratory. Backfill materials tested included plastic concretes with various cement contents, as well as a cement-bentonite mix with a high cement content. The first test series included unconfined compression tests and triaxial permeability tests. Stress-strain test results from unconfined compression tests are summarized in Figure 7. Triaxial permeability results for the trial mixes ranged from 3×10^{-7} cm/s for cement-bentonite to 5×10^{-8} cm/s for plastic concrete. From these results, either a low strength plastic concrete or a cement-bentonite mix was judged to provide the desired level of ductility.

The mixes were then subjected to erosion testing. Cylindrical samples were split lengthwise in a splitting tensile fashion. The two halves of the sample were mounted 1/16 inch (1.5 mm) apart, and water was forced through the gap under 30 psi (207 kPa) pressure. None of the mixes showed significant erosion during this test. A more severe test was devised by subjecting each specimen to a jet of water from a 1/8 inch (3 mm) nozzle under 45 psi (310 kPa) pressure. Under these conditions, a 3/4 inch (19 mm) diameter hole was eroded 1/2 inch (13 mm) deep in the cement-bentonite sample in 24 hours. The plastic concrete specimens did not erode under the severe jet erosion test.

The mix selected for the project consisted of an unusual low strength plastic concrete. The aggregates used were angular crushed waste rock from the mine and a natural unprocessed silty beach sand found at the site. The maximum size of the aggregate was limited to 1/2 inch (13 mm) to maintain adequate workability. The mix final design had a very high bentonite/cement ratio of 0.22, a cement/water ratio of 0.36, a cement/aggregate ratio of 9 percent, and a slump of 8 to 10 inches (20 to 25 cm). The design mix yield was:

	lb/yd³	kg/m³
Cement	239	143
Coarse aggregate	1330	798
Fine aggregate	1330	798
Bentonite	53	32
Water	667	400

This resulted in an average unconfined compressive strength of about 144 psi (993 kPa) at 7 days, 220 psi (1517 kPa) at 28 days, and an unconfined tangent modulus of 9,400 kips/ft² (450 MPa) at 7 days and 12,900 kips/ft² (618 MPa) at 28 days. The final design mix had a permeability of 4×10^{-7} cm/s. Because of the limited precedent for such a low strength plastic concrete, careful monitoring of the mix during construction was called for in the specifications.

CONSTRUCTION

Construction Procurement

Due to the difficult and unusual nature of the construction, the mine operators chose an innovative procurement process. Seven specialty contractors indicated interest in performing the work, and four of these were prequalified. Two-stage technical and cost proposals were received from three of these four contractors. After lengthy technical and cost negotiating, a contractor was selected and a contract was negotiated. This process allowed the engineer and contractor to illuminate the key uncertainties in the project and allow the contractor to propose innovative solutions to the technical problems rather than add large

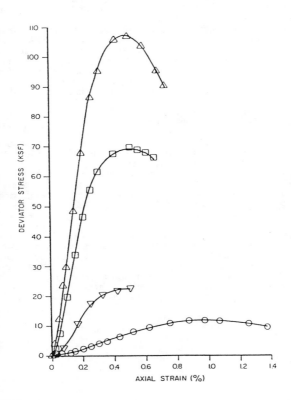

L E G E N D

	MIX	B/W	C/W	C/A	S/A	B/A	w	γd	AGGREGATE
○	CEMENT BENTONITE	6	0.38	-	-	-	180	28.2	-
□	MIX A PLASTIC CONC.	4.7	0.6	16.7	23.1	1.3	17.5	112.7	45% CWR 55% NS
△	MIX B PLASTIC CONC.	3.5	0.68	16.3	9.8	0.8	15.6	116.5	45% CWR 55% NS
▽	MIX E PLASTIC CONC.	6	0.6	16.7	30.1	1.7	25.3	97.6	OTHER PROJ. PIT RUN

B BENTONITE WEIGHT   A AGGREGATE WEIGHT   γd DRY UNIT WEIGHT (LB/FT^3)
W WATER WEIGHT   S BENTONITE-WATER WEIGHT   CWR COARSE WASTE ROCK WEIGHT
C CEMENT WEIGHT   w WATER CONTENT   NS NATURAL SAND WEIGHT

FIG. 7 -- Representative unconfined compression
test results on slurry wall backfill mixes

contingencies in his bid or plan for large claims to recover his excess costs.

Wall Excavation

Excessive slurry loss -- The first problem to be worked out during construction was how to excavate slurry wall panels through the very loose waste rock dump. Rotary drilling during the geotechnical investigations had lost from 200 to 1000 percent of the drilling fluids going through the dump materials. A slurry loss test program was conducted both in the laboratory and in field drill holes. The laboratory phase consisted of mixing Tower Gel 90 (90 yield bentonite), Slurry Ben 125 (125 yield bentonite), Salt Gel (Attapulgite clay), and Volclay Saline Seal (70 yield bentonite) with four different waters: distilled water, fresh process water from the mine's supply system, ground water from a test trench near the planned slurry wall alignment, and sea water taken near the site. The results of viscosity, filter press testing, flocculation observations and field performance in 10 inch (25 cm) diameter drill holes indicated that high yield (125 barrels/per ton) bentonite would provide the most stable slurry and best filtrate properties.

Despite a fairly thick bentonite slurry mix and careful attention to the mixing properties, overall, the project lost an average of 25 pounds (11.3 kg) of bentonite per square foot of wall area with a maximum of almost 100 lb/ft^2 (690 kPa). This represented a serious problem in supply logistics since transportation onto the island is restricted to barge or ferry. Rapid slurry losses during excavation were common. Attempts to plug leaks ranged from adding loose, dry, well-graded till to the open panel to adding cement to gel the bentonite slurry. Extreme problems require extreme solutions, and more than once an entire pallet of cement was added (all at once) to attempt to stop a leaking panel. This addition of cement was not without detrimental side effects, as will be discussed below.

Trench collapse - - Early attempts to excavate panels resulted in several severe trench collapses. Several panels resulted in continuing collapse problems and needed to be backfilled with a lean concrete mix and re-excavated. Problems culminated when a completed panel being desanded prior to concrete placement collapsed behind the guidewalls opening a hole so large that the desanding unit fell into the panel trench (Figure 8).

The first attempts by the contractor to stabilize the upper dump materials consisted of augering 30 inch (76 cm) diameter holes between the guidewalls to a depth of 10 feet (3 m) and backfilling with a lean concrete mix. This proved to be ineffective since the treated material was removed during subsequent excavations. The next attempt made was to pre-trench between the guidewalls to a depth of 10 feet (3 m) with a backhoe, and backfill with a lean concrete mix. During this operation, a 100 foot (30 m) long section of the guidewalls collapsed into the excavation. In repairing these guidewalls, and in constructing all subsequent guidewalls, a trench was pre-excavated to a depth of 10 feet (3 m) and backfilled with lean-mix concrete prior to construction of the guidewalls.

To help stabilize the excavations in the dump materials, panel lengths were limited to a single clamshell bite (about 10 feet (3 m) of panel after placing endstops) for primary panels, and about 20 feet (6 m) for secondary panels. Even with these stabilization efforts, excavations often grew up to 4 to 6 feet (1.4 to 1.8 m) in width. The project had consistent overpours of 50 to 60 percent. On two occasions, the waste rock dump caved during excavation burying a clamshell. The clamshells were eventually retrieved. Once excavation through the dump was complete, caving was typically not observed.

FIG. 8 -- Trench collapse and loss of desanding unit

Difficult Excavation - - The most effective excavation tools proved to be large, 13-ton, cable-hung "Rochester Way" clamshells, but even these could not break boulders which were too large to fit between the guidewalls. To break boulders, the contractor used 10,000 pound star chisels. However, the effectiveness of the chisels was significantly reduced by the loose nature of the dump matrix. Often, the operator would use the chisel to "chase" the same boulder down through the matrix as the excavation progressed.

Excavations for the toe of the cutoff in the very dense glacial till represented another problem. The same clamshells, supplemented by chisels, were used to excavate the till early in the project, with very slow production rates. A crawler-mounted caisson auger rig was brought onsite to pre-drill the embedment in till prior to excavation with a clamshell. Although this improved excavation rates marginally, it was surmised that excavations with the clamshell would quickly fill in the pre-drilled holes, negating their effectiveness. This method was eventually abandoned, in favor of using a 24 inch (61 cm) wide "Manic" clamshell for the embedment excavation instead of the 30 inch (76 cm) clamshells used for the overburden excavations.

Panel Cleaning

Panels were typically cleaned by mucking the bottom of the excavation with a clamshell bucket to remove large debris and vacuumed with an air-lift pipe. Air-lifting was continued during desanding until the sand content of the slurry was below 5 percent. Cleaning of the slurry prior to concrete placement required special attention due to the thick mix properties, cement contamination, and the extreme measures taken during excavation to stop slurry losses. Several panels needed to have the slurry replaced by pumping out the excavation slurry and wasting it while replacing it with fresh slurry. End stop pipes were inserted prior to cleaning so that any material knocked into the panel bottom would be removed during air-lifting.

Early during construction, it was common practice to allow fully excavated panels to sit open for several days prior to backfilling. During backfilling of two panels after a holiday shutdown, a layer of contaminated bentonite was observed on top of the concrete at the end of the pours. This layer was the result of excessive build-up of flocculated filter cake due to the addition of large quantities of cement to prevent slurry losses during excavation. As the bentonite lost its ability to maintain a stable filter cake and the duration a panel was left open increased, trench concrete underpours became more common indicating limited trench collapse or inward movement. Coating along joints of contaminated slurry was also a concern. A scratcher was used to clean joint surfaces. The practice of adding cement to stabilize slurry losses was eventually discontinued, and panels were mandated to be backfilled one day after excavation was completed.

Additional instrumentation was installed near these panels with theoretical concrete underpours during backfill placement. During drilling with a Becker hammer casing advancement rig to install a piezometer adjacent to a newly poured panel, the bit on the drill casing became blocked, and a surge of high pressure compressed air was used to clean the tip. This resulted in air bubbles appearing on both sides of the slurry wall. It was postulated that the panel either had a pre-existing defect or the weak backfill had been hydraulically fractured by the high pressure air. It was decided to replace this panel; however, re-excavation was not started for approximately two weeks. Maintaining panel verticality during this re-excavation was very difficult since the hardened backfill was significantly stronger than the surrounding soil. This problem was overcome by advancing pilot holes with the drop chisel and backfilling the panel with mine waste rock or lean concrete as necessary. Prompt re-excavation would have avoided this problem.

Backfill Placement

Backfill mixing -- Mixing of the backfill under field conditions proved to be another obstacle for the contractor to overcome. The first attempts involved dry-mixing the cement and bentonite with the aggregates before adding water. This method often resulted in balls of dry unmixed sand and bentonite. The unusually high percentage of bentonite in the mix made dry batching impossible to maintain a uniform mix. To overcome this problem the contractor and engineer together devised a method to first mix the bentonite with the mixing water in a high speed colloidal mixer, place this very thick mixture with a porridge consistency into a concrete ready-mix truck, and add the aggregate and cement at the ready-mix plant. This procedure allowed the bentonite to hydrate in the truck prior to adding cement and aggregate. While this resulted in a much more uniform material, the mix was still very difficult to maintain at a consistent balance between the slump needed for proper placement and the low strength necessary to provide ductility in the finished wall.

End stops -- Special end stops were developed by the contractor for this project to form a longer seepage path joint and protect the relatively weak plastic concrete during excavation of the adjacent panel. The end stops shown in Figure 9 were comprised of two elements: a steel tube miter joint form and a steel plate which was placed along the form with guides.   Both elements were lowered into the panel prior to concreting and left in-place for approximately 8 hours at which time the plastic concrete reached an initial set sufficient to be stable. At this time the form was removed before it became permanently set in the panel, but the protective plate was left in place to protect the plastic concrete formed joint. The plate was later removed after the adjacent panel bite excavation was completed.

The backfill in one panel collapsed due to a construction error when the end stop pipe was removed 4.5 hours after completion of the pour. The end of the backfill settled 2.5 feet (0.7 m), tension cracks could be measured to a depth of over 8 feet (2.4 m), and backfill material had slumped into the end stop hole to a depth of 28 feet (8.5.m). This panel was re-excavated and backfilled immediately with no verticality problems.

FIG. 9 -- End stops for joint forms in plastic concrete

QUALITY CONTROL

Quality control was an important element in the success of this project by providing panel by panel verification that the design intent was being achieved in construction. The most important elements of the quality control program were monitoring of excavation spoils to confirm that the embedment depth criteria in clayey till was achieved, testing of trench slurry properties such as filtrate to maintain adequate trench stability, verification of verticality, joint continuity and bottom cleanliness conditions to avoid building seepage paths into the wall, and monitoring of backfill mixing and placement to achieve a relatively uniform and fluid mix.

A significant program of backfill sample testing was implemented to confirm that the design mix properties were being achieved in the field. This testing included backfill slump at the trench, unconfined compression at various ages (7 days, 28 days and older), and triaxial compression tests. The unconsolidated undrained triaxial tests were conducted on 6-inch (15 cm) diameter specimens which had been submerged cured. Interestingly, as shown in Figure 10, the stress-strain characteristics of the plastic concrete resemble a ductile clayey till rather than a brittle concrete. This testing was excellent verification that a ductile mix was achieved that matched the deformation characteristics of the surrounding soil mass.

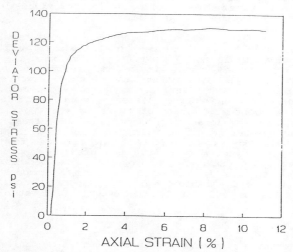

FIG. 10 -- Triaxial stress strain curve for 6-in. (15cm) specimen of plastic concrete backfill

INSTRUMENTATION

The Island Copper seepage barrier wall was heavily instrumented. A typical instrumented section is shown in Figure 3. The total instrumentation inventory consists of:

- 12 inclinometer/extensometer installations placed in the wall

- 43 vibrating wire (VW) piezometers in 15 multiple-level strings and 15 standpipe (SP) piezometers

- Settlement/movement points along 12 instrument lines with three locations on each line (wall, crest of soil slope, and crest of rock slope)

- Flow meters on ground water discharge pumps and flow weirs on seepage collection ditches.

Inclinometers were installed by coring holes directly in the wall. This was an effective way to maintain alignment of the drill hole, but the very hard nature of the coarse aggregate in a weak plastic concrete matrix resulted in very poor core recovery, which was not truly representative of the in situ backfill material. Piezometers were installed with a Becker hammer drill rig, which was able to relatively efficiently penetrate the dump material.

DEWATERING

After the slurry wall was completed and prior to pit slope excavation, the dump and beach and fluvial sands had to be dewatered inside the wall. In addition to allowing a stable excavation, dewatering also provided an excellent test of the seepage barrier effectiveness of the wall. The large number of instruments, and the flow net and finite element analysis predictions made during design, provided an opportunity to check that the design intent was achieved.

Originally six 8-inch (20 cm) diameter PVC deep wells were installed approximately 50 feet (15 m) downstream of the slurry wall. They were installed approximately 10 to 20 feet (3 to 6 m) into the till layer. Pumping began in October 1989 and, within about two months, approximately 40 to 50 feet (12 to 15 m) of drawdown was achieved, dewatering the dump and sands. The pumping rate continued to drop from a maximum of 1,700 igpm (7.7 m³/min) to a steady-state rate of between 100 to 300 igpm (0.45 to 1.36 m³/min). Eventually, most of the flow was contributed from a single well no. 7, which apparently tapped into an outwash zone beneath the wall. During dewatering, approximately 0.5 inches (1.2 cm) of lateral deflection was measured (see Figure 11). This compares favorably to the range of 0.2 to 0.84 inches (0.5 to 2 cm) predicted by design finite element analyses. Settlement of the top of the wall during dewatering ranged from 0.2 to 0.4 inches (0.5 to 1 cm), compared to design predictions of 0.2 to 0.4 inches. In 1991, two additional wells were added in the vicinity of well no. 7 in an attempt to dewater this outwash zone.

SLOPE EXCAVATION

Slope excavation proceeded within 50 feet (15 m) of the slurry wall at a slope of approximately 30° through the overburden soils and generally 40 to 45° in the rock wall (Figure 3). Between May and August 1990 when the bulk of the soil bench was excavated, the incremental lateral deflections ranged from 0.5 to 0.7 inches (1.2 to 1.7 cm), see Figure 11, with a total deflection of 1 to 1.4 inches (2.5 to 3.5 cm). This compares to 0.6 to 2 inches (1.5 to 5 cm) of total lateral deflection predicted in the design finite element analyses (Figure 6). Setlements of the top of the wall ranged from 0.5 to 0.6 inches (1.2 to 1.5 cm) compared to design predictions of 0.2 to 0.5 inches (0.5 to 1.2 cm). The excavation slope was stable and water flow has not increased, indicating that the wall is functioning as intended in design.

CONCLUSIONS

The owner, design team and contractor have succeeded in constructing an unprecedented slurry wall installation. Several key elements were responsible for this success. The owner made a concerted effort to become educated on the subject. The design team identified and quantified the difficulties well in advance. The remote location of the site, combined with the difficult nature of the subsurface deposits presented the contractor and design team with new challenges every day, such as:

- Unusual requirement for ductile, low permeability and erosion-resistant wall capable of sustaining relatively large deformations and high gradients in a salt water environment.

- Very difficult excavation conditions in loose dump with boulders and hard till, excessive slurry loss, and severe collapse problems.

- Problems with mixing and placing a low strength backfill with high bentonite content.

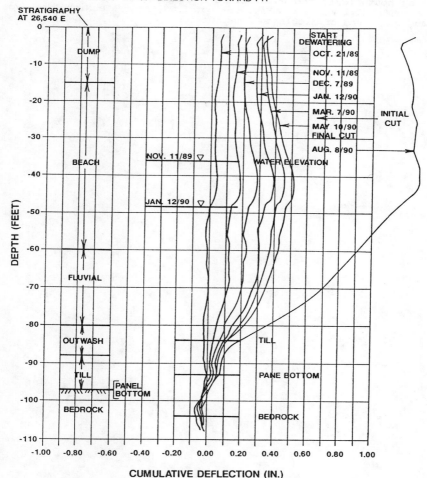

FIG. 11 -- Inclinometer deformation profile

However, these challenges were attacked with a spirit of partnership and willingness to try various technical solutions to solve the problems. This project expanded the range of practical slurry wall solutions to seepage problems in a loose, highly pervious and heterogeneous rock dump with a ductile, low strength plastic concrete.

ACKNOWLEDGEMENTS

The willingness of all parties involved to work through each problem together, providing the necessary expertise and resources, was the major reason for the success of the project. The project team was comprised of the authors and the following key individuals: Andy Robertson and John Barton - Bridges of SRK; Jean-Yves Perez, Richard Ladd, Tom Kelley and Danny Roybal of Woodward-Clyde; Chris Brown, Kevin O'Kane and John Hanna of Island Copper; G. Wayne Clough and Eric Leika of Virginia Tech; our consulting board of Milton Harr, Gilbert Tallard and Rick Call; Arturo Ressi, Nick Cavalli and Mario Marcasoli of ICOS; and Pete Nicholson, Joe Pratt and Don Bruce of Nichloson Construction.

Majed A. Khoury, Philippe H. Fayad, and Richard S. Ladd

DESIGN, CONSTRUCTION AND PERFORMANCE OF A SOIL-BENTONITE CUTOFF WALL
CONSTRUCTED IN TWO STAGES

REFERENCE: Khoury, M.A., Fayad, P.H., and Ladd, R.S., "Design,
Construction and Performance of a Soil-Bentonite Cutoff Wall
Constructed in Two Stages", Slurry Walls: Design, Construction
and Quality Control, ASTM STP 1129, David B. Paul,
Richard R. Davidson, and Nicholas J. Cavalli, Eds., American
Society for Testing and Materials, Philadelphia, 1992.

ABSTRACT: Soil-bentonite seepage cutoffs constructed by the
slurry-trench method in earth embankments present serious design
and construction concerns that need to be adequately addressed in
order to assure overall embankment safety. The paper describes
the various phases of the installation and performance monitoring
of a 1,500 m (4,900 ft) long S-B cutoff wall in a dam and dike
constructed of sandy material. The cutoff wall extended to a
maximum depth of 23 m (75 ft) and had a width of 0.9 m (3 ft),
except for a 305 m (1,000 ft) long section where the width was
increased to 1.5 m (5 ft) to accommodate hydraulic heads in excess
of 9 m (30 ft). Construction of the wall was performed in two
stages. The lower stage was constructed when the dam reached
about 75 percent of its maximum height while the upper stage was
constructed when the dam was close to its final height. This is
believed to be the first use of an S-B cutoff constructed in two
stages as the main barrier in a new embankment. The paper also
discusses the lessons learned from this two-stage construction and
post-construction performance based on the collected
instrumentation data.

KEYWORDS: Cutoff wall, embankment, soil-bentonite backfill,
slurry trench, design, laboratory testing, staged construction,
instrumentation, hydraulic fracturing, earth dam.

INTRODUCTION

A slurry trench soil-bentonite (S-B) wall was installed within the
Manasquan dam and dike in New Jersey, USA as the main barrier to
seepage through the relatively pervious embankment and foundation
soils. The 23 m (75 ft) maximum depth cutoff wall was constructed in
two stages. A lower stage was built when the dam reached a maximum
height of 14 m (45 ft). The upper stage was implemented when the dam
was 17 m (55 ft) high and this stage keyed a minimum of 0.9 m (3 ft)
into the lower stage.

The three authors are Senior Associate, Assistant Project Engineer
and Senior Associate, respectively, all with Woodward-Clyde
Consultants, 201 Willowbrook Boulevard, Wayne, New Jersey, U.S.A.,
07470.

Detailed studies and laboratory testing were conducted during the design phase to establish the geometry and backfill mix of the cutoff wall. The construction of the wall was carefully checked with a comprehensive quality control testing program. Performance of the cutoff wall was monitored during and after the filling of the reservoir with a series of settlement plates, total stress cells and vibrating-wire piezometers. Instrumentation data have indicated that the cutoff wall has effectively reduced the seepage through the embankments and foundation.

S-B cutoff walls constructed by slurry trench method are being used more frequently to reduce seepage in old and new embankments. Although this method has been in existence for many decades, its application for cutoff walls in earth dams presents serious design concerns associated with the applied hydraulic gradients and with stability and quality control during construction. These concerns need to be adequately addressed to assure proper performance of the wall and consequently the safety of the embankments. The design, construction and performance of the Manasquan S-B cutoff wall involved problems and considerations which are important to designers of similar installations. This paper describes the various phases of this project and presents an evaluation of the performance of the cutoff wall and the lessons learned.

DESCRIPTION OF SITE AND EMBANKMENTS

Site and Foundation Characteristics

The Manasquan Reservoir is located near Farmingdale in Monmouth County, New Jersey. The 15.9 million m³ (12,890 acre-foot) reservoir is part of a pumped storage water supply system that provides water to County users; therefore, allowing reduction in the demand for the limited groundwater resources in this coastal area of New Jersey.

The reservoir is formed by an 18 m (60 ft) high dam constructed across Timber Swamp Brook (a tributary to the Manasquan River) and an adjacent 9 m (30 ft) high dike constructed across a topographically low area south of the dam. The reservoir and embankments are underlain by Coastal Plain sediments. The major geologic formations of direct importance to this project consist of the Kirkwood, Manasquan and Vincentown formations. The Kirkwood formation includes an upper, predominantly sandy stratum, and a lower stratum with alternate layers of silt, clay and sand. The Kirkwood is underlain by the Manasquan formation which includes the major base clay layer beneath the reservoir. This layer is a high plasticity glauconitic clay at the top and grades to a sandy layer at the bottom. The Vincentown formation underlies the Manasquan formation and is predominantly sandy at the top and forms the main regional aquifer immediately below the reservoir. Most of the above-described formations underlying the site are also known to contain acidic soils.

The Kirkwood formation is under phreatic water table conditions with groundwater roughly governed by topography. The Vincentown formation is a semi-confined aquifer exhibiting artisian water pressures in the dam vicinity. A generalized profile along the dam alignment is shown on Figure 1.

Embankment Characteristics

The dam and dike were constructed of the predominantly fine sands of the upper Kirkwood formation obtained from on-site borrow areas. Within a portion of Timber Swamp Brook that included the centerline of

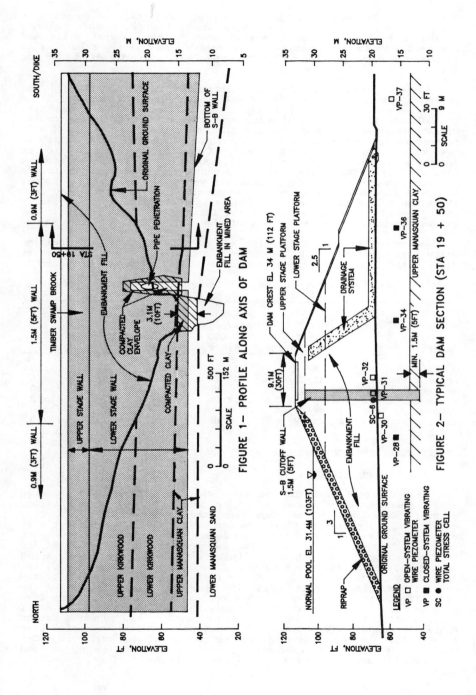

FIGURE 1— PROFILE ALONG AXIS OF DAM

FIGURE 2— TYPICAL DAM SECTION (STA 19 + 50)

the dam, the Manasquan clay had been mined for fertilizer sometime in the 19th Century. This mined area was filled with soft organic sediments that had to be excavated down to the natural soils and replaced with compacted soils including a blanket of imported clay to restore the mined portion of the Manasquan clay, immediately under the dam.

Seepage control within the homogenous sandy embankments was provided mainly by the S-B cutoff wall which keyed a minimum of 1.5 m (5 ft) into the Manasquan clay layer (or the compacted clay blanket). In addition, an internal drainage system consisting of a chimney drain, blanket drain and toe drain was installed downstream of the cutoff wall to control residual seepage and maintain downstream slope stability in case of a failure in the S-B cutoff. A typical dam cross-section is shown in Figure 2. A 3.1 m (10 ft) diameter Prestressed Reinforced Concrete Pipe (PRCP) horizontally penetrates the dam at about the original ground elevation, immediately south of Timber Swamp Brook. The PRCP pipe was constructed in an envelope of compacted clay into which the S-B cutoff keyed (see Figure 1). The pipe is connected to the upstream outlet tower, houses the inlet pipe to the reservoir and allows for the emergency drawdown of the reservoir at the same time.

Ranges of typical properties of the embankment and foundation soils are presented in Table 1. The range in particle-size distribution curves for the embankment soils is presented in Figure 3.

TABLE 1 -- Typical Properties of Embankment and Foundation Soils

Material Type	USCS Classification	Percent Passing No. 200 Sieve	Plasticity Index	Hydraulic Conductivity, cm/sec
Upper Kirkwood	SP-SM/SM	10-23	NP	$1 \times 10^{-3} - 1 \times 10^{-4}$
Lower Kirkwood	CH/ML/MH/CL/SM	33-84	10-39	$1 \times 10^{-3} - 1 \times 10^{-5}$
Manasquan Clay	CH	> 50	50	$5 \times 10^{-6} - 5 \times 10^{-7}$
Manasquan Sand	SM/SP-SC/SC	14-25	NP-30	$1 \times 10^{-2} - 1 \times 10^{-6}$
Vincentown Sand	SM/SP-SM/SC	9-29	NP	$1 \times 10^{-2} - 1 \times 10^{-3}$
Embankment Sand	SP-SM/SM	5-35	NP	$1 \times 10^{-3} - 1 \times 10^{-4}$

DESIGN CONSIDERATIONS AND LABORATORY TESTING

Critical Design Factors

An S-B cutoff wall for the Manasquan dam and dike was selected after considering a number of other possible methods of seepage control. Other methods considered included: a cement-bentonite (C-B) cutoff wall, a compacted clay core and an upstream inclined wet clay core. The S-B cutoff wall was determined to provide the most technically feasible and cost effective method of seepage control for this embankment. The S-B wall alternative was preferred over a C-B wall mainly because the S-B method allowed the formation of a filter cake along the trench walls which was believed to be beneficial to the overall performance of the wall, its hydraulic conductivity and the stability of the excavated trench (reduces the potential slurry loss through the unsaturated, relatively pervious embankment sands). Also, the S-B wall allowed a much easier achievement of the required design hydraulic conductivity (discussed later) and was less expensive than a C-B wall. However, the main disadvantage of an S-B wall over a C-B wall was associated with the impact of differential settlements between the backfill and the embankment on the long-term performance of the wall.

The design studies and associated laboratory testing were directed toward selecting a cutoff geometry and an S-B backfill that met the following criteria:

1. The long-term hydraulic conductivity of the wall was not to exceed 1 x 10^{-6} cm/sec (about 1,000 times smaller than the expected horizontal hydraulic conductivity of the embankment sands). A maximum laboratory hydraulic conductivity of 5 x 10^{-7} cm/sec, at an effective confining pressure of 48 kPa (0.5 tsf) was selected for construction quality control to account for field variabilities in backfill mixes.

2. The wall had to be compatible with the local soil and water environments. The design of the backfill mix had to maximize the use of on-site soils.

3. The wall had to be compatible with the hydraulic gradients imposed on it. The wall should therefore be designed to reduce the potential for development of concentrated leaks by hydraulic fracturing and to control downstream erosion that would result from these concentrated leaks.

4. The open slurry-filled trench had to be stable during construction to preserve the safety and integrity of the embankments.

Laboratory Testing to Select a Backfill Mix

The S-B wall had to be excavated in a profile consisting of soils with different characteristics such as the compacted embankment sands, the sands, silts and clays of the Kirkwood formation, and the clays of the Manasquan formation. As a result, the amount of fines available in the excavated soils was expected to vary significantly along the cutoff alignment, thus requiring at some locations the addition of dry bentonite or the importation of borrow soils with more fines (two costly alternatives) in order to achieve the required hydraulic conductivity of the backfill mix. The laboratory testing program was designed to address these concerns and to provide information on the hydraulic conductivity, consolidation and strength characteristics of the S-B mix needed for engineering analyses.

Various S-B mixes were prepared using on-site material and representing the expected soil conditions along the excavated trench. A laboratory testing program (following accepted ASTM or U.S. Corps of Engineers standards) was conducted to develop the relevant S-B backfill mix characteristics. These characteristics are summarized in Table 2 and Figures 4 and 5. Laboratory data from D'Appolonia (1980) are shown on Figures 4 and 5 for comparison purposes. The S-B backfill volumetric strains measured during initial consolidation of the hydraulic conductivity samples are also reported in Table 2.

A series of compatibility tests were also performed with acid water as permeant. About 3 pore volumes of acid water (pH = 2.9) were permeated through one S-B test specimen (mix No. 5 in Table 2). The test indicated that the hydraulic conductivity of this specimen remained basically unchanged after this permeation.

The laboratory tests confirmed that a backfill mix using on-site soils, with at least 30 percent fines, can achieve the hydraulic conductivity required for construction quality control. However, the test results (i.e., compression ratios and volumetric strains) indicated that, at the required percent fines, the S-B backfill would have high compressibility, resulting in relatively large settlements. It should be mentioned that the measured volumetric strains were comparable to values measured on S-B backfills from other similar

TABLE 2 -- Laboratory Data On Soil-Bentonite Backfill Mixes

Soil-Bentonite Mix Characteristics	Mix 1	Mix 2	Mix 3	Mix 4	Mix 5
A. General Mix Data					
• Slump, cm (in.)	12.7(5)	13.3(5.25)	12.1(4.75)	12.7(5)	12.7(5)
• Percent Bentonite by dry weight*	1.08	0.87	1.05	1.18	1.65
B. Index and Physical Properties					
• Passing No. 200 Sieve, percent	8.7	23.4	30.5	37.6	72.5
• Water Content, Percent	23.8	32.5	31.0	39.0	62.1
• Total Unit Weight, KN/m³ (pcf)	19.0(121.3)	18.2(115.8)	18.2(115.9)	17.6(111.8)	15.7(100.0)
• Undrained Shear Strength by laboratory vane, kPa (psf)	-	-	-	1.0(20)	2.0(42)
• pH	6.6	-	6.2	3.4	3.2
C. Engineering Properties					
• Hydraulic Conductivity, cm/sec [Volumetric strain, percent]					
-- at 48 kPa (0.5 tsf) confining pressure	1.2×10^{-5}	1.1×10^{-6} [6.9]	4.1×10^{-7} [11.6]	2.9×10^{-7} [13.6]	1.9×10^{-7} [15.9]
-- at 96 kPa (1.0 tsf) confining pressure	-	9.2×10^{-7} [13.3]	3.2×10^{-7} [15.4]	2.2×10^{-7} [18.0]	1.2×10^{-7} [18.4]
-- at 287 kPa (3.0 tsf) confining pressure	-	6.4×10^{-7} [16.1]	1.9×10^{-7} [16.5]	1.3×10^{-7} [21.4]	4.5×10^{-8} [29.0]
• Consolidation					
-- Compression Ratio	-	-	0.077	0.091	0.137
-- Swell Ratio	-	-	0.005	0.006	0.010
-- Coeff. of Consol. for 96-192 kPa (1-2 tsf), 1×10^{-4} cm²/sec	-	-	85.9	63.3	20.6

* Based on adding slurry with a 6 percent bentonite to water ratio (by weight) to achieve the required backfill slump.

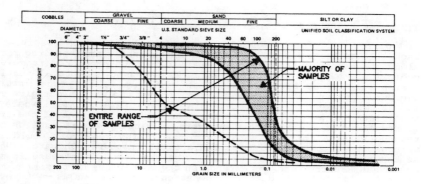

FIGURE 3— TYPICAL PARTICLE— SIZE RANGE
FOR EMBANKMENT SOILS

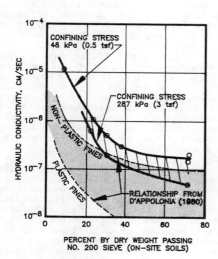

FIGURE 4— HYDRAULIC
CONDUCTIVITY OF
S—B BACKFILL
RELATED TO ON—SITE
FINES CONTENT

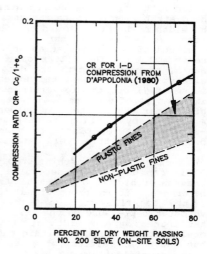

FIGURE 5— COMPRESSIBILITY
OF S—B BACKFILL
RELATED TO ON—
SITE FINES CONTENT

projects. Furthermore, additional laboratory testing demonstrated that unreasonably large percentage of gravel (at least 30 percent) would have to be mixed with the S-B backfill to achieve a beneficial reduction in volumetric strain and to reduce the potential for large settlement.

Hydraulic Fracturing Evaluations

Differential settlement between the relatively compressible S-B backfill and the compacted more rigid embankment generates drag forces along the trench wall. The S-B backfill is thus prevented from fully consolidating under its own weight. As a result, the total vertical stress within the backfill does not build up to its true vertical overburden value. This arching action across the wall might give rise to the development of horizontal thin cracks in the backfill where the total vertical stress acting on the near horizontal plane of the crack is reduced. If the hydrostatic reservoir water pressure exceeds this reduced vertical stress, water from the rising reservoir could seep through the crack resulting in a hydraulic fracture (Sherard, 1986). As the reservoir continues to rise, the crack could increase in size and erode. Further erosion depends on the conditions of the embankment material located immediately downstream of the wall. However, according to Sherard (1985): "Leaks caused by hydraulic fracturing usually do not cause erosion, either because the velocity is too low or because they discharge into effective filters" and "both experience with dam behavior and recent laboratory research show conclusively that concentrated leaks (from hydraulic fracturing) are reliably controlled and sealed by adequate filters, even under the most extreme conditions."

The estimation of vertical stresses within a narrow cutoff trench filled with relatively compressible backfill is not well established. The distribution of these stresses with depth depends significantly on the width of the trench and the shear stresses that develop along the trench walls, among other factors. In the case of S-B walls, the magnitude of wall shear stresses is affected by the filter cake on the trench walls. The filter cake tends to lubricate the wall of the trench, thereby reducing the drag forces on the wall and helping the build-up of total vertical stresses. The method of S-B backfill placement (i.e., tremie versus dozer filling), the coarseness of the mix and type of embankment material, all influence the preservation of this filter cake. There is evidence to suggest that this filter cake is not destroyed during the displacement of the bentonite slurry by the S-B backfill when placed by pushing into the trench with a dozer. However, very little field data exists on this issue.

Terzaghi simple arching theory and suggestions proposed by Blight (1973) can be used to determine the distribution of total vertical stresses within the S-B trench. Assuming that: 1) shear stresses along the trench wall are proportional to the effective vertical stresses and 2) the backfill pore pressure is proportional to the effective hydrostatic pressure on the wall, it can be demonstrated theoretically that increasing the width of the wall results in an increase of the total vertical stresses within the wall. These analyses also confirm that the total vertical stresses in a narrow trench can become, with depth, significantly smaller than the overburden stresses.

In practice, such stress analyses are rarely performed. Instead, engineers have limited the differential hydraulic gradient acting on the S-B wall using experience and sometimes the results of blowout tests. The objective of these tests is to establish the gradient at which the S-B fines "pipe" into the downstream embankment shell (Xanthakos, 1979). The U.S. Corps of Engineers (1986) recommends using a trench width equal to 0.1 of the maximum differential hydraulic head acting on the S-B wall. This recommendation is based on a factor of safety of 3 and a blowout gradient of 30. For this project, a laboratory blowout test was performed to confirm the gradient at which a sharp increase in flow occurs through a 10 cm (4 in.) thick layer of S-B backfill overlying a 10 cm (4 in.) thick layer of compacted embankment sand. The test was conducted in a flexible wall triaxial cell having a diameter of 10 cm (4 in.). The test indicated that no blowout occurred for applied hydraulic gradients up to 160. A different type of laboratory tests, however, has been used by Sherard and Dunningan (1989) to evaluate penetration of fines into downstream filters.

Based on all of the above considerations, a 0.9 m (3 ft) thick S-B wall was selected for hydraulic heads up to 9 m (30 ft) and a 1.5 m (5 ft) thick wall was selected for hydraulic heads greater than 9 m (30 ft). Additionally, the compacted embankment sand downstream of the S-B wall was expected to act as a filter to control concentrated flows from possible hydraulic fractures or other leaks (if they occur). The D_{15} of the embankment sand (see Figure 3) is less than the 0.7 mm size recommended by Sherard and Dunningan (1989) for downstream filters against sandy silts and clays and silty and clayey sands (i.e., soil Group 2 in their classification which is comparable to the S-B backfill in the Manasquan cutoff). Finally, a drainage system was also incorporated into the downstream shell of the embankments as a third line of defense for controlling potential leaks.

CONSTRUCTION METHODS AND QUALITY CONTROL

Two-Stage Construction

Construction of the cutoff wall was executed in two stages. The original design called for a one stage construction. The lower stage had a maximum depth of 19.5 m (64 ft) with an average depth of 17 m (56 ft) and was keyed 1.5 m (5 ft) into the Manasquan Clay. The upper stage averaged a depth of 5.5 m (18 ft) and was keyed a minimum of 0.9 m (3 ft) into the lower stage S-B backfill. The upper stage wall was constructed two months after the completion of the lower stage wall.

The contractor preferred the two stage construction because, in his opinion, the reduction of the depth of the excavated trenches would improve stability, would create more room on top of the embankment to mix the backfill on the side of the trench (on-site mixing), and would limit the continuous need for a clamshell to excavate the trench. However, the two stage construction resulted in added quality control testing and monitoring and in the creation of a connection between the upper and lower walls.

Lower Stage Trench

A hydraulic Koehring 1266D backhoe with an extended 23 m (75 ft) long dipper stick was used to excavate the majority of the lower trench. Construction started from the north abutment of the dam toward the south abutment of the dike. The excavated material was stockpiled on top of the embankment adjacent to the trench where it was mixed with the bentonite slurry pumped from the trench. The mixing was performed with several passes of a CAT D5H-L6P dozer mounted on wide tracks equipped with pyramidal shape cleats. The mixed backfill was then pushed back into the slurry filled trench.

A 53 cm (21 in.) diameter tremie pipe was used at two locations for backfill placement: at the startup of the trench and on the south side of the PRCP penetration into the dam. At this later location, the vertical trench keys on each side of the clay envelope (see Figure 1) necessitated the drilling of two open shafts under bentonite slurry. The augered shafts had a diameter of 1.5 m (5 ft) and were used as open slots to guide the backhoe bucket as it approached (or departed) the northern (or southern side) of the penetration.

The trench excavation proceeded in 6 m to 9 m (20 ft to 30 ft) long sections with the toe of the excavation kept at least 6 m (20 ft) ahead of the leading edge of the backfill slope. The average progress rate for the lower stage trench was 455 m^2 (4,900 ft^2) per day and 440 m^2 (4,700 ft^2) per day for the 0.9 m (3 ft) wide trench and the 1.5 m (5 ft) wide trench, respectively. The bentonite-water slurry was mixed in a 54,500 L (12,000 gallon) tank with a continuous Venturi tube high shear mixer. Bentonite was delivered in bulk by trucks to a large capacity silo parked near the mixing tank. Open ponds were used for hydration, circulation and storage of the bentonite-water slurry before pumping to the open trench.

The sand content of the bentonite slurry in the trench was regularly monitored. An efficient slurry recirculation method was followed whereby fresh slurry was pumped to the leading edge of the excavation and the slurry needed in the backfill was pumped from the trench near the backfill toe. However, a Caviem desanding unit had to be used on few occasions to further reduce the sand content, especially when only a very small amount of fresh slurry was pumped to the trench. The suction point of the desanding unit was located at approximately a depth of 12 m (40 ft) within the trench.

The cleanliness of the bottom of the trench and the top of the backfill slope were also regularly monitored for sand sediment accumulation and, when necessary, a clamshell moving behind the backhoe was used to perform the required clean up.

Upper Stage Trench

The same 1266D Koehring hydraulic backhoe with a standard dipper stick was used to excavate the upper trench. The average progress rate was 670 m^2 (7,200 ft^2) per day and 640 m^2 (6,900 ft^2) per day for the 0.9 m (3 ft) and the 1.5 m (5 ft) wide trench, respectively. Since the excavated material consisted entirely of embankment sand, lower Kirkwood silty/clayey material was imported from on-site borrow areas to increase the amount of fines for most of the trench alignment. Furthermore, the cleanliness of the bottom of the trench was strictly maintained to avoid leaving a relatively pervious sandy zone at the connection between the upper and lower trenches.

Quality Control Testing

Quality control testing during the construction of the S-B wall was the responsibility of the contractor. The engineer provided regular check testing to confirm the contractor's data. The project contract documents established the quality control testing program, including the methods or standards for the tests, the frequency of testing and the required testing values. The trench was tested every 3 m (10 ft) intervals for depth and every 6 m (20 ft) intervals for penetration into the keying stratum and for deviation from the planned alignment. The actual trench alignment remained within 0.3 m (1 ft) from the specified alignment. The trench deviation from verticality was tested every day and did not exceed 1.5 percent of the trench depth.

The bentonite-water slurry was tested for viscosity, density, filtration and pH at both the pump location (mixing point) and in the trench. A submarine sampler was used to collect slurry samples from different depths within the trench.

The S-B backfill was sampled at the leading edge of the advancing backfill slope and was tested for slump, density, fraction passing the No. 200 sieve, and hydraulic conductivity. A 72 N (50 lb) grab sampler was used to collect these S-B backfill samples as well as the samples from the backfill slope. The operation of this heavy sampler was quite involved, but was found very helpful in checking the backfill quality. Although, the flexible wall permeameter constituted the basis for acceptance of the backfill, a rigid wall permeameter was used for more frequent and rapid testing and as an indicator of the quality of the backfill. However, the rigid wall permeameter resulted in hydraulic conductivities about one order of magnitude higher than the values obtained in the flexible wall permeameter.

The slope of the backfill was also measured regularly, and found to be on the average 2 times flatter in the 1.5 m (5 ft) wide trench than in the 0.9 m (3 ft) wide trench. Table 3 presents a summary of the results of the quality control testing during construction of the two-stage S-B wall. In summary, the test results in this table indicated that construction met the intent of the contract documents. Also, these tests formed the basis for adjusting construction methods such as the need for desanding, cleaning the bottom of the trench and backfill slope, as well as adjusting the slurry and backfill constituents.

SETTLEMENT OBSERVATIONS

Construction of the S-B cutoff in two stages necessitated the detailed monitoring of the backfill settlement in order to establish when the majority of this settlement had occurred and to decide when the placement of the overlying embankment material could begin. However, the observed settlements provided added insight into the long-term behavior of the cutoff wall as discussed later in the paper.

Temporary settlement plates were installed 15 cm (6 in.) below the surface of the lower stage backfill as shown in Figure 6. They consisted of 61 cm x 91 cm (2 ft x 3 ft) size galvanized steel plates having a thickness of 1.3 cm (0.5 in.). The plates were connected to a 2.5 cm (1 in.) diameter riser pipe inserted in a 5.1 cm (2 in.) diameter PVC sleeve. The settlement plates were installed in both the 0.9 m (3 ft) wide trench and the 1.5 m (5 ft) wide trench. However, construction scheduling difficulties led to a delay of several days in the installation of these plates, therefore missing some of the initial backfill settlement. The magnitude of this settlement had to be back estimated based on visual observations and settlement data (strains) observed in the upper stage backfill.

Temporary settlement plates consisting of 30 cm x 30 cm (1 ft x 1 ft) wooden boards were installed on the top of the upper stage backfill within 24 hours of the backfill placement. In addition, Borros points were pushed through the upper stage backfill and were anchored in the lower stage backfill to monitor the settlement of this backfill during construction of the upper trench.

Settlement observations in the upper and lower stage backfills are shown in Figure 7. Interpretation of the data presented in Figure 7 indicates that:

1. Most of the settlement of the lower (deeper) stage S-B backfill occurred during the first 2 months and 3 weeks after backfilling of the 1.5 m (5 ft) wide trench and the 0.9 m (3 ft) wide trench, respectively.
2. The measured settlement of the S-B backfill in the 1.5 m (5 ft) wide trench was about 2 to 3 times the measured settlement of the backfill in the 0.9 m (3 ft) wide trench.

TABLE 3 -- Summary of Quality Control Testing*

Component/Property	Frequency	Lower State Trench		Upper Stage Trench		Specified
		Range	Average	Range	Average	Value
A. Bentonite-Water Slurry (pump)						
• Viscosity, sec	2/day	40-50	43.3	37-47	42.3	40-45 sec
• Density, kN/m^3 (pcf)	2/day	10-11.6 (63.5-74)	10.2 (65.2)	10.1-11.5 (64-73.5)	10.5 (66.6)	min. 10.1 kN/m^3 (min. 64.3 pcf)
• Filtrate loss, ml	2/day	10.5-19	13.5	12-15.5	13.1	max. 25 ml in 30 min at 4.8 kPa (100 psi)
• pH	2/day	7-9	7.3	7-8	7.3	7-10
B. Bentonite-Water Slurry (trench)						
• Viscosity, sec	2/day	43-105	58	41-78	57.8	35-60 sec
• Density, kN/m^3 (pcf)	2/day	10.2-13.5 (65-86)	12.1 (77.3)	11.6-13.7 (74-87)	12.6 (80.1)	10.1-14.2 kN/m^3 (64.3-90.5 pcf)
• Filtrate loss, ml	1/day	11.5-23	16.1	13-18	15.4	N/A
• pH	2/day	6.4-8.6	7.2	6.3-7.4	6.7	N/A
• API Sand Content, percent	-	9.0-34	22.8	18.5-36	25.5	N/A
B. Soil-Bentonite Backfill						
• Slump, cm (in.)	2/day	9.5-17.8 (3.75-7)	13.5 (5.3)	9.5-16.5 (3.75-6.5)	13.5 (5.3)	10.2-15.2 cm (4-6 in.)
• Density, kN/m^3 (pcf)	2/day	17.1-18.1 (109-115)	17.7 (112.7)	18.1-18.7 (115-119)	18.4 (117.3)	3.1 kN/m^3 (20 pcf) above slurry density
• Passing No. 200 Sieve, percent	1/week	17.4-50.3	39.3	31.9-47.1	40.0	N/A
• Flexible Wall Hydraulic Cond., cm/sec	1/week	2.0×10^{-7} 5.2×10^{-8}	9.4×10^{-8}	2.8×10^{-7} 1.0×10^{-7}	1.5×10^{-7}	max. 5×10^{-7} cm/sec
• API fixed Wall Hydraulic Cond., cm/sec	1/day	2.1×10^{-6} 3.8×10^{-8}	8.5×10^{-7}	1.5×10^{-6} 2.9×10^{-7}	9.2×10^{-7}	N/A
• Backfill Slope	1/day	10H:1V for 0.9 m(3 ft) trench and 19H:1V for 1.5 m(5 ft) trench				5H:1V - 10H:1V

*Testing in accordance with American Petroleum Institute Specifications (API RP 13A an 13B), American Society of Testing and Materials standards (ASTM) and U.S. Army Corps of Engineers Manual (EM1110-2-1906).

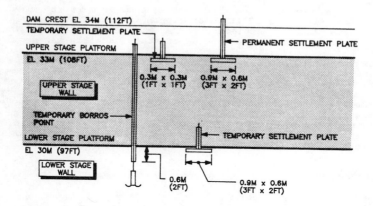

FIGURE 6— SETTLEMENT INSTRUMENTS
IN S—B BACKFILL

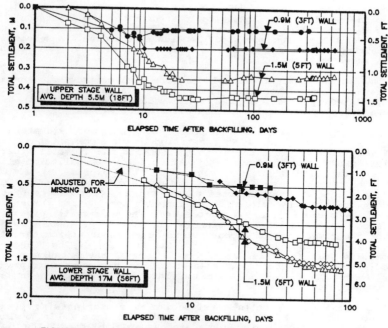

FIGURE 7— OBSERVED SETTLEMENT OF S—B BACKFILL
FROM TEMPORARY SETTLEMENT PLATES

3.   Vertical strains measured in the S-B backfill were about 7 to
     9 percent and 3 to 4 percent in the 1.5 m (5 ft) wide trench
     and the 0.9 m (3 ft) wide trench, respectively.
4.   The measured settlement of the lower stage backfill following
     the construction of the upper stage backfill was negligible.

Construction of the embankment above the completed trench resumed
after measurements indicated that most of the backfill settlement had
occurred. However, fill placement operations above the completed lower
stage trench proceeded cautiously and heavy equipment did not operate
over the trench until about 1.5 m (5 ft) of fill was placed over the
S-B backfill. The top of the backfill in the upper stage 1.5 m (5 ft)
wide trench was reinforced with geogrids to allow the use of heavy
equipment over the trench and to improve the long-term condition of the
paved road along the crest of the dam.

INSTRUMENTATION AND POST-CONSTRUCTION MONITORING

Instrument Types and Locations

     The completed S-B cutoff was instrumented as part of the overall
instrumentation system for the embankments. The objective of the
instrumentation was to monitor the performance of the cutoff wall and
to verify the design assumptions. The cutoff related instruments
included: permanent settlement plates on top of the S-B backfill, a
series of piezometers inside the backfill and in the embankment
upstream and downstream of the cutoff, a series of total stress cells
inside the backfill and flow weirs located at the two discharge points
of the dam toe drain. The instruments were concentrated in 5 study
sections at the dam and one study section at the dike. A schematic of
the instrument types and locations along a typical study section in the
dam is shown on Figure 2.

     The permanent settlement plates were similar to those installed
temporarily in the lower stage trench. The plates were laid on top of
the completed upper stage backfill immediately after removal of the
temporary plates and Borros points discussed previously.

     Piezometers in the S-B backfill consisted of vibrating-wire
sensors (Geokon Model No. 4500S) installed inside a conventional 3.2 cm
(1.25 in.) diameter well point tip pushed into the backfill after the
completion of the upper stage construction. This installation allowed
for easy replacement of the sensors at the expense of a longer
piezometer response time. Five piezometers were installed at different
elevations adjacent to the total stress cells. Piezometers upstream
and downstream of the cutoff included either open-system (embankment)
or closed-system (foundation) piezometers. The open-system piezometers
consisted of vibrating-wire sensors (Geokon Model 4500S) inserted
through the riser pipe of a conventional Casagrande piezometer with a
0.6 m (2 ft) long porous plastic filter tip. The Casagrande
piezometers were installed after completion of the embankment. The
closed-system piezometers consisted of Telemac vibrating wire pressure
cells (Model CL-1) and were buried into the foundation prior to
embankment construction.

     The total stress cells consisted of a vibrating-wire pressure
transducer (Geokon Model 4500) connected to a 5 cm (2 in.) wide by
10.2 cm (4 in.) long fluid filled stainless steel bladder. The bladder
was connected to an EW-size drill rod pushed into the S-B backfill
after completion of the upper stage construction. At 2 locations
within the 1.5 m (5 ft) wide wall, the cells were oriented in
2 directions, i.e.,. parallel and perpendicular to the dam alignment.
These stress cells were found to be very sensitive to ambient
temperatures and required important temperature corrections. A
temperature correction curve was developed by the manufacturer on 3

cells similar to those installed. The built-in cell thermistors allowed to make in situ temperature measurements and to correct the measured pressures accordingly. Unfortunately, 2 of the 7 installed cells developed significant calibration problems and became unreliable.

Instruments in S-B wall were positioned at the centerline of the wall. All cables from the vibrating wire sensors were carried to junction boxes at the top of the embankments and then were carried to a Remote Monitoring Unit (RMU) at the inlet/outlet tower. The signals were sent via radio frequency from the RMU to a Central Network Monitor (CNM) at the Reservoir Administration Building where all data management and reporting took place.

Instrumentation Data

Construction of the dam and dike embankments was completed in September 1989. Reservoir filling began on February 1990, the reservoir reached elevation 31.1 m (102 ft) in July 1990 and has fluctuated around this elevation since then. The rate of filling averaged about 15 cm (0.5 ft) per day during the first month and decreased to approximately half this rate until June 1990. All instruments were monitored manually prior to, and during the initial filling of the reservoir (until April 1990) and automatically thereafter.

Data collected from the settlement plates on top of the S-B backfill indicated that no appreciable settlement of the backfill had occurred after completion of the upper stage cutoff wall construction. The total flow rate recorded at the flow weirs at the dam has consistently remained below 45 L/min (12 gpm) and did not show any increase as the reservoir filled up. Only seasonal fluctuations were observed in the flow weirs due to rainfall.

Figure 8 shows plots of the measured total heads in piezometers installed at dam station 19+50 which corresponds to a dam height of 15.2 m (50 ft) and 1.5 m (5 ft) wide cutoff. These plots are representative of the other instrumentation study sections (not reported herein) and indicate the following:

1. The total heads upstream of the cutoff wall increased with reservoir filling and remained at, or slightly below the reservoir levels.
2. The total heads downstream of the cutoff wall were controlled by the blanket drain (or were slightly above the top of the blanket in the zone located between the cutoff wall and the upstream edge of the blanket drain).
3. The total heads in the cutoff wall were intermediate between the total heads upstream and downstream of the cutoff. The head drop observed between the upstream piezometers and the piezometers in the cutoff wall corresponds to approximately 40 percent of the total 10 m (33 ft) head drop across the wall. Similar observations were made at other instrumented study sections except that the total head drops across the 0.9 m (3 ft) wall were smaller than 7.5 m (25 ft). Therefore, the maximum gradients observed across both walls were less than 10.

Figure 9 shows plots of the measured horizontal total stresses in the stress cells installed in the S-B backfill. These stress measurements represent 2 elevations in the 1.5 m (5 ft) wide trench: elevation 16.8 m (55 ft) for 2 directions and elevation 19.8 m (65 ft) for 2 directions; and one elevation in the 0.3 m (3 ft) wide trench,

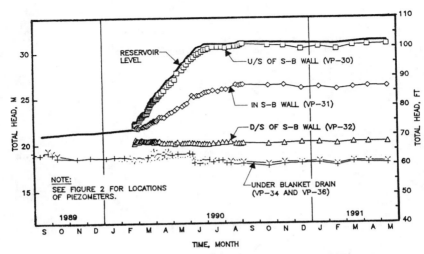

FIGURE 8— PIEZOMETRIC HEADS AT STA 19+50

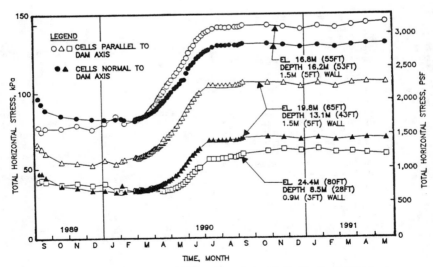

FIGURE 9— TOTAL HORIZONTAL STRESSES IN S—B WALL

i.e., 24.4 m (80 ft) for one direction.   Figure 9 indicates the following:

1. The observed increase in total horizontal stress in the backfill followed the reservoir rise. This increase was approximately equal to the increase in total head in the companion backfill piezometers.

2. The stress cells installed parallel to the dam axis (or facing the reservoir) measured higher horizontal stresses than cells installed perpendicular to the dam axis.

3. The horizontal stresses increased with depth.

Figure 10 presents a summary plot of the variation with depth of the total piezometric heads and total horizontal stresses in the S-B wall.   The data in Figure 10 suggests that the measured total horizontal stresses from cells facing the reservoir are approximately equal to or slightly greater than the normal pool reservoir pressure. Similar observations were made in Britain, however, within narrow puddle clay embankment cores and for about the same ratios of measurement depth to wall thickness (Charles, 1990).

Due to the elevation of the cells, direct comparisons of horizontal stresses at similar depths could not be made between the 1.5 m (5 ft) wall and the 0.9 m (3 ft) wall. However, the smaller magnitude of total settlements observed in the 0.9 m (3 ft) wall suggests that the transfer of total vertical stress with depth could be less than observed in the wider wall. This is consistent with theoretical analysis using simple arching theories. Therefore, total horizontal stresses at depths greater than 8.5 m (28 ft) within the 0.9 m (3 ft) wall (i.e., deepest cell elevation) may be smaller than the stresses measured below this depth in the 1.5 m (5 ft) wall (i.e., less than reservoir pressure).

The total vertical pressures can be estimated from the measured piezometric heads and total horizontal pressures (normal to the dam axis) using an assumed lateral earth pressure coefficient of 0.5. These estimated vertical pressures in the S-B backfill are shown on Figure 10 and indicate values greater than reservoir hydrostatic pressures, but smaller than total overburden pressures. However, the actual lateral earth pressure coefficient is unknown and could be less than 0.5, resulting in total vertical stress values smaller than those shown in Figure 10.

CONCLUSIONS AND RECOMMENDATIONS

General Conclusions

1. The installation of the S-B seepage barrier by the slurry trench method has effectively reduced seepage through the Manasquan embankments and their foundation. This is supported by the observed reduction in piezometric heads across the cutoff wall and the extremely low discharge from the downstream flow weirs.

2. The careful implementation of a detailed quality control program during construction required the cooperation of the contractor. This was essential to the construction of a relatively homogenous cutoff, therefore reducing the potential for "windows" or major defects in the wall. Furthermore, the collected quality control data allowed the timely adjustment of backfill constituents and construction methods to meet field conditions.

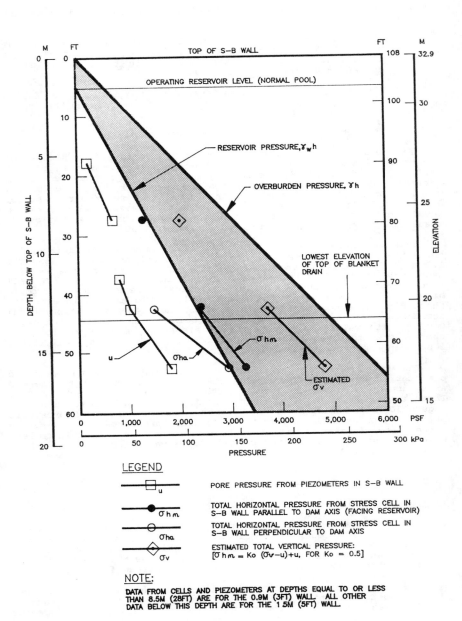

FIGURE 10 — TOTAL PRESSURES IN S—B WALL

3. Installation of the wall in two stages resulted in some construction advantages (in terms of cost and schedule). However, these benefits may have been somewhat offset by additional quality control monitoring to ensure proper tie-in and clean up of an additional working platform within the embankments.

4. Increasing the width of the cutoff wall induced more settlement of the S-B backfill during construction. The maximum total settlement of the S-B backfill observed in the 1.5 m (5 ft) wall was 2 m (6.6 ft). This was twice the maximum total settlement of 1 m (3.2 ft) observed in the 0.9 m (3 ft) wall.

5. Most of the observed S-B backfill settlement occurred within less than 2 months after placement. However, the observed maximum settlement in the shallow upper stage wall was reached faster (i.e., within two weeks) than in the deeper lower stage wall.

6. The gradation of the S-B backfill was a major variable in the amount of observed total settlement. The addition of gravel was not found economical for reducing the compressibility of the S-B backfill. However, it may be advantageous in other cases to modify the original gradation of the backfill (if practical) to achieve the compressibility reduction.

7. Stress cells installed in the S-B backfill facing the reservoir suggest total horizontal stresses that are approximately equal to or slightly greater than the normal pool reservoir pressure. In the 0.9 m (3 ft) wall, these stresses could be less than reservoir pressure below a depth of about 8.5 m (28 ft).

Recommendations

The instrumentation data presented in this paper suggests that narrow S-B cutoff walls may be susceptible to the development of horizontal cracks or separations due to differential settlement between the backfill and embankment soils. This susceptibility is increased with depth. The presence of these cracks could lead to hydraulic fracturing when the reservoir is filled and if piping is not prevented downstream of the wall. The use of S-B cutoff walls wider than the conventional 0.9 m (3 ft) width appears to reduce the potential for cracking. However, there is a practical limit to the construction of wide S-B cutoffs by the slurry trench method, especially when such widths are required for high dams. In these situations, other types of cutoffs have to be considered.

Additional in situ investigations, such as direct measurement of vertical stresses (Watts and Charles, 1988) or cone penetration testing to detect weak strength zones (Engemoen and Hensley, 1986) in completed S-B walls would improve our understanding of stress transfer in these walls and are recommended. Detailed stress analyses and settlement computations should be used only as indicators of potential cracking. If such potential exists, it would be poor engineering not to design adequate filters and drainage zones to control internal erosion in the embankment shell downstream of the S-B cutoff wall.

Finally, the authors would like to emphasize that careful construction quality control of S-B cutoff walls is as important as the above considerations to the successful performance of the cutoff.

ACKNOWLEDGEMENTS

The work discussed in this paper was performed by Woodward-Clyde Consultants as part of the engineering services provided by the team of Metcalf and Eddy and Woodward-Clyde to the New Jersey Water Supply Authority for the Manasquan Reservoir System. Inquip Associates, Inc. of McLean, Virginia, U.S.A., was the S-B cutoff wall subcontractor.

The authors wish to acknowledge the contributions to this work of their colleagues Christopher Adams, Richard Davidson, Artie Harris, Jr., Harry Horn, Robert Kirby, and Jean-Yves Perez. Dr. Melvin Esrig of Woodward-Clyde reviewed the final manuscript and provided valuable suggestions.

REFERENCES

Blight, G.E., 1973, "Stresses in Narrow Cores and Core Trenches in Dams," Transactions of the 11th International Congress on Large Dams, ICOLD, Madrid, Spain, pp. 63-79.

Charles, J.A., 1990, "Deterioration of Clay Barriers: Case Histories," Proceedings of the Conference on Clay Barriers for Embankment Dams, Institution of Civil Engineers, London, October 18, 1989, Thomas Telford, London, pp. 109-129.

D'Appolonia, D.J., June 1980, "Soil Bentonite Slurry Trench Cutoffs," Journal of Geotechnical Engineering, ASCE, Vol. 106, No. 6, pp. 399-417.

Engemoen, W.O, and Hensley, P.J., June 1986, "ECPT Investigation of a Slurry Trench Cutoff Wall," Proceedings of In Situ 86, a Specialty Conference on the Use of In Situ Tests in Geotechnical Engineering, ASCE, Blackburg, Virginia, pp. 514-528.

Sherard, J.L., October 1986, "Hydraulic Fracturing in Embankment Dams," Journal of Geotechnical Engineering, ASCE, Vol. 112, No. 10, pp. 905-927.

Sherard, J.L., and Dunningan, L.P., May 1985, "Filters and Leakage Control in Embankment Dams," Proceedings of the Conference on Seepage and Leakage from Dams and Impoundments, ASCE, Denver, Colorado, pp. 1-30.

Sherard, J.L., and Dunningan, L.P., July 1989, "Critical Filters for Impervious Soils," Journal of Geotechnical Engineering, ASCE, Vol. 115, No. 7, pp. 927-947.

U.S. Army Corps of Engineers, September 1986, Engineering and Design Seepage Analysis and Control for Dams, Engineer Manual EM 1110-2-1901.

Watts, K.S., and Charles, J.A., 1988, "In Situ Measurement of Vertical and Horizontal Stress from a Vertical Borehole". Geotechnique, Vol. 38, No. 4, pp. 619-626.

Xanthakos, P.P., 1979, Slurry Walls, McGraw Hill, New York.

Richard R. Davidson[1], Jacques Levallois[2], and Kenneth Graybeal[3]

SEEPAGE CUTOFF WALL FOR MUD MOUNTAIN DAM

REFERENCE: Davidson, R.R., Levallois, J., and Graybeal, K., "Seepage Cutoff Wall for Mud Mountain Dam," <u>Slurry Walls: Design, Construction and Quality Control</u>, ASTM STP 1129, David B. Paul, Richard R. Davidson and Nicholas J. Cavalli, Eds., American Society for Testing and Materials, Philadelphia, 1992.

ABSTRACT: Monitoring of instrumentation of the 50-year old Mud Mountain Dam indicated to the U.S. Army Corps of Engineers (Seattle District) that the core of the 120-meter high earth-rockfill dam possessed defects that could lead to a potential piping failure. Therefore, a concrete cutoff wall was constructed using hydrofraise slurry wall construction techniques to correct this problem. During construction of the slurry wall, severe slurry losses and cracking of the dam occurred. A sophisticated recompression grouting program was implemented to fill existing openings and recompress the distressed core material to prevent hydraulic fracturing by the head of slurry in the trench. Once the grouting program was finished, the cutoff wall was completed without incident to a new world record depth of 122.7 meters.

KEYWORDS: Slurry wall, earth-rockfill dam, cutoff, hydrofraise, grouting, concrete, seepage, piping, hydraulic fracturing, arching.

DESCRIPTION OF THE PROJECT

Mud Mountain Dam was constructed in 1941 on the White River at the base of Mt. Ranier, 8 km upstream and southeast of Enumclaw, Washington. The drainage area above the dam is 1,035 km[2]. Tacoma, Washington offers a significant downstream hazard. The project is a single purpose flood control dam, constructed and operated by the Seattle District, U.S. Army Corps of Engineers. The dam is a zoned earth and rockfill structure 120 m high, with a crest length of 213 m. The top of the dam is at elevation 381 m. The general configurations of the project are shown on Fig. 1.

Foundation

The dam is constructed across a narrow canyon with steep (near vertical) rock walls more than 60 m high on both sides. The rock in the canyon floor and walls is a moderately hard to hard andesitic volcanic agglomerate, consisting of angular blocks of andesite within a welded tuff and ash matrix. Unconfined compressive strengths in the rock range as high as 140,000 kPa.

[1] Senior Associate, Woodward-Clyde Consultants, Stanford Place 3, Suite 1000, 4582 South Ulster Street Parkway, Denver, Colorado, 80237

[2] Project Manager, Soletanche, Inc., 6 Rue de Watford, 9200 Nanterre, France

[3] Design Engineer, U.S. Army Corps of Engineers, Seattle District, Seattle, Washington

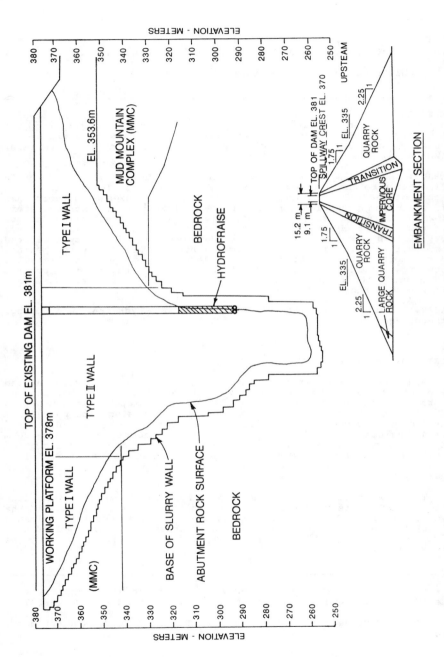

FIG. 1 -- Mud Mountain Dam cutoff wall.

The upper canyon walls are chiefly Mud Mountain Complex (MMC) material. The MMC is an overburdened assemblage of relatively competent mudflows, containing cobbles, gravels, sands, silts and highly variable amounts of clay, boulders, wood fragments and pumice. The cobbles and boulders have measured unconfined compressive strengths as high as 185,000 kPa.

Dam Embankment

The centrally located dam core is a broadly graded mixture of sands and gravels containing 15% to 20% fines. The fines vary from non-plastic silts to moderate plastic clays. Upstream and downstream transition zones, separating the core from the nearly symmetrical rock shells, have gradations that do not provide filter protection to the core material. This is especially a problem for that portion of core above elevation 320 m, which is predominantly composed of silty sand.

Core Deterioration

Observation of a single piezometer during the early 1980s suggested deterioration of the core resulting in increasing seepage gradients. The geotechnical investigation which followed indicated the presence of numerous defects throughout the core. Near the bottom of the dam, within the reach of normal reservoir fluctuations, defects consisted of water-bearing zones of clean gravel matrix with no fines, suggestive of a gravelly core material with the fines removed by reservoir flushing and/or by piping. Loss of fines probably resulted from the rapidly fluctuating low level reservoir, possibly in connection with open jointing in the rock. Although fractures and openings in the vertical abutment rock walls were gravity grouted, soil infilling materials were not removed, providing erodible future seepage paths. This loss of fines could have been prevented by proper filter design and construction.

In the upper more sandy portion of the core, defects appear to be loose zones and cracks, apparently the result of differential settlement and arching. Prior to cutoff wall excavation, observation during the removal of the top 3 m of dam revealed the presence of numerous subvertical longitudinal cracks. A 1.8 m diameter access shaft, excavated and cased to a depth of 58 m below the top of dam, indicated three separate zones of thin water-filled diagonally transverse cracks. Each zone consisted of a set of several closely spaced cracks. Historical records indicate that transverse cracks were observed adjacent to the abutments following construction, which were subsequently filled and not observed again. Furthermore, the upper 30 m of the dam has never been subjected to reservoir loading.

The arching of the soil core material, within the narrow steep-sided canyon, and in the narrow upper portion of the core between the stiffer rockfill shells reduced stresses below typical K_o conditions, making the soil susceptible to hydraulic fracturing, cracking and piping. Careful inflow tests into piezometers, with head limited to minimize hydraulic fracture, indicated relatively rapid hydraulic communication between the various piezometers throughout much of the dam core. Similar problems with central earth core/rockfill shell dams have been observed by Bertram (1967), Kjaernsli and Torblaa (1968), Sherard (1973), Vaughan et al. (1970) and Biarez et al. (1970).

Cutoff Wall Design

After consideration of various alternatives, the decision was made to construct a cutoff wall having a specified minimum thickness of 61 cm and keyed no less than 4.5 m into the canyon walls. The reason for this relatively large keying was because of the presence of numerous joints and overhangs, the unknown degree to which these had been treated during the original construction, and the apparent open nature of the rock joints.

The wall was divided into type I and type II walls. Type I represented the shallow wall on both shoulders of the canyon where standard cutoff wall techniques could be used with few restrictions. Type II wall was in the area of the deep canyon and its steep walls (Fig. 1). The steep hard rock and the unprecedented depth of the cutoff wall caused a great deal of concern about the ability of any construction method to provide assurance of continuity between individual wall elements. For this reason, the specifications required that the type II wall be constructed using primary and secondary elements and that the primary elements must contain a structural steel member which was to act as a positive guide for excavation of the secondary elements. A minimum continuity of 61 cm between primary and secondary panels was required.

Initially, the Corps planned to specify plastic concrete for the cutoff wall because of the anticipated deformation under the pool loading. However, the decision was made to use conventional structural concrete, about which a great deal is known, and accepting the fact that some cracking of the wall would probably occur. Cracking is not believed to be a serious problem. However, wall movements are being monitored by instrumentation.

The contract was awarded in July 1988 to Soletanche Inc., who intended to use a special Hydrofraise for excavating the cutoff wall.

THE MUD MOUNTAIN DAM HYDROFRAISE

A Hydrofraise is a down-the-hole reverse circulation rig which excavates a rectangular trench 2.8 m long under slurry, with widths ranging from 0.6 m to 1.2 m. The rig comprises a heavy steel body (45 tons) with two down-the-hole hydraulic motors that rotate two cutter drums in opposite directions. The soil and rock is cut by pic cutter teeth mounted on the drums. The cutters excavate a serrated surface directly in adjacent primary panel concrete to provide a joint with excellent structural and seepage path elongation characteristics. A submersible pump is located immediately above the wheels to move the cuttings in the drilling slurry to the surface and through a pipeline to the desanding plant. Hydraulic power is supplied by a power pack mounted on a heavy crane which supports and manipulates the machine; a pipeline linking the rig to a desanding unit continuously feeds clean, new, or desanded slurry to the excavation.

The hard andesite bedrock of the Mud Mountain Dam required special pic cutter teeth to be developed to cut the rock. Also, because of the presence of nearly vertical canyon walls, the contractor added special features including a body extension to increase the length of the Hydrofraise to 24 m and longitudinal guides operated by jacks to take reaction opposite to the canyon cliff in order to avoid deflection (Fig. 2).

CUTOFF CONTINUITY

The requirement for a steel guide in the primary panels was deleted in response to a Value Engineering Proposal from the contractor in which continuity of the cutoff wall would be assured and controlled by the three following means.

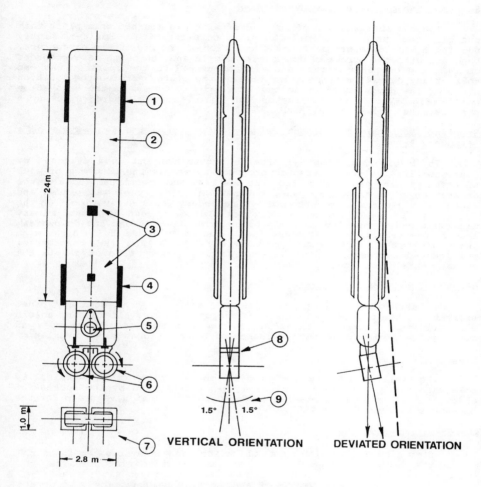

1. UPPER LONGITUDINAL GUIDE OPERATED WITH
    JACKS
2. UPPER BODY
3. DOUBLE INCLINOMETER
4. LOWER LONGITUDINAL GUIDE OPERATED WITH
    JACKS
5. PUMP SECTION
6. CUTTER WHEELS
7. BASE PLAN
8. TILT PLATE
9. RANGE OF LATERAL INCLINATION +/-1.5°

FIG. 2 -- Hydrofraise 12,000 machine.

Steering Capability of the Hydrofraise

The two cutter drums of the Hydrofraise are mounted on a plate that can tilt the cutters 1.5° off the plane of excavation. Built-in highly sensitive inclinometers monitor the position of the rig; these parameters, together with the torque of the cutter wheels and the depth, are recorded on tape and on paper. They are also displayed to the operator who can correct any deviation tendency by tilting the plate, varying the rotation speed of the drums and jacking the longitudinal frames on the excavation walls (Fig. 2). The contractor can also set the Hydrofraise on a predetermined non-vertical path.

Sampling Concrete of Adjacent Primary Panels from the Excavation of a Secondary Panel

To double-check the Hydrofraise recordings and show evidence of panel continuity, the contractor proposed to sample the concrete of each adjacent primary panel 61 cm from the upstream and downstream faces of the excavation of a secondary panel bottom. A guide frame was placed and centered by jacks at the bottom of the secondary panel excavation. On the frame, two 50 mm ID curved guide pipes aiming at each adjacent primary panel are positioned respectively 61 cm from the upstream and downstream face of the secondary panel excavation. The angle of the guide pipes with the primary panel surface was approximately 23°. A 19 mm (RW) core barrel was lowered successively in the four guide pipes to core or sample the primary panel concrete.

Black and Red Dye in Concrete

To assess adjacent primary panel overlap by the secondary panel excavation, the primary panel bottom concrete was dyed alternating colors black or red. During excavation of the secondary panel bottom, dyed cuttings were removed showing evidence of both adjacent panel overlap.

Precedent

The ability of the Hydrofraise to maintain tight verticality tolerances in a very deep excavation was demonstrated by the successful completion of an approximate 120 m deep cutoff wall at Navajo Dam for the Bureau of Reclamation in 1987.

SLURRY WALL EXCAVATION

After site preparation work, which included excavation to lower the top of the dam by 3 m to provide an adequate working platform area, the Hydrofraise was assembled and suspended to a Manitowoc 4100 crane (Fig. 3). Guidewalls were constructed and work proceeded from a concrete working platform slab. The desanding plant was located on the spillway just upstream from the crest along with the maintenance facility for the Hydrofraise.

First Slurry Losses

On May 17, 1989, excavation of a primary element in relatively shallow type II three-bite panel (6.7 m long) was begun near the top of the left canyon wall. After excavating to a depth of 9.5 m, the crew took a lunch break. When they returned, they found that the slurry had leaked from the excavation, which then was partially backfilled with sand and gravel and refilled with slurry. On the following day, the second bite of the same primary panel was attempted and an abrupt slurry loss was experienced at a depth of 8.5 m, requiring backfill and replacement of slurry. The day after, a similar slurry loss occurred on a primary panel several meters away, at a depth of 9 m, and as the excavation was being backfilled, a vortex appeared in one of the previously refilled

excavations. As the slurry dropped, a diagonal crack could be seen in the
excavation sidewall. After experiencing other slurry losses at deeper
levels, both panels were completed.

FIG. 3 -- Hydrofraise excavation of slurry wall.

Cracking of the Dam

Work continued for several weeks on the shallow left abutment
panels, with occasional slurry loss, requiring backfilling and re-
excavation. An attempt was made to locate and treat dam core defects by
a series of about 20 borings drilled using bentonite mud, with the
intention of gravity grouting in zones where mud was lost. Only six of
these borings experienced significant mud losses; however, some of those
accepted as much as 60 m³ of grout. Subsequent panel excavations disrupted
by slurry losses indicated that this program had failed, probably because
of the inability of the isolated 125 mm diameter drill holes to intersect
all of the defects in the core.

In mid-June 1989, excavation of a shallow panel above the right
canyon shoulder was attempted. Excavation reached a depth of 35 m, when
suddenly all slurry was lost within a few minutes and vertical cracks
opened at each end of panel excavation. The panel was backfilled, re-
excavated and concreted the week after without further incident. The next
panel excavated in the same area encountered an abrupt slurry loss at 38
m accompanied by cracking, with three parallel cracks extending across the
entire dam crest up to the opposite river bank.

Total loss of slurry during this period approached 3,800 m³, with
individual losses exceeding 700 m³. Apparently, much of this lost slurry
was temporarily stored in the upstream shell of the dam. After a period

of weeks, a spring of diluted bentonite slurry appeared at the upstream toe. Fortunately, being of glacial origin, the river carries a normal bedload of glacial silt and the slurry did no environmental damage.

Problem Evaluation and Solution

At this point, it became evident that the dam core was hydraulic fracturing under the slurry pressure in the trench even at shallow depth and that the slurry was charging pre-existing cracks in the core with full hydrostatic pressure. There was serious concern that the repeated slurry losses and dam cracking would lead to a cave-in of the trench wall, possibly trapping the Hydrofraise and even leading to loss of life. In addition, the flood season was approaching and it was evident that the ability of the dam to safely withstand a high pool had diminished rather than improved as a result of the work thus far. Instead of calling in attorneys and establishing an adversarial posture, the contractor and Corps adopted a teamwork approach to solve the problem technically. After several open and frank meetings, the contractor proposed the following:

1.   Reduce all type II panels to single-bite panels to minimize excavation size, the time each panel is open, and hence the risk of cave-in.

2.   Reduce the penetration of the key in the rock from 4.5 m to 1.5 m to reduce time of excavation and exposure of dam core to slurry pressure.

3.   Temporarily stop work with the Hydrofraise until completion of a comprehensive program of recompression grouting designed to fill pre-existing cracks and increase the lateral stresses in the core to a level sufficient to resist the hydraulic fracturing pressure from the slurry-filled trench.

The Corps agreed to items 1 and 3, but disagreed to change the key in the rock.

RECOMPRESSION GROUTING PROGRAM

Grouting Approach

Two grouting techniques were considered to recompact and restress the core of the dam:

-    Compaction grouting consisting of placing a stiff cement mortar under high pressure within the soil; and

-    Recompression grouting by controlled hydraulic fracturing with rigidified cement-bentonite grout.

Compaction grouting is a proven technique for depths not exceeding 40 m, but the intrusion of a stiff mortar under high pressure can create unfilled cracks and hence a path for water seepage. This technique did not appear applicable for a dam core recompaction.

Recompression by controlled hydraulic fracturing with a rigidified grout is a relatively sophisticated technique not commonly used in the United States. Outside the United States it has been used in soils after ground failure or to prevent ground loss in shaft and tunnel excavation (e.g., the Caracas subway). In addition, this technique has been used for constructing cutoffs under dams such as the Sheak Peak Dam (Hong Kong). Depths of 120 m were uncommon, but similar grout treatments at this depth had been performed in Mexico City for shaft excavation in 1971. At Balderhead Dam (UK), a grouting treatment for dam core restoration had been performed prior to slurry cutoff wall construction (Vaughan et al. 1970).

The technique relies basically on the creation of grout-filled plane surfaces intersecting in all directions; planes first develop perpendicularly to the lowest soil stress and recompact the adjacent soil. Regrouting through sleeve pipes creates new planes developing in other directions (usually perpendicularly to the previous fracture). The repetition of grouting stages in the same area creates the desired multidirectional fracturing and recompression. A concern with this type of grouting is to limit the travel of the grout through the hydraulic fractures. Uncontrolled hydraulic fracturing would waste large volumes of grout and potentially further deteriorate the core. Therefore, special controls on grout setting time, pressure and volume were required for controlled hydraulic fracturing. A variety of very thick to very fluid grout mixes can be pumped through the grout pipes. This provides flexibility to achieve both recompression and a reduction in permeability from the grouting treatment.

Based on these considerations, the contractor implemented a grouting program consisting of two succeeding sequences:

1.   Sealing the cracks and fissures created (or pre-existing) in the dam core by gravity grouting; and

2.   Drilling and pressure grouting two lines of grout holes located respectively 1.5 m and 2.5 m upstream and downstream of the cutoff wall.

Gravity Grouting Program

This program was performed by drilling 125 mm diameter holes with a bentonite-cement slurry mix which would set after drilling. Holes were located on the centerline of the cutoff wall at 1.5 m spacing. In case of the slurry loss, silicate was added to the mix to provide rigidity and short setting time to avoid channeling away of the grout. Grouting was performed until the level of the slurry in the hole began rising.

This program successfully sealed off the main cracks and voids, except in the left bottom corner of the canyon. The large amount of grout placed locally was indicative of a high and unpredictable deterioration of the dam core. Figure 4 provides an indication of the areas of the core which accepted grout during the gravity grouting program.

Recompression Grouting Program

Recompression grout holes extended to the bedrock with a 1.8 m spacing between holes of the same row. It was planned to drill and grout primary holes at 3.6 m spacing prior to drilling the intermediary secondary holes.

Grout pipes -- The grout holes were equipped with 50 mm ID sleeve pipes with lateral perforation placed every 60 cm, covered with a rubber or a plastic sleeve acting as a non-return valve. The grout pipe was lowered within a casing into a hole previously drilled with bentonite slurry. When withdrawing the casing, a bentonite-cement sleeve grout was injected in the annulus displacing the bentonite slurry and sealing the grout pipe. High pressure grout usually requires steel grout pipes to avoid deformation. At Mud Mountain Dam, heavy-duty plastic pipes were placed below 45 m depth to avoid possible later interference with the Hydrofraise if they deviated into the path of the panel excavation.

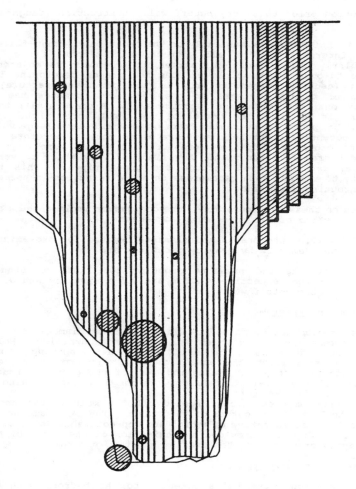

FIG. 4 -- Results of gravity grouting program.

Drilling grout holes with the Enpasol -- In the 1950s, the oil drilling industry attempted to correlate drilling parameters such as rate of drilling and the torque of the drilling rig with the characteristics of the drilled formation. Empirical formulas have been established by authors such as Teale, Somerton, etc. (Pfister 1985). The Enpasol recordings rely on the same basic principle. The Enpasol is a "black box" monitoring up to 8 drilling parameters of a blind drilled hole. Every 5 mm of depth, the digitized data are recorded on tape. Raw parameters are printed on paper. Computer processing of the parameters provides a representation of the stratigraphy of the drilled formations since the drilling parameters are influenced by the permeability and density of the soil. On grouting projects, the Enpasol recordings provide an indication of which portions of the stratigraphy are distressed or permeable and will accept grout penetration.

At Mud Mountain Dam, the grout holes of the upstream row were drilled with a Schramm drilling rig equipped with an Enpasol. Enpasol recording did not slow down production drilling as would more commonly used water testing. The following parameters were recorded:

- rate of drilling,
- thrust on the drilling bit,
- counterthrust,
- torque, and
- pressure of the drilling fluid.

Recordings of the last parameter indicated that the Mud Mountain Dam core had little or no cohesion. The three other parameters were combined by an Enpasol expert in an empirical formula highly sensitive to the looseness and permeability of the dam core material.

Figure 5 shows a print-out of the computer processing of a grout hole Enpasol recording. It appears that the upper portion of the hole has deteriorated, as well as the lower part, which is close to an andesite cliff.

The systematic Enpasol recording of the upstream row of grout hole provided a grouting map of the Mud Mountain Dam core prior to initiating the recompression grouting program. It appeared that the upper 60 m of the dam core were decompressed and the upper 45 m very decompressed. The abutment rock-dam core interface was loose on the upper left canyon wall within 0.7 m of the rock wall. The same interface on the right canyon wall was in a surprisingly good condition. Except locally, the lower 50 m of dam core within the narrow canyon walls appeared not to be distressed; but the most damaged area was located in the neighborhood of the left deep canyon cliff.

Recompression grouting parameters -- The following parameters were monitored closely and controlled at the grouting plant. A typical circular chart recording of flow rate and pumping pressure is shown in Figure 6.

• Rate of Pumping. A slow pumping rate favors the multidirectional hydrofracturing process. Because a solidified grout cannot progress any further in a crack, fresh grout coming from the same sleeve creates new cracks in other directions. The rate of pumping at Mud Mountain Dam was limited to 0.7 m^3 per hour.

• Pressures. Pressure recordings of the first grouted holes were thoroughly scrutinized. A limiting pressure of 2000 kPa (including approximately 300 kPa of headloss) was set in order to ensure adequate recompression of the dam core but limit hydraulic fracturing. This pressure is high compared to U.S. standards, but it is inherent to the technique of soil recompression by multidirectional hydrofracturing.

• Grout Mixes. Two basic stable grout mixes were used on the site:

Grout A		Grout B	
Portland cement:	300 kg	Portland cement:	500 kg
Bentonite:	60 kg	Bentonite:	60 kg
Water:	1,000 kg	Water:	1,000 kg

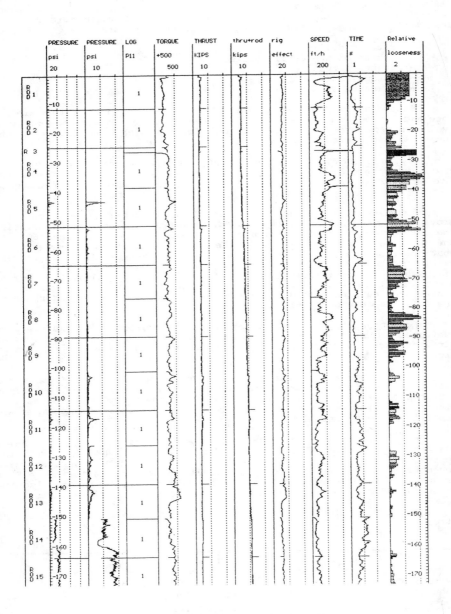

FIG. 5 -- Digital Enpasol recording.

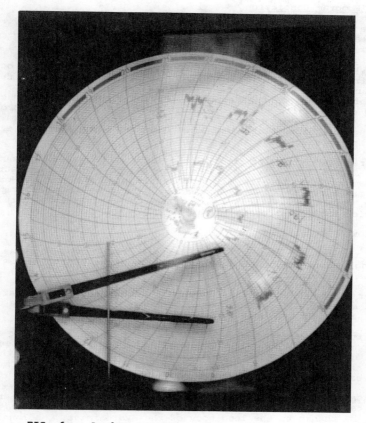

FIG. 6 -- Analog recording of grouting parameters.

In both mixes, a limited quantity of silicate was introduced to provide rigidity and achieve a setting time ranging from 30 minutes to 1 hour. In the upper 45 m, this short setting time was not sufficient to avoid channeling up to the platform level. To prevent such leaks, silicate and grout were pumped simultaneously in the same hole. It achieved a flash setting time of 2 minutes.

Each grout program was limited to 200 litres per sleeve, except in the neighborhood of the abutment rock-dam core interface where double quantities were injected. Successive stages of grouting with the same quantities were performed in the same holes at the same depths until achieving the required limit pressure. Delay between two succeeding programs was a minimum of 36 hours to allow the grout to set sufficiently.

In the lower part of the canyon, one grouting stage was generally sufficient to reach the limit pressure and achieve recompression. From 60 m to 45 m depth, two to three stages were performed with very thick grout mixes. The largest grout quantities were placed in the neighborhood of the deep left canyon cliff, confirming the findings of the Enpasol recordings. The number of grout stages performed on the downstream row was proportional to the thickness of the Enpasol recording lines (Figure 5).

Grouting Program Conclusion

The recompression grouting program started in late August 1989 and was completed on December 1, 1990. The volume of grout injected amounted to an average of 9.1% of the theoretical volume of soil treated. This is in the high bracket, compared to similar recompression programs in soils (5 to 7%). In addition, large variations of grout volume occurred, ranging from 4.8% in the lower dam core to 15% and more in the upper dam core. Guidance by the Enpasol recordings was a major asset to avoid a blind overtreatment of the dam core. During subsequent construction of the deep cutoff wall, one minor slurry loss occurred, which proves the grouting program was successful but not overachieved. This large recompression treatment of a dam core is unprecedented, and the extensive use of fast-setting grout at such depth is also not common.

During recompression grouting the guide wall settled by about 15 cm, probably due to consolidation of the upper dam core while the upstream and downstream rockfill shells did not settle significantly. Horizontal displacements of the guide wall reached 2 to 4 cm during recompression grouting. These observations support the arching phenomenon postulated as a cause for the low stresses in the core.

EXCAVATION OF THE DEEP PANELS

In the changed design, the deep panels excavation length was limited to a single bite or 2.8 m, with an overlap increased to 36 cm between primaries and secondaries. Excavation was performed smoothly, in spite of bentonite slurry pollution by the grout which required extensive chemical treatment of the mud. Gravels impregnated with grout were excavated along the left canyon cliff, indicative of an extensive washout of the dam core material at this location.

Fifteen panels reached a depth over 100 m below the working surface. The deepest panel ended at a depth of 122.5 m which is currently the world's deepest slurry wall panel. Three panels drove more than 30 m through the andesite rock of the canyon walls and two through more than 50 m of canyon rock.

Excavation of the two primary panels placed on the left and right subvertical cliffs was performed with a deviation of less than 10 cm in over 100 m, thanks to the long body of the Hydrofraise, the longitudinal guides and the steering capability of the rig. This remarkable achievement was accomplished through hard andesite, dental concrete, grout pipes and rock bolts.

For the secondary panels, a cautious approach was adopted to ensure proper overlap between adjacent panels. The Hydrofraise readouts were double-checked by in situ tests performed during excavation. The Hydrofraise cutting wheels were equipped with soft drill bits (bits without carbide tip). The heavy wear of the teeth biting into the concrete of the adjacent panels imprinted on the cutting wheels the exact relative position of the two panels. At rock level, the same tests were performed with bits equipped with cylindrical rock samplers to collect material into which the bit was cutting. On the last secondary panels, the soft drill bit test superseded the concrete sampling, since this test determined the actual overlap between panels. It confirmed the high accuracy of the Hydrofraise in deep excavation. The relative deviation between two adjacent panels did not exceed 20 cm (less than 0.2%).

CONCLUSIONS

During construction of the cutoff wall, the concerns about the condition of the dam core were graphically confirmed. The presence of an extensive network of cracks, large washed out zones and voids in the distressed dam core were confirmed by the large slurry losses during trench excavation, as was the inadequacy of the filter protection. The need for a positive concrete cutoff wall was demonstrated since a grout curtain alone would not have prevented further deterioration of the core because of its inability to intersect every defect in the core.

Deep embedment of the cutoff wall in rock was found to be essential because of the extremely variable condition of the rock and the core deterioration at the rock interface.

The recompression grouting program, as designed and carried out by the contractor using sophisticated technology relatively new to the United States, was highly successful in increasing the lateral stress conditions in the dam to permit resumption of slurry wall construction.

The Hydrofraise 12,000 machine achieved, without difficulty, a highly accurate excavation to unprecedented depth under extremely difficult conditions. The maximum deviation of the excavation was less than 0.2 percent.

The experience of constructing a cutoff wall through Mud Mountain Dam has underlined the importance of teamwork between owner, designer and contractor. This cooperative "can do" attitude turned a major disaster into a successful precedent of useful construction technologies for the construction industry in the United States.

REFERENCES

Bertram, G.E. (1967). "Experience with Seepage Control Measures in Earth and Rockfill Dams," Transactions 9th Congress on Large Dams, Istanbul, Vol. 3, p. 91.

Biarez, J., J.L. Bordes et P. Londe (1970). La fissuration des noyaux des barrages en enrochement ou en alluvions. CIGB 10 Montreal, Q 36, R 3.

Graybeal K., and J. Levallois (1991). Construction of Cutoff Wall With Hydrofraise Through The Core of Mud Mountain Dam (USA). ICOLD 17, Vienna, Q 66, R 49.

Kjaernsli, B. and I. Torblaa (1968). "Leakage Through Horizontal Cracks in the Core of Hyttejuvet Dam," Publication No. 80, Norwegian Geotechnical Institute, Oslo, Norway.

Pfister, P. (1985). "Recording Drilling Parameters in Ground Engineering." Ground Engineering, April.

Sherard, J.L. (1973). "Embankment Dam Cracking," Embankment Dam Engineering - The Casagrande Volume, John Wiley & Sons, Inc., New York.

Vaughan, P.R., D.J. Kluth, M.W. Leonard, and H.H.M. Pradoura (1970). "Cracking and Erosion of the Rolled Clay Core of Balderhead Dam and the Remedial Works Adopted for its Repair," Proceedings 10th International Congress on Large Dams, Vol. 3, pp. 73-93.

Han C.M. Breek[1]

THE CONSTRUCTION OF "THIN" SLURRY WALLS AND THE SUPPOR-
TING LIQUID SLURRIES USED

REFERENCE: Breek, H.C.M., **"The construction of "thin
walls and supporting liquid slurries used"**[2], Slurry
walls: Design, Construction and Quality Control, ASTM STP
1129, David B. Paul, Richard R. Davidson, and Nicholas J.
Cavalli, Eds., American Society for Testing and Materials, Philadelphia, 1992.

ABSTRACT: A method to make a thin slurry trench or wall
in the ground, based on the US patent number 4,877,357,
whilst using different supporting fluids.
The slurry trench or wall will be formed into the ground
by driving a beam section and simultaneously and entirely
filling up the trench, formed by soil displacements with
a supporting fluid. The wall is formed by driving a steel
beam sectional to the required depth after which it is
subsequently pulled out of the soil with a vibrating
movement, which is obtained by delivering blows to the
beam at a suitable frequency, by vibrator or vibratory
hammer. Whilst the beam is extracted, sufficient supporting fluid is supplied to fill up the trench/wall formed
by the beam.

KEYWORDS: Slurry walls, thin slurry walls, ground
displacing slurry walls, driven beam method, cast-in-situ
"thin" slurry walls

INTRODUCTION

In this article attention will be paid to the
various aspects, which are of importance when constructing ground displacing, cast-in-situ "thin" slurry walls.
Also attention will be paid to the supporting liquid
slurries used. In the last couple of years more and more
slurry walls are being applied to:

[1]Director of Funderingstechnieken Verstraeten B.V.,
P.O. Box 55, 4500 AB OOSTBURG, Holland

[2]"United States of America patent nr. 4, 887, 357",
October 1989, Verstraeten A.J.

a)   The construction of depressed roads in builtup
     areas.
b)   Increasing the water impermeability and decreasing
     the water seepage at river dikes and dams.
c)   Isolating polluted ground, contaminated mud-basins
     and refuse dumpsites.

Up to date in general an excavated wall or diaphragm
wall was used, however I would like to illustrate the
construction of ground displacing "thin" slurry walls.

THE PRINCIPLE OF A SLURRY WALL

In the construction of depressed roads.

When there are one or more closed clay-layers apparent of sufficient density, at a not too great depth, an
open channel construction can be realized by means of a
slurry wall. By constructing a road in this way in other
words depressed, the available space taken up will be
less. The noise from the traffic is considerably reduced.
Moreover the visual pollution is less.

Increasing the water impermeability and decreasing the
water seepage at river dikes and dams.

To increase the impermeability and decrease seepage
at river dikes, in order to increase the safety, a slurry
wall can be constructed in the dike. Since the method of
construction is ground displacing, the ground displacement will increase the impermeability.

For the isolation of pollution in the ground.

To prevent the pollution from spreading through the
ground by means of ground water streams, the isolation by
the use of slurry walls is an excellent solution. The
great advantage of this ground displacing system by
constructing slurry walls, is the fact that no polluted
ground is allowed out, which would require purification
or protected storage.

THE CONSTRUCTION OF A SLURRY WALL

To construct separation screens in the ground, there
are two different techniques possible, namely:
1.   Ground replacing method.
2.   Ground displacing method.

The first "ground replacing" method can be constructed as follows. A wall is dug under a mixture of bentoni-

te-cement. This mixture will harden after the digging and
will serve as a separation-screen. This method uses
approximately 1,5 times the volume of the wall of bentonite-cement mixture per square meter, since it is partly
spoiled with the excavated soil. This method is therefore
rather expensive due to the consumption of cement and
bentonite. Depending on the composition, the mixture has
a specific gravity of ± 1,25 and a permeability of ± 10^{-9}
m/sec.

Another ground replacing method is to dig under
bentonite and to replace the bentonite afterwards by the
final mixture of which the separation-wall is being
formed. This can be concrete or a heavy mixture of bento-
nite-stoneflour, fly-ash and cement. The ground replacing
method has the following disadvantage. When a screen is
made in polluted ground, this ground is brought to the
surface during digging, with all the consequences and
problems such as transportation of polluted ground to
special dumpsites or soil-treatment installations involving high costs.

The "ground displacing" method has a great advantage
as mentioned before, there is no exposure of polluted
soil. A screen can be made with a beam-profile which is
installed by a vibrator, the so-called "vibrated-beam
method". The wearing of the steel beam-profile is very
high, especially in sandy layers, while several types of
soil limit this technique such as hard clay-layers and
cohesive soils. Also, the slurry mix used with this
technique, needs a certain viscosity to be pumped. This
results in a slurry with a limited specific gravity. The
thickness of the screen is restricted to a maximum of 4
inches.

This technique was revised and we developed the
"driven-beam method" which excludes the disadvantages of
the "vibrated-beam method" and with our technique it is
possible to construct slurry walls up to a thickness of
(8") 20 cm. The slurry is a rather thick "yoghurt-like"
mixture and is pumped with a concrete-pump. The slurry
has a high specific gravity (1,5) and with a high K-value
of up to 10^{-11}m/sec. The penetration of most known soil-
layers causes no problem for this method, especially not
for clay-layers and such.
This method works as follows: (see also Fig. 1)

There is an H-beam (1) with a hammering device (2)
on top of the body. To one flange a continuous nose (3)
is welded, which runs in the already made trench. At the
bottom-end steel plates (4) are welded on both sides of
the H-beam. These steel plates determine the thickness of
the final slurry wall. There are also two or four tubes

(5) welded on to the beam which end in the "room" formed
by the two inserted plates. These tubes are connected to
a pump with a variable capacity, which is able to pump
very stiff, thick mixtures. Under the H-beam a bottom
plate (6) is placed which overlaps the trench thickness
plate by approx. 9,5 mm (3/8") on both sides. The hammer
starts to drive so that the beam penetrates the soil. At
the same time slurrymix is pumped and fills up the trench
as it is formed. When the beam has reached the required
depth, the slurry stands in the trench up to the top. The
beam is pulled out of the ground, where necessary using a
vibrator leaving the footplate in place at the bottom of
the trench. The shape of the trench thickness plates are
such that the sides of the slurry wall are sealed by the
sloping form on the upper side (see Fig. 2)

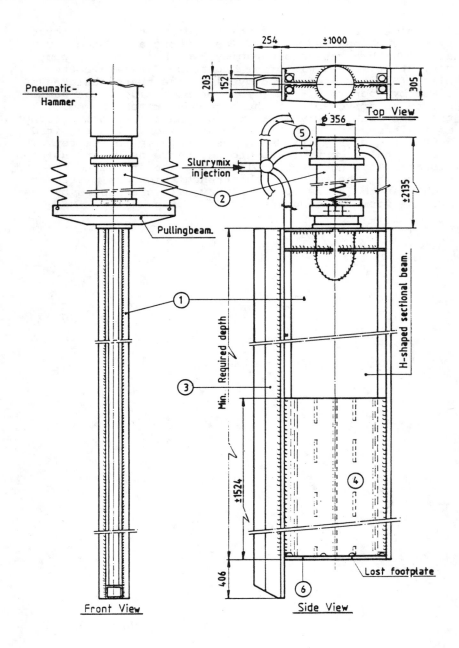

Fig. 1   Driven Beam apparatus

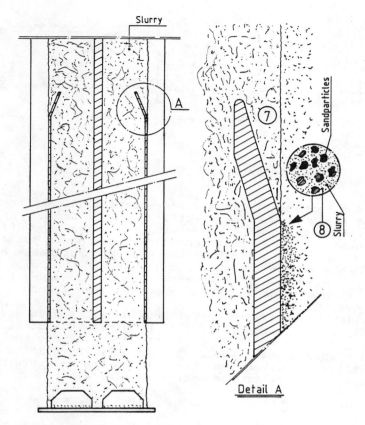

Vertical cross-section over trench
bottom part.

Fig. 2   View during beam withdrawl

Furthermore the wedge-action [detail A (7)] pushes the mixture into the wall an the pores (8) are filled. As soon as the beam is out of the ground, it is moved one beam width. A (new) bottomplate is attached and the H-profile is driven into the ground again. The continuous guidance nose (3) follows the previous trench (9), while the flange of the H-beam follows in the previous flange position (10) to prevent deviation from the earlier formed trench. The working method is then repeated (see Fig. 3) The slurry of the last trench of the day needs to be mixed with a retarder in order to continue the next day.

This technique is very suitable for the use of mixes with a high specific gravity and has many advantages.

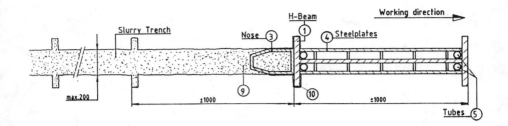

Fig. 3   <u>Panel Construction Sequence</u>

First the K-value of these slurry-mixes is higher than
that of a mix with a low specific gravity. Second, an
ideal composition can be made with very fine sand, flyash, rockflour and cement-bentonite, keeping it pumpable.
The high specific gravity of the slurry, preferably equal
to or greater than the specific gravity of the soil, in
which the slurry wall is constructed, is necessary to
support the side walls and to guarantee the trench
thickness.
With a lower specific gravity the side walls have greater
tendency to come together. It is possible to install a
synthetic reinforcement such as tensar grid into the
trench with a special tool. This is very interesting,
especially for earthquake areas, since the wall stays
together by the reinforcement. (see Fig. 4)

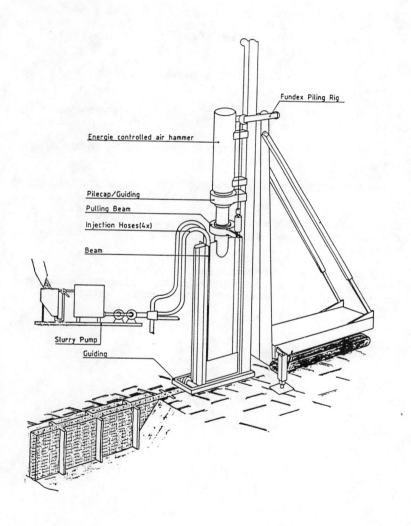

Fundex Piling Rig

Energie controlled air hammer

Pilecap/Guiding

Pulling Beam

Injection Hoses(4x)

Beam

Slurry Pump

Guiding

Fig. 4   Oblique View of Thin Slurry Wall Construction

ADVANTAGES OF THE SYSTEM

1) No removal of polluted soil.

2) Application of heavy slurry mixes is possible, which guarantees sufficient impermeability.

3) Trench thicknesses from 10 to 20 cm are possible.

4) Steel or synthetic reinforcement of the slurry trench is possible.

5) High production capacity depending on the soil condition.

6) Extreme soil layers, which cannot be penetrated by a vibrator, can be penetrated by a driven profile.

7) Can be installed up to great depths, greater than when using a vibrator.

8) Cement-bentonite slurry is a non polluting application.

9) Cement-bentonite slurry is supposed to be resistant to mechanical and chemical erosion under "normal" circumstances.

This method of constructing of ground displacing slurry walls has been patented in the United States of America under nr. 4, 887, 357, dated October 31 1989.

Steven R. Day[1] and Christopher R. Ryan[1]

STATE OF THE ART IN BIO-POLYMER DRAIN CONSTRUCTION

REFERENCE: Day, S. R. and Ryan, C. R., "State of the Art in Bio-Polymer Drain Construction," Slurry Walls: Design, Construction, and Quality Control, ASTM STP 1129, David B. Paul, Richard R. Davidson, and Nicholas J. Cavalli, Eds., American Society for Testing and Materials, Philadelphia, 1992.

ABSTRACT: A common feature of civil engineering design is the "french drain," a trench intended to intercept and collect groundwater and transfer it laterally to a sump. The environmental marketplace has created a larger demand for these drains for the purpose of the collection of contaminated groundwater. Traditional construction methods that use trench boxes or shoring, sometimes in combination with dewatering systems, present a number of problems, particularly if the trenches have depths in excess of about five meters.

The Bio-Polymer Slurry Drain (BP Drain) has provided a new method for constructing deep drains that eliminates shoring and dewatering. It does not require a wide excavation, reducing spoil disposal and does not require trench entry by workers, improving safety.

The system uses basic slurry trench technology but, instead of bentonite clay slurry, a guar-gum based slurry is used to maintain the open trench. Once the trench is dug to full depth, it is backfilled with a pervious material such as gravel. Wells can be inserted, pipe laterals can be placed and filter fabric inserted, all under slurry. When the trench is filled, the slurry is chemically and biologically "broken", allowing the slot to collect water.

[1]Steven R. Day, District Manager and Christopher R. Ryan, President, Geo-Con, Inc., P.O. Box 17380, Pittsburgh, PA 15235.

This paper reviews the current practice as illustrated by these case studies: a collection trench for oil, another for a chemical containment, and a drain constructed inside a slurry wall at a landfill site. The authors believe that this methodology will be subject to wide application once all of its features and advantages are fully realized.

KEYWORDS: Bio-Polymer, drains, groundwater, collector wells, slurry, construction

---

INTRODUCTION

One of the most difficult civil engineering projects has always been the construction of deep drains. By definition, these are constructed through soil profiles with flowing groundwater. Control of the excavation side slopes and construction dewatering are difficult problems. Trench collapse is a leading cause of construction worker injury and death.

The concept of trenching under a slurry has been an intriguing technology. The use of slurries to hold open trenches for impervious barriers and structural concrete slurry walls has been common practice for more than thirty years. In a drain application, however, the bentonite clay slurries commonly used would seal the trench walls from water inflow and defeat the purpose of the drain.

Use of biodegradable slurries has changed the technology. Now trenches can be excavated under slurry, backfilled with a pervious mixture, and the slurry degraded to allow for water infiltration.

To the authors' knowledge, the first U.S. use was a project in San Jose, California. A BP Drain, 17m deep and 200m long, was constructed to collect a diesel spill (Hanford and Day, 1988). Numerous additional applications have been completed in the U.S. market, almost all for environmental cleanups (Day, 1990). A similar process had apparently earlier been used to construct drains for dewatering and slope stabilization in France (Bachy, 1982).

The BP Drain technique provides numerous advantages over conventional construction, some of which are listed below:

Economy--Because the technique does not require dewatering nor sheeting and shoring, it is considerably cheaper to install. Typically it costs less than half of conventional construction.
Schedule--For the same reasons, the time of construction is much less than for conventional trenching methods.

Safety--Since no one enters the excavation with the BP Drain method, the method is much safer. There is also less potential for damage to surrounding structures from excavating or dewatering activities.

Environmental--Since most applications are on contaminated sites, another important advantage of the BP Drain is that it is narrower and generates less excavation spoil. There is also no water generated by temporary dewatering systems.

In the following sections, we look at construction methods, technical factors, and several example case studies.

CONSTRUCTION METHODS

A bio-polymer slurry drainage trench (or BP Drain) is constructed using a modified version of the slurry trench technique. The trench is excavated under slurry using an extended reach hydraulic excavator creating relatively narrow (0.5 to 1.0 meters) trenches up to 20 meters deep. Trench stability is temporarily provided by a polymer based slurry. A permeable backfill (gravel) and extraction structures (wells) are placed in the trench, through the slurry, to complete the construction. Later, the slurry degrades, permitting groundwater to flow through the trench for extraction or injection.

Polymer Slurry

Critical to successful BP Drain construction is the maintenance and control of the slurry. Guar gum based slurries normally remain effective for only about one day unless treated with additives. Slurry life is affected by atmospheric conditions, soil types and construction expertise. Typically, a mud engineer or slurry trench specialist trained in the use and control of bio-polymer systems directs the slurry mixing. Standard tests include viscosity and filtrate (API 13B) along with other slurry tests specified by ASTM D4380. Slurry treatment primarily consists of the addition of pH modifiers and preservatives which can extend the life of the slurry to as much as a few weeks.

Guar gum-based slurries provide a high gel strength (viscosity >40cP) and low water loss (filtrate < 25 ml) which permits the efficient transfer of the elevated hydrostatic head of the slurry to the trench walls thereby providing stability. Most soil types can be supported, as long as a slurry head of 1 meter or more can be maintained in the trench over the local groundwater table.

As an alternative to the guar slurries, there are some synthetic polymers that can be degraded in a similar fashion. To date, synthetic polymers have seen only limited use and only in applications where trench stability is not critical. Synthetic polymers have a very low gel strength (viscosity <15cp) and high water loss (filtrate >50 ml); therefore, they are limited to cases with more stable trench geometry and inherently stable soils. Care must be used in the selection of synthetic polymers since some create toxic byproducts when degraded. With continued research, synthetic polymers may prove useful on a wider variety of sites.

After the trench is backfilled, the bio-polymer slurry must be treated to initiate degradation and the trench flushed to develop the drain. The efficiency of trench flushing is a function of site conditions and the efforts of the contractor. A highly permeable soil and warm weather will encourage rapid flushing and result in limited excess slurry for disposal. Usually, degraded slurry is used to flush and develop the drain by pumping and recirculating at least three pore volumes of the trench. Simple drawdown tests can be used to demonstrate the effectiveness of the development.

In most cases, a small proportion of degraded slurry will remain as excess and must be evaporated, solidified, or disposed of at a waste water treatment facility. The BOD (biological oxygen demand) and COD (chemical oxygen demand) of the degraded slurry are similar and initially in the range of 3000 to 6000 mg/l. As the degradation continues and with successful initial degradation, the BOD may decrease to 1000 mg/l in a week and eventually (about six months) to background levels.

Backfill

Depending on the purpose and design of the drainage trench, different materials can be placed through the slurry into the trench to serve as the permanent, permeable backfill. A typical backfill is a clean, washed gravel such as pea gravel or crushed stone. A backfill with an engineered gradation or a filter fabric envelope can be used when the surrounding soil conditions would cause plugging or silting.

The backfill is placed through the slurry via tremie pipe or by sliding the backfill down the slope of the previously placed backfill to displace the slurry and minimize segregation. Sands and finer backfills must be prewetted to be tremied while coarser backfills, such as pea gravels, can be placed dry. Tremie placement should be used around wells and other structures to ensure accurate alignment.

Woven filtration fabrics are preferred over other geotextiles since the degraded slurry can be flushed from the weave. Placement of geotextiles in a slurry-filled trench requires special equipment and procedures. Geotextiles will naturally float and so they must be weighted to be placed through slurry. Concrete weights and temporary frames are most often used to facilitate placement and provide ballast. End tubes may also be used to still wave action in the trench which can disturb placement efforts. Continuity of the geotextiles is provided by overlapping the sheets.

Usually, the backfill is extended up to near the surface and always above the water table. Typically, the top 1 to 2 meters of the trench is backfilled with excess trench spoil or other soil to cap the trench and limit surface water infiltration. This zone may also support buried vaults, discharge piping and pump controls.

Extraction Structures

The most economical means of removing collected groundwater in a BP Drain is through well casings with pumps. With a permeable backfill, wells can be spaced about 100 meters apart. Stainless steel, galvanized steel, polyvinylchloride and polyethylene well casings have all been used successfully. Groundwater chemistry may dictate the selection of nonmetallic materials or other special considerations in extremely corrosive groundwaters. Inexpensive submersible, progressive cavity, or ejector pumps are available which can operate in corrosive groundwaters and pump at the very low extraction rates (35 lpm or less) required in most applications.

For a limited number of cases, a horizontal drainage pipe may be required along the bottom of the trench. The utility of horizontal pipes for groundwater collection is often overestimated. Drain pipes must have perforations which may be more restrictive than gravel alone in transmitting groundwater. Closer well spacing and deeper trenches can almost always provide equal performance and a lower initial cost and with reduced maintenance costs. In most groundwater extraction applications, the presence of pipe in a gravel-filled trench does not affect the performance of the system and is redundant.

In those few instances where a drainage pipe is required, special pipe-laying equipment of a design similar to cable-laying equipment is used. The pipe, of course, must be fully flexible and corrugated for strength. A separate pipe-laying machine travels over the slurry-filled trench behind the excavator, laying the pipe through the slurry while simultaneously bedding and backfilling around the drain pipe through a tremie. Pipe grade is controlled by survey control of the pipe laying boom. Small diameter sumps or wells (100 to 600 mm diameter) are either attached directly to the drain pipe or placed directly beside the drain pipe perforations for continuity.

Experience has shown that laying a drain pipe using weighted sections can also be used but only in very short (15 meters or less) trenches which can be placed in a single step. In longer sections the buoyancy of the flexible pipe creates folds at the end of each weight, which become crimped when the trench is backfilled. Since all work is performed in the blind, under slurry, breaks in the pipe cannot be easily detected and repairs are extremely difficult and costly. Purpose-built pipe-laying equipment is recommended for all but the shortest trenches.

In general, conventional manholes or lift stations are not recommended for a number of reasons. First, conventional manholes constitute a confined space which can allow unauthorized access. Second, pumps, control facilities and access to same can be provided through conventional well equipment at a much lower installation cost. Duplex systems can be provided using multiple well casings for backup pumps. Third, conventional manholes must be constructed by conventional means (sheeting, shoring and dewatering) negating a significant portion of the savings provided by the BP Drain installation. Finally, concrete manholes are sealed structures which are only attached to the drain field through the perforated pipe. A much larger radius of influence can be provided by using a perforated sump or well, and in the case of failure of the drainage pipe, the perforated sump or well provides a safety factor for ensuring the continued service of the drainage trench.

CASE STUDIES

Most BP Drains are installed to collect contaminated groundwater where the depth of the excavation makes conventional trenching impractical and soil conditions make well fields ineffective. A wider application of the BP Drain method is possible when the designer and the specialty contractor work together to fully exploit the advantages of the technique. The following case studies portray some of the more complicated systems installed to date and illustrate the potential for BP Drains on other sites.

Oil Skimmer in South Texas

A refinery had to collect floating waste oil which was leaving the site and appearing as a sheen on the adjoining Houston Ship Channel. A high water table, numerous utility lines, fill soils and limited working space made conventional excavation difficult and expensive. The BP Drain method was selected to create a deep trench in which was placed a geomembrane barrier to block oil seepage, while still allowing clean groundwater to pass under and into the waterway. Wells were placed in the trench to remove floating product which was collected by the barrier. Figure 1 shows a schematic of the completed system.

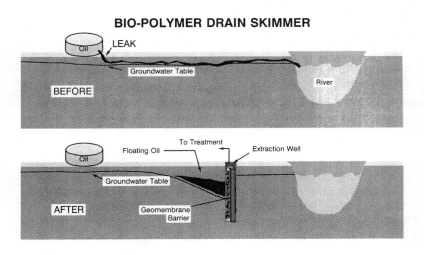

BIO-POLYMER DRAIN SKIMMER

FIG. 1--Schematic of Oil Skimmer Interceptor Trench

Geomembrane panels were prefabricated and HDPE joints welded to the membrane. The panels were stretched over frames which held the geomembrane during installation and jointing. An interlocking dovetail joint was used which was later grouted to complete the seal.

A trench 400 meters long and 6 meters deep was constructed between the waterway and the plant access roadway. The installation sequence for placing the geomembrane panels is shown in Figures 2 and 3. Due to the presence of the geomembrane, extensive development of the drain was required to ensure adequate flushing behind the barrier. The installation schedule was about one month.

GEOMEMBRANE/BIO-POLYMER INSTALLATION

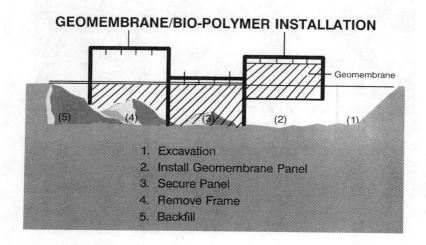

1. Excavation
2. Install Geomembrane Panel
3. Secure Panel
4. Remove Frame
5. Backfill

FIG. 2--Sequence for Installation of Geomembrane in Bio-Polymer Trench

Collection Trench in Northern California

A major manufacturing plant needed to contain a plume of spilled processing chemicals. An onsite treatment and containment system was designed which called for a down-gradient, soil-bentonite slurry wall and BP Drain. Due to regulatory requirements, a horizontal drainage pipe was included in the design. Well casings were placed at 100 m intervals, and cleanouts for the pipe were provided near the wells. A cross-section of the parallel trenches is shown in Figure 4.

A drought in the area made it necessary to use runoff water as the slurry mixing water. The water had to be sterilized to limit biological growth and along with the hot summer weather increased additive requirements to protect the slurry from premature degradation.

FIG. 3--Installation of Geomembrane Panel

CROSS SECTION OF GROUNDWATER
CONTAINMENT AND EXTRACTION SYSTEM

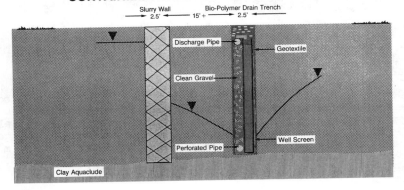

FIG. 4--Cross Section of Groundwater Containment System

The BP Drain was constructed through clays and silts up gradient and parallel to the cutoff wall. The trench was excavated 0.75 meters wide and about 9 meters deep and lined with a woven geotextile. The pipe laying machine (Figure 5) laid and bedded a 150 mm diameter perforated pipe through the slurry. Extraction wells 300 mm in diameter and 100 mm diameter monitoring wells were placed in the trench alongside the perforated pipe. Construction time for the project was less than two months.

FIG. 5--View of Pipe Installation in Bio-Polymer Trench

Landfill Dewatering in Ohio

A nuclear fuels processing plant had a mixed waste landfill that required closure. Plumes of contaminates were caused by the fluctuations in the groundwater table saturating the base of the landfill. The remedy was to construct a soil-bentonite slurry wall up gradient and a BP Drain parallel to the landfill to divert groundwater and finally cap the landfill to prevent infiltration. A schematic of the dewatering plan is shown in Figure 6.

Regulatory deadlines made it imperative to perform the construction in the winter. The cold weather made it difficult to pump and mix the slurry and complicated efforts to degrade the slurry.

A soil-bentonite slurry wall 250 meters long and two 125 meter long BP Drains were constructed up to 15 meters deep. Each BP Drain was one meter wide, lined with a woven geotextile, and equipped with a single extraction well. After nearly a year of operation, each trench produces a steady 19 lpm (5 gpm). A photo of the installation is shown in Figure 7. Construction of all trenches required less than one month.

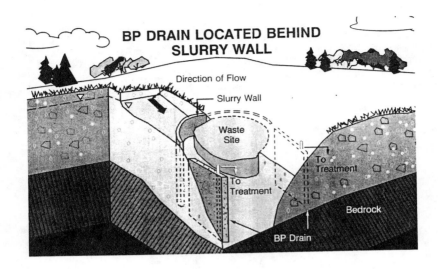

FIG. 6—Schematic of Slurry Wall and Bio-Polymer System
to Dewater Landfill

FIG. 7—View of Slurry Trench Installation

CONCLUSION

The BP Drain methodology provides a new means for constructing difficult deep drains. Where appropriate, they also provide significant savings of time and money, as well as improving worker safety and general environmental exposure. The projects completed to date have generally been for environmental containment purposes, although the process lends itself to civil works as well. We see a considerable potential for future applications of this technique.

REFERENCES

[1] Hanford, R. W. and Day, S. R., Installation of a Deep Drainage Trench by the Bio-Polymer Slurry Drain Technique, National Water Well Association Conference Proceedings, Las Vegas, NV, May, 1988.

[2] Day, S. R., Deep Groundwater Collection Trenches by the Bio-Polymer Drain Method, HMCRI Superfund Conference Proceedings, November, 1990.

[3] Bachy, Deep Draining Trench Brochure, SIF Bachy, Levallois Perret, France, 1982.

[4] American Petroleum Institute, "Recommended Practice for Standard Procedure for Field Testing Water-Based Drilling Fluids", Specification RP13B-1, Washington, D.C., First Edition, June 1, 1990.

Structural

Nancy A. Bono, Thomas K. Liu, and Cetin Soydemir

PERFORMANCE OF AN INTERNALLY BRACED SLURRY-DIAPHRAGM WALL FOR EXCAVATION SUPPORT

REFERENCE: Bono, N.A., Liu, T.K., and Soydemir, C., "Performance of an Internally Braced Slurry-Diaphragm Wall for Excavation Support," Slurry Walls: Design, Construction, and Quality Control, ASTM STP 1129, David B. Paul, Richard R. Davidson, and Nicholas J. Cavalli, Eds., American Society for Testing and Materials, Philadelphia, 1992.

ABSTRACT: This paper presents the construction performance of an internally braced diaphragm wall constructed by the slurry trench method at a waterfront site on the Boston Harbor in Massachusetts. Due to the proximity of an existing building, waterfront structures and the harbor, as well as the unfavorable subsoil conditions, a cross-lot bracing system was selected for excavation support. The earth support system was instrumented by inclinometers and strain gages, and the existing abutting building was monitored by settlement reference points. Instrumentation data allowed monitoring of performance of the excavation support system as well as settlements in the existing adjacent building during the foundation construction.

The performance data indicated significantly unsymmetrical lateral displacements of the opposite diaphragm walls resulting from the unequal loads imposed by the building surcharge on one side as well as the limited soil mass on the opposite harbor side. Also, the daily collected data made it possible to take quick remedial action on the lateral support system at the time of a critical incident.

KEYWORDS: slurry diaphragm wall, excavation support, internal bracing, geotechnical instrumentation

---

Ms. Bono and Drs. Liu and Soydemir are Staff Engineer, Chairman, and Vice President, respectively, at Haley & Aldrich, Inc., 58 Charles Street, Cambridge, Massachusetts 02141.

PROJECT DESIGN AND CONSTRUCTION

General

Flagship Wharf Building, an eleven-story structure with a five level below-grade parking structure was constructed during 1988-1990 at a waterfront site on the Boston Harbor in Charlestown, Massachusetts. Excavation for the garage substructure, 30 m by 76 m in plan area and 15 m in depth was undertaken utilizing internally braced reinforced concrete diaphragm wall panels constructed with the conventional slurry trench technique (Figure 1). The 15 m deep excavation was within 4.5 m of an existing sheet pile bulkhead facing the harbor along one of the 76 m long sides, and within 1.5 m of an existing seven-story building supported by belled caissons on the opposite side, as shown in Figure 2. Due to the proximity of the existing building and the harbor, as well as the unfavorable subsoil conditions, a cross-lot bracing system had to be selected in lieu of a typically less costly external bracing system for the excavation support.

Since the two opposite 76 m long walls of the excavation were not symmetrically loaded, frequent monitoring of the wall performance during construction was especially important. Movements of the walls were surveyed by inclinometers installed within the reinforced concrete diaphragm panels. Stresses in selected bracing members were measured by vibrating-wire type strain gages. In addition, settlements in the existing adjacent building were monitored by level survey of reference points installed on the exterior line of columns.

Subsurface Conditions

The project site is underlain from ground surface down by:
        Miscellaneous Fill
        Organic Deposit
        Glacio-Marine Deposit
        Glacial Till

Average soil strata are shown in Figure 2. The glacio-marine deposit was relatively thin and not present at all locations, it is therefore not included in the profile.

Miscellaneous Fill: A layer of miscellaneous fill ranging from about 1.5 to 8 m in thickness blanketed the site. The fill consisted of a loose to dense mixture of gravel, sand, silt and clay with brick, glass, wood, cinders and other construction debris. Within the soil matrix were remnants of the site's history as a Navy Yard including granite block seawalls, timber bulkheads, wood cofferdams, pile supported crane rails, and building foundations.

Organic Deposit: Underlying the surficial fill was typically a layer of loose to very loose organic sandy silt. It ranged from 0 to about 7 m in thickness, and typically had SPT blow-counts, (N values)

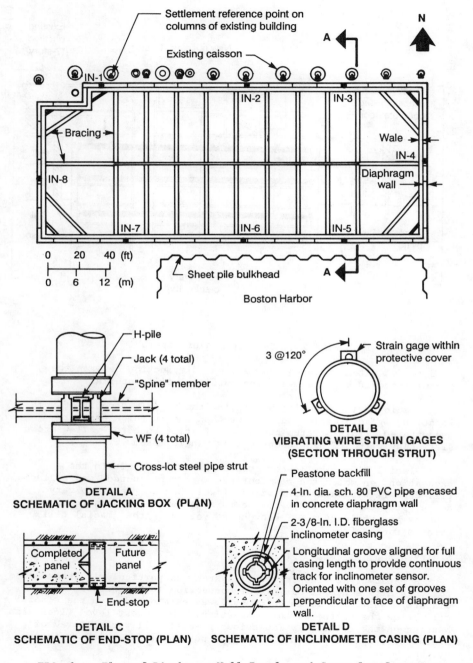

FIG. 1 -- Plan of Diaphragm Wall Panels and Cross-Lot Struts

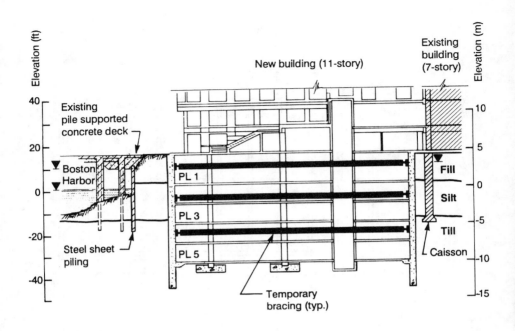

FIG. 2 -- Section A-A of Figure 1

of 3 to 7. Often there was not a clear distinction between the organic deposit and the overlying surficial fill material.

Glacio-Marine Deposit: Underlying the organic deposit at some locations, glacio-marine soils less than 2 m in thickness were encountered. This stratum consisted of stiff to hard, yellow-brown silty clay with SPT blow-count values ranging from 12 to 42.

Glacial Till: The lowest stratum encountered within the excavation, on which the new footings were constructed, was a glacial till deposit typically consisting of well-bonded, dense to very dense, gray to brown silty coarse to fine sand with occasional cobbles and boulders. SPT blow count values in the glacial till stratum ranged from 38 to 141.

Slurry-Diaphragm Wall

A water-tight diaphragm wall system was particularly recommended for this site since it has direct connection to the harbor. The diaphragm wall, 760 mm in thickness, was extended 3 m in the glacial till below the bottom of the excavation. The lowest level floor slab bearing on the relatively impervious glacial till was relieved of hydrostatic uplift pressure through a permanent underslab drainage system.

The 760 mm thick diaphragm wall panels were provided with reinforcing steel cages. The reinforcing steel included plates on the inside face of the wall to allow positive connection to the wales of the internal bracing system.

The 18 m deep diaphragm wall system was constructed of 46 individual panels, ranging in length from approximately 3 to 5.5 m. Both a kelly-bar mounted clam-shell bucket and a cable operated clam-shell bucket were utilized to excavate for the panels. A chisel was used when obstructions which could not be excavated by the bucket were encountered. One and two end-stops, for secondary and primary panels, respectively, were then installed at design locations. The end-stops used by the Contractor consisted of three 6 m long segments of rectangular steel section with a triangular shaped wedge along the center, as depicted in Figure 1.

The end-stops contained openings which allowed the slurry to flow laterally from the panel zone while concrete was being placed, and also facilitated the use of jacks to lift the end-stops from the trench excavation following concrete placement. In addition, the end-stops could accommodate a water stop membrane. When used, the membrane was inserted partially into the slot within the triangular wedge portion of the end-stop. Following placement and setting of the concrete for the panel, the end-stop would be lifted out of the trench excavation with the membrane remaining partially embedded in the concrete. The adjacent panel would then be cast around the extruding portion of the water stop membrane. Typically water stops were not used in this project.

The individual panel excavations (i.e., trenches) were supported by bentonite slurry which was maintained at a minimum of 0.6 m above the groundwater level. The slurry was desanded prior to placing concrete by tremie methods, utilizing a combination shaker screen and desanding cone type unit. Standard tests were conducted at specified intervals to determine the properties of the slurry, including viscosity, sand content, pH, and specific gravity.

During and upon completion of the excavation, water tightness of the panel joints was monitored, and drilling and chemical grouting was undertaken along some joints to control seepage.

Cross-Lot Bracing System

Site and subsurface conditions dictated the choice of an internal bracing system. The rectangular shape of the excavation resulted in designing a cross-lot bracing arrangement since a system utilizing three levels of rakers was not feasible due to the limited dimensions of the excavation. The cross-lot bracing members consisted of three levels of steel pipe struts spaced at 6 m center to center as shown in Figures 1 and 2. Each steel pipe strut spanned approximately 15 m from a wale to a center steel H-pile, which besides the strut also supported a specially designed jacking box. There were nine pairs of struts at each bracing level; 610 mm in diameter at the upper level, 760 mm at the mid level, and 910 mm at the lowest level. The thickness of the pipe sections were 9.5 mm at the upper level and mid level, and 13 mm at the lowest level. Other bracing members included three levels of steel wales, nine corner braces at each level, and three levels of horizontal steel "spine" members spanning east-west across the excavation.

A schematic of the jacking box is depicted in Figure 1. The jacks were placed between wide flange steel members at the ends of the pipe struts, welded on the closure plates, as shown, and a pre-load of approximately 40% of the design load was applied. The maximum design loads estimated for the individual struts ranged from 1,423 kN at the upper level to 4,448 kN at the lowest level. Steel plates (shims) were then forced in and welded into place to "lock-in" the pre-load. Due to the configuration of the end-bay struts, and the length of the site, it was not feasible to pre-load the system in the longitudinal direction. Similarly, the diagonal, corner struts were not pre-loaded.

Sequence of Excavation

The planned panel construction schedule allowed excavation to begin at the west end of the site prior to completing all the slurry wall panels. The initial excavation included a perimeter trench to the upper bracing level to allow installation of the top wales. Simultaneously, an excavation in the east-west orientation was conducted at the center of the site to the mid-level bracing elevation, leaving a 2 horizontal to 1 vertical berm against the diaphragm walls. The central excavation allowed installation of the first and second level "spine" members, and east and west end-bay struts. Throughout this excavation, truck access was maintained along the north and south sides of the site to expedite excavation rates.

Installation of the upper level cross-lot struts was then commenced, allowing excavation of the full area of the site progressively to the second bracing level elevation, however, obstructing truck access to the center of the site thereby slowing the excavation rates. Following completion of the upper level cross-lot struts, the remaining excavation was conducted utilizing shovel-dozers which moved the soil to a particular location to be removed from the excavation by a clam-shell operating from ground surface.

PERFORMANCE OF THE WALL-BRACING SYSTEM

Instrumentation

The performance of the diaphragm wall and the internal bracing system was surveyed by means of inclinometers, building settlement reference points, and strain gages. The data obtained was utilized to monitor performance of the excavation support system during construction to allow advanced warning of potential "problems". The following sections discuss the installations and the measurements in parallel with the construction progress.

Instrumentation Installations

Inclinometers: Eight inclinometer casings (IN-1 through IN-8) were installed in selected panels, as indicated in Figure 1, to allow measurements of horizontal movements of the diaphragm walls during excavation. PVC pipe casings were secured to the reinforcing steel prior to installing the "cage" into the slurry stabilized trench in order to allow installation of the smaller diameter fiberglass inclinometer casing. The annular space between the PVC pipe and inclinometer casing was backfilled with pea stone to stabilize the casing.

Initial readings of the inclinometers were taken prior to commencement of excavation to establish the reference bases for lateral movements. Subsequent readings were typically taken on a weekly basis, with frequency being increased if an accelerated rate of movement was observed. The data was analyzed by assuming fixity at the bottom of the inclinometer casing. It may be noted that the bottom of the inclinometer is not necessarily stationary, and where more precision is required the top of the inclinometer should be surveyed independently relative to a fixed reference line and the surveyed inclinometer movements be corrected accordingly.

Strain Gages: A total of sixteen vibrating-wire strain gages were installed on selected bracing members. The locations were arranged to obtain a representative set of data from each of the three bracing levels. The three strain-gage arrangement at 120 degrees apart (Figure 1) allows correction for bending of the steel members. The three strain gage arrangement was installed on three struts, one at each of the three bracing levels. At other locations, one or two gages were installed on the selected struts.

Building Reference Points: Reference points were established at each column location along the exterior column line of the existing seven-story building abutting the excavation. These reference points were monitored by level survey typically on a weekly basis, and daily when accelerated rates of movement were observed up through the removal of the bracing.

Performance of Inclinometers

Figures 3, 4 and 5 show inclinometer data at the mid-points of the opposite 76 m long walls during the months of March, April and May 1989. Typically, the greatest displacements were measured at the center inclinometers (IN-2 and IN-6), this is expected to be due to the restraining effects of the corners on the shorter walls.

Prior to March 1989 with the upper level cross-lot struts installed, and excavation having progressed to the mid-level cross-lot struts, measured movements were relatively small, (1.25 cm

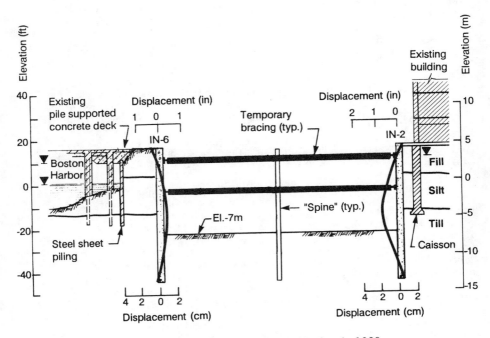

FIG. 3 -- Inclinometer Data: 27 March 1989

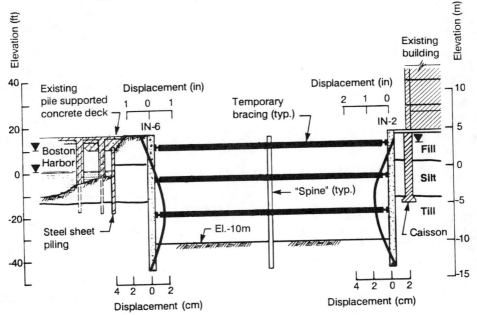

FIG. 4 -- Inclinometer Data; 6-7 April 1989

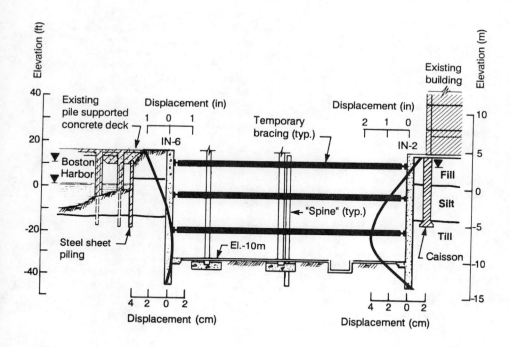

FIG. 5 -- Inclinometer Data: 17 May 1989

or less) with maximum displacements occurring at the east and west walls. This could be attributed to the fact that the end-bay struts and "spine" members were not pre-loaded, and that the bracing system in the east-west direction was subject to relatively elastic compression.

As shown in Figure 3, by the end of March 1989 excavation had progressed to El. -7 m, and the upper and mid-level cross-lot struts had been installed. At this stage, maximum wall deflections were less than 2 cm and toward the excavation. Approximately two weeks later, the lowest level cross-lot struts had been installed, and the excavation had proceeded to El. -10 m. As shown in Figure 4, through 6-7 April 1989 the surveyed maximum wall movements were still under 2 cm, however the location of the maximum displacements had shifted to lower elevations while excavation advanced from El. -7 to El. -10 m.

During the last week of April 1989, local overstressing and associated deformations of mid level and lower level jacking boxes were observed. The resulting wall movements were immediately confirmed with inclinometer readings. Figure 5 shows the wall displacements as of the second week of May. As shown, the north wall, adjacent to the existing structure had undergone a total of approximately 4.4 cm of displacement toward the excavation, with the maximum displacement occurring just below the lowest level struts.

Also as of the second week of May, along the south wall, adjacent to the harbor, the maximum movements, which had previously been observed at the level of the lowest level struts, were observed to shift to the upper portion of the wall, and were observed to be away from the excavation. The magnitude of these displacements away from the excavation was observed to be approximately 2.5 cm. In parallel, displacements at the level of the lowest-level struts, which had been measured to be 1.25 cm toward the excavation on 6-7 April, was observed to reduce to 0.3 cm toward the excavation. In summary the direction of the displacements had reversed along the south wall during the excavation.

Upon discovery of local overstressing in several of the jacking boxes, corrective measures were taken to strengthen the jacking boxes, and subsequent inclinometer readings reflected a decrease in rate of wall movements.

Figure 6 shows the maximum displacements with directions at each of the eight inclinometer locations surveyed during September 1989 after the wall movements had stabilized. The general trend of displacements toward the harbor could be explained by suggesting that the building surcharge and the active pressures from the north wall exceeded the active resistance from the south wall and forced it to the passive mode in order to maintain force equilibrium in the horizontal direction.

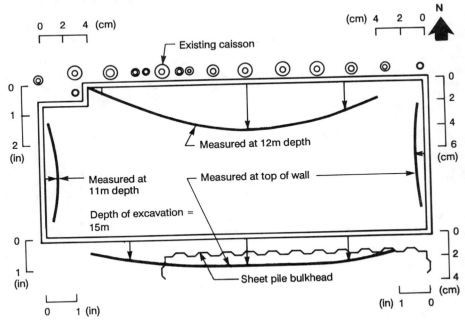

FIG. 6 -- Measured Maximum Displacements

Performance of Strain-Gages

    Strain gages on selected struts were monitored on selected
struts throughout the duration of excavation. Typical data for the
mid-level and lowest-level cross-lot struts are presented in Figures
7 and 8, respectively. These struts were both instrumented with
three strain gage arrangements. The strut load data in Figures 7 and
8 have also been corrected for temperature effects, assuming that the
walls are non-yielding. This correction is necessary to distinguish
between the load increase due to earth pressures and the thermal
stresses in the steel struts. Since the bulk of the excavation was
performed during a period of warming spring months, measured loads
were affected by both sources.

    As shown in Figures 7 and 8, the strut loads dropped to
approximately one-half of the pre-load shortly after installation of
the struts. This is possibly due to creep occurring in the
bracing-wall-soil system resulting in stress relaxation within a few
days of applying the pre-load. The observation also suggests that
pre-loading was effective in reducing future wall displacement as
excavation proceeded.

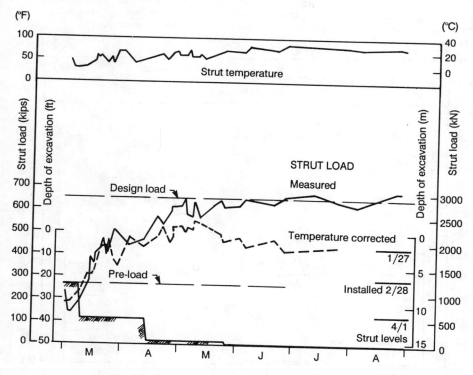

FIG. 7 -- Vibrating Wire Strain Gage Data - Mid-Level

As the depth of the excavation increased, the strut loads were observed to increase as expected. The measured maximum strut loads at the mid-level struts (Figure 7) were quite close to the design load. The design estimates for the uniform lateral effective soil pressure were 4H kN per square meter above groundwater, and 2H kN per square meter below groundwater, where H equals the depth of the excavation in meters, plus static water pressure, traffic-construction surcharge, and surcharge loads induced through the caissons of the existing building. The design load of the struts did not include the thermal loading which was measured to be as high as 30% of the total measured load (or 910 kN) at the mid-level struts.

The maximum measured strut loads at the lowest-level struts (Figure 8) were approximately 65% of the design load, estimated as stated above. This may be due to the relatively rigid support provided by the glacial till through the 10 ft. embedded section of the diaphragm wall. Due to the larger cross-sectional area of the lowest level struts, ambient temperature increase resulted in relatively larger load increases (up to 36% of the total load, or 1925 kN).

When measured loads of the mid-level struts reached the level of the design load, steps were taken by the Contractor by hanging tarpaulins to minimize direct sunlight on the steel members.

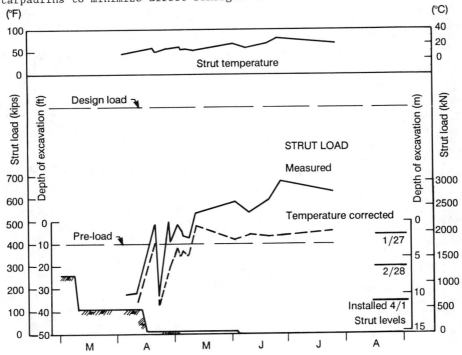

FIG. 8 -- Vibrating Wire Strain Gage Data - Lowest Level

Performance of Building Settlement Reference Points

Building settlement reference points were installed at column locations along the exterior column line of the existing building abutting the excavation as shown in Figure 1. The reference points were monitored by level survey typically on a weekly basis, and daily when accelerated rates of movement were observed. As shown in Figure 9, maximum settlements of about 1 cm were measured through the last week of March 1989. At this point, the excavation had progressed to just below the lowest-level bracing El. -7 m, to allow installation of the struts.

By the early part of April a total settlement of about 2.75 cm was measured. By the end of April, the total settlement reached to about 4 cm approximately at the mid-point of the north diaphragm wall. This total settlement can be directly related to the observed displacement of the slurry wall of 4.4 cm toward the excavation during the period of the local overstressing observed in several of the jacking boxes. Although the problem with the jacking boxes were corrected shortly following its detection (25 April) settlement of the existing structure continued at a decreased rate for several weeks as indicated in Figure 9.

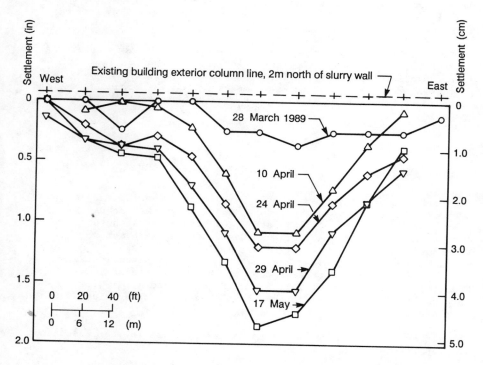

FIG. 9 -- Settlement Performance of the Existing Building

CLOSURE

Construction of the Flagship Wharf Project including a five-level below grade parking garage adjacent to the Boston Harbor was successfully completed in 1990 by utilizing a slurry diaphragm wall and a cross-lot bracing system for support of the 30 m by 76 m by 15 m excavation. Challenging site constraints including an existing seven-story building, only 1.5 m from the north face of the excavation, and an existing steel sheet pile bulkhead forming the harbor line adjacent to the south face of the excavation led the selection of a perimeter diaphragm wall to be an internal bracing system necessary for excavation support.

Since the existing unsymmetrical external loads and available soil masses behind the two opposing north and south diaphragm walls would result in non-symmetrical wall displacements a field instrumentation program was implemented for construction monitoring. Collected performance data made it possible to monitor the progressive wall movements, bracing loads and settlements of the existing adjacent building supported on belled caissons only several inches from the north diaphragm wall. Instrumentation also served to detect and diagnose an overstressing problem in the bracing system, and allowed to monitor the effectiveness of the implemented remedial measures.

Strain gages mounted on the cross-lot struts besides providing data on the strut loads associated with the excavation, jacking (i.e., pre-loading), they performed an important function by indicating the effect of ambient temperature on the strut loads which happened to be quite significant and required the Contractor to take special action.

ACKNOWLEDGMENTS

The following organizations participated in the development of the project: Raymond Development, Inc., Charlestown, Massachusetts, Owner; The Architects Collaborative, Cambridge, Massachusetts, Architect; Weidlinger Associates, Cambridge, Massachusetts, Structural Engineers; Haley & Aldrich, Inc., Cambridge, Massachusetts, Geotechnical Engineers; Turner Construction Company, Boston, Massachusetts, General Contractor; Case International, Roselle, Illinois, Slurry Wall Subcontractor; and A. A. Will, Corporation, Randolph, Massachusetts, Excavation and Bracing System Subcontractor.

The authors gratefully acknowledge Ms. Laura Gross for her assistance in preparation of the graphics.

David A. Schoenwolf[1], Robert V. Whitman[2], Eldon L. Abbott[3], and
James M. Becker[4]

POST OFFICE SQUARE GARAGE PROJECT - A CASE HISTORY OF INSTRUMENTED
SLURRY WALL PERFORMANCE

REFERENCE: Schoenwolf, D. A., Whitman, R. V., Abbott, E. L., and
Becker, J. M., **"Post Office Square Garage Project - A Case History of
Instrumented Slurry Wall Performance,"** Slurry Walls: Design, Con-
struction, and Quality Control, ASTM STP 1129, David B. Paul, Richard
R. Davidson, and Nicholas J. Cavalli, Eds., American Society for Test-
ing and Materials, Philadelphia, 1992.

ABSTRACT: This paper presents the results of the monitored performance of a reinforced concrete diaphragm wall (slurry wall) while making a seven-level, 24.4 m (80 ft) deep excavation in downtown Boston
for the construction of an underground garage using the "top-down"
construction technique. In developing the design and construction
methodology, ground movement control was considered to be an important
aspect in design of the excavation support system. Finite element analyses were performed to model the anticipated soil and adjacent building
movements. Observed movements during construction were compared to the
values generated during design to judge the performance of the excavation support system. Modifications to the construction sequence were
made to help reduce future movements. The owner's commitment of resources necessary to support the program played an important role in
achieving the desired goals.

KEYWORDS: slurry walls, finite element analyses, top-down construction, inclinometer, observational approach

---

[1]Vice President, Haley & Aldrich, Inc., 4909 Cordell Ave.,
Bethesda, MD 20814.

[2]Member of Technical Advisory Committee, Friends of Post Office
Square and Professor of Civil Engineering, Massachusetts Institute of
Technology, Cambridge, MA 02139.

[3]Vice President, Parsons Brinckerhoff Quade & Douglas, Inc.,
120 Boylston Street, Boston, MA 02116.

[4]President of Beacon Construction Co. and Chairman of the
Construction Committee, Friends of Post Office Square, Inc., 50 Federal
Street, Boston, MA 02110.

INTRODUCTION

The Post Office Square Garage is a new 1,400 car garage, with seven levels of below-grade structure, constructed in the heart of Boston's financial district. At the ground surface, the garage is covered with a 6070 m^2 (1.5 acre) park. The Owner of the project is the Friends of Post Office Square, Inc., a non-profit organization composed of 19 Boston civic and business organizations. In 1982, the Friends of Post Office Square formulated a proposal to replace an aging City-owned garage with a public park and underground parking facility. The proposal met the important need for public green space in Downtown Boston, while offering office workers and downtown shoppers a convenient and expanded underground parking facility. The $80 million project was developed through a unique public/private partnership. Once the capital costs of the project are repaid to the investors, ownership of the garage will revert to the City of Boston.

The ownership set a high priority on minimizing construction risks and related impacts on adjacent areas. However, it was recognized that overly conservative design or construction methods would not be cost-effective. Therefore, the adopted philosophy was to allow methods which did not overly penalize construction efficiency, with the provision that contingency measures could be implemented, if necessary. Therefore, the observational approach was adopted; design on the basis of expected conditions, envision all possible adverse conditions that might arise, plan for how to deal with them if necessary, and monitor the information during construction so that mitigation measures could be implemented as required. This approach relied heavily upon the implementation of sophisticated engineering predictions of performance and close monitoring, as described herein. Both the design and construction procedures were frequently challenged, through a series of checks and balances, to achieve success.

PROJECT SITE AND SUBSURFACE CONDITIONS

Site Conditions

Located in Boston's Financial District, the project site is bordered on all sides with streets, utilities and buildings. One of the major project concerns was the potential impact of the planned construction on the adjacent buildings which were as close to the project perimeter as 18 m (60 ft). In order to help assess the impact, the locations and foundation types of the buildings immediately surrounding the site were researched. As shown on Figure 1, 8 of the 12 adjacent buildings are supported on foundations which typically bear about 6.1 to 7.6 m (20 to 25 ft.) below ground surface, on or in the near-surface clay stratum.

Subsurface Soil, Rock and Groundwater Conditions

Subsurface soil, rock and groundwater conditions in the project vicinity are summarized below (Refer to Figure 2):

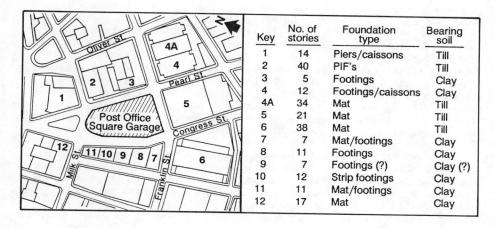

Key	No. of stories	Foundation type	Bearing soil
1	14	Piers/caissons	Till
2	40	PIF's	Till
3	5	Footings	Clay
4	12	Footings/caissons	Clay
4A	34	Mat	Till
5	21	Mat	Till
6	38	Mat	Till
7	7	Mat/footings	Clay
8	11	Footings	Clay
9	7	Footings (?)	Clay (?)
10	12	Strip footings	Clay
11	11	Mat/footings	Clay
12	17	Mat	Clay

FIG. 1--Site location and adjacent buildings.

Fill: A surface layer of miscellaneous fill consisting of fine SAND to sandy GRAVEL with varying amounts of brick, concrete, and granite blocks. The fill varied in thickness from 0.6 to 4.0 m (2 to 13 ft).

Clay: Below the fill, a clay deposit ranges in thickness from 10.6 to 15.2 m (35 to 50 ft). This deposit is classified as a gray silty CLAY, having frequent to occasional partings, lenses and layers of sand and silt. The undrained shear strength is 48.8 to 73.2 kPa (0.5 to 0.75 tsf).

Sand: A sand layer was encountered in most borings, described as a medium dense to very dense, coarse to fine SAND with varying amounts of coarse to fine gravel. The deposit varied in thickness from 0.3 to 5.8 m (1 to 19 ft) where encountered.

Glacial Till: Glacial till underlies the site and generally consists of hard, clayey to gravelly SILT to very dense silty coarse to fine SAND, ranging in thickness from 1.5 to 11.6 m (5 to 38 ft).

Bedrock: The bedrock is described as a very soft to moderately hard, completely to very slightly weathered, ARGILLITE and SANDSTONE.

Water levels recorded in the observation wells indicated groundwater levels varying from 2.4 to 3.7 m (8 to 12 ft) below street level. The piezometric levels in the sand, glacial till and bedrock were typically about 6.1 to 7.6 m (20 to 25 ft) below ground surface.

PROJECT CONSTRUCTION

Construction of the new garage began in October 1988 with the demolition of an aging City of Boston Garage. The new garage was con-

structed on approximately the same footprint as the previous garage
using an advanced state-of-the-art technique known as "top-down" construction or the Milan method [1]. This method was selected to minimize risk with regard to potential construction-related effects on the
surrounding environment, since it provides a stiff, permanent wall
bracing system as excavation proceeds. It also offered many construction advantages for the Owner and Contractor. It eliminated tiebacks
and temporary internal bracing. In addition, the use of the top-down
method allowed the Contractor to cast the roof of the garage initially,
and utilize it as a staging platform throughout construction, thereby
minimizing traffic tie-ups on adjacent streets.

Top-down construction involves constructing a cast-in-place concrete diaphragm wall (slurry wall) around the garage perimeter to serve
as the permanent foundation wall (a in Figure 2A). All interior columns
and foundation supports were installed prior to general excavation.
Slurry filled slots (b in Figure 2A), typically 0.9 x 3.0 m (3 x
10 ft), were excavated from ground surface to bearing in rock at depths
of 25.9 to 29.0 m (85 to 95 ft). The reinforcing cage for each load
bearing element (LBE), with steel column attached (c in Figure 2A), was
lowered into the slot and the portion below the lowest floor slab level
was tremie concreted (d in Figure 2A). The slot above was backfilled
with a cement-bentonite mixture.

The roof slab and the seven lower floors were then cast in sequence from the top down; the earth below each slab level was excavated
in a mining operation and removed through temporary openings in the
slabs. Movable concrete forms, attached to the columns and slurry
wall, were lowered into position as each floor was excavated (Figures
2B and 2C).

Construction/Monitoring Organization

To oversee the construction/monitoring process, the Owner assembled a Technical Advisory Committee, drawing on the expertise of its
various members as well as local academics and professionals. This
committee further delegated its oversight to a series of subcommittees
which were served by professional staff. To facilitate the desired
dynamic check and balance process, the Owner retained its own geotechnical engineer and also required that both the designer and contractor
retain their own geotechnical consultants. In addition, the structural
check engineer, mandated by the City of Boston and retained by the
Owner, was a foundation engineering firm. All four of these firms
participated in the design and analysis process and the design of the
extensive instrumentation efforts that were headed by the Owner's
geotechnical consultant.

To ensure that the data collected were interpreted and fed back
into the construction process, a Geotechnical Monitoring Subcommittee
was formed. It was important that such a committee was separate from
the day to day exigencies of construction, so that it could raise concerns to the ownership when necessary.

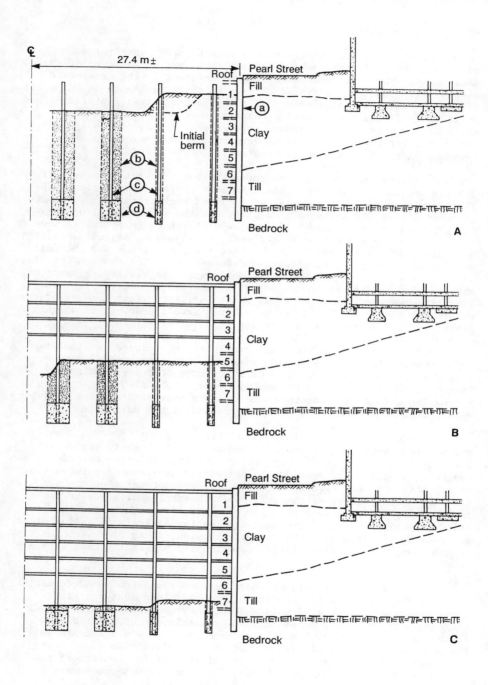

FIG. 2--Cross-section through Pearl Street looking north

FINITE ELEMENT ANALYSES

One of the geotechnical-related uncertainties concerning the proposed method of construction and the long-term performance of the facility was the magnitude of the inward movement of the concrete dia- phragm wall, and the associated effects of these movements on the verti- cal and horizontal displacements of the adjacent streets, utilities and buildings. In order to quantify the magnitude of these movements, estimates of expected performance were made as a guide to design and construction planning. Movements were predicted using the two-dimensional finite element programs SOILSTRUCT and JFEST.

Undrained analyses were performed by both Parsons Brinckerhoff Quade & Douglas and Massachusetts Institute of Technology using SOIL- STRUCT, with their own estimates of soil and rock properties. Results of these SOILSTRUCT analyses indicated that the maximum wall deforma- tions were similar, although there were differences in estimated move- ments at the top and bottom of the wall. Analyses were also performed to evaluate the influence of the assumed soil properties and the influ- ence of wall stiffness on predicted deformations. The range of predict- ed movements are shown on Table 1. Horizontal and vertical ground surface deformations at the building face across the street from the excavation were on the order of 25 mm (1 in.). Horizontal movements within the surficial fill layer were, in general, equal to or slightly greater than the vertical deformation.

While undrained analyses may reasonably be assumed to simulate conditions during and immediately after construction, provided no pro- longed workstoppage occurs, it is difficult to properly simulate long-term conditions using drained analyses in SOILSTRUCT. Attempts at estimating movements by drained analyses for post-construction behavior were performed and showed essentially no additional movement.

In addition, finite element analyses using SOILSTRUCT did not account for consolidation due to drawdown of the phreatic surface in the clay during and after construction. The consolidation deformations due to dewatering must be added to the excavation-induced deformations to estimate the total ground movement. To account for these time-dependent pore water changes, finite element analyses were per- formed using the program JFEST [2]. The program accounts for the con- solidation of the soil in the load-deformation analysis of geotechnical problems by coupling the equations of transient fluid flow with those of the "Cam Clay" elastic-plastic constitutive material stress-strain model.

JFEST was used to perform undrained and consolidation deformation analyses for the project. Results of the undrained analyses yielded about the same magnitude of wall and soil movements as the SOILSTRUCT program, with an estimated consolidation settlement of about 25 mm (1 in.) approximately 12.2 m (40 ft) from the concrete diaphragm wall. The analyses also indicated that most of the deformation would occur in the first half of the excavation. Therefore, careful construction procedures during the initial stages of excavation were necessary.

INSTRUMENTATION/MONITORING PROGRAM

The 24.4 m (80 ft) deep excavation was in close proximity to nearby streets, utilities and structures. It was recognized that the performance of the excavation was contingent on many construction-dependent variables which could not be fixed in advance, and that adjustments might be necessary depending upon observations made during the course of construction. Hence, the Project Team developed and implemented an extensive instrumentation program to observe and document the excavation performance [3]. The instrumentation program consisted of inclinometer, ground and building settlement reference points, observation wells and piezometers installed in and adjacent to the project site as described below:

Inclinometers

Inclinometers were installed in selected slurry wall panels, immediately behind selected slurry wall panels and across the street from the excavation in front of nearby buildings. A total of 13 inclinometer casings were installed within PVC sleeves cast in selected diaphragm wall panels (Figure 3A). At each location, a borehole was advanced through the 102 mm (4 in.) diameter sleeve to a typical depth of 7.6 to 9.1 m (25 to 30 ft) below the bottom of the wall. A 70 mm (2-3/4 in.) outer diameter inclinometer casing was installed to the full depth of the hole and backfilled with a cement/bentonite mixture. The inclinometers were extended below the bottom of the wall in order that fixity could be assumed.

A total of seven inclinometers were installed at locations in front of nearby buildings to monitor lateral soil movements associated with wall movements (Figure 3A). These inclinometers were advanced to depths of 33.5 to 36.6 m (110 to 120 ft), terminating in the bedrock. The casing sizes and installation details were as described above. In addition, four inclinometers were installed in the soil immediately outside the diaphragm wall at selected locations to monitor potential soil movements as the slurry wall panels were excavated (Figure 3A).

Ground and Building Settlement Reference Points

To monitor vertical movements within the potential area of influence of the deep excavation, a total of 84 surface reference points were established prior to construction. The surface points were typically PK nails in the pavement or sidewalk or points on utilities (Figure 3B). The reference points on buildings were typically drilled-in pins installed on vertical faces or existing building features. The selected locations were both on the front, side and rear limits of the buildings, in order to record differential settlement, should it occur (Figure 3C). Optical survey procedures were used. A permanent bench mark was installed into the bedrock 32.3 m (106 ft) below ground surface.

Observation Wells and Piezometers

Observation wells and piezometers were installed inside and outside the perimeter slurry wall in all the various strata (Figure 3D) to monitor the construction-related effects on the local groundwater regime.

RECORDED SLURRY WALL MOVEMENTS

Horizontal movements deduced from slope inclinometer readings varied significantly around the site, both in magnitude and the manner in which they developed during construction. This variation was the

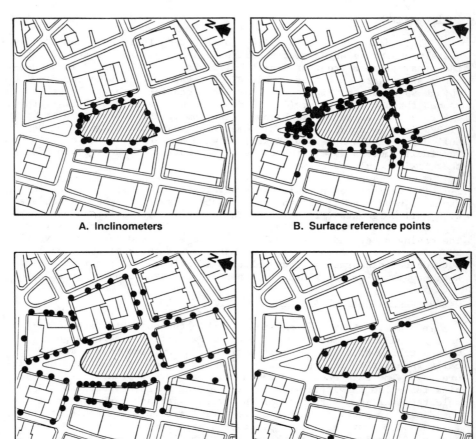

A. Inclinometers   B. Surface reference points

C. Building reference points   D. Observation wells, piezometers

FIG. 3--Instrumentation location plan

result of a number of factors: the site was irregularly shaped; at the Milk Street end the roof was cast on grade before any excavation; the sequencing of excavation, forming and placing of floors varied along the length of the site; etc. Utility tunnels under the adjacent streets may also have had an influence. It is not possible to explain fully all of the variations of horizontal movement, but a number of important factors can be identified.

Congress and Franklin Streets

Perhaps the most typical pattern of movement was recorded at Inclinometer 5 along Congress Street. Figure 4B shows horizontal movements at various stages of construction. The eight curves in this figure correspond to the completion of excavation for the roof, for lower level one, etc. on to the final excavation.

As shown on Figure 4B, the movement at the top was somewhat in excess of 25 mm (1 in.) up to and through the completion of Lower Level 3 (LL3), then subsequently decreased. At the end of excavation for LL2, movement at mid-depth exceeded that of the top, with the point of maximum movement progressing downward as excavation proceeded. Once excavation reached the bottom of the clay (after completion of LL5), additional movements during excavation for LL6 and LL7 were small. The final recorded movement near the top was between 13 and 25 mm (0.5 and 1 in.), with a maximum movement of about 38 mm (1.5 in.), occurring near the bottom of the clay at El. -10 m (El. 33 ft.). Movements at Inclinometer 3 on Congress Street, and Inclinometer 21 and 23 along Franklin Street (final movements are shown in Figures 4A, 4G and 4H, respectively), were quite similar to those at Inclinometer 5.

Pearl Street

At Inclinometer 16, situated along Pearl Street, the lateral movements were quite different, as is seen from the plot in Figure 4F. During the initial excavation, movement at the top was much larger than along Congress and Franklin Streets. Movements continued to be larger as excavation proceeded, and maximum deflections reached about 51 mm (2 in.). Again the rate of deflection decreased substantially once excavation reached the bottom of the clay.

The exact cause of these larger movements is not entirely clear, and appears to have resulted from a combination of factors.

o   The initial excavation for the roof was along Pearl Street. This first cut was particularly deep, and the contractor was allowed to keep only a short 7.6 m (25 ft) wide berm, as shown by the dotted line in Part A of Figure 5. Once the large movements were observed, the contractor agreed to maintain berms with a minimum width of 12.2 m (40 ft). This more conservative practice was followed for the initial excavations along Congress and Franklin Streets. (For subsequent stages of excavation, the contractor was asked to use even wider berms, leaving only a narrow trench

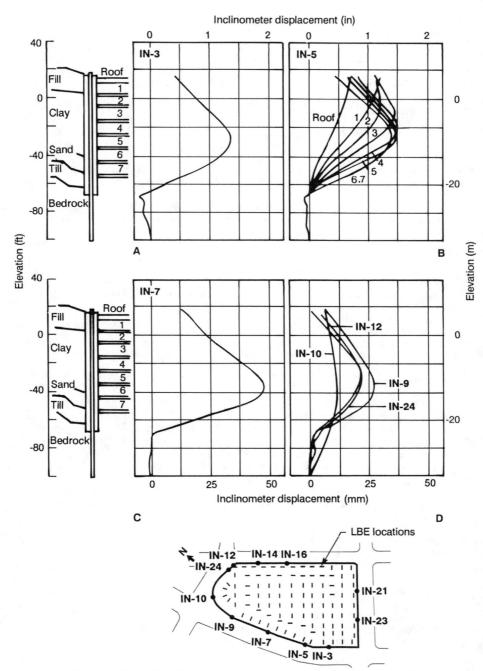

FIG. 4--Recorded horizontal movements of diaphragm wall

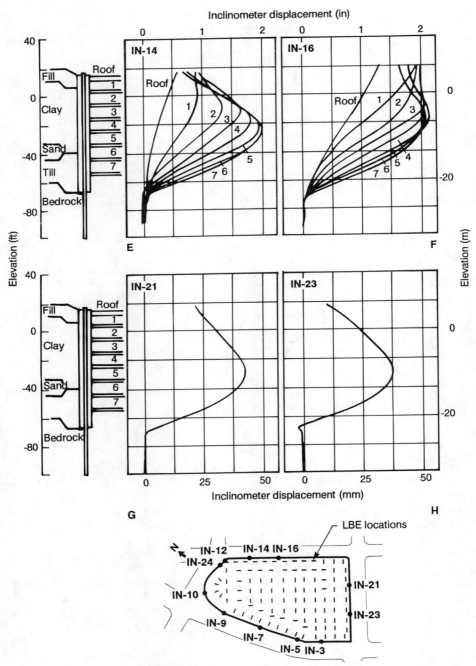

FIG. 4 (cont.)--Recorded horizontal movements of diaphragm wall

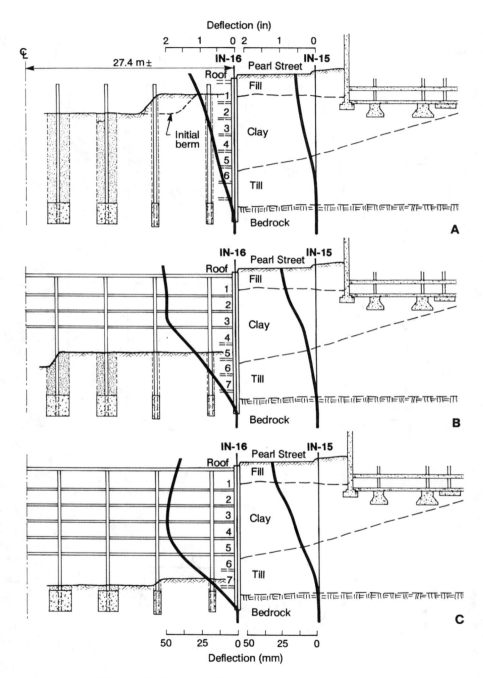

FIG. 5--Wall and soil movements, IN No. 15 & 16

through the center of the site for equipment movement; see Part B
of Figure 5.)

o   The excavation along Pearl Street was open for a long period of
      time (longer than along Congress Street) before the bracing pro-
      vided by the roof was completed. Forming and pouring of the roof
      presented several special difficulties, as it was necessary to
      develop experience in the use of the moveable forms. As a re-
      sult, there was also some delay in the installation of temporary
      bracing (pipe struts) across the roof opening for access and
      egress ramps.

o   Still another explanation has to do with the effect of the LBE
      slots near Pearl Street. Here there was a double row of slots
      oriented parallel to the wall (Figure 4) which removed a greater
      portion of the resisting soil from in front of the wall than
      where the LBEs were oriented perpendicular to the wall. Moreover,
      tests showed that the strength of the cement-bentonite backfill
      in these slots was particularly low. This situation might ex-
      plain the larger movements both initially and during subsequent
      increments of excavation.

o   Finally, some temperature effects appear to contribute to the
      larger movements, as discussed below.

      Figure 4E also summarizes movements at Inclinometer 14 along
Pearl Street. Here the horizontal deflections at the top were within
the range generally found along Congress and Franklin Streets. The
proximity to the cast-on-grade roof slab at the Milk Street end may
have provided additional support. However, the maximum movements at
depth were similar to those at Inclinometer 16. A final maximum movement of about 51 mm (2 in.) at depth was also recorded at Inclinometer
7 along Congress Street (Figure 4C). Inclinometer 7, 14 and 16 were
all located in long, straight stretches of diaphragm wall, and this
situation may have contributed to the greater maximum movements at
these locations.

Milk Street

      A different situation existed at the Milk Street end of the exca-
vation, where the roof slab was cast-on-grade before excavation commenced. Since the northern portion of the project was constructed
under Milk Street, that portion of the roof slab was constructed as the
first order of work in order to restore traffic on Milk Street. Not
only was the top of the diaphragm wall braced from the outset, but the
arching action of the curved wall combined to reduce the horizontal
movements. Figure 4D summarizes the final movements at four inclinometers in this portion of the wall. Note that movements are smallest at
Inclinometer 10 in the middle of the arch, and increase toward Congress
and Pearl Streets.

Temperature Effects

One factor contributing to the larger than expected initial movements of the top of the walls was a sharp temperature drop shortly
after completion of the roof. Figure 6 plots both the daily range in
temperature during this interval and the inward movement of the top of
the wall. A clear association of temperature change and movement is
noted. At this stage, steel pipe struts were used to brace across
slots left in the roof, along both Pearl and Congress Streets, at the
locations of access and egress ramps. The calculated change in length
of these struts as a result of the temperature drop agreed well with
the observed increments of movement.

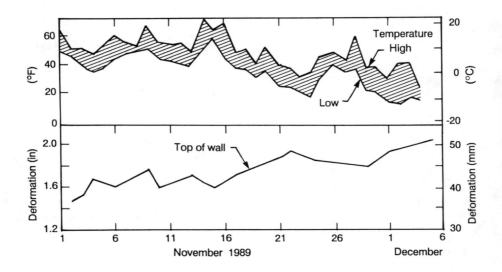

FIG. 6--Top of wall movements versus temperature

Shrinkage of Roof and Floors

It was recognized prior to construction that the roof and floors
would creep and shrink following placement, thus permitting additional
wall movements. The concrete mix was designed to minimize this effect,
and tests were carried out in the laboratory to assess the possible
delayed movement. Estimates for this movement ranged from 8 to 12 mm
(0.3 to 0.5 in.) for each floor. Evaluations of actual creep/shrinkage
measurements, based on the inclinometer data, indicated that at the
roof, there was a rather large initial increase followed, at the lower
levels, by a gradual decrease. The increase is, in part, the result of
the temperature effect discussed in the previous paragraph, and the
subsequent decrease may reflect the gradual warming trend during the

latter stages of construction. There was a time-delayed movement at all floor levels, on the average about 8 mm (0.3 in.) [4].

Slurry Trench Construction

Initially there was some concern about horizontal movements of the ground toward the excavation during excavation for the diaphragm wall. Hence four inclinometers were placed, before any work on the wall, at locations several feet outside the projected line of the wall. Recorded ground movements during excavation of monitored panels were less than 8 mm (0.3 in.) toward the excavation, and there was a small net outward movement as a result of concreting the panel.

Comparisons to Initial Predictions

Considering the various complications discussed above, the final recorded movements accord quite well with the theoretical predictions made in advance of excavation. Omitting the measurements at Milk Street and ignoring the large observed top-of-wall displacement at Inclinometer 16, the comparisons may be summarized as shown in the following Table 1:

TABLE 1--Comparison of Predicted Versus Observed Movements

Location	Predicted-mm[a]	Observed-mm[a]
Top	8 to 20	12 to 25
Maximum	33 to 36	38 to 50
Bottom	5 to 13	-3 to 3

[a] 1 inch = 25 mm

None of the advance predictions considered the effects of ambient temperature changes. It is clear that the stiffness of the rock strata to resist horizontal movements in the embedded portion was underestimated. Displacements from the first stage of excavation were generally larger than predicted, partly because of temperature effects and partly because the excavation at this stage was deeper than originally planned.

MOVEMENTS OF ADJACENT BUILDINGS

While a discussion of the vertical and horizontal movements of adjacent buildings is beyond the scope of this paper, they were quite small and there was no reported damage. Whatever the explanation for the larger movements of the diaphragm wall at Inclinometer 16, the horizontal movements in front of the building across Pearl Street were significantly smaller, as may be seen in Figure 5. The maximum settlement at this building was about 13 mm (0.5 in.), and there has been no movement subsequent to construction. The inclinometer in front of the buildings across Congress Street showed maximum horizontal displacements of 8 mm (0.3 in.) or less. The maximum settlement recorded on these buildings was 8 mm (0.3 in.). For comparison, the settlement predicted using SOILSTRUCT and JFEST, ignoring consolidation, ranged from 10 to 30 mm (0.4 to 1.2 in.).

GOALS ACHIEVED

Clearly the goals of the Friends of Post Office Square have been achieved. The deepest building excavation in the history of Boston has been carried out in the heart of the City with minimal disruption. This was carried out as a team effort that was achieved by focusing on both the public spirited nature of the project as well as the state-of-the-practice design and construction effort.

ACKNOWLEDGMENTS

The authors gratefully acknowledge the Friends of Post Office Square, Inc. for permission to publish the results of this project. In addition, the writers wish to acknowledge Mr. Chris Erikson, Haley & Aldrich, Inc. and Mr. Robert Rawnsley, Parsons Brinckerhoff Quade and Douglas, Inc. who worked long hours on the construction site recording construction progress, instrument data and helping to make reasonable interpretations of the results.

REFERENCES

[1]   Becker, James M. and Haley, Mark X., "Up/Down Construction - Decision Making and Performance," Design and Performance of Earth Retaining Structures, Geotechnical Special Publication No. 25, American Society of Civil Engineers, New York, NY, 1990.

[2]   Finno, R. J., "Response of Cohesive Soil to Advance Shield Tunnel," a dissertation submitted to the Department of Civil Engineering and the Committee of Graduate Studies of Stanford University in partial fulfillment of the requirements for the degree of Doctor of Philosophy, July 1983.

[3]   Whitman, R.V., Johnson, E.G., Abbott, E.L., Becker, J.M., "Field Instrumentation Program Vital to Deep Excavation Project," ASCE Geotechnical Engineering Congress, Boulder, CO June 1991.

[4]   Hashash, Y., Personal communication, PhD. Thesis at Massachusetts Institute of Technology, in progress (1991).

Kuang-Hsiung Lee,[1] Chin-Der Ou,[2] and Kuei-Wu Tsai[3]

QUALITY CONTROL IN CONSTRUCTION OF STRUCTURAL DIAPHRAGM WALL JOINTS

REFERENCE: Lee, K.H., Ou, C.D., and Tsai, K.W., "Quality Control in Construction of Structural Diaphragm Wall Joints," _Slurry Walls: Design, Construction, and Quality Control, ASTM STP 1129_, David B. Paul, Richard R. Davidson, and Nicholas J. Cavalli, Eds., American Society for Testing and Materials, Philadelphia, 1992.

ABSTRACT: Diaphragm wall with leaky or defective joints have been identified as one of the main reasons that lead to ground loss and associated structural distress of adjacent buildings. In recent years, improvements in joint details and construction procedures have been proved successful in achieving watertightness requirements of structural diaphragm walls for deep excavation projects in Taiwan. The various factors which lead to leaky or defective joints and possible preventive measures are addressed.

KEYWORDS: diaphragm wall joints, deep excavation, quality control, slurry, watertightness

The diaphragm wall has been adopted by the Taiwan construction industry since early 1970 as an earth retaining structure for deep excavation as well as a part of the permanent underground structure. For diaphragm walls used as permanent structures, an overlapping joint (Fig. 1) is routinely designed to provide better resistance against lateral force induced by earthquakes. The primary panel shown in Fig. 1 is first constructed with reinforcing bars stretching out of the partition plate. The reinforcing cage of the secondary panel is then lowered down to provide overlapping at the joints.

[1] President, Ground Engineering and Construction Co., 3/Fl, 28, Lane 102, An-Ho Rd., Sec. 1, Taipei, Taiwan.
[2] Director General, Taiwan Area National Expressway Engineering Bureau, 5/Fl, 141, Min Sheng E. Rd., Sec. 2, Taipei, Taiwan.
[3] Professor, Civil Engineering Department, San Jose State University, One Washington Square, San Jose, CA 95192-0083.

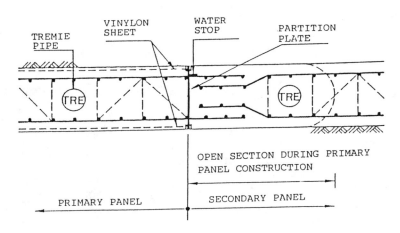

FIG. 1--Layout of an overlapping joint.

The main concern regarding the use of such continuous joints has been quality control problem. Incidents related to leaky or defective joints such as construction schedule delays or ground failure are not uncommon. With all the major construction projects such as rapid transit system planned for the next decade, more than 1,500,000 square meters of diaphragm walls are to be constructed to accommodate relevant underground construction. An utmost important task for Taiwan local diaphragm wall contractors is to devise effective quality control measures to guard against possible defective joints. It is therefore the purpose of this paper to give a detailed account of the state-of-the-art measures adopted in Taiwan for ensuring a watertight joint. The possible mechanism which leads to a defective joint is also discussed.

COMMON JOINT DEFECTS

For overlapping joints, three common defects are generally observed near or on the partition plate; which are cavities, exposed reinforcing bars, or weak bentonite concrete zone.

Cvaities are soft pockets filled by bentonite mud, slime and impurities trapped between panels. Depending on the amount of trapped material, cavities can be further divided into partial cavities (Fig. 2) or complete cavities (Fig.3). Partial cavities consist of isolated pockets of trapped material, while complete cavities possess pockets transversing throughout the wall thickness.

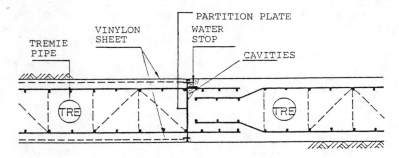

FIG. 2--Schematic diagram of partial cavities.

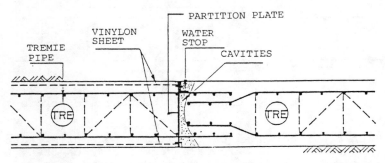

FIG. 3--Schematic diagram of complete cavities.

Fig. 4 is a schematic diagram of the exposed reinforcing bars, which shows the outside portion of overlapping
reinforcing bars is occupied by filtration film or
impurities rather than concrete. During subsequent
excavation, the filtration film or impurities would simply
peel off the wall, leaving this part of reinforcing bars
unprotected.

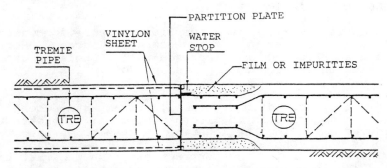

FIG. 4--Schematic diagram of exposed reinforcing bars.

Instead of forming cavities, the bentonite mud and slime trapped between joints may also intermixed with tremie concrete to form a weak bentonite concrete zone as shown in Fig. 5. compared with fresh tremie concrete, this contaminated material is low in strength. Due to the existence of this contaminated material and subsequent deformation of diaphragm wall, cracks tend to develop at the joints, resulting in ground water leakage through the wall.

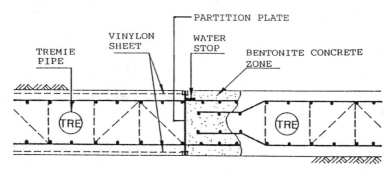

FIG. 5--Schematic diagram of bentonite concrete zone.

When constructed as part of the permanent structure, the presence of joint defects severely reduces the efficiency of diaphragm wall by causing more seepage than permitted through the joints and by reducing the overall stiffness of diaphragm wall. The defective joint itself is a weak spot. Deformation of diaphragm wall due to excavation or high ground water pressure often lead to cracks at these defective joints, resulting in leakage of ground water through joints. In severe cases, the leaking ground water is accompanied by large amount of granular material, causing subsidence of ground and distress of adjacent buildings.

FACTORS THAT LEAD TO DEFECTS

Diaphragm walling is a complicated operation which requires special attentions to ensure its success. However, inherent shortcomings of diaphragm wall techniques or negligence on construction procedures often lead to defective joints.

For a typical diaphragm wall, primary and secondary panels are constructed in alternating order. Construction procedures including the lowering of steel cage into trench and subsequent concrete tremieing are all carried out under water/slurry, denying the contractor access to treat the joint fully to ensure a strong bonding between primary and secondary panels. Moreover, steel plate with a smooth surface is usually adopted as partition plate to reduce the amount of mud/slime trapping, and it is apparent that as an undesired side effect, the bonding capacity between partition plate and tremie concrete will be reduced.

Other mechanisms may also contribute to the weakening of diaphragm wall joints. For example, tremie concrete at the slurry/concrete interface will be diluted by slurry/water even under normal tremie condition, resulting in a low strength concrete with high water/cement ratio that provides poor bonding capacity between panels. As for an abnormal tremie condition, large amount of non-concrete materials such as bentonite mud, sediments and contaminated concrete would rest on top of the fresh concrete. Instead of rising with the fresh concrete, these non-concrete materials would be pushed toward and trapped at the joints or trench faces. As a result, the fresh concrete is virtually separated from the partition plate by the entrapped materials, and the continuity of diaphragm wall is interrupted.

A discussion of various factors that may cause defects are given below.

Inadequate Control of Slurry

Quality of slurry is a major issue directly related to the quality of diaphragm wall joints. Fail to control the slurry quality often results in defective joints. For example, a slurry with high sand content or density may affect the flow pattern of tremie concrete, which may in turn lead to an accumulation of impurities/slime near the joints. In addition to the concern for high sand content in the slurry, the influen of silt content can not be overlooked either. Field experience showed that the silt particles or clayey debris suspended within slurry would also interact with tremie concrete and produce a large amount of contaminated concrete.

In pervious soil, a slurry with high filtration loss may create a thick film cake on trench face if the slurry quality is not well controlled. The film cake would inevitably reduce the effective cross sectional area of the finished diagram wall, exhibiting a defect pattern similar to the one shown in Fig. 4.

Inappropriate Concrete Tremieing Porcess

Special attention must be given to the pouring of concrete to ensure the integrity of diaphragm wall. Poor workability or flowability of concrete may lead to accumulation of impurities near the joints as a result of undesired flow patterns [1]. Inappropriate pouring procedures, including interruptions during concreting, premature withdrawing of the tremie pipe, wrong spacing or location of tremie pipes, and uneven pouring rate also lead to an undesired flow pattern of the tremie concrete. Other negligences during concrete pouring, such as leaky tremie pipes or overflowed concrete, would also increase the possibility of producing a defective joint. Leaky tremie pipes would result in a low strength tremie concrete of high water/cement ratio. While the overflowed concrete would drop directly into diaphragm wall trench and lead to gelation of slurry. The slurry gelation and low strength concrete would eventually lead to defective joints.

Insufficient Joint Sweeping

As a standard practice, joint section must be swept to remove as much as possible the accumulated slime/impurities before tremieing the secondary panel. Joint cleaner in the form of scraper, brush wheel or water jets can be adopted for this purpose (Fig. 6). However, it is physically impossible to thoroughly clean the joint section on certain occasions, implying the existence of slim/impurities even before the placement of tremie concrete.

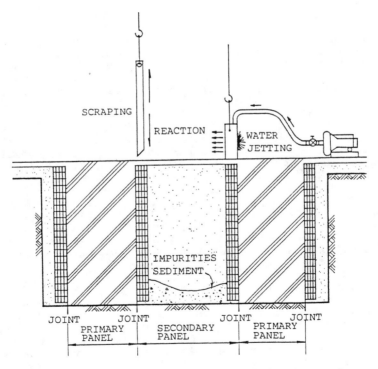

FIG. 6--Schematic diagram of joint sweeping.

Excessive Amount of Sediments

The slurry of a newly excavated trench contains large amount of soil debris or suspending particles, a period of 1-2 hours is usually required for the debris or particles to settle. The sedimentation is then removed by the use of air lift, suction pump or trench excavation machine. This process has to be repeated until the amount of sediments are controlled within specified limits. Otherwise, it is inevitable to have a diaphragm wall with leaky or defective joints.

Blockage of Reinforcing Bars

A steel cage is required to provide reinforcement for diaphragm wall. However, the steel cage is an object blocking the free flow of tremie concrete especially near the overlapping area where heavy reinforcement is likely to make the free flow of tremie concrete even more difficult. Another phenomenon is the leakage of mortar/cement through the annular gaps of the drilled holes on partition plate. This phenomenon, according to field experience, would lead to the gelation of slurry in secondary panels. From the above discussions, it is of little doubt that the presence of steel cage is another factor leading to defective joints.

Poor Trench Excavation Tolerance

Trenches of poor verticality often pose a problem for steel cage placement. The steel cage tends to scratch soil off trench face and produce extra amount of sediments. It is very difficult to remove the extra sediments from trench before concrete tremieing. A direct impact is the reduction in diaphragm wall panel depth, quality of joint is to be affected as well.

Concrete Leakage

While tremieing the primary panel, concrete may leak to the open area just outside the partition plate due to a burst partition plate or broken vinylon sheet. As a consequence, steel cage of the secondary panel can not be lowered to the designated location to meet design require- ment. A possible remedy is to chip off the concrete that leaks to the open area by physical means, but a complete chip-off may not be possible if the concrete hardens. Moreover, the chip-off action usually results in a full scale contamination of slurry. Diaphragm wall joints constructed under such circumstance are of course very poor in quality.

Deflection of Wall During Excavation

The diaphragm wall joints it a weak spot from a

structural point of view. Bonding between tremie concrete
and partition plate is generally poor, and the entrapped
slime/impurities make the bonding capacity even worse. As a
result, deformation of wall due to excavation and/or earthquake often lead to cracks at joints.

QUALITY CONTROL MEASURES

For Taiwan local diaphragm wall construction industry,
the most significant advance on the improvement of joint
quality has been the application of a specially designed
joint. As mentioned in previous section, the partition
plate is generally made of smooth steel plate. The smooth
plate face is low in bonding capacity and may behave as an
ideal route for leaking ground water. In order to
strengthen the bonding capacity and at the same time cut off
ground water leakage, a special joint is developed based
upon local experience [2]. In physical form, the special
joint is comprised of pair of metallic hooks wielded to the
partition plate (Fig. 7). This pair of hooks, which is
embedded in tremie concrete, serve as a joint stiffener and
a water stop. Bonding capacity between partition plate and
tremie concrete is significantly increased, possible leakage
route is effectively cut off as well. One additional
benefit is that the L-shaped hooks behave as ideal guide
rails for various type of joint cleaners, enabling a
thorough cleaning of diaphragm wall joint. Field experience
has shown that with the use of a special joint, the
structural behavior and watertightness of diaphragm wall are
both significantly improved [3].

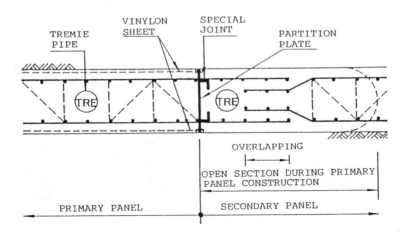

FIG. 7--Schematic diagram of a special joint.

In addition to the use of a special joint by Taiwan local contractors, relevant or complementary measures which are essential to the quality control of diaphragm wall joints are also addressed below.

Improvement on Excavation Tolerance

Modern excavation systems are usually equipped with sensors and alignment adjust plates. The verticality of diaphragm wall trench can be maintained within a tolerance of 1/300-1/500 for moderate excavation depth (Fig. 8). A tolerance of 1/1000 can even be achieved for diaphragm wall more than 50 m in depth. With the improvement on vertical tolerance, soil on trench face is less likely to be scratched off during steel cage placement. The vinylon sheet wrapped around the steel cage is more likely to remain intact as well due to a reduced friction between steel cage and trench face.

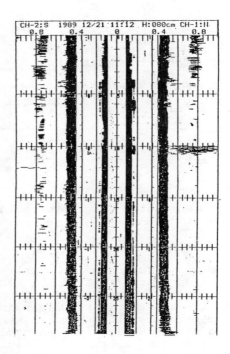

FIG. 8--A typical supersonic profile of diaphragm wall trench.

Sufficient Joint Sweeping

Adoption of the specially designed joint made the
thorough cleaning of diaphragm wall joint possible. As
shown in Fig. 7, a pair of hooks wielded to the partition
plate serve as ideal guide rails for the scraper, and the
repeated upward/downward movements of scraper can be carried
out without deviation. If water jets are adopted for joint
cleaning instead, this pair of hooks provide reaction to the
jet flows so that nozzle locations can be maintained to exert
constant jet pressure. Mud or slime attached to the
partition plate can therefore be completely scratched off
as a result. Impurities trapped between trench face and
extended reinforcement bars can also be scratched off by the
use of a custom-made flat joint cleaner (Fig. 9), and
intergrity of the joints can therefore be preserved.

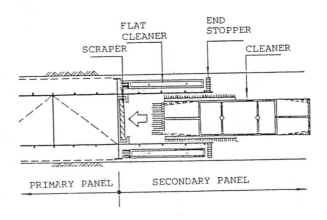

FIG. 9 -- A schematic diagram of joint cleaning.

Adequate Sediment Treatment

A mandatory settling period of 2 hours is observed in
the field. This action allows most of the suspending
particles and soil debris to settle down at the bottom of
trench. The sediments are then carefully removed by using
trench excavation machine, suction pump or air lift (Fig.
10). A deep ground water sampler is then used to take
slurry sample at the bottom of trench for sand content
check. The sand content must be less then specified before
terminating the sediment removal process. The subsequent
steel cage placement and concrete tremieing would therefore
encounter less amount of slime/impurities.

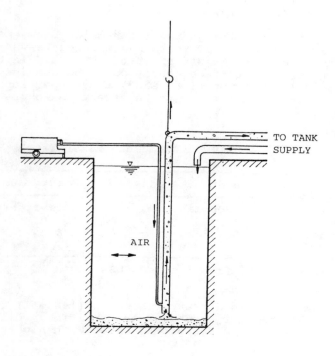

FIG. 10--Sediment treatment by air lift.

Special Steel Cage Treatment

Epoxy is applied to seal off the holes drilled on partition plate of primary panels. This seemingly trivial action greatly improved the slurry quality of secondary panels, leading to a construction joint of better quality.

The partition plate and vinylon sheet of primary panel are tightly secured to the steel cage, thus reducing the possibility of concrete leakage.

Quality Control of Concrete

To provide a better workability and ensure a desirable flow pattern for tremie concrete, the requirements shown in (Table 3) are usually adopted for Taiwan local diaphragm wall construction. Special mix may be required for adverse ground conditions.

Control of Slurry Quality

Better understanding on the interaction between slurry and soils over the past few years had enabled Taiwan local contractors to master the use of stability fluid in the field. For local subsurface conditions, which mainly consists of silty clay or silty sand, the proportionings shown in (Table 1) were found to be effective in most cases.

TABLE 1--<u>Proportionings of slurry.</u>

	Bentonite Based	Polymer Based
Tap Water	1000 liters	1000 liters
Bentonite*	30-100 kg	10-40 kg
Polymer(CMC)	0.5-3 kg	1-6 kg
Thinner(FBL)	0.5-3 kg	...

* Sodium Bentonite from Wyoming, USA.

The bentonite based slurry shown in (Table 1) is mainly used for regular ground water condition, while the polymer based slurry is for ground water with high salinity content.

In order to achieve satisfactory performance in the field, physical properties of the slurry must be controlled within the limits as shown in (Table 2).

TABLE 2--<u>Slurry requirements.</u>

Physical Properties	Limits
Density (g/cm^3)	1.02-1.10
pH value	<11.5
Filtrate loss (cm^3)	10-50
Filter cake thickness (mm)	3-15
Marsh funnel viscosity (sec)	21-25
Sand content (%)	0-3

The lower range for density and Marsh funnel viscosity appear low, however, the authors' experience on diaphragm walling indicated that the slurry requirements shown above are ideal for the silty material found in the subsurface of Taipei and Kaohsiung metropolitan areas.

TABLE 3--Concrete requirements.

Physical Properties	Limits
Slump (cm)	18-20
Water/cement ratio	0.48-0.53
Diameter of	
Coarse aggregate (mm)	<25
Cement quantity (kg/m^3)	>350

Relocation of Tremie Pipes

The authors also found that the location of tremie pipes played an important role regarding the quality of diaphragm wall joints. If the tremie pipes were relocated to a position closer to the partition plate as shown in Fig. 7 rather than the original position shown in Fig. 1, the tremie concrete would be more effective in pushing slime/impurities away from the joints Realizing the benefit of relocating tremie pipes, Taiwan local contractors now adopt the tremie pipes layout shown in Fig. 7 as part of the standard practice.

Treatment of Concrete Leakage

Concrete leakage is a rarely occurring but disastrous incident. In the event of concrete leakage, a more effective remedial measure is to break up the concrete into small pieces by high pressure water jets. The concrete is allowed to harden before applying the water jets Easy break-up of the concrete and minimal amount of slurry contamination is expected.

CONCLUSIONS

Various factors have been identified in the formation of defective or leaky joints. Preventive or counter measures as described above have also been found to be effective in avoiding problems. Among the preventive measures, adoption of the special joint as well as the relocation of tremie pipes contribute most in improving the joint quality. The special joint provides additional bonding capacity to resist the development of tension cracks; therefore a complete watertightness is achieved. Adopting the special joints, the diaphragm walls also exhibit improved structural behavior during excavations in various site conditions. However, the extent of improvement can only be qualitatively assessed at the current stage, and further study is required to reach a quantitative conclusion regarding the structural behavior of an improved joint. Though the special joint has been found useful, standard construction procedures and other fine details must also be observed to ensure the quality of joints.

Admittedly, quality of diaphragm wall is sensitive to all sorts of tangible and intangible factors which are often beyond control. However, by stringently following the measures mentioned above, the first author experienced minimal amount of joint related problems for a total area of 200,000 m02diaphragm walls with various thickness and depth over the past years. Joints of diaphragm wall were virtually watertight in any case.

Though a perfect specification for diaphragm wall construction is yet to be written, the authors believed that in addition to following the specifications closely, a sound understanding on the factors that lead to defective joints and a commitment for excellence are the key to water-proof diaphragm wall joints.

REFERENCES

[1] Gerwick, B. and Holland, T., "Concrete Placed Under Water," Concrete Construction, November, 1986, pp 943-945.

[2] Ou, C.D. and Lee, K.H, "Watertightness of the Diaphragm Wall at Vertical Joints," Proceedings of the Eighth Asian Regional Conference on Soil Mechanics and Foundation Engineering, Kyoto, Japan, 1987, pp 309-312.

[3] Tsai, K.W., Ou, C.D. and Lee, K.H., "Watertight and Earthquake Resistant Joints for Diaphragm Walls," Proceedings of the Geotechnical Engineering congress, Boulder, Colorado, June, 1991, Accepted for Publication.

Donald A. Bruce, Patrick H. C. Chan and George J. Tamaro

DESIGN, CONSTRUCTION AND PERFORMANCE OF A DEEP CIRCULAR DIAPHRAGM WALL

Reference: Bruce, D.A.,   Chan, P.H.C.,   and   Tamaro, G.J.   "Design,
Construction and Performance of a Deep Circular Diaphragm Wall," Slurry
Walls: Design, Construction, and Quality Control, ASTM STP 1129, David B.
Paul, Richard R. Davidson, and Nicholas J. Cavalli, Eds., American Society
for Testing and Materials, Philadelphia, 1992.

ABSTRACT: The new Richmond Avenue Pump Station in Staten Island NY was
successfully constructed to a depth 27m below existing grade within a
16.5m circular, 50m deep slurry wall cofferdam. Construction was carried
down through water bearing sands with minimal dewatering of the interior
of the cofferdam and with no distress to the surrounding residential
structures. This paper describes the design, construction and performance
of the slurry wall and the general excavation.

KEYWORDS: Slurry Walls, Cofferdams, Pump Stations, Excavation, Dewatering

INTRODUCTION

    The new Richmond Avenue Pump Station on Staten Island, New York, is
an integral feature of the Borough's Oakwood Beach Water Pollution Control
Project (City of New York, Department of Environmental Protection,
Contract T-7A Foundation).   The permanent shaft was built within a
circular reinforced concrete slurry wall structure, approximately 16m in
diameter.   The shaft connects new 1.2m diameter influent and effluent
sewer lines (Figure 1). The specifications did not permit the temporary
slurry wall cofferdam to be utilized as part of the permanent structural
wall of the Pump Station.

    The shaft, located within two blocks of the ocean, was constructed
through fine sandy soils with the natural ground water level found within
4.6m of the existing ground surface.   Dewatering operations associated
with other adjacent sewer construction provided some relief of water head
during construction. The close proximity of a residential neighborhood
and the effects and cost of deep prolonged pumping increased the risks
associated with dewatering necessary for the construction of the shaft
"in the dry" using conventional soldier beams and lagging.   Following
detailed review of several construction options, including driven sheet
piles and ground freezing, the General Contractor, John P. Picone, Inc.,

    Donald A. Bruce is Technical Director at Nicholson Construction
Company; Patrick H. C. Chan is a Design Engineer and George J. Tamaro is
a Partner at Mueser Rutledge Consulting Engineers.

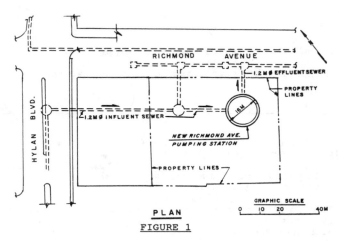

PLAN

FIGURE 1

selected a scheme proposed by Nicholson Construction featuring the use of a structural diaphragm wall constructed by the slurry trench method. Given the need to avoid "blow in" of the silty fine sands at the designed subgrade elevation of -21.6m (Elevations refer to Borough of Staten Island sewer datum which is 970mm above USGS Mean Sea Level at Sandy Hook, NJ), and to generally reduce seepage into the shaft excavation, options were examined to extend a cut off below subgrade elevation into a relatively impermeable hard silty clay, at Elevation -47.3m. Various schemes, including different types of grouting, were examined, but the most suitable option in this instance was simply to continue the diaphragm wall, unreinforced, down to elevation -47.3m. This decision was influenced by the dewatering difficulties experienced by other contractors working on adjacent shafts.

The diaphragm wall installed by Nicholson Construction was 16m in internal diameter, 50m deep, and 600mm thick, making it, at the time, the deepest such structure installed by conventional diaphragm wall equipment in the United States. Mueser Rutledge Consulting Engineers provided geotechnical services, designed the slurry wall and inspected installation of the wall.

This paper summarizes the subsurface conditions, design, construction and performance of the wall and the subsequent excavation.

SITE CONDITIONS

Surface Access

The available work area at this site was limited considering the space needed for the equipment and materials of construction, including reinforcing steel storage and cage fabrication areas (see Figure 1). In addition, strict environmental controls were placed on the handling, transport and disposal of excavated debris and waste bentonite slurry.

To facilitate excavation operations, the ground level immediately around the shaft was lowered 2 meters to Elevation +3.8m for installation of a crushed stone work platform. This level was slightly above the final top of wall (El +3.0m) after removal of guide walls and bentonite contaminated concrete.

Subsurface Conditions

The stratum boundaries dipped gently across the site. The following major units were identified by the additional site investigation undertaken after award of the contract. The uppermost stratum (G-1) is a Recent glacial deposit, whereas the bulk of the sequence comprised Cretaceous beach sand deposits, summarized as follows:

El +3 to +1.5 (G1) - Medium compact red-brown silty fine to medium sand, trace gravel, roots (SM). SPT 13-28 (Avg 19), Water content 18%.

El +1.5 to -29m (C2) - Loose to very compact yellow, gray, tan, red and brown, fine to medium sand (SP, SM) trace silt, occasional silty clay layers (ML), stiff, grey, trace lignite. Very occasional micaceous, hard, black, white, silty clay (CL). Very occasional soft grey silty clay (CL). SPT for sands 28-114 (Avg 74), for others 5-22 (Avg 13), water content 17-29%.

El -29m to -36.6m (C1) - Compact to very compact, silty or clayey yellow, brown and grey, fine, medium sand (SP, SC, SM), occasional silty clay layers, medium sand (SM). SPT values 57 to 114 (Avg 81), water content 20-22%.

El -36.6m to Avg -39.6m (C2) - Light grey, fine, medium sands, trace silt, trace clay (SP, SM, CL). SPT from 46-70 (Avg 53), water content 22%.

El Avg -39.6m to Avg -47.3m (C1) - Grey, fine-medium sands, trace silt, clay (SP, SC, SM). Occasional seams of dark grey clay and silty clay (CL). Overall SPT values 36-85 (Avg 56), water content 24-29%.

Below Avg -47.3m (C3) - Hard to very hard, dark grey, silty clay (CL), trace silt, water content 24-26%.

Standard Penetration Test (STP) values relate to a 64 kg. hammer and a drop of 760mm.

Permeability

The wall was designed to toe 0.6m to 1.5m into the hard, relatively impermeable C3 stratum. During excavation, the ground water level averaged about Elevation -4.6m, with a 0.6m to 0.9m variation, attributed to tidal effects and the adjacent dewatering efforts of another shaft contractor. The silty sands generally had in situ permeabilities (vertical) in the range of 8×10^{-4} to 3×10^{-6} cm/sec, based on laboratory testing of Pitcher barrel undisturbed samples. Values of 2×10^{-3} to 2×10^{-4} cm/sec were calculated from field falling head tests in piezometers (horizontal), and 2×10^{-2} cm/sec was estimated from an analysis of drawdown data on adjacent contracts. The piezometer test data was affected by dewatering within 60m of the site and the dewatering analysis was influenced by the proximity of the ocean.

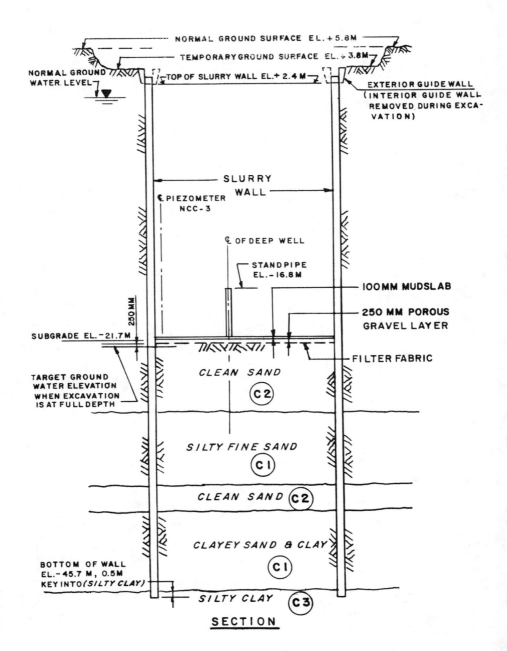

SECTION

FIGURE 2

DESIGN CONSIDERATIONS

Water Cutoff

Two dimensional flow net analyses were conducted to estimate ground water flow during construction. These studies indicated that an adequate factor of safety against base heave, boils or piping could be obtained if the toe of the wall was established at Elevation -39.6. Continuous dewatering would have been required if the wall were terminated at a higher elevation. The anticipated presence of cleaner, more permeable sands at Elevation -36.6m to -39.6m, and the proximity to the ocean, caused concern that higher groundwater flows than predicted by the general analysis would, in fact, occur. For safety and economic reasons, it was therefore decided to continue the diaphragm wall cut-off to Elevation - 47.3m where a more certain water cutoff was obtained from the low permeability C3 material.

An uplift stability analysis was also conducted on the finished base slab. The groundwater within the shaft had to be maintained below the gravel drainage layer until such time as the 2.1m thick base slab concrete reached an Unconfined Compressive Strength of 21 kPa. Thereafter, hydrostatic uplift forces, corresponding to a water level of Elevation - 16.8m, could be resisted with a factor of safety of 1.05. An open standpipe was installed to Elevation -16.8m to ensure that the pressure beneath the slab did not exceeded that level: overflow from this pipe would merely add weight to the structure and increase overall stability. Full hydrostatic pressure could be resisted with a factor of safety of 1.1 when the outside walls reached Elevation -3.4m and interior concrete reached Elevation -14m. Upon completion of the whole structure, the factor of safety against uplift was calculated to be 1.4 for structural weight alone (including the weight of the slurry walls), and 2.9 assuming side friction on the slurry walls.

The interior walls of the pump station were connected to the slurry walls by keyways and dowels designed to transfer the weight of the slurry wall to the permanent structure in an uplift condition. The factor of safety against uplift was thus improved for both construction and the permanent structure. The cost of pumping beneath the base slab during concreting of the permanent shaft was reduced and the pumps could be shut down earlier.

Slurry Wall Panel Geometry

Available excavation equipment dictated that the wall be laid out in segments of seven panels, each consisting of three chords (Figure 3). The deflection angle at the joint between adjacent panels was sufficiently large to accommodate minor variation in plan geometry without fear of local buckling "snap through". Panel joints were formed by 50m long, 600mm deep wide flange beams. Panels were heavily reinforced to a depth of 32.6m with steel cages comprised of 25mm horizontal bars and 20mm, 22mm, and 25mm vertical bars.

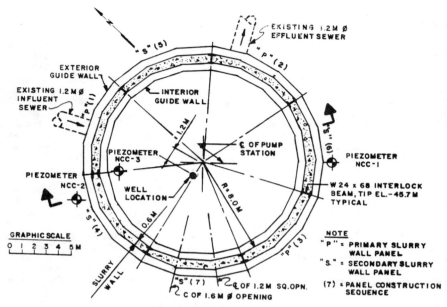

GENERAL PLAN

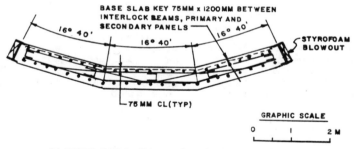

SLURRY WALL PRIMARY PANEL
PLAN

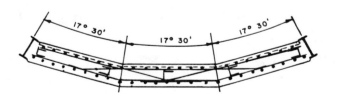

SLURRY WALL SECONDARY PANEL
PLAN
FIGURE 3

Analysis and Design

The structural design considered the behavior of the shaft as a cylindrical shell constructed in chord segments and then as a cylinder of discrete segments with misalignments of up to 150mm at the panel joints. Longitudinal (vertical) and transverse (horizontal) bending was also examined.

In the first case, the wall was assumed to be constructed perfectly aligned, without ring beams or any other internal bracing. The structure was analyzed as a cylindrical shell under axisymmetric loading (triangular distribution). Both ends of the shell were assumed unrestrained. Soil pressures were calculated assuming at rest soil conditions (K_o = 0.5 to a depth of 21.3m and 1.0 below 21.3m). The maximum radial displacement computed was 3mm, a movement too small to mobilize the soil into a K_a situation. Ground movements associated with panel excavation were not considered to be sufficient to significantly reduce at rest radial soil pressures. The longitudinal bending moment associated with this case was small, as expected, since the shell resists load in direct compression. This case did not govern the design.

The second case considered the possibility of significant panel misalignments occurring during construction requiring the installation of ring beams for supplemental bracing. A panel was assumed to be misaligned to the extent that arch action was no longer sufficient to fully support the load. In this analysis, the panel was analyzed as a continuous beam with ring beams as internal supports. Contrasting with the first case, K_a was assumed since displacements associated with bending of the cylinder would be larger than displacements associated with ring compression.

For the transverse analysis, a 150mm maximum horizontal misalignment of adjacent panels was assumed. The wall section was designed as a column resisting ring compression axial force and a bending moment generated by the 150mm eccentricity. Reinforcement was provided to withstand the horizontal bending moments associated with misalignment of joints and the bending of panels between future stabilizing ring beams. External pressure, ring compression and moment varied linearly with depth to subgrade, with the density of horizontal reinforcing varying accordingly. This assumed construction defect governed the design but did not develop in the field. As a result, ring beams were not installed. A cap beam was installed at the very top of the shaft to finish the top of the wall and to provide stability to the individual panels at the top.

CONSTRUCTION

The Sequence of Shaft Construction was divided into six stages,outlined as follows:

    I.   Site Preparation
        1.   Excavate to site working level (approx El +3.8m) and place crushed stone as a working platform.
        2.   Layout center of shaft and guide walls.
        3.   Excavate and install guide walls.

   II.   Diaphragm Wall Construction
        1.   Excavate Primary panel.
        2.   Maintain bentonite slurry in excavation with top of slurry at El +2.1m or higher.

3. Desand slurry at completion of panel construction.
4. Fabricate reinforcing cage and attach interlock beams.
5. Install reinforcing cage and interlock beams as a unit.
6. Displace bentonite slurry continuously with concrete tremied from bottom of panel, with tremie outlet at least 2.4m below slurry interface.
7. Excavate and cast remaining two Primary panels in sequence indicated in Figure 2.
8. Excavate Secondary panels (4 each), allowing adjacent Primary panels to cure a minimum of two days before starting excavation. Install cage to a "right fit" between existing interlock beams. Secondary panel S4 requires one interlock beam installed with the cage.

III. Control Groundwater
1. Install and develop deep well, minimum 125mm i.d., to El -54.9, at position shown in Figure 3. Install submersible pump.
2. Install piezometer (NCC 3) within shaft as shown in Figure 3 to El -27.4m. (Note: Both to be sealed through base slab when cast.)
3. Test effectiveness of the wall as a cut-off by activating the pump and monitoring drawdown in the shaft. Determine if daytime pumping can maintain groundwater in shaft continuously below target piezometer level. If not, increase number of wells and pump capacity. (Note: This step may be executed as part of shaft excavation, Step IV, 3, below.)

IV. Excavate Shaft
1. Remove interior guide wall.
2. Excavate soil within shaft, taking care to maintain both well and piezometer casings to surface.
3. Continuously maintain groundwater within the shaft below excavation level.

V. Construction of Base Slab
1. Continue excavation to subgrade at El -22.7m.
2. Place filter fabric on subgrade and install clean porous crushed aggregate drainage layer on fabric and adjacent to well screen. Place plastic vapor barrier membrane over drainage layer and cast concrete mudmat.
3. Cast base slab of permanent structure and key into slurry wall. Allow slab to cure to minimum f'_c of 21 kPa while maintaining groundwater below El -22.3m. Extend 125mm well casing standpipe up to El -16.8m and 50mm riser pipe for piezometer to El -13.7m.

VI. Construct Permanent Structure
1. Limit uplift pressures on base slab by allowing water to rise in standpipe and flow into shaft if necessary. Dewater shaft as needed, but not less than daily. Operate deep well during the day to maintain water pressure on the slab to a pressure no higher than a head at El -16.8, as measured by riser pipe.
2. Construct pump station walls, followed by interior, while continuing Step VI, 1, above.

3.   After outside walls of pump station reach at least El +3.4m, and interior construction has reached at least El -10.7m, the piezometer, riser pipe, well and standpipe may be sealed, allowing full hydrostatic pressure to develop on the base of the slab.

Diaphragm Wall Construction

The guide walls were of standard design and construction, 900mm deep by 450mm wide, reinforced longitudinally and with sufficient tolerance for the 600mm wide bucket to pass unencumbered.

A 140 tonne capacity Manitowoc 4000 crane operated the 13 tonne Keller mechanical excavating grab (Photograph 1). This grab was extended by guides to a length of 9.8m to aid verticality control and was capable of a 2.7m bite in one pass. Verticality measurements were made every 3.0m of excavation depth by checking the position of the lifting cables. In addition, at least twice in each panel, piano wires were attached to the grab to measure panel deviation or twisting. Panel deviation was readily corrected by use of a specially designed chisel. A tolerance of 1% of verticality and 150mm horizontal planar misalignment was permitted.

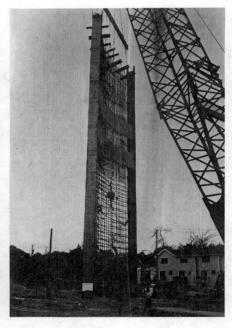

Photograph 1. Cable Suspended excavating grab, showing long frame extension.

Photograph 2. Placement of re-enforcing cage and transverse beams. Note wood and styrofoam for blockouts & joint keys.

Bentonite slurry was prepared in a jet mixer before being pumped to storage tanks or ponds. Typically the specific gravity was about 1.02, the pH 8, and the Marsh Cone reading about 42 seconds. Panels were excavated in three bites per panel, with the middle section following about 9m behind the end bites. Production rates were considerably lower than what had been anticipated on the basis of the geological logs. The grab's teeth were modified to improve "bite" efficiency. The clay seams encountered at 44m and 48m proved relatively easy to excavate. There was minor loss of bentonite slurry throughout the job, attributable to drawdown from adjacent dewatering. Desanding of each panel took about 10-25 hours. This was accomplished at three plan positions per panel and featured a double tube pipe system providing vigorous agitation and scouring of the base and removal of the suspended sands (from 16% to less than 2%) before concreting.

The 50m long ASTM A36 interlock beams (WF 24x68) were delivered in three pieces and bolted or welded together. The 38m long steel ASTM Grade 60 rebar cages, were fabricated in two sections on site. A total of 175 tonne of ASTM A615 reinforcing steel was used. A special lifting bed was designed and built to handle the segmented long cage. Wood and styrofoam blockouts were attached to the cages to form keyways in the exposed slurry wall (Photograph 2).

Photograph 3. Tremie concreting of Primary panel.

Concrete was supplied by ready mix trucks and had a maximum aggregate size of 20mm, a target 28-day f'_c of 28 kPa, a slump of 180mm and 4% air entrainment.   Typical mixes contained 420 kg of cement, 780 to 830 kg of fine aggregate (natural sand), 980 to 1000 kg of coarse aggregate (crushed rock) and 165 l-180 l of water per cubic yard. Various types and proportions of additives were used to entrain air and to retard/plasticize. Seven-day strength tests indicated cube strengths of 31 kPa-38 kPa, increasing to 38 kPa-50 kPa at 28 days.   Concrete was placed by tremie, via two 250mm diameter tremie pipes in each panel, at an average rate of 31m^3 3/hour (Photograph 3).   The overpour on the job averaged 15%.

After completion of all panels the General Contractor removed the upper 3m of soil from within the shaft and installed a 750mm deep ring beam to secure and finish the upper part of the slurry wall.

PERFORMANCE

The dewatering pump was activated prior to the start of excavation and operated for only a day or two before it "ran dry", highlighting the watertightness of the structure and supporting the decision to embed the wall in the low permeability clays.

Excavation proceeded smoothly to subgrade and the gravel drain, mudmat and overlying structures were placed without incident.   Pumping was occasionally required for about 1 to 2 hours every few days.   The soil at subgrade was reported dry without noticeable seepage through the soil (with the well inoperative).

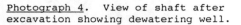

Photograph 4. View of shaft after excavation showing dewatering well.

Photograph 5.   View from bottom after completion.

Primary panels were found to be completely vertical with the Secondaries out by only 100 to 150mm, as measured at the panel centers. The ends of the Secondaries were, on average, slightly further out: the beams were square to the Primaries which possibly made the keying of the Secondaries much more difficult.

The keyways lined up well except at one joint where there the key was 600mm out of position. Small water seeps were noted at a local joint misalignment (S5 and P2) and at a point of minor concrete segregation (P1). These seeps produced about 8 to 20 lph prior to sealing and proved no problem during construction. After completion of excavation, the dewatering well was operated about once per week, and then for a only few hours, until it was effectively "dry". Photographs 4 and 5 show the completed excavation.

CONCLUSIONS

The 16m diameter Oakwood Beach shaft was successfully constructed within an extremely limited site, under difficult soil and groundwater conditions, using the slurry trench method of construction . Design requirements related to base stability and water inflow dictated that the wall be keyed into an impermeable strata 24.4m below the subgrade elevation of the permanent structure, a total depth of 50m.

Excavation within the slurry wall cofferdam confirmed the suitability and quality of the structure. The permanent structure was built without incident within the excavation, without the need for internal bracing and with a limited amount of dewatering from within the cofferdam.

ACKNOWLEDGEMENTS

The authors acknowledge the contributions of their colleagues in the preparation of this paper.

Arun Patel[1] and Raymond Castelli[2]

PERMANENT SLURRY WALLS AT BALTIMORE
METRO'S SHOT TOWER STATION

REFERENCE: Patel, A. and Castelli, R. , "Permanent Slurry Walls at Baltimore Metro's Shot Tower Station", Slurry Walls: Design, Construction, and Quality Control, ASTM STP 1129, David B. Paul, Richard R. Davidson, and Nicholas J. Cavalli, Eds., American Society for Testing and Materials, Philadelphia, 1992.

ABSTRACT: The general approach and State-of-the Art methods used for the design of the permanent slurry walls for an underground transit station are presented. The design included alternative studies, geotechnical investigations, seepage analysis, structural design, constructability aspects and architectural interface in selecting slurry walls as the station's permanent walls. The station's wall design also required the installation of jet grout walls in lieu of slurry wall panels where existing underground 115 kV electric lines crossed the station. The paper addresses evaluation and analytical methods used in resolving significant issues that confronted the designers in adoption of slurry walls as the station's permanent walls, and presents preliminary findings of the construction instrumentation monitoring program.

KEYWORDS: station, slurry walls, earth pressures, buoyancy, jet grout columns, support of excavation, instrumentation.

INTRODUCTION

Baltimore Metro's Charles Center Station, constructed from 1975 to 1978, utilized concrete slurry walls for support of the station excavation. The use of slurry walls eliminated the need for costly underpinning of adjacent high rise buildings [1]. The slurry walls for Charles Center Station, however, provided only temporary support for the construction period. Once excavation was completed, approximately 1.2 m (4 ft.) thick cast-in-place concrete walls were installed for permanent support of lateral soil and water loads.

As part of an extension of the Baltimore Metro system, the current construction of Shot Tower Station in downtown Baltimore again utilizes slurry wall technology. However, reflecting a trend observed elsewhere in the country, the slurry walls for Shot Tower Station are designed as both the temporary and permanent support for the structure. This paper discusses the significant issues considered in the selection of the permanent slurry walls for Shot Tower Station, describes the design criteria and methodology for this structure, and presents preliminary findings of the construction instrumentation monitoring program.

---

[1] Chief Structural Engineer, ICF Kaiser Engineers, Inc., 201 N. Charles Street, Baltimore, Maryland 21201

[2] Senior Professional Associate, Parsons Brinckerhoff Quade and Douglas, Inc., One Penn Plaza, New York, N.Y. 10119

PROJECT

The Baltimore Metro is the result of planning and design development programs that began in the late 1960s. Section A, extending approximately 12 km (7.5 miles), opened for revenue service in 1983. The Metro system nearly doubled in length when the 9.66 km (6 miles) Section B extension was opened in 1987. Section C, which is currently in construction, extends the system from the existing downtown Charles Center Station to Johns Hopkins Hospital (Fig. 1). Section C consists of 1,910 m (6,270 ft.) of twin earth tunnels and two underground stations.

One of these stations, the Shot Tower Station, has been designed using slurry walls for the permanent station walls (Fig. 2 and 3). As of December, 1991, this station was under construction with all slurry wall panels in-place, and the excavation at full depth at the west end of the station.

STATION CONFIGURATION

Shot Tower Station is located along Baltimore Street at the intersection with the I-83 Expressway (Fig. 2). The nationally known Inner Harbor is approximately 0.8 km (0.5 miles) south of the station. The station site is surrounded by open parking areas, six-lanes of the I-83 expressway, historically significant Shot Tower, and 7 to 10 story commercial buildings and townhouses. The station site crosses a 75 year old triple-cell culvert known as Jones Falls Conduit, a 2.5 m (98 in.) elliptical sewer, a twin cell concrete storm drain and 115-kV live electric lines.

Shot Tower Station is 183 m (600 ft.) long, 18.3 m (60 ft.) wide and 16.2 m (53 ft.) deep from roof to invert. The station roof had to be deep enough, generally 2 m (7 ft.) to 4.6 m (15 ft.) to allow clearance for the Jones Falls Conduit. The mezzanine had to have a high enough ceiling, about 6.4 m (21 ft.), to accommodate structural framing, architectural ceiling, and electrical and mechanical ducts. The two tunnels entering the station are 5.8 m (19 ft.) in diameter, and spaced 11.3 m (37 ft.) apart horizontally to provide a 8 m (26 ft.) wide column free space for a center platform.

SUBSURFACE CONDITIONS

The Jones Falls channel, across which the Shot Tower Station is being constructed, forms a local topographic depression. Although much of this area has been filled during the historical development of Baltimore, the ground surface at the station site ranges only from about EL.+2.3 to +4.6 m (+7.5 to +15 ft.) (MSL datum). The low lying nature of the site has resulted in several subsurface features of particular importance to the design of the station (Fig. 4). These include:

o   A shallow groundwater table at depths ranging from 1.2 to 3.4 m (4 to 11 ft.)

o   The presence of 3.7 to 7.9 m (12 to 26 ft.) of miscellaneous manmade fill.

o   Local zones of soft organic soils up to 3 m (10 ft.) thick trapped beneath the fill.

The fill is a heterogeneous mix of loose to medium dense sand, silt, gravel and debris with Standard Penetration Test (SPT) N-values generally ranging from 4 to 18 blows per 30 cm (blows per foot). The organic deposits are composed of organic silt, clay and peat with SPT N-values generally less than 10.

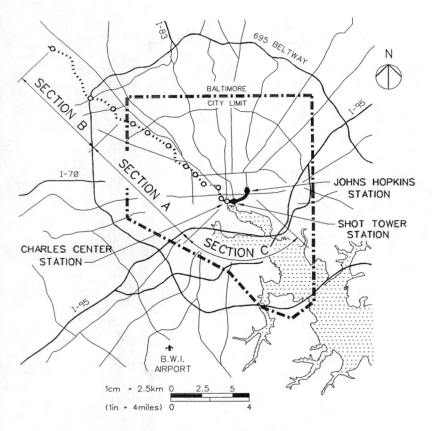

FIG. 1 -- Baltimore Metro System

Underlying the fill and organic soils, and extending to approximately El.-12 m (-40 ft.), are dense to very dense Cretaceous deposits composed primarily of sand and gravel, and silty sand. These soils are designated as "C1" and "C2" soils, respectively, according to the Baltimore Metro classification system. The Cretaceous soils have SPT N-values typically ranging from 40 to more than 100.

The Cretaceous soils are underlain by residual soils and then by highly weathered rock. The residual soils, designated as "RS", are generally less than 1.5 m (5 ft.) thick and are composed of very dense silty sand. The highly weathered rock, designated as "RZ-1", is derived from the decomposition of amphibolites and gneisses, and generally consists of a silty sand with rock fragments and relict rock structure. The residual soil and highly weathered rock generally have SPT N-values ranging from 55 to more than 100. Generally, RS and RZ-1 materials can be excavated with soil excavation techniques, but special excavation tools are occasionally required for local areas of partially weathered or fresh rock.

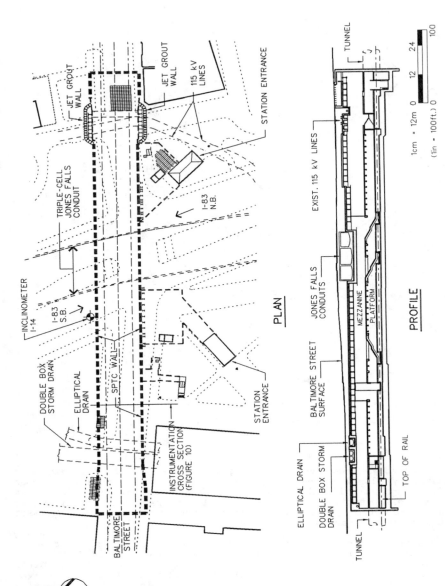

FIG. 2 -- Shot Tower Station plan and profile

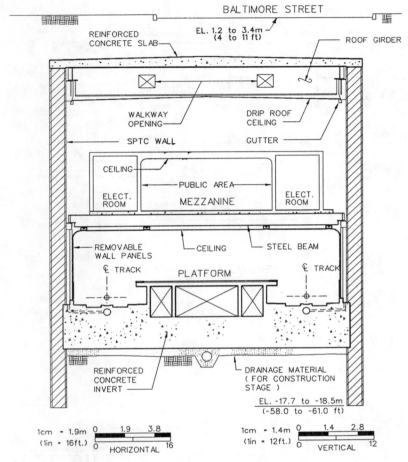

FIG. 3 -- Typical Shot Tower Station section

Design properties for the various soil strata are presented in Table 1.

TABLE 1 - Summary of design soil properties.

Stratum	Moist Unit Weight (kg/m³)	Effective Friction Angle (degrees)	Permeability k_h (cm/sec)	k_h/k_v
Fill	1930	28	1×10^{-3}	2
Cretaceous (C1, C2)	2000	35	1×10^{-3}	2
Residual Soil (RS)	2000	25-35	1×10^{-5}	3
Weathered Rock (RZ-1)	2000	35-40	1×10^{-5}	3

k_h = Coefficient of permeability in horizontal direction
k_v = Coefficient of permeability in vertical direction

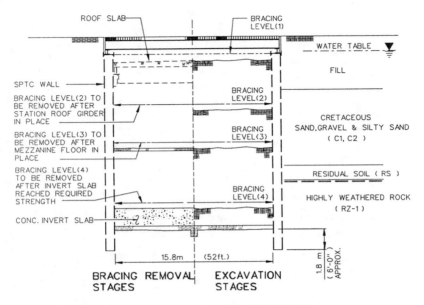

FIG. 4 -- Construction condition

NOTE: CONTRACTOR WAS PERMITTED TO REMOVE INTERMEDIATE
STRUT LEVEL BETWEEN LEVEL(3) AND LEVEL(4).

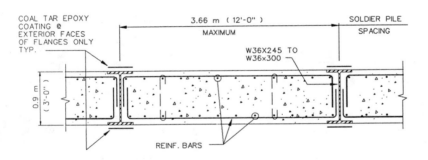

FIG. 5 -- Typical SPTC wall panel plan

ALTERNATIVE CONSTRUCTION METHODS

The use of a soldier pile and lagging support system was rejected for Shot Tower Station since the extensive dewatering required for such a system would likely result in significant settlement of many of the surrounding buildings due to compression of the underlying soft organic soils.   Therefore, excavation within a water tight wall with minimum dewatering was considered mandatory. Use of sheet piling was eliminated due to the difficulty in installing the sheeting for a depth of 21 m (70 ft.) through fill, dense soil and weathered rock. In addition, buried obstructions such as debris in the fill, abandoned basement walls and utilities precluded the use of sheet piling.

Various types of concrete diaphragm walls were investigated including precast concrete panels, cast-in-situ reinforced concrete walls and cast-in-situ concrete walls with soldier piles [2].   The precast concrete slurry wall panels were rejected due to the difficulty in transportation of large size panels (approximately 21 m or 70 ft. long) and the inability to achieve watertight joints between the panels.

Cast-in-situ reinforced concrete slurry walls, although reasonably watertight, required larger than usual wall thickness, typically 1.2 to 1.5 m (4 to 5 ft.) to transmit high bending moments and shear forces imposed by the soil and full hydrostatic pressures.   Also, moment connections using reinforcing bar bends, field bending and field welding offered major structural problems [2].

The type of wall selected for Shot Tower Station consisted of vertical soldier pile sections set in a slurry stabilized slot with a reinforcing bar cage placed between the soldier piles. This type of the wall known as "Soldier-Pile-Tremie-Concrete" (SPTC) wall, provides a relatively watertight wall, significant strength in the vertical direction, greater flexibility in moment connections, and relatively easy connections for temporary cross lot bracing and wales (Fig. 4 and 5).

In addition to providing temporary support during construction, the SPTC wall described above was also designed as the final structural wall for Shot Tower Station. The use of the SPTC wall for permanent support resulted in a considerable savings in cost due to elimination of a heavy secondary cast-in-place concrete wall as had been used for the Charles Center Station in Section A of the Baltimore Metro.

Use of tie backs in lieu of cross-lot bracing was precluded due to possible leakage through the slurry walls at the tie back locations.

STRUCTURAL DESIGN CONSIDERATIONS

Lateral Earth Pressure

Since the Shot Tower Station SPTC wall initially acts as excavation support and ultimately as the station's permanent exterior walls, the walls had to be designed for different loading conditions. As shown in Figure 6, four different soil loading conditions were applied on the structure. They are:

o   Construction condition using temporary bracings during excavation. (Case I Loading)

o   Short term loading condition with the normal water table. (Case II Loading).

o   Long term final condition based on at-rest earth pressure with the highest water table. (Case III Loading).

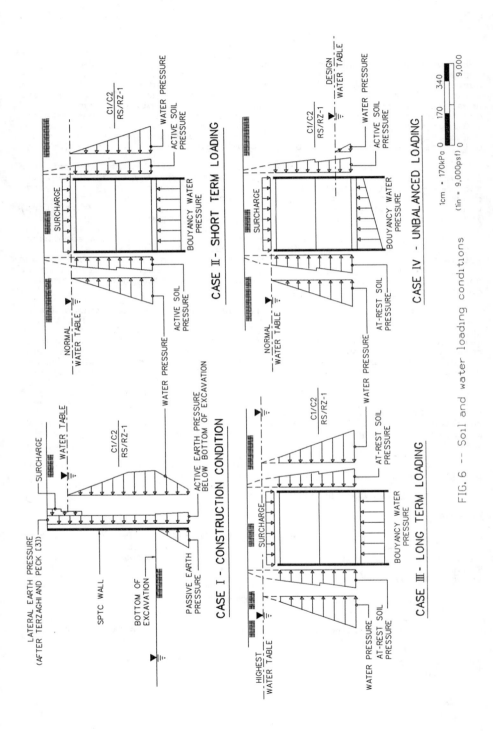

FIG. 6 -- Soil and water loading conditions

o   Unequal soil loading condition due to a possible future braced excavation on one side (Case IV Loading).

The construction condition (Case I Loading) considered a variety of loadings corresponding to the sequencing of station excavation, strut installation, concrete placement, and strut removal (Fig. 4). Also, during construction, the contractor was permitted to dewater to El.-3 m (-10 ft.) to reduce the loading on level 4 struts. To guide the contractor in his design of the temporary bracing system for these various construction stages, the bid documents provided criteria for vertical and horizontal spacing of bracing, and for soil and hydrostatic pressures. Design parameters were established for removal of temporary bracing as well as installation of permanent mezzanine and roof beams. Deflection of the soldier piles was required to be not more than 13 mm (0.5 in.) during installation and removal of temporary bracings.

Frame Analysis

For the permanent station structure design, both rigid and non-rigid structural framing concepts were analyzed and compared. Compared to the rigid frame design concept, the non-rigid frame required a large positive moment in roof and mezzanine beams and therefore required slightly heavier steel beams. Even though the rigid frame concept offered slight reduction in beam weight, the moment connections between steel beams and soldier piles required extremely heavy size field welding and accurately fitted assemblies to accomplish a tight fit. Moment connections (rigid frame concept) thus proved to be very difficult and therefore were rejected. Shear connections using field welded brackets to the soldier piles with beams supported on brackets were found to be the most practical design (Fig. 7). Further economy in the weight of beams was achieved by utilizing composite construction of concrete slab and steel beam using shear stud developers.

Seepage Analysis

With the excavation extending approximately 17.0 m (55 ft.) below the groundwater table, lateral water pressure became the major load on the SPTC wall. Use of full hydrostatic pressure for design of the wall for the Case I loading condition, however, was considered overly conservative and inappropriate since seepage into the excavation from beneath the wall would considerably reduce the groundwater pressure during construction, particularly along the lower part of the wall where the pressure is greatest. A seepage analysis was therefore performed to better estimate these pressures, and to establish loading criteria for design of the wall. The seepage analysis was also used to assess potential drawdown of the groundwater level which could impact nearby structures, and to estimate the quantity of seepage into the excavation for defining internal dewatering requirements.

The seepage analysis was performed using the two dimensional finite element computer program "SEEP". Taking advantage of symmetry, the mesh was developed to model one-half of the station cross-section. In addition, the mesh modeled the geometry of the SPTC wall and the soil stratification. A mesh boundary was established at a distance of 152 m (500 ft.) from the SPTC wall, corresponding to the maximum radius of influence for drawdown derived from an on-site pumping test. The bottom boundary was established at a depth below the groundwater table approximately equal to twice the submerged depth of the wall. The coefficient of horizontal permeability and ratio of horizontal to vertical permeability values estimated for the various soil strata are shown in Table 1.

The water pressure distribution obtained from the above analysis is

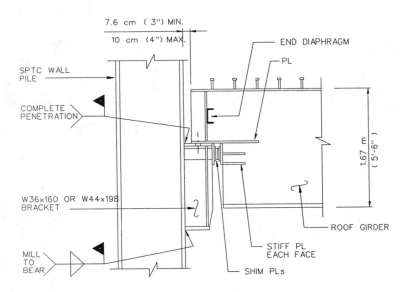

ROOF BEAM CONNECTION

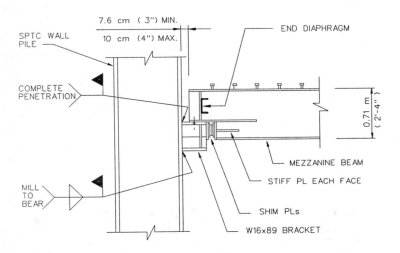

MEZZANINE BEAM CONNECTION

FIG. 7 -- Connection details

shown in Figure 6 for Case I. As illustrated in this figure, seepage beneath the slurry wall resulted in a reduction of lateral water pressure of approximately 20 percent at the base of the excavation compared to the hydrostatic condition. Below this point, the net water pressure was assumed to reduce linearly to zero at the mid-point of the wall base.

Buoyancy

The high water table made buoyancy of the station box a primary design consideration. Several alternatives were considered to resolve the structure floatation issue. They included:

o   A heavier invert slab, approximately 1.8 to 2.8 m (6 to 9 ft.) thick, without an underdrain pressure relief system.

o   A thinner invert slab, 0.6 m (2 ft.) thick, with a permanent underdrain and backup pumping installation.

o   Tie down rock anchors with thin slab and no provision for an underdrain system.

The possibility of deterioration from corrosion made tie down anchors unacceptable. The reliability of the permanent drainage and pump installation with backup system was considered doubtful.   It was determined, therefore, that the most positive method for controlling uplift of the station was by adding dead weight of the invert slab. By keying the invert slab into the SPTC walls, the weight of the entire station structure is utilized to resist buoyancy. The design factor of safety against buoyancy for the normal groundwater table condition is 1.05 considering the weight of the structure but ignoring soil friction on the sides of the structure.

Wall Details

The soldier piles in the SPTC wall consisted of 14.2 cm (36 in.) wide flange steel beams spaced at 2.1 to 2.8 m (7 to 9 ft.). Reinforcing bars between the soldier piles were designed to laterally transmit soil and water pressures to the soldier piles, and to meet the minimum requirements for temperature and shrinkage stresses (Fig. 5). Concrete of 27.6 MPa (4,000 psi) compressive strength was used in the design. Since no moment connections between floors and walls were used, embedded recesses were provided to develop bearing connections. Structural concrete in the SPTC slurry wall was installed up to an elevation below the roof slab. Above this elevation, the walls were installed with lean mix of bentonite and cement mixture to facilitate future excavation and installation of the concrete roof slab.

Allowable Wall Tolerances

Allowable tolerances for SPTC wall construction are summarized below:

o   Location of soldier piles in each direction.   ± 5 cm (± 2 in.)
o   Out of plumbness of wall in each direction.   0.5%
o   Angular rotation of soldier piles.   5.0°
o   Location of recesses.   ± 7.6 cm (± 3 in.)

A maximum construction tolerance of ± 15 cm (± 6 in.) was allowed. This includes the cumulative effect of the above tolerances.

Waterproofing Considerations

Slurry wall construction does not permit the installation of positive waterproofing membranes on wall surfaces in contact with soil. For such permanent type slurry wall construction, leakage of water and waterproofing details therefore required special consideration. For Shot Tower Station, the architectural finish wall was separated from the structural SPTC wall (Fig. 3). Details were developed to restrict the path of water from coming into contact with finish surfaces. In addition, the following measures were also included in the design:

o   Provide performance criteria for acceptable leakage.

o   Include reasonable cost in construction budget for unforeseen grouting program to correct any leakage.

o   Use cavity walls and provide drain collectors at invert slab.

o   Design removable type architectural facade wall panels for periodic inspection of the SPTC wall.

o   Stop migration of water from walls into floors using gaps between contacting surfaces. Use drip moulds on wall and beam connections.

o   Design the station ceiling to work as a roof drip pan.

A leakage rate of less than 0.57 litre (0.15 gallons) per minute for 30.5 m (100 ft.) length of wall, 0.04 litre (0.01 gallons) per minute for a leak in 3.0 m (10 ft.) of wall, and 0.02 litre (0.005 gallons) per minute for any single leak was considered acceptable.

As of December, 1991 the excavation inside the station walls has reached full depth at the west end of the station. Exposed west end wall panels are relatively dry except occasional minor leaks which have been sealed by cast-in-place concrete patches and grouting. These panels are installed within the specified construction tolerances except the recesses for slab connections are displaced vertically and horizontally by approximately 7.6 to 15 cm (3 to 6 in.).

JONES FALLS CONDUIT CROSSING

During the concept design phase, several underpinning methods were evaluated for construction of the station structure beneath the Jones Falls Conduit, but these methods proved costly. Potential damage during underpinning of the old conduit structure remained a critical problem. A method requiring staged removal and reconstruction of each cell, and support of the new conduit on the station structure proved to be the most practical.

The reconstruction of Jones Falls Conduit required removing one cell at a time by diverting the flow into the two other cells. Drainage characteristics and hydrological investigations were made to meet the drainage requirements for the highest flood level (100 years). Extra precautions were considered in the design for emergency measures in case of such flooding. The empty cell was then removed so that slurry wall panels on the north and south sides of the station box could be constructed. The permanent station roof was constructed and supported on the slurry wall panels. Upon completion of the station roof structure, the removed cell was reconstructed. Staging the slurry wall construction beneath the conduit required careful coordination with the demolition and reconstruction work. Brick and mastic waterproofing was used between the base of the conduit cells and the station roof slab. High density polyethylene (HDPE) membrane sheets were installed at the outside faces of conduit and at the junction of the SPTC wall with the conduit cells.

JET GROUT CUT-OFF WALL

The four 115 kV power lines crossing the Shot Tower Station site, as shown in Figure 2, could not be relocated or temporarily put out of

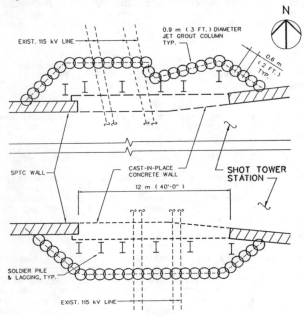

FIG. 8 -- Jet grout cut-off wall plan

service. With these power lines left in place, however, it was not possible to construct the SPTC wall through this location. As a result, there was a 12 m (40 ft.) wide gap in the SPTC walls on both the north and south sides of the station. These gaps were closed using a jet grout seepage cut-off wall in combination with a conventional soldier pile and lagging excavation support system (Fig. 8).

Jet grouting, a relatively new technique in the United States, utilizes rotary drilling tools to mix cement grout with the in situ soil to create soilcrete columns. A specialized nozzle at the tip of the drill stem injects a high pressure air and water jet to cut the in situ soil and mix it with cement grout. Waste soil and grout returns to the surface through the borehole annulus for off-site disposal. The diameter of the constructed columns is governed by several factors including the composition of the soil, the jet pressure, the rotation speed and lift rate of the drill rod, and the grout flow. The primary advantage of jet grouting is that it can be used to stabilize a broad range of soils, including materials which are not suitable for conventional cement or chemical grouting.

The jet grout closure walls for Shot Tower Station consisted of a single row of 0.9 m (3 ft.) diameter columns spaced 0.6 m (2 ft.) on-center. The columns extended through the permeable Cretaceous soils and into the residual soil and weathered rock strata which have significantly lower permeability. A total of 56 columns were installed with lengths ranging from 18.9 to 20.7 m (62 to 68 ft.). Installation procedures used for the jet grout columns were based on the contractor's previous experience and on the results of a test program conducted at the site prior to production drilling. These procedures are summarized below:

o Rotation rate   10 RPM
o Lift rate   30 cm/min.
o Grout flow rate   120 liters/min.
o Jet water flow rate (2.6 mm nozzle)   86 liters/min.
o Jet water pressure at drill   400 bars
o Air pressure at drill   7 bars

The grout used was a cement-bentonite mix, with a water cement ratio of 0.67 by weight, a bentonite content of 2 to 2.5 percent by weight of cement, and a specific gravity of 1.67 ± 0.05.

As shown in Figure 8, the jet grout columns formed a seepage cut-off wall outside the soldier pile support system. The soldier piles and attached bracing were designed to support the full Case I water pressure in addition to the acting earth pressure. The soldier piles were located outside the limits of the station walls to allow construction of a permanent cast-in-place concrete closure wall in the gap between the adjoining slurry wall sections.

SPTC WALL CONSTRUCTION

Prior to excavation of the slurry wall panels, a test boring was drilled at each panel location to verify that the panels would be founded on very dense residual soil or weathered rock. SPT split spoon samples obtained at 76 cm (2.5 ft.) intervals or continuous rock core samples were recovered for a 3 m (10 ft.) depth below the required panel base. Where necessary, the panel embedment was increased to obtain suitable bearing.

The slurry wall for Shot Tower Station had an average height of 20.8 m (68 ft.) and a total plan length of 383 m (1258 ft.). The wall was excavated in a total of 82 panels, with individual panel lengths generally ranging from 3.4 to 5.5 m (11 to 18 ft.). These panels were excavated using a cable operated, clam type grab bucket suspended from a 90 metric tons (100 ton) crawler crane. The grab bucket had a jaw opening of 3.7 m (12 ft.) and a weight of 11 to 13 metric tons (12 to 14 tons). Locally, a drop chisel was used to penetrate rock, boulders or hard soil.

The bentonite slurry used to stabilize the panel trench was composed of natural Wyoming bentonite conforming to API Standard 13A. The contract specifications required the bentonite slurry to have the following specific properties:

o   Viscosity as measured by the Marsh Funnel Viscometer of not less than 40 seconds nor more than 70 seconds prior to placing concrete.

o   pH between 7 and 10.

o   Specific gravity not to exceed 1.1 when freshly mixed.

o   Sand content not to exceed five percent by API test RP-13B prior to placing concrete.

At the completion of excavation, the bottom of the panel was cleaned and the slurry cycled until the entire volume of slurry in the panel had been replaced by fresh slurry. This was accomplished by pumping from the bottom of the panel while adding fresh slurry to the top. Throughout the excavation operation, the bentonite slurry was maintained within 0.6 m (2 ft.) from the top of the guide walls, and not less than 0.9 m (3 ft.) above the natural groundwater surface.

The soldier piles were installed in the excavated panel using a template at the surface to position the piles. Since the top of the piles are below the ground surface, an extension was attached to the piles and extended 0.6 m (2 ft.) above the guide walls. The base of the pile was held in position using the weight of the pile bearing on the trench bottom. Styrofoam fillers were placed between the pile flanges at the ends of the panel to facilitate excavation of adjoining panels.

After setting the soldier piles, the reinforcing cage was lowered into the trench and hung from the guide walls. Concrete with a slump between 15 and 20 cm (6 and 8 in.) was then tremied to the bottom of the trench using 25 cm (10 in.) diameter tremie pipes. Slurry displaced during concreting was conveyed to a holding tank for future use.

PRELIMINARY INSTRUMENTATION DATA

Since excavation and strut installation was still in progress at the time this paper was written, only preliminary results are available from the construction instrumentation program. Some typical results are presented in Figures 9 and 10.

Figure 9 presents a plot of lateral ground displacements for inclinometer I-14 located approximately 1.8 m (6 ft.) beyond the north SPTC wall (see Fig. 2 for plan location). The inclinometer casing was extended about 4.6 m (15 ft.) below the bottom of the SPTC wall to provide a base reference point outside the zone of movement. Positive values of displacement are in a southern direction, toward the station excavation.

Figure 10 presents strain gage readings for excavation support struts at a cross section on the west side of the station where the excavation had reached full depth (see Fig. 2 for plan location). Shown are plots of load versus time for struts 2G, 3G and 4E3 in the second, third and fourth bracing levels, respectively. The strut loads were determined using vibrating wire strain gages, placed symmetrically on the principle axes of the struts. The loadings shown represent the average of four strain gages for struts 2G and 3G, and two gages for strut 4E3. At this cross section, the struts in the second and third bracing levels had a horizontal spacing of 3.66 m (12.0 ft.), whereas the fourth level struts were spaced at 2.44 m (8.0 ft.). The struts were required to be preloaded to 25 percent of the strut design load determined from the loading criteria shown for Case I in Figure 6, except for bracing level 4 for which partial dewatering was permitted to reduce the external water pressure. The corresponding target preload forces for struts 2G, 3G, and 4E3 were 300, 580 and 920 kN (68, 130 and 207 kips), respectively.

Following are some of the preliminary findings obtained from the available data.

o   Maximum lateral ground displacement was generally less than about 10 mm (0.4 in.), which is equivalent to about 0.06 percent of the excavation depth. This small lateral displacement is likely due to both the high strength of the existing soils and the high stiffness of the SPTC wall. These small lateral displacements were obtained despite the large span of 6.5 m (21.4 ft.) between the third and fourth bracing levels, and despite the relatively low preload level.

o   With the excavation at full depth, the loads in struts 2G, 3G and 4E3 were at 32, 73 and 31 percent of their respective design loads

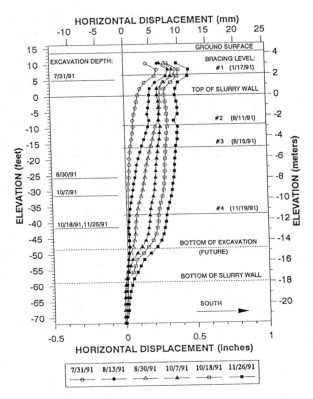

FIG. 9 -- Lateral ground displacement at inclinometer I-14

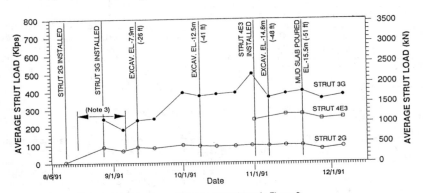

Notes: 1) Strut levels are similar to those shown in Figure 9.
2) Horizontal spacing for level 2 and 3 struts (2G and 3G)
   was 3.66m (12 ft), and for level 4 struts (4E3) was 2.44m (8 ft).
3) Wells activated for partial dewatering to EL. -3m (-10 ft).

FIG. 10 -- Typical strut loads during station excavation

with the excavation at full depth. The higher percentage in strut 3G was due to a modification of the bracing design during construction which increased the vertical span between the third and fourth bracing levels from 3.7 to 6.5 m (12 to 21.4 ft.).

o   Two factors contributing to the low loads measured in the struts as compared to the design values were a) the high strength of the existing soils, and b) the relatively low strut preload level.

SUMMARY

Use of slurry walls as permanent station walls for Shot Tower Station provided an interesting design challenge. A successful design of such an underground structure depends on the ability to coordinate the interfacing design functions between the geotechnical, structural, architectural and the construction engineers including the slurry wall construction companies. Waterproofing, development of details to limit the path of water from coming in contact with interior finishes and the utilization of removable finish wall panels to permit periodic inspection of walls were considered an integral part of the station design.

It was concluded that the greatest economy in the use of slurry walls can be realized when the retaining wall structure becomes part of the station final structure. Advancing technological improvements in slurry wall construction and waterproofing systems will bring further economy in the construction.

Preliminary results from an instrumentation monitoring program demonstrate successful performance of the SPTC wall during excavation for the Shot Tower Station.

ACKNOWLEDGEMENTS

Funding for the project was provided by the Urban Mass Transit Administration (UMTA) and the State of Maryland Department of Transportation (MDOT). Mass Transit Administration (MTA), an agency of MDOT, is directing the design and construction of the project. A joint venture team consisting of Daniel, Mann, Johnson and Mendenhall, ICF Kaiser Engineers, Inc. and Parsons Brinckerhoff Quade and Douglas, Inc. (DKP) was the Design Consultant and the Construction Manager. Keiwit/Shea, a joint venture, was the General Contractor. Case International Company was the slurry wall Subcontractor, and the GKN-Hayward Baker Company installed the jet grout columns.

REFERENCES

[1]   Bencor Corporation of America, Subcontractor for Temporary Slurry Wall Construction, Charles Center Station, Baltimore Metro, 1978, Design and Shop Drawings Submittals.

[2]   Xanthakos, Petus P., 1979, Slurry Walls, McGraw-Hill, Inc.

[3]   Terzaghi, Karl and Peck, Ralph B., Soil Mechanics in Engineering Practice, Second Edition, John Wiley & Sons, Inc., New York, 1967, pp 399-403.

Author Index

Subject Index

A

ACNA Organic Chemical Plant,
    Italy, 181
Arching, 309
Attapulgite, 69

B

Backhoe, 225
Baltimore, MD, Harborplace,
    foundation wall, 151
Baltimore, MD, underground transit
    system, 403
Barrettes, 207
Beam, driven, method, 324
Bentonite, 3, 26, 69, 78, 86, 194
Biopolymers, 69, 333
Boston, MA, 194, 207, 347, 361
Bracing system, cross-lot, 347
Building protection, during
    construction, 103, 117,
    128, 140, 151, 164, 194, 361
    construction using slurry walls,
    194, 403

C

Calcium bentonite, 172
Cement, 172
Cement-bentonite, 42, 140, 225
Charles Center Station,
    Baltimore, MD, 403
Church of the Epiphany,
    Washington, DC, 164
Clamshell, 3, 271
Clay, 69, 103, 225, 251
Cofferdam, 391
Collector wells, 333
Colloids, 86
Composites, 78, 103, 181
Concrete, 26, 151, 207, 235, 309,
    361
Conductivity, 172
Construction, thin slurry walls, 324
Contaminants, 69, 78, 103, 172,
    181, 333

Copper mine, cutoff walls, 271
Cutoff walls, 3, 42, 69, 140, 181
    Island Copper Mine, 271
    Mud Mountain Dam, 309
    plastic concrete, 271
    Sacramento River, 225
    soil-bentonite, 289
    Wister Dam, 251
CWS system, 16

D

Dams
    cutoff walls for, 289, 309
    slurry walls for, 235, 251
Dewatering, 391
Diaphragm walls, 128
    concrete, 151, 361
    internally braced, 347
    joints, 16, 377
    pump station, 391
    specifications for, 42
    trenching method, 86
    Wells Dam, 235
Drainage, 181
Drains, french, 333
Driven beam method, 324

E

Earth pressures, 403
    lateral, 151, 347
Embankments, 225, 289
    dam, 235, 251
Erosion, 140, 235
Excavation, 26, 86, 207, 271, 377,
    391
    support, 117, 164, 347, 361,
    403

F

Filter, sand, 251
Filtrate, 86
Finite element analyses, 361
Fluids, supporting, 324
Fly ash, 172